Welcome Home Diabetic Cookbook

450 Easy-to-Prepare Recipes for the Slow Cooker, Stovetop, and Oven

Hope Comerford

PHOTOS BY
BONNIE MATTHEWS

Good Books

New York, New York

Copyright © 2018 by Good Books, an imprint of Skyhorse Publishing, Inc.
Photos by Bonnie Matthews

Good Books books may be purchased in bulk at special discounts for sales promotion, corporate gifts, fund-raising, or educational purposes. Special editions can also be created to specifications. For details, contact the Special Sales Department, Good Books, 307 West 36th Street, 11th Floor, New York, NY 10018 or info@skyhorsepublishing.com.

Good Books is an imprint of Skyhorse Publishing, Inc.®, a Delaware corporation.

Visit our website at www.goodbooks.com.

10 9 8 7 6 5 4 3 2 1

Library of Congress Cataloging-in-Publication Data is available on file.

Cover design by Mona Lin
Cover photos by Bonnie Matthews

Print ISBN: 978-1-68099-351-6
Ebook ISBN: 978-1-68099-364-6

Printed in China

Table of Contents

About *Welcome Home Diabetic Cookbook*

We understand that having dietary restrictions can be challenging, but that should not stop you from enjoying your food. When you're diabetic, it's important to manage your calorie, carb, fat, and sodium counts. That's why we've put together hundreds of recipes, each with nutritional information included, so you and your loved ones can enjoy your meals without the guesswork. Each recipe is followed by its Exchange List Values, which list carbs, fats, starches, etc. and the Basic Nutritional Values as well.

Calculating the Nutritional Analyses

If the number of servings is given as a range, we used the higher number to do the nutritional analyses calculations.

The nutritional analysis for each recipe includes all ingredients except those labeled "optional," those listed as "to taste," or those calling for a "dash." If an ingredient is listed with a second choice, the first choice was used in the analysis. If a range is given for the amount of an ingredient, the first number was used. Foods listed as "serve with" at the end of a recipe, or accompanying foods listed without an amount, were not included in the recipe's analysis. In recipes calling for cooked rice, pasta, or other grains, the analysis is based on the starch being prepared without added salt or fat, unless indicated otherwise in the recipe. Please note, too, that the nutritional analyses do not cover the ingredients included in the Tips and Variations that follow some of the recipes.

The analyses were done assuming that meats were trimmed of all visible fat, and that skin was removed from poultry, before being cooked.

Tips for Healthier, Happier Eating

How to Plan Healthy Meals

Healthy meal planning is an important part of diabetes care. If you have diabetes, you should have a meal plan specifying what, when, and how much you should eat. Work with a registered

dietitian to create a meal plan that is right for you. A typical meal plan covers your meals and snacks and includes a variety of foods. Here are some popular meal-planning tools:

1. **An exchange list** is a list of foods that are grouped together because they share similar carbohydrate, protein, and fat content. Any food on an exchange list may be substituted for any other food on the same list. A meal plan that uses exchange lists will tell you the number of exchanges (or food choices) you can eat at each meal or snack. You then choose the foods that add up to those exchanges.

2. **Carbohydrate counting** is useful because carbohydrates are the main nutrient in food that affects blood glucose. When you count carbohydrates, you simply count up the carbohydrates in the foods you eat, which helps you manage your blood glucose levels. To find the carbohydrate content of a food, check the Nutrition Facts label on foods or ask your dietitian for help. Carbohydrate counting is especially helpful for people with diabetes who take insulin to help manage their blood glucose.

3. **The "Create Your Plate" method** helps people with diabetes put together meals with evenly distributed carbohydrate content and correct portion sizes. This is one of the easiest meal-planning options because it does not require any special tools—all you need is a plate. Fill half of your plate with non-starchy vegetables, such as spinach, carrots, cabbage, green beans, or broccoli. Fill one-quarter of the plate with starchy foods, such as rice, pasta, beans, or peas. Fill the final quarter of your plate with meat or a meat substitute, such as cheese with less than 3 grams of fat per ounce, cottage cheese, or egg substitute. For a balanced meal, add a serving of low-fat or nonfat milk and a serving of fruit.

No matter which tool you use to plan your meals, having a meal plan in place can help you manage your blood glucose levels, improve your cholesterol levels, and maintain a healthy blood pressure and a healthy weight. When you're able to do that, you're helping to control—or avoid—diabetes.

Learning Portion Control

Portion control is an important part of healthier eating. Weighing and measuring your foods helps familiarize yourself with reasonable portions and can make a difference of several hundred calories each day. You want to frequently weigh and measure your foods when you begin following a healthy eating plan. The more you practice weighing and measuring, the easier it will become to estimate portion sizes accurately.

You'll want to have certain portion-control tools on hand when you're weighing and measuring your foods. Remember, the teaspoons and tablespoons in your silverware set won't give you exact measurements. Here's what goes into your portion-control toolbox:

- Measuring spoons for ½ teaspoon, 1 teaspoon, ½ tablespoon, and 1 tablespoon
- A see-through 1-cup measuring cup with markings at ¼ , ⅓, ½ , ⅔, and ¾ cup
- Measuring cups for dry ingredients, including ¼ ⅓, ½, and 1 cup.

You may already have most of these in your kitchen. Keep them on your counter—you are more likely to use these tools if you can see them. Get an inexpensive food scale for foods that are measured in ounces, such as fresh produce, baked goods, meats, and cheese. When you're weighing meat, poultry, and seafood, keep in mind that you will need more than 3 ounces of raw meat to produce a 3-ounce portion of cooked meat. For example, it takes 4 ounces of raw, boneless meat—or 5 ounces of raw meat with the bone—to produce 3 cooked ounces. About 4½ ounces of raw chicken (with the bone and skin) yields 3 ounces cooked. Remember to remove the skin from the chicken before eating it.

There are other easy ways to control your portions at home in addition to weighing and measuring:

- Eat on smaller plates and bowls so that small portions look normal, not skimpy.
- Use a measuring cup to serve food to easily determine how much you're serving and eating.
- Measure your drinking glasses and bowls, so you know how much you're drinking or eating when you fill them.
- Avoid serving your meals family-style because leaving large serving dishes on the table can lead to second helpings and overeating.
- Keep portion sizes in mind while shopping. When you buy meat, fish,

or poultry, purchase only what you need for your meal.

When you're away from home, your eyes and hands become your portion-control tools. You can use your hand to estimate teaspoons, tablespoons, ounces, and cups. The tip of your thumb is about 1 teaspoon; your whole thumb equals roughly 1 tablespoon. Two fingers lengthwise are about an ounce, and 3 ounces is about the size of a palm. You can use your fist to measure in cups. A tight fist is about half a cup, whereas a loose fist or cupped hand is closer to a cup. These guidelines are true for most women's hands, but some men's hands are much larger. The palm of a man's hand is often the equivalent of about 5 ounces. Check the size of your hand in relation to various portions.

Remember that the more you weigh and measure your foods at home, the easier it will be to estimate portions on the road.

Controlling your portions when you eat at a restaurant can be difficult. Try to stay away from menu items with portion descriptors that are large, such as "giant," "supreme," "extra-large," "double," "triple," "king-size," and "super." Don't fall for deals in which the "value" is to serve you more food so that you can save money. Avoid all-you-can-eat restaurants and buffets.

You can split, share, or mix-and-match menu items to get what you want to eat in the correct portions. If you know that the portions you'll be served will be too large, ask for a take-home container when you place your order and put half of your food away before you start eating.

Gradually, as you become better at portion control, you can weigh and measure your foods less frequently. If you feel like you are correctly estimating your portions, just weigh and measure once a week, or even once a month, to check that your portions are still accurate. A good habit to get into is to "calibrate" your portion-control memory at least once a month, so you don't start overestimating your portion sizes. Always weigh and measure new foods.

Frequently Asked Questions about Diabetes and Food

1. *Do people with diabetes have to eat a special diet?*
No, they should eat the same foods that are healthy for everyone—whole grains, vegetables, fruit, and small portions of lean meat. Like everyone else, people with diabetes should eat breakfast, lunch, and dinner and not put off eating until dinnertime. By then, you are ravenous and will eat too much. This sends blood sugar levels soaring in people with diabetes, and doesn't allow them to feel hungry for breakfast the next morning.

2. *Can people with diabetes eat sugar?*
Yes, they can. Sugar is just another carbohydrate to the body. All carbohydrates, whether they come from

dessert, breads, or carrots, raise blood sugar. An equal serving of brownie and of baked potato raise your blood sugar the same amount. If you know that a rise in blood sugar is coming, it is wise to focus on the size of the serving. The question of "how much sugar is too much?" has to be answered by each one of us. No one who wants to be healthy eats a lot of sugar.

3. *What natural substances are good sugar substitutes? Are artificial sweeteners safe for people with diabetes?*

Honey, agave nectar, maple syrup, brown sugar, and white sugar all contain about the same amount of calories and have a similar effect on your blood glucose levels. All of these sweeteners are a source of carbohydrates and will raise blood glucose quickly.

If you have diabetes, you can use these sweeteners sparingly if you work them into your meal plan. Be aware of portion sizes and the carbohydrate content of each sweetener:

- 1 tablespoon honey = about 64 calories, 17 grams of carbohydrate
- 1 tablespoon brown sugar = about 52 calories, 13 grams of carbohydrate
- 1 tablespoon white sugar = about 48 calories, 13 grams of carbohydrate
- 1 tablespoon agave nectar = about 45 calories, 12 grams of carbohydrate
- 1 tablespoon maple syrup = about 52 calories, 13 grams of carbohydrate
- 1 packet of artificial sweetener = about 4 calories, <1 gram of carbohydrate

Artificial sweeteners are a low-calorie, low-carb option. Because they are chemically modified to be sweeter than regular sugar, only a small amount is needed to sweeten foods and drinks. There are several different artificial sweeteners available under various brand names: stevia, aspartame, acesulfame-K, saccharin, or sucralose. With the direction of your health care provider, these may be safe options for people with diabetes when used in moderate amounts.

4. *How many grams of carbohydrates should someone with diabetes eat per day? How many at each meal?*

This is a very common question. About 45–60 grams of carbohydrates per meal is a good starting point when you are carb-counting. If you follow that recommendation, you will be eating a total of 135–180 grams of carbohydrates per day. However, some people may need more, and some may need less. Talk with your health care team to create an individualized meal plan to help you meet your health goals.

5. *What types of fruit can I eat? Is canned or fresh fruit better for people with diabetes?*

You can eat any type of fruit if you work it into your meal plan. Fruits are loaded with vitamins, minerals, and fiber. Fresh, canned, or frozen fruit without added sugars are all good options. You get a similar amount of nutrients from each. When you buy canned fruit, be sure the fruit has been canned in water or juice—not in syrup.

Fruit is nutritious, but it is not a "free food." The following portions have about 15 grams of carbohydrates:

- 1 small piece of whole fruit such as a small apple, small orange, or kiwifruit
- ½ cup of frozen or canned fruit
- ¾–1 cup of fresh berries or melon
- ⅓–½ cup 100% no-sugar-added fruit juice
- 2 tablespoons of dried fruit

6. *Besides meat, what can I eat to make sure I get enough protein?*

There are many protein sources. Proteins that are low in saturated and trans fats are the best options. Choose lean sources of protein like these:

- Eggs, egg whites, and egg substitutes
- Vegetarian proteins: beans, soy products, veggie burgers, nuts, and seeds
- Low-fat or nonfat dairy products
- Fish and shellfish
- Poultry without the skin
- Cheeses with 3 grams of fat or less per ounce
- When you do eat meat, choose lean cuts

People with diabetes can follow a vegetarian or vegan diet. Plant-based diets that include some animal products like eggs and milk can be a healthy option. However, animal products are not necessary. A mix of soy products, vegetables, fruits, beans, and whole grains provides plenty of protein and nutrients.

7. *Why should I eat whole grains instead of refined grains?*

Even a food made with 100 percent whole wheat flour will raise your blood glucose levels. All grains—whole or not—affect blood glucose because they contain carbohydrates. However, you shouldn't completely avoid starchy foods. People with diabetes need some carbohydrates in their diet.

Whole grains are a healthy starch option because they contain fiber, vitamins, and minerals. Choose whole wheat or whole-grain foods over those made with refined grains, but watch your portion sizes.

8. *Can people with diabetes eat potatoes and sweet potatoes?*

Yes! Starchy vegetables are healthy sources of carbohydrates. They also provide you with important nutrients like potassium, fiber, and vitamin C. You can include them in your meal plan as part of a balanced meal. Just pay attention to portion sizes and avoid unhealthy toppings. If you are carb counting, remember that there are about 15 grams of carbohydrates in:

- ½ cup of mashed potatoes
- ½ cup of boiled potatoes
- ¼ of a large baked potato with the skin

9. *Without salt and fat, food tastes bland. What can I do?*
When you are preparing healthy foods, try to limit added fats and extra salt. Look for recipes that use herbs (fresh or dried) and spices for flavor instead. There are many spice blends available in the baking aisle at the grocery store—choose salt-free blends. Other healthy ways to flavor your foods include:

- Squeezing lemon or lime juice on vegetables, fish, rice, or pasta
- Using onion and garlic to flavor dishes
- Baking meats with sugar-free barbecue sauce or any low-fat marinade
- Adding low-fat, low-calorie condiments, such as mustard, salsa, balsamic vinegar, or hot sauce

10. *Are gluten-free products okay for people with diabetes to eat?*
About 1 percent of the total population has celiac disease, which is an allergy to gluten—a protein found in wheat, rye, and barley. About 10 percent of people with type 1 diabetes also have celiac disease. People with celiac disease or gluten intolerance should follow a gluten-free diet. However, unless you have one of these conditions, following a gluten-free diet is unnecessary and can make meal planning more difficult. Gluten-free products may contain more grams of carbohydrates per serving than regular products. For example, gluten-free bread can have twice as many grams of carbohydrates as whole wheat bread. You can use gluten-free products and recipes, but just be sure to check the carbohydrate content and calories.

Tips for Using Your Slow Cooker

Not all slow cookers are created equal . . . or work equally as well for everyone!
Those of us who use slow cookers frequently know we have our own preferences when it comes to which slow cooker we choose to use. For instance, I love my programmable slow cooker, but there are many programmable slow cookers I've tried that I've strongly disliked. Why? Because some go by increments of 15 or 30 minutes and some go by 4, 6, 8, or 10 hours. I dislike those restrictions, but I have family and friends who don't mind them at all! I am also pretty brand-loyal when it comes to my manual slow cookers because I've had great success with those and have had unsuccessful moments with slow cookers of other

brands. So, which slow cooker(s) is/are best for your household?

It really depends on how many people you're feeding and if you're gone for long periods of time. Here are my recommendations:

For 2–3 person household   3–5-quart slow cooker
For 4–5 person household   5–6-quart slow cooker
For a 6+ person household   6½–7-quart slow cooker

Large slow cooker advantages/ disadvantages:

Advantages:
You can fit a loaf pan or a baking dish into a 6- or 7-quart, depending on the shape of your cooker. That allows you to make bread or cakes, or even smaller quantities of main dishes. (Take your favorite baking dish and loaf pan along when you shop for a cooker to make sure they'll fit inside.)

You can feed large groups of people, or make larger quantities of food, allowing for leftovers, or meals, to freeze.

Disadvantages:
They take up more storage room. They don't fit as neatly into a dishwasher. If your crock isn't ⅔–¾ full, you may burn your food.

Small slow cooker advantages/ disadvantages:

Advantages:
They're great for lots of appetizers, for serving hot drinks, for baking cakes straight in the crock, and for dorm rooms or apartments.
Great option for making recipes of smaller quantities.

Disadvantages:
Food in smaller quantities tends to cook more quickly than larger amounts. So keep an eye on it. Chances are, you won't have many leftovers. So, if you like to have leftovers, a smaller slow cooker may not be a good option for you.

My recommendation:
Have at least two slow cookers; one around 3 to 4 quarts and one 6 quarts or larger. A third would be a huge bonus (and a great advantage to your cooking repertoire!). The advantage of having at least a couple is you can make a larger variety of recipes. Also, you can make at least two or three dishes at once for a whole meal.

Manual vs. Programmable
If you are gone for only six to eight hours a day, a manual slow cooker might be just fine for you. If you are gone for more than eight hours during the day, I would highly recommend purchasing a programmable slow cooker that will switch to warm when the cook time you set is up. It will allow you to cook a wider variety of recipes.

The two I use most frequently are my 4-quart manual slow cooker and my 6½-quart programmable slow cooker. I like that I can make smaller portions in my 4-quart slow cooker on days I don't need or want leftovers, but I also love how my 6½-quart slow cooker can accommodate whole chickens, turkey breasts, hams, or big batches of soups. I use them both often.

Get to know your slow cooker . . .
Plan a little time to get acquainted with your slow cooker. Each slow cooker has its own personality—just like your oven (and your car). Plus, many new slow cookers cook hotter and faster than earlier models. I think that with all of the concern for food safety, the slow-cooker manufacturers have amped up their settings so that "High," "Low," and "Warm" are all higher temperatures than in the older models. That means they cook hotter—and therefore, faster—than the first slow cookers. The beauty of these little machines is that they're supposed to cook low and slow. We count on that when we flip the switch in the morning before we leave the house for ten hours or so. So, because none of us knows what kind of temperament our slow cooker has until we try it out, nor how hot it cooks—don't assume anything. Save yourself a disappointment and make the first recipe in your new slow cooker on a day when you're at home. Cook it for the shortest amount of time the recipe calls for. Then, check the food to see if it's done. Or if you start smelling food that seems to be finished, turn off the cooker and rescue your food.

Also, all slow cookers seem to have a "hot spot," which is of great importance to know, especially when baking with your slow cooker. This spot may tend to burn food in that area if you're not careful. If you're baking directly in your slow cooker, I recommend covering the "hot spot" with some foil.

Tips and Tricks
Slow cookers tend to work best when they're ⅔ to ¾ of the way full. You may need to increase the cooking time if you've exceeded that amount, or reduce it if you've put in less than that. If you're going to exceed that limit, it would be best to reduce the recipe, or split it between two slow cookers. (Remember how I suggested owning at least two or three slow cookers?)

Keep your veggies on the bottom. That puts them in more direct contact with the heat. The fuller your slow cooker, the longer it will take its contents to cook. Also, the more densely packed the cooker's contents are, the longer they will take to cook. And finally, the larger the chunks of meat or vegetables, the more time they will need to cook.

Keep the lid on! Every time you take a peek, you lose 20 minutes of cooking time. Please take this into consideration each time you lift the lid! I know, some of you can't help yourself and are going to lift anyway. Just don't forget to tack on 20 minutes to your cook time for each time you peeked!

Sometimes it's beneficial to remove the lid. If you'd like your dish to thicken a bit, take the lid off during the last half hour to hour of cooking time.

If you have a big slow cooker (7- to 8-quart), you can cook a small batch in it by putting the recipe ingredients into an oven-safe baking dish or baking pan and then placing that into the cooker's crock. First, put a trivet or some metal jar rings on the bottom of the crock, and then set your dish or pan on top of them. Or a loaf pan may "hook onto" the top ridges of the crock belonging to a large oval cooker and hang there straight and securely, "baking" a cake or quick bread. Cover the cooker and flip it on.

The outside of your slow cooker will be hot! Please remember to keep it out of reach of children and keep that in mind for yourself as well!

Get yourself a quick-read meat thermometer and use it! This helps remove the question of whether or not your meat is fully cooked, and helps prevent you from overcooking your meat as well.

Internal Cooking Temperatures:
Beef—125–130°F (rare); 140–145°F
  (medium); 160°F (well-done)
Pork—140–145°F (rare); 145–150°F
  (medium); 160°F (well-done)
Turkey and Chicken—165°F
Frozen meat: The basic rule of thumb is, don't put frozen meat into the slow cooker. The meat does not reach the proper internal temperature in time. This especially applies to thick cuts of meat! Proceed with caution!

Add fresh herbs 10 minutes before the end of the cooking time to maximize their flavor.

If your recipe calls for cooked pasta, add it 10 minutes before the end of the cooking time if the cooker is on High; 30 minutes before the end of the cooking time if it's on Low. Then the pasta won't get mushy.

If your recipe calls for sour cream or cream, stir it in 5 minutes before the end of the cooking time. You want it to heat but not boil or simmer.

Approximate Slow-Cooker Temperatures (Remember, each slow cooker is different):

High—212°F–300°F
Low—170°F–200°F
Simmer—185°F
Warm—165°F

Cooked beans freeze well. Store them in freezer bags (squeeze the air out first) or freezer boxes. Cooked and dried bean measurements: 16-oz. can, drained = about 1¾ cups beans
19-oz. can, drained = about 2 cups beans
1 lb. dried beans (about 2½ cups) = 5 cups cooked beans

Appetizers

Appetizers

Jalapeño Popper Dip

**Jamie Mowry
Arlington, TX**

Makes 12 servings, about ¼ cup per serving
Prep. Time: 15 minutes
Baking Time: 30 minutes

2 8-oz. pkgs. fat-free cream cheese, softened

1 cup light mayonnaise

4-oz. can chopped green chilies, drained

2-oz. can diced jalapeño peppers, drained

½ cup freshly grated Parmesan cheese

½ cup panko bread crumbs

1. Mix cream cheese and mayonnaise in large bowl until smooth. Stir in chilies and peppers.

2. Pour pepper mixture in a greased baking dish.

3. Combine Parmesan and panko. Put on top of pepper mixture.

4. Bake at 350°F for 30 minutes until golden and bubbly.

Serving suggestion:
Serve with veggies, pita chips, or regular corn chips, or whatever "dipper" you like.

Exchange List Values
- Carbohydrate 0.5
- Lean Meat 1.0
- Fat 0.5

Basic Nutritional Values
- Calories 105
  (Calories from Fat 55)
- Total Fat 6 gm
  (Saturated Fat 1.2 gm,
  Trans Fat 0.0 gm,
  Polyunsat Fat 2.7 gm,
  Monounsat Fat 1.6 gm)
- Cholesterol 15 mg
- Sodium 480 mg
- Potassium 130 gm
- Total Carb 6 gm
- Dietary Fiber 0 gm
- Sugars 2 gm
- Protein 6 gm
- Phosphorus 230 gm

Buffalo Chicken Dip

Deb Martin
Gap, PA
Donna Treloar
Muncie, IN

Makes 26 servings, ¼ cup per serving
Prep. Time: 15 minutes
Cooking Time: 20–60 minutes

10-oz. can chunk chicken, drained

¾ cup Frank's RedHot Original Cayenne
   Pepper Sauce

2 8-oz. pkgs. fat-free cream cheese, softened

1 cup light ranch dressing

1½ cups shredded cheddar Jack cheese,
   divided

tortilla chips

1. Heat chicken and hot sauce in a large frying pan over medium heat until heated through.

2. Stir in cream cheese and ranch dressing. Cook, stirring, until well blended and warm.

3. Mix in half of shredded cheese.

4. Transfer the mixture to a small slow cooker. Sprinkle the remaining cheese over the top.

5. Cover and cook on Low setting until hot and bubbly. Serve with tortilla chips.

Variation:

Replace hot sauce with 1 cup Buffalo wing sauce. Spread cream cheese in bottom of small shallow baking dish. Layer with shredded chicken, Buffalo wing sauce, ranch dressing, and shredded cheese. Bake at 350°F for 20 minutes or until cheese is melted.
                —Donna Treloar, Muncie, IN

Exchange List Values
- Lean Meat 1.0
- Fat 0.5

Basic Nutritional Values
- Calories 75
  (Calories from Fat 35)
- Total Fat 4 gm
  (Saturated Fat 1.1 gm,
  Trans Fat 0.0 gm,
  Polyunsat Fat 0.8 gm,
  Monounsat Fat 0.9 gm)
- Cholesterol 15 mg
- Sodium 475 mg
- Potassium 90 gm
- Total Carb 2 gm
- Dietary Fiber 0 gm
- Sugars 1 gm
- Protein 6 gm
- Phosphorus 160 gm

Hot Cheese and Bacon Dip

Lee Ann Hazlett
Freeport, IL

Makes 25 servings
Prep. Time: 15 minutes
Cooking Time: 1 hour
Ideal slow-cooker size: 1-qt.

9 slices bacon, diced

2 8-oz. pkgs. fat-free cream cheese, cubed and softened

8 oz. shredded reduced-fat mild cheddar cheese

1 cup fat-free half-and-half

2 tsp. Worcestershire sauce

1 tsp. dried minced onion

½ tsp. dry mustard

½ tsp. salt

2–3 drops Tabasco sauce

1. Brown and drain bacon. Set aside.

2. Mix remaining ingredients in slow cooker.

3. Cover. Cook on Low 1 hour, stirring occasionally until cheese melts.

4. Stir in bacon.

Exchange List Values
• Lean meat 1.0

Basic Nutritional Values
• Calories 54 (Calories from Fat 28)
• Total Fat 3 gm (Saturated Fat 1.5 gm, Polyunsat Fat 0.2 gm, Monounsat Fat 1.1 gm)
• Cholesterol 11 mg
• Sodium 273 mg
• Total Carb 2 gm
• Dietary Fiber 0 gm
• Sugars 1 gm
• Protein 6 gm

Cheesy Hot Bean Dip

**John D. Allen
Rye, CO**

Makes 20 servings
Prep. Time: 10 minutes
Cooking Time: 2 hours
Ideal slow-cooker size: 3-qt.

16-oz. can refried beans

1 cup salsa

1 cup shredded reduced-fat Monterey Jack

1 cup reduced-fat Cheddar cheese

1 cup fat-free sour cream

3-oz. pkg. fat-free cream cheese, cubed

1 Tbsp. chili powder

¼ tsp. ground cumin

1. Combine all ingredients in slow cooker.

2. Cover. Cook on High 2 hours. Stir 2–3 times during cooking.

Serving suggestion:
Serve warm from the cooker with tortilla chips.

Exchange List Values
- Carbohydrate 0.5
- Fat 0.5

Basic Nutritional Values
- Calories 65
  (Calories from Fat 22)
- Total Fat 2 gm
  (Saturated Fat 1.5 gm,
  Polyunsat Fat 0.1 gm,
  Monounsat Fat 0.7 gm)
- Cholesterol 11 mg
- Sodium 275 mg
- Total Carb 6 gm
- Dietary Fiber 1 gm
- Sugars 2 gm
- Protein 6 gm

NOTES

This bean dip is a favorite. Once you start on it, it's hard to leave it alone. We have been known to dip into it even when it's cold.

Party Starter Bean Dip

Leona M. Slabaugh
Apple Creek, OH

Makes 16 servings, ¼ cup per serving
Prep. Time: 20–25 minutes
Baking Time: 20 minutes
Standing Time: 5 minutes

16-oz. can Old El Paso refried beans or
  vegetarian refried beans

8-oz. pkg. fat-free cream cheese, softened

12-oz. jar salsa, *divided*

nacho tortilla chips

1. Spread beans into bottom of a 9-inch pie pan or a decorative pan, spreading up the sides a bit.

2. In a bowl, beat cream cheese, then add ⅔ cup salsa and beat until smooth.

3. Spread cream cheese mixture over beans. Bake 20 minutes at 350°F.

4. Spread remaining salsa over dip which has set for 5 minutes. Serve with nacho chips.

Good Go-Alongs:
This is nice with a good dish of fruit and assorted snack crackers when eaten as a snack.

Exchange List Value
- Carbohydrate 0.5

Basic Nutritional Values
- Calories 40
  (Calories from Fat 0)
- Total Fat 0 gm
  (Saturated Fat 0.1 gm,
  Trans Fat 0.0 gm,
  Polyunsat Fat 0.0 gm,
  Monounsat Fat 0.1 gm)
- Cholesterol 0 mg
- Sodium 345 mg
- Potassium 180 gm
- Total Carb 6 gm
- Dietary Fiber 2 gm
- Sugars 1 gm
- Protein 3 gm
- Phosphorus 105 gm

Hot Crab Dip

Cassandra Ly
Carlisle, PA
Miriam Nolt
New Holland, PA

Makes 20 servings
Prep. Time: 15 minutes
Cooking Time: 3–4 hours
Ideal slow-cooker size: 3- or 4-qt.

½ cup milk

⅓ cup salsa

3 8-oz. pkgs. fat-free cream cheese, cubed

2 8-oz. pkgs. imitation crabmeat, flaked

1 cup thinly sliced green onions

4-oz. can chopped green chilies

assorted crackers or bread cubes

1. Combine milk and salsa. Transfer to greased slow cooker.

2. Stir in cream cheese, imitation crabmeat, onions, and chilies.

3. Cover. Cook on Low 3–4 hours, stirring every 30 minutes.

4. Serve with crackers or bread.

Exchange List Values
- Carbohydrate 0.5
- Meat, Very Lean 1.0

Basic Nutritional Values
- Calories 60
  (Calories from Fat 4)
- Total Fat 0 gm
  (Saturated Fat 0.1 gm,
  Polyunsat Fat 0.2 gm,
  Monounsat Fat 0.1 gm)
- Cholesterol 9 mg
- Sodium 410 mg
- Total Carb 5 gm
- Dietary Fiber 0 gm
- Sugars 4 gm
- Protein 8 gm

Cheesy New Orleans Shrimp Dip

Kelly Amos
Pittsboro, NC

Makes 20 servings
Prep. Time: 25 minutes
Cooking Time: 1 hour
Ideal slow-cooker size: 1-qt.

1 slice bacon

3 medium onions, chopped

1 clove garlic, minced

4 jumbo shrimp, peeled and deveined

1 medium tomato, peeled and chopped

7 oz. reduced-fat Monterey Jack cheese,
   shredded

4 drops Tabasco sauce

⅛ tsp. cayenne pepper

dash black pepper

milk to thin dip, *optional*

chips

Exchange List Value

• Lean Meat 1.0

Basic Nutritional Values

• Calories 43
   (Calories from Fat 18)
• Total Fat 2 gm
   (Saturated Fat 1.5 gm,
   Polyunsat Fat 0.1 gm,
   Monounsat Fat 0.6 gm)
• Cholesterol 13 mg
• Sodium 90 mg
• Total Carb 2 gm
• Dietary Fiber 0 gm
• Sugars 2 gm
• Protein 4 gm

1. Cook bacon until crisp. Drain on paper towel. Crumble.

2. Sauté onions and garlic in skillet sprayed with nonfat cooking spray. Drain on paper towel.

3. Coarsely chop shrimp.

4. Combine all ingredients except chips in slow cooker.

5. Cover. Cook on Low 1 hour, or until cheese is melted. Thin with milk if too thick. Serve with chips.

Shrimp Dip

Joyce Shackelford
Green Bay, WI

Makes 1½ cups, 9 servings, 2 Tbsp. per
  serving
Prep. Time: 15 minutes
Chilling Time: 1 hour

3-oz. pkg. Neufchâtel (⅓-less-fat) cream
  cheese, softened

1 cup fat-free sour cream

2 tsp. lemon juice

1-oz. pkg. Italian salad dressing mix

2 Tbsp. green pepper, finely chopped

½ cup cooked shrimp, finely chopped

1. Blend all ingredients together.

2. Chill at least 1 hour.

3. Serve with chips or crackers.

Exchange List Values
- Carbohydrate 0.5
- Fat 0.5

Basic Nutritional Values
- Calories 65
  (Calories from Fat 20)
- Total Fat 2.5 gm
  (Saturated Fat 1.4 gm,
  Trans Fat 0.0 gm,
  Polyunsat Fat 0.1 gm,
  Monounsat Fat 0.6 gm)
- Cholesterol 25 mg
- Sodium 385 mg
- Potassium 70 gm
- Total Carb 7 gm
- Dietary Fiber 0 gm
- Sugars 3 gm
- Protein 4 gm
- Phosphorus 65 gm

Hot Pizza Dip

Linda Abraham
Kimberly, OR
Beverly High
Bradford, PA

Makes 8 servings
Prep. Time: 20 minutes
Cooking/Baking Time: 5–20 minutes

8-oz. pkg. fat-free cream cheese, softened

½ tsp. dried oregano

½ tsp. dried parsley

¼ tsp. dried basil

¾ cup shredded part-skim mozzarella cheese, *divided*

¼ cup freshly grated Parmesan cheese, *divided*

½–1 cup pizza sauce

2 Tbsp. chopped green bell pepper

2 Tbsp. sliced black olives, *optional*

¼ cup chopped onions, *optional*

1. In a small bowl, beat together cream cheese, oregano, parsley, and basil.

2. Spread mixture in bottom of greased 9-inch glass pie plate.

3. Sprinkle 6 Tbsp. mozzarella and 2 Tbsp. Parmesan cheese on top of cream cheese mixture.

4. Spread the pizza sauce over all.

5. Sprinkle with remaining cheese.

6. Top with green pepper, olives, and onions.

7. Cover and microwave 5 minutes or bake at 350°F for 20 minutes.

Exchange List Values
- Lean Meat 1.0
- Fat 0.5

Basic Nutritional Values
- Calories 70
  (Calories from Fat 20)
- Total Fat 2.5 gm
  (Saturated Fat 1.5 gm,
  Trans Fat 0.0 gm,
  Polyunsat Fat 0.2 gm,
  Monounsat Fat 0.7 gm)
- Cholesterol 15 mg
- Sodium 340 mg
- Potassium 155 gm
- Total Carb 4 gm
- Dietary Fiber 0 gm
- Sugars 2 gm
- Protein 7 gm
- Phosphorus 220 gm

Cheesy Chorizo Dip

Hope Comerford
Clinton Township, MI

Makes about 8 servings, ¼ cup per person
Prep. Time: 15 minutes
Cooking Time: 2 hours
Ideal slow-cooker size: 1½–2-qt.

12 oz. Velveeta cheese

8 oz. chorizo, browned

½ cup salsa

1. Spray crock with nonstick spray.

2. Place the Velveeta cheese in the crock and place the chorizo and salsa on top.

3. Cover and cook on Low for 2 hours, or until all is melted. Turn to warm. Serve.

Exchange List Values
- Med-Fat Meat 0.5
- Fat 0.5
- Milk 0.5

Basic Nutritional Values
- Calories 135
  (Calories from Fat 82)
  Total Fat 9 gm
  (Saturated Fat 5.2 gm,
  Trans Fat 0 gm,
  Polyunsat Fat 0.5 gm,
  Monounsat Fat 2.0 gm)
- Cholesterol 15 mg
- Sodium 581 mg
- Potassium 166 gm
- Total Carb 3.6 gm
- Dietary Fiber 0.2 gm
- Sugars 2.9gm
- Protein 7.4 gm
- Phosphorus 242 gm

Quick and Easy Nacho Dip

Kristina Shull
Timberville, VA

Makes 20 servings
Prep. Time: 15 minutes
Cooking Time: 2 hours
Ideal slow-cooker size: 3-qt.

½ lb. 85%-lean ground beef

pepper, *optional*

onion powder, *optional*

2 cloves garlic, minced, *optional*

2 16-oz. jars salsa (as hot or mild as you like)

15-oz. can fat-free refried beans

1½ cups fat-free sour cream

1½ cups shredded reduced-fat sharp
   cheddar cheese, *divided*

tortilla chips

1. Brown ground beef. Drain. Add pepper, onion powder, and minced garlic, if desired.

2. Combine beef, salsa, beans, sour cream, and 1 cup cheese in slow cooker.

3. Cover. Heat on Low 2 hours. Just before serving, sprinkle with ½ cup cheese.

4. Serve with tortilla chips.

Exchange List Values
- Carbohydrate 0.5
- Lean Meat 1.0

Basic Nutritional Values
- Calories 80
  (Calories from Fat 27)
- Total Fat 3 gm
  (Saturated Fat 1.5 gm,
  Polyunsat Fat 0.2 gm,
  Monounsat Fat 1.0 gm)
- Cholesterol 14 mg
- Sodium 298 mg
- Total Carb 8 gm
- Dietary Fiber 2 gm
- Sugars 3 gm
- Protein 6 gm

Easy Layered Taco Dip

Lindsey Spencer
Morrow, OH
Jenny R. Unternahrer
Wayland, IA

Makes 10 servings
Prep. Time: 15 minutes

8-oz. fat-free cream cheese, softened

8-oz. fat-free sour cream

8-oz. taco sauce or salsa

4 cups shredded lettuce

1 cup chopped tomato

chopped green pepper, *optional*

1 cup reduced-fat shredded Mexi-blend
   cheese

tortilla chips

TIP

1. If you can, add the lettuce, tomato
   and cheese at the last minute so
   the lettuce doesn't get soggy.
   —Jenny R. Unternahrer, Wayland, IA
2. Omit salsa and lettuce. Add 3 Tbsp.
   taco seasoning to the sour cream
   and cream cheese and add a layer
   of chopped onion.
   —Barbara J. Bey, Hillsboro, OH

1. Blend cream cheese and sour cream
until smooth. Spread in bottom of a 9x13-inch
dish.

2. Layer taco sauce over sour cream
mixture, then lettuce, tomato, pepper (if
using), and cheese.

3. Serve with tortilla chips.

Exchange List Values
- Carbohydrate 0.5
- Lean Meat 1.0

Basic Nutritional Values
- Calories 90
  (Calories from Fat 20)
- Total Fat 2.5 gm
  (Saturated Fat 1.5 gm,
  Trans Fat 0.0 gm,
  Polyunsat Fat 0.1 gm,
  Monounsat Fat 0.6 gm)
- Cholesterol 10 mg
- Sodium 415 mg
- Potassium 175 gm
- Total Carb 9 gm
- Dietary Fiber 1 gm
- Sugars 3 gm
- Protein 7 gm
- Phosphorus 205 gm

Taco Appetizer Platter

Rachel Spicher Hershberger
Sarasota, FL

Makes 15 servings, about 1½ oz. per serving
Prep. Time: 20 minutes
Cooking Time: 10 minutes

1 lb. 90%-lean ground beef

½ cup water

7 tsp. salt-free taco seasoning

2 8-oz. pkgs. cream cheese, softened

¼ cup fat-free milk

4-oz. can chopped green chilies, drained

2 medium tomatoes, seeded and chopped

1 cup chopped green onions

lettuce, *optional*

½ cup honey barbecue sauce

1 cup shredded 75%-less-fat cheddar cheese

corn chips

1. In a skillet, cook beef over medium heat until no longer pink. Drain. Add water and taco seasoning; simmer for 5 minutes.

2. In a bowl, combine the cream cheese and milk; spread on 14-inch serving platter or pizza pan. Top with meat mixture. Sprinkle with chilies, tomatoes, and onions. Add lettuce, if desired.

3. Drizzle with barbecue sauce. Sprinkle with cheddar cheese. Serve with corn chips.

TIP

I put this on my cake server with a pedestal. It looks great.

Exchange List Values
- Carbohydrate 0.5
- Lean Meat 2.0

Basic Nutritional Values
- Calories 115
  (Calories from Fat 30)
- Total Fat 4 gm
  (Saturated Fat 1.4 gm,
  Trans Fat 0.2 gm,
  Polyunsat Fat 0.2 gm,
  Monounsat Fat 1.2 gm)
- Cholesterol 25 mg
- Sodium 350 mg
- Potassium 285 gm
- Total Carb 7 gm
- Dietary Fiber 1 gm
- Sugars 5 gm
- Protein 12 gm
- Phosphorus 260 gm

Hot Artichoke Dip

Mary Wheatley
Mashpee, MA

Makes 30 servings, ¼ cup each
Prep. Time: 20 minutes
Cooking Time: 1–4 hours
Ideal slow-cooker size: 4-qt.

2 14-oz. jars marinated artichoke hearts,
   drained

1 cup fat-free mayonnaise

1 cup fat-free sour cream

1 cup water chestnuts, chopped

2 cups freshly grated Parmesan cheese

¼ cup finely chopped green onions

1. Cut artichoke hearts into small pieces. Add mayonnaise, sour cream, water chestnuts, cheese, and green onions. Pour into slow cooker.

2. Cover. Cook on High 1–2 hours or on Low 3–4 hours.

Serving suggestion:
Serve with crackers or crusty French bread.

Exchange List Values
- Carbohydrate 0.5
- Fat 0.5

Basic Nutritional Values
- Calories 57
  (Calories from Fat 26)
- Total Fat 3 gm
  (Saturated Fat 1.2 gm,
  Polyunsat Fat 0.7 gm,
  Monounsat Fat 0.9 gm)
- Cholesterol 6 mg
- Sodium 170 mg
- Total Carb 5 gm
- Dietary Fiber 0 gm
- Sugars 2 gm
- Protein 3 gm

Slow-Cooked Salsa

Joleen Albrecht
Gladstone, MI

Makes 34 servings, ¼ cup each
Prep. Time: 15–20 minutes
Cooking Time: 3 hours
Ideal slow-cooker size: 3-qt.

10 fresh Roma, or plum, tomatoes, chopped coarsely

2 cloves garlic, minced

1 onion, chopped

2 jalapeño peppers

¼ cup cilantro leaves

½ tsp. salt

1. Place tomatoes, garlic, and onion in slow cooker.

2. Remove stems from jalapeños. Remove seeds, too, if you prefer a milder flavor. Chop jalapeños. Stir into slow cooker.

3. Cover. Cook on High 2½–3 hours, or until vegetables are softened.

4. Allow to cool.

5. When cooled, combine cooked mixture with cilantro and salt in a blender or food processor. Blend or process to the consistency that you like.

Exchange List Value

• Free Food

Basic Nutritional Values

• Calories 10
  (Calories from Fat 0)
• Total Fat 0 gm
  (Saturated Fat 0 gm,
  Polyunsat Fat 0 gm
  Monounsat Fat 0 gm
  Cholesterol 0 mg),
• Sodium 35 mg
• Total Carb 2 gm
• Dietary Fiber 0 gm
• Sugars 1 gm
• Protein 0 gm

Pineapple Salsa

**Lorraine Stutzman Amstutz
Akron, PA**

Makes 2½ cups, 10 servings, ¼ cup per serving
Prep. Time: 30 minutes

1½ cups fresh pineapple

1 cup cucumber

¼ cup red onion

2–4 tsp. jalapeño

1 tsp. garlic

2 Tbsp. fresh cilantro

¼ cup lime juice

1 tsp. grated lime peel

1 tsp. sugar

¼ tsp. salt

TIP

1. Serve with your favorite tortilla chips.
2. If you don't have a food processor, simply chop the pineapple, cucumber, onion, jalapeño, garlic, and cilantro. Combine with lime juice and peel, sugar, and salt.

1. Pulse ingredients together in food processor until just chopped.

Exchange List Value
- Carbohydrate 0.5

Basic Nutritional Values
- Calories 20 (Calories from Fat 0)
- Total Fat 0 gm (Saturated Fat 0.0 gm, Trans Fat 0.0 gm, Polyunsat Fat 0.0 gm, Monounsat Fat 0.0 gm)
- Cholesterol 0 mg
- Sodium 60 mg
- Potassium 55 gm
- Total Carb 5 gm
- Dietary Fiber 1 gm
- Sugars 3 gm
- Protein 0 gm
- Phosphorus 5 gm

Texas Caviar

Elaine Rineer
Lancaster, PA

Makes 7½ cups, 30 servings, ¼ cup per serving
Prep. Time: 15 minutes
Cooking Time: 10 minutes
Chilling Time: 12–24 hours

½ cup sugar

¼ cup oil

salt and pepper, to taste

¾ cup apple cider vinegar

1 Tbsp. water

15½-oz. can black-eyed peas, rinsed

2 11-oz. cans white shoepeg corn

15½-oz. can black beans, rinsed

8-oz. jar chopped pimento

small green bell pepper, finely diced

small red onion, chopped

1. In saucepan, combine sugar, oil, salt, pepper, vinegar, and water. Heat until boiling, then cool.

2. Mix together peas, corn, beans, pimento, green pepper, and onion. Pour cooked sauce over mixture. Stir. Serve cold.

TIP

1. Best if refrigerated 24 hours before serving.
2. Serve with scoop Fritos or corn chips.

Variations:

1. Add 1 can Ro*Tel diced tomatoes and chiles, 2 diced Roma tomatoes, and 2 sliced avocados. Omit corn and pimento. As dressing, use 1 cup zesty Italian dressing with a squeeze of lime juice.
   —Angie Van Steenvoort, Galloway, OH

2. For dressing, boil together ½ cup olive oil, ½ cup apple cider vinegar, and ½ sugar until sugar is dissolved. Cool.

3. Reduce pimento to 2 oz. and add 1 cup chopped celery.

4. Serve as a salad or dip.
   —Amy Bauer, New Ulm, MN

Exchange List Values
- Starch 0.5
- Fat 0.5

Basic Nutritional Values
- Calories 70
  (Calories from Fat 20)
- Total Fat 2 gm
  (Saturated Fat 0.2 gm,
  Trans Fat 0.0 gm,
  Polyunsat Fat 0.6 gm,
  Monounsat Fat 1.2 gm)
- Cholesterol 0 mg
- Sodium 85 mg
- Potassium 125 gm
- Total Carb 11 gm
- Dietary Fiber 2 gm
- Sugars 4 gm
- Protein 2 gm
- Phosphorus 40 gm

Fruit Salsa with Cinnamon Chips

Jackie Halladay
Lancaster, PA

Makes 12 servings, 6 chips and about ⅓ cup
  salsa per serving
Prep. Time: 45 minutes
Baking Time: 12 minutes

Cinnamon Chips:
6 6-inch flour tortillas
butter flavor cooking spray
¾ tsp. cinnamon
2 Tbsp. sugar

Salsa:
1 orange, peeled and chopped
1 apple, chopped
1 kiwi, peeled and chopped
1 cup chopped strawberries
½ cup blueberries
2 Tbsp. honey
1/4 cup orange juice
2 Tbsp. sugar-free jam (any flavor)
¼–½ tsp. cinnamon
¼ tsp. nutmeg
pinch salt

1. To make cinnamon chips, cut tortillas into 12 wedges and arrange on a baking sheet. Lightly mist with cooking spray.

2. Mix cinnamon and sugar together.

3. Sprinkle tortilla wedges with the cinnamon sugar.

4. Bake for 10 minutes at 350°F, then broil for 2 minutes. Remove from pan until cool.

5. To make salsa, toss all prepared fruit together in a large bowl.

6. In a smaller bowl, mix honey, orange juice, jam, cinnamon, nutmeg, and salt.

7. Stir honey mixture into fruit. Tastes best when allowed to marinate in the refrigerator for several hours.

TIP

1. A food processor helps with all the chopping.
2. You can really use any combination of fruit.
3. Whole wheat tortillas make it even healthier.

Exchange List Values
- Starch 0.5
- Fruit 0.5
- Carbohydrate 0.5

Basic Nutritional Values
- Calories 95
  (Calories from Fat 15)
- Total Fat 2 gm
  (Saturated Fat 0.3 gm,
  Trans Fat 0.0 gm,
  Polyunsat Fat 0.3 gm,
  Monounsat Fat 0.7 gm)
- Cholesterol 0 mg
- Sodium 95 mg
- Potassium 125 gm
- Total Carb 21 gm
- Dietary Fiber 2 gm
- Sugars 10 gm
- Protein 2 gm
- Phosphorus 30 gm

Pretty Fruit Kabobs with Dip

Anya Kauffman
Sheldon, WI

Makes 40 servings, 1 kabob and 2 Tbsp. dip
per serving
Prep. Time: 30 minutes

8-oz. Neufchâtel (⅓-less-fat) cream cheese, softened

9-oz. fat-free frozen whipped topping, thawed

6 oz. marshmallow cream

1 tsp. vanilla extract

¼ cup fat-free milk

1 honeydew, cut in 80 pieces

1 pineapple, cut in 80 pieces

2 lbs. strawberries, cut in 40 pieces

1 lb. red grapes

1 lb. green grapes

40 8-inch skewers

1. Beat cream cheese until fluffy.

2. Fold in whipped topping and marshmallow cream. Add vanilla and milk.

3. Refrigerate until ready to serve.

4. For kabobs, thread green grape, pineapple, red grape, honeydew, strawberry, honeydew, red grape, pineapple, green grape on skewers. Serve.

TIP

Tester stuck the kabobs in a foam block placed in a low pan and covered with lettuce, making a "fruit bouquet."

NOTES

A bright, delicious combination! Fresh fruit is always a big hit, especially if there are guests with diet restrictions.

Exchange List Values
- Fruit 0.5
- Carbohydrate 0.5

Basic Nutritional Values
- Calories 80
  (Calories from Fat 15)
- Total Fat 2 gm
  (Saturated Fat 0.8 gm,
  Trans Fat 0.0 gm,
  Polyunsat Fat 0.1 gm,
  Monounsat Fat 0.3 gm)
- Cholesterol 5 mg
- Sodium 40 mg
- Potassium 175 gm
- Total Carb 16 gm
- Dietary Fiber 1 gm
- Sugars 12 gm
- Protein 1 gm
- Phosphorus 30 gm

Strawberry Yogurt Dip

Teresa Koenig
Leola, PA

Makes 5½ cups, 22 servings, ¼ cup per
serving
Prep. Time: 20 minutes

8-oz. frozen light whipped topping, thawed

2 6-oz. cartons light strawberry yogurt

1–1½ cups mashed strawberries, fresh or
thawed frozen

sliced fruit

TIP

Also tastes good with pretzels or as a
topping for scones.

1. Combine whipped topping, yogurt, and
mashed berries.

2. Serve with variety of sliced fresh fruit.

Exchange List Value
- Carbohydrate 0.5

Basic Nutritional Values
- Calories 35
  (Calories from Fat 15)
- Total Fat 2 gm
  (Saturated Fat 1.2 gm,
  Trans Fat 0.0 gm,
  Polyunsat Fat 0.0 gm,
  Monounsat Fat 0.1 gm)
- Cholesterol 0 mg
- Sodium 15 mg
- Potassium 45 gm
- Total Carb 6 gm
- Dietary Fiber 0 gm
- Sugars 5 gm
- Protein 1 gm
- Phosphorus 25 gm

Creamy Caramel Dip

**Mary Kay Nolt
Newmanstown, PA**

Makes 40 servings, 1 Tbsp. per serving
Prep. Time: 20 minutes
Chilling Time: 1 hour

8-oz. fat-free cream cheese, softened

¾ cup brown sugar

1 cup fat-free sour cream

2 tsp. vanilla extract

1 cup fat-free milk

3.4-oz. pkg. instant vanilla pudding mix

Serving suggestion:
Serve as a dip for pineapples, apples, grapes, strawberries, etc.

1. Beat cream cheese and brown sugar.

2. Add sour cream, vanilla, milk, and pudding mix. Mix together.

3. Chill at least 1 hour.

Exchange List Value
• Carbohydrate 0.5

Basic Nutritional Values
• Calories 30
  (Calories from Fat 0)
• Total Fat 0 gm
  (Saturated Fat 0.0 gm,
  Trans Fat 0.0 gm,
  Polyunsat Fat 0.0 gm,
  Monounsat Fat 0.0 gm)
• Cholesterol 0 mg
• Sodium 80 mg
• Potassium 40 gm
• Total Carb 7 gm
• Dietary Fiber 0 gm
• Sugars 5 gm
• Protein 1 gm
• Phosphorus 60 gm

Fruit Dip

Michelle D. Hostetler
Indianapolis, IN

Makes 10 servings, 2 Tbsp. per serving
Prep. Time: 10 minutes

1 cup fat-free sour cream

2 Tbsp. brown sugar

½ tsp. cinnamon

¼ tsp. vanilla extract

1. Mix ingredients together.

2. Serve with cut-up apples, grapes, and bananas (not included in nutritional info).

Warm Memories:
People always take seconds and rave over it.

Exchange List Value
(not including fruit)
- Carbohydrate 0.5

Basic Nutritional Values
(not including fruit)
- Calories 30
  (Calories from Fat 0)
- Total Fat 0 gm
  (Saturated Fat 0.1 gm,
  Trans Fat 0.0 gm,
  Polyunsat Fat 0.0 gm,
  Monounsat Fat 0.0 gm)
- Cholesterol 0 mg
- Sodium 30 mg
- Potassium 35 gm
- Total Carb 7 gm
- Dietary Fiber 0 gm
- Sugars 4 gm
- Protein 1 gm
- Phosphorus 25 gm

Father Todd's Favorite Baked Brie

Nanci Keatley
Salem, OR

Makes 60 servings, 1 Tbsp. per serving
Prep. Time: 15 minutes
Baking Time: 20–25 minutes

16-oz. round Brie

½ cup Splenda Brown Sugar Blend

¼ cup amaretto

½ cup chopped pecans

¾ cup dried cherries

1. Place Brie in round oven-safe casserole or pie plate.

2. Mix brown sugar and amaretto together; spread on top of cheese.

3. Sprinkle with pecans and cherries.

4. Bake at 375°F for 20–25 minutes.

Serving suggestion:
Serve with French bread slices.

TIP

You can use Grand Marnier or a hazelnut liqueur instead. You can also use macadamia nuts or filberts instead of pecans.

Warm Memories:
I've made this for many occasions. The best was when we celebrated our renewing of vows and our priest, Father Todd, came to the small party we had. He loved the baked Brie so much that I changed the recipe's name to honor him!

Exchange List Value
• Fat 1.0

Basic Nutritional Values
• Calories 45
  (Calories from Fat 20)
• Total Fat 2.5 gm
  (Saturated Fat 1.3 gm,
  Trans Fat 0.0 gm,
  Polyunsat Fat 0.2 gm,
  Monounsat Fat 1.0 gm)
• Cholesterol 5 mg
• Sodium 55 mg
• Potassium 25 gm
• Total Carb 4 gm
• Dietary Fiber 0 gm
• Sugars 2 gm
• Protein 1 gm
• Phosphorus 25 gm

Festive Fruit and Nut Spread

Lucille Hollinger
Richland, PA

Makes 24 servings, 1 Tbsp. per serving
Prep. Time: 15 minutes
Chilling Time: 30 minutes

8-oz. Neufchâtel (⅓-less-fat) cream cheese, softened

¼ cup orange juice

½ cup dried cranberries

½ cup pecans, chopped

Good Go-Alongs:
Good with crackers or spread on bagels

1. In a small mixing bowl, beat cream cheese and orange juice until smooth.

2. Fold in cranberries and pecans.

3. Cover and refrigerate 30 minutes.

Exchange List Value
• Fat 1.0

Basic Nutritional Values
• Calories 50
  (Calories from Fat 35)
• Total Fat 4 gm
  (Saturated Fat 1.4 gm,
  Trans Fat 0.0 gm,
  Polyunsat Fat 0.6 gm,
  Monounsat Fat 1.5 gm)
• Cholesterol 5 mg
• Sodium 40 mg
• Potassium 30 gm
• Total Carb 3 gm
• Dietary Fiber 0 gm
• Sugars 2 gm
• Protein 1 gm
• Phosphorus 20 gm

Baked Brie
with Cranberry Chutney

Amymarlene Jensen
Fountain, CO

Makes 25 servings
Prep. Time: 25 minutes
Cooking Time: 4½ hours
Ideal slow-cooker size: 1-qt.

1 cup fresh, or dried, cranberries

½ cup brown sugar

⅓ cup cider vinegar

2 Tbsp. water or orange juice

2 tsp. minced crystallized ginger

¼ tsp. cinnamon

⅛ tsp. ground cloves

oil

8-oz. round of Brie cheese

1 Tbsp. sliced almonds, toasted

crackers

1. Mix together cranberries, brown sugar, vinegar, water or juice, ginger, cinnamon, and cloves in slow cooker.

2. Cover. Cook on Low 4 hours. Stir once near the end to see if it is thickening. If not, remove top, turn heat to High, and cook 30 minutes without lid.

3. Put cranberry chutney in covered container and chill for up to 2 weeks. When ready to serve, bring to room temperature.

4. Brush shallow baking dish or ovenproof plate with vegetable oil; place Brie, still in rind, on plate.

5. Bake uncovered at 350°F for 9 minutes, until cheese is soft and partially melted. Remove from oven.

6. Top with half the chutney and garnish with almonds. Serve with crackers.

Exchange List Value

· Fat 1.0

Basic Nutritional Values

· Calories 38
  (Calories from Fat 23)
· Total Fat 3 gm
  (Saturated Fat 1.5 gm,
  Polyunsat Fat 0.1 gm,
  Monounsat Fat 0.8 gm)
· Cholesterol 8 mg
· Sodium 67 mg
· Total Carb 3 gm
· Dietary Fiber 0 gm
· Sugars 3 gm
· Protein 1 gm

Cheese and Olive Spread

Suzanne Yoder
Gap, PA

Makes 2 cups, 1 Tbsp. per serving
Prep. Time: 15 minutes
Chilling Time: 1 hour

8-oz. pkg. reduced-fat
  shredded mild cheddar cheese

4 oz. Neufchâtel (⅓-less-fat) cream cheese,
  softened

4 oz. fat-free cream cheese, softened

½ cup light mayonnaise

¼ cup stuffed green olives, chopped

¼ cup green onions, chopped

2 Tbsp. lemon juice

¼ tsp. ground red pepper, or to taste

1. Mix ingredients.

2. Refrigerate at least an hour.

Serving suggestion:
Serve with Ritz crackers.

TIP

I usually have these ingredients on hand so it's simple to have a little something ready for unexpected guests. It tastes even better after 1–2 days.

Exchange List Value
• Fat 1.0

Basic Nutritional Values
• Calories 45
  (Calories from Fat 30)
• Total Fat 4 gm
  (Saturated Fat 1.5 gm,
  Trans Fat 0.0 gm,
  Polyunsat Fat 0.6 gm,
  Monounsat Fat 0.9 gm)
• Cholesterol 10 mg
• Sodium 145 mg
• Potassium 25 gm
• Total Carb 1 gm
• Dietary Fiber 0 gm
• Sugars 0 gm
• Protein 3 gm
• Phosphorus 65 gm

Sweet Cheese Ball

Mary Ann Lefever
Lancaster, PA

Makes 35 servings, 2 Tbsp. per serving
Prep. Time: 10 minutes
Chilling Time: 4 hours

2 8-oz. pkgs. fat-free cream cheese, softened

3.4-oz. pkg. French vanilla instant pudding mix

15-oz. can fruit cocktail, well drained

4 Tbsp. orange juice

1 cup sliced almonds

1. Mix cream cheese, pudding, fruit, and juice.

2. Refrigerate to set up, approximately 4 hours.

3. Shape into a ball and roll in almonds.

4. Store in refrigerator.

Serving suggestion:
Serve with buttery crackers such as Town House, graham crackers, or apple slices.

Warm Memories:
A friend always brought this to get-togethers or served at her home and would not give out the recipe. Finally she got tired of me asking and gave me the recipe. Always a hit at get-togethers.

Exchange List Value
• Carbohydrate 0.5

Basic Nutritional Values
• Calories 40
  (Calories from Fat 15)
• Total Fat 2 gm
  (Saturated Fat 0.1 gm,
  Trans Fat 0.0 gm,
  Polyunsat Fat 0.3 gm,
  Monounsat Fat 0.8 gm)
• Cholesterol 0 mg
• Sodium 120 mg
• Potassium 65 gm
• Total Carb 5 gm
• Dietary Fiber 0 gm
• Sugars 3 gm
• Protein 2 gm
• Phosphorus 100 gm

Roasted Pepper and Artichoke Spread

Sherril Bieberly
Sauna, KS

Makes 24 servings
Prep. Time: 20 minutes
Cooking Time: 1 hour
Ideal slow-cooker size: 1-qt.

1 cup grated Parmesan cheese

½ cup reduced-fat mayonnaise

8-oz. pkg. fat-free cream cheese, softened

1 clove garlic, minced

14-oz. can artichoke hearts, drained and chopped finely

⅓ cup finely chopped roasted red bell pepper

crackers, cut-up fresh vegetables, or snack-bread slices

1. Combine Parmesan cheese, mayonnaise, cream cheese, and garlic in food processor. Process until smooth. Place mixture in slow cooker.

2. Add artichoke hearts and red bell pepper. Stir well.

3. Cover. Cook on Low 1 hour. Stir again.

4. Use as spread for crackers, cut-up fresh vegetables, or snack-bread slices.

Exchange List Value
- Fat 1.0

Basic Nutritional Values
- Calories 49
  (Calories from Fat 29)
- Total Fat 3 gm
  (Saturated Fat 1.3 gm,
  Polyunsat Fat 0.7 gm,
  Monounsat Fat 0.9 gm)
- Cholesterol 8 mg
- Sodium 209 mg
- Total Carb 2 gm
- Dietary Fiber 0 gm
- Sugars 1 gm
- Protein 4 gm

Chicken Salad Spread

Lois W. Benner
Lancaster, PA

Makes 8 servings, about ¼ cup per serving
Prep. Time: 20 minutes

2 cups shredded, cooked chicken

½ cup reduced-fat light mayonnaise

½ tsp. cream-style horseradish

½ tsp. prepared mustard

½ tsp. Worcestershire sauce

1 tsp. white sugar

½ tsp. salt

1 Tbsp. finely chopped onion

1 Tbsp. finely chopped celery

1. Prepare cooked chicken by removing all skin, bones, and tendons. Save broth and chunks of chicken. Shred chicken chunks in blender. Set aside and cool thoroughly.

2. Combine all other ingredients.

3. Add cooled, shredded chicken to mayonnaise mixture. If consistency is too thick to spread easily, add small amounts of chicken broth until it spreads easily.

Serving suggestion:
Spread filling generously between bread or rolls.

Exchange List Values
- Lean Meat 2.0
- Fat 0.5

Basic Nutritional Values
- Calories 105
  (Calories from Fat 55)
- Total Fat 6 gm
  (Saturated Fat 1.2 gm,
  Trans Fat 0.0 gm,
  Polyunsat Fat 2.6 gm,
  Monounsat Fat 1.9 gm)
- Cholesterol 35 mg
- Sodium 310 mg
- Potassium 100 gm
- Total Carb 2 gm
- Dietary Fiber 0 gm
- Sugars 1 gm
- Protein 10 gm
- Phosphorus 75 gm

Reuben Spread

Clarice Williams
Fairbank, IA
Julie McKenzie
Punxsutawney, PA

Makes 52 servings
Prep. Time: 15 minutes
Cooking Time: 1–2 hours
Ideal slow-cooker size: 3-qt.

½ lb. corned beef, shredded or chopped, all visible fat removed

16-oz. can sauerkraut, well drained

1 cup shredded Swiss cheese

1 cup shredded cheddar cheese

1 cup mayonnaise

bread slices

Thousand Island dressing, *optional*

1. Combine all ingredients except bread and Thousand Island dressing in slow cooker. Mix well.

2. Cover. Cook on High 1–2 hours until heated through, stirring occasionally.

3. Turn to Low and keep warm in cooker while serving. Put spread on bread slices. Top individual servings with Thousand Island dressing, if desired.

Variation:
Use dried beef instead of corned beef.

Exchange List Value
- Fat 1.0

Basic Nutritional Values
- Calories 58
  (Calories from Fat 49)
- Total Fat 5 gm
  (Saturated Fat 1.5 gm,
  Polyunsat Fat 1.9 gm,
  Monounsat Fat 1.6 gm)
- Cholesterol 10 mg
- Sodium 113 mg
- Total Carb 1 gm
- Dietary Fiber 0 gm
- Sugars 0 gm
- Protein 2 gm

NOTES

Low-fat cheese and mayonnaise are not recommended for this spread.

Molded Crab Spread

Marsha Sabus
Fallbrook, CA

Makes 12 servings
Prep. Time: 10 minutes
Cooking Time: 5–7 minutes
Chilling Time: 4 hours

1-oz. envelope unflavored gelatin

3 Tbsp. cold water

10¾-oz. can lower-fat, lower-sodium cream of mushroom soup

8-oz. fat-free cream cheese, softened

1 cup light mayonnaise

6-oz. can crab

1 cup chopped celery

2 green onions, chopped

Serving suggestion:
Serve with crackers or bread.

TIP

You can also substitute shrimp for crab.

1. In a small microwave-safe bowl, sprinkle gelatin over cold water. Let stand 1 minute. Microwave uncovered on High 20 seconds. Stir. Let stand 1 minute or until gelatin is completely dissolved.

2. In a large saucepan, combine soup, cream cheese, mayonnaise, and gelatin. Cook and stir over medium heat for 5–7 minutes or until smooth.

3. Remove from heat and add crab, celery, and onions.

4. Transfer to a 5-cup ring mold, lightly greased. Cover and refrigerate 4 hours or until set.

5. Unmold onto serving platter.

Exchange List Values
- Carbohydrate 0.5
- Lean Meat 1.0
- Fat 0.5

Basic Nutritional Values
- Calories 95
  (Calories from Fat 45)
- Total Fat 5 gm
  (Saturated Fat 0.8 gm,
  Trans Fat 0.0 gm,
  Polyunsat Fat 2.9 gm,
  Monounsat Fat 1.5 gm)
- Cholesterol 20 mg
- Sodium 430 mg
- Potassium 290 gm
- Total Carb 5 gm
- Dietary Fiber 0 gm
- Sugars 2 gm
- Protein 6 gm
- Phosphorus 145 gm

Liver Paté

Barbara Walker
Sturgis, SD

Makes 12 servings, 2 Tbsp. each
Prep. Time: 20 minutes
Cooking Time: 4–5 hours
Ideal slow-cooker size: 3-qt.

1 lb. chicken livers

½ cup dry wine

1 tsp. instant chicken bouillon

1 tsp. minced parsley

1 Tbsp. instant minced onion

¼ tsp. ground ginger

½ tsp. seasoning salt

1 Tbsp. light soy sauce

¼ tsp. dry mustard

¼ cup light, soft tub margarine

1 Tbsp. brandy

Serving suggestion:
Serve with crackers or toast.

1. In slow cooker, combine all ingredients except margarine and brandy.

2. Cover. Cook on Low 4–5 hours. Let stand in liquid until cool.

3. Drain. Place livers in blender or food grinder. Add margarine and brandy. Process until smooth.

Exchange List Value
• Lean Meat 1.0

Basic Nutritional Values
• Calories 61
  (Calories from Fat 28)
• Total Fat 3 gm
  (Saturated Fat 0.6 gm,
  Polyunsat Fat 0.6 gm,
  Monounsat Fat 1.2 gm)
• Cholesterol 137 mg
• Sodium 235 mg
• Total Carb 1 gm
• Dietary Fiber 0 gm
• Sugars 0 gm
• Protein 6 gm

Basic Deviled Eggs and Variations

Makes 12 halves; serving size is 2 egg halves
Prep. Time: 30 minutes
Cooking Time: 20 minutes

Below are instructions for making deviled eggs of any variety. For specific recipes and ingredients, see pages 40 and 41.

To hard-boil eggs:

1. Place eggs in a single layer in a lidded pan.

2. Fill the pan with cold water to just cover the eggs.

3. Bring to a full boil over high heat, covered.

4. As soon as the water begins the full boil, immediately turn the heat down to low for a simmer. Allow to barely simmer for exactly 18 minutes.

5. Pour off hot water. Run cold water and/or ice over the eggs to quickly cool them.

To make deviled eggs:

1. Cut eggs in half lengthwise. Gently remove yolk sections into a bowl.

2. Discard two yolks if using a recipe for 6; discard 4 yolks if using a recipe for 12. Mash remaining yolk sections together with a fork. Stir in remaining ingredients with yolk mixture until smooth.

3. Fill empty egg whites. The filling will make a little mound in the egg white. Garnish, optional.

4. Refrigerate.

Basic Deviled Eggs

Joanne Warfel
Lancaster, PA

6 large eggs, hard-boiled and peeled

¼ cup light mayonnaise

1 tsp. vinegar

1 tsp. prepared mustard

⅛ tsp. salt

sprinkle of pepper

paprika

parsley sprigs, for garnish

Exchange List Value

- Med-Fat Meat 1.0

Basic Nutritional Values

- Calories 75
  (Calories from Fat 55)
- Total Fat 6 gm
  (Saturated Fat 1.4 gm,
  Trans Fat 0.0 gm,
  Polyunsat Fat 2.0 gm,
  Monounsat Fat 1.9 gm)
- Cholesterol 125 mg
- Sodium 205 mg
- Potassium 70 gm
- Total Carb 1 gm
- Dietary Fiber 0 gm
- Sugars 1 gm
- Protein 6 gm
- Phosphorus 70 gm

Dill Pickle Eggs

Jan Mast
Lancaster, PA

6 large eggs, hard-boiled and peeled

¼ cup fat-free plain yogurt or light mayonnaise

1 Tbsp. pickle relish

1 tsp. dill weed

1 tsp. vinegar

1 tsp. prepared mustard

¼ tsp. salt

¼ tsp. Worcestershire sauce

⅛ tsp. pepper

paprika

pickle slice, to garnish

Exchange List Value
• Med-Fat Meat 1.0

Basic Nutritional Values
• Calories 65
  (Calories from Fat 30)
• Total Fat 4 gm
  (Saturated Fat 1.1 gm,
  Trans Fat 0.0 gm,
  Polyunsat Fat 0.6 gm,
  Monounsat Fat 1.3 gm)
• Cholesterol 125 mg
• Sodium 205 mg
• Potassium 95 gm
• Total Carb 2 gm
• Dietary Fiber 0 gm
• Sugars 2 gm
• Protein 6 gm
• Phosphorus 85 gm

Tex-Mex Eggs

Jan Mast
Lancaster, PA

6 large eggs, hard-boiled and peeled

¼ cup fat-free plain yogurt or light
   mayonnaise

1 Tbsp. finely diced onion

1 tsp. lemon juice

1 tsp. prepared mustard

1 tsp. taco seasoning

¼ tsp. salt

Exchange List Value
- Med-Fat Meat 1.0

Basic Nutritional Values
- Calories 60
  (Calories from Fat 30)
- Total Fat 4 gm
  (Saturated Fat 1.1 gm,
  Trans Fat 0.0 gm,
  Polyunsat Fat 0.7 gm,
  Monounsat Fat 1.2 gm)
- Cholesterol 125 mg
- Sodium 215 mg
- Potassium 95 gm
- Total Carb 2 gm
- Dietary Fiber 0 gm
- Sugars 1 gm
- Protein 6 gm
- Phosphorus 90 gm

Stuffed Mushrooms

Melva Baumer
Mifflintown, PA

Makes 10 servings, 2 mushroom caps per
   serving
Prep. Time: 25 minutes
Baking Time: 20–30 minutes

20 fresh mushrooms, about 1 lb.

2 Tbsp. finely chopped onion

¼ cup trans-fat-free tub margarine

½ cup Italian seasoned bread crumbs

¼ cup freshly grated Parmesan cheese

2 Tbsp. oil

Warm Memories:
This is a simple dish to prepare and to shop
for. But it is fabulous.

1. Wash mushrooms; remove stems but
don't throw them out. Place mushrooms in
greased baking pan, stem-side up.

2. Finely chop 2 tablespoons of the
mushroom stems. Discard the rest. Sauté
onion and chopped mushroom stems in
margarine. Turn off heat and stir in crumbs.

3. Fill each mushroom cap with mixture.
Sprinkle Parmesan cheese over all. Drizzle
with oil.

4. Bake at 350°F for 20–30 minutes.

Exchange List Values
- Carbohydrate 0.5
- Fat 1.5

Basic Nutritional Values
- Calories 90
  (Calories from Fat 65)
- Total Fat 7 gm
  (Saturated Fat 1.5 gm,
  Trans Fat 0.0 gm,
  Polyunsat Fat 1.8 gm,
  Monounsat Fat 3.3 gm)
- Cholesterol 0 mg
- Sodium 150 mg
- Potassium 145 gm
- Total Carb 6 gm
- Dietary Fiber 1 gm
- Sugars 1 gm
- Protein 3 gm
- Phosphorus 55 gm

Variation:
To plain cracker crumbs, add 1 Tbsp. dried
parsley, ½ tsp. garlic salt, 3 Tbsp. minced
onion, 2 Tbs. melted butter, pepper to taste,
and minced mushroom stems. Do not sauté
stuffed mushroom caps and proceed as listed.
   —Melva Baumer, Mifflintown, PA

Veggie Pizza

Jean Butzer
Batavia, NY
Julette Rush
Harrisonburg, VA

Makes 18 servings, 2x3-inch rectangle per serving
Prep. Time: 20–30 minutes
Cooking Time: 9–12 minutes
Chilling Time: 30 minutes

2 8-oz. pkgs. refrigerated crescent rolls

8-oz. pkg. fat-free cream cheese, softened

½ cup fat-free mayonnaise

1 tsp. dill weed

1/2 tsp. onion salt

¾–1 cup broccoli florets

¾–1 cup finely chopped green pepper or mushrooms

¾–1 cup finely chopped tomato, membranes and seeds removed

½ cup sliced ripe olives

½ cup finely chopped sweet onion or red onion

¾ cup cheddar cheese, shredded fine, *optional*

1. Separate dough into 4 rectangles.

2. Press onto bottom and up sides of 10x13-inch jelly roll baking pan to form crust.

3. Bake 9–12 minutes at 350°F or until golden brown. Cool.

4. Mix cream cheese, mayonnaise, dill, and onion salt until well blended.

5. Spread over cooled crust, but not too thickly.

6. Top with chopped vegetables and optional cheese.

7. Press down lightly into cream cheese mixture.

8. Refrigerate. Cut into squares to serve.

TIP

1. Add veggies of your preference and availability.
2. Do not put the cream cheese mixture on too thick. There may be ¼ cup left after spreading it on the crescent rolls. This can be saved to use as a dip with any leftover vegetables you have.

Exchange List Values
- Starch 1.0
- Fat 1.0

Basic Nutritional Values
- Calories 130 (Calories from Fat 65)
- Total Fat 7 gm (Saturated Fat 1.5 gm, Trans Fat 0.0 gm, Polyunsat Fat 0.8 gm, Monounsat Fat 4.1 gm)
- Cholesterol 0 mg
- Sodium 400 mg
- Potassium 110 gm
- Total Carb 12 gm
- Dietary Fiber 1 gm
- Sugars 3 gm
- Protein 3 gm
- Phosphorus 150 gm

Reuben Appetizer Squares

Mary Ann Lefever
Lancaster, PA

Makes 24 servings, 2-inch square per
   serving
Prep. Time: 20 minutes
Baking Time: 12–15 minutes

2 cups baking mix

½ cup fat-free milk

2 Tbsp. vegetable oil

1 cup sauerkraut, well drained

2½-oz. pkg. thinly sliced smoked corned
   beef, coarsely chopped

⅔ cup light mayonnaise

1 Tbsp. pickle relish

1 Tbsp. ketchup

1½ cups reduced-fat shredded Swiss cheese
   (about 6 oz.)

Warm Memories:
These squares are very different for church
suppers and well received.

Exchange List Values
- Starch 0.5
- Fat 1.0

Basic Nutritional Values
- Calories 90
  (Calories from Fat 45)
- Total Fat 5 gm
  (Saturated Fat 1.1 gm,
  Trans Fat 0.0 gm,
  Polyunsat Fat 1.4 gm,
  Monounsat Fat 1.9 gm)
- Cholesterol 5 mg
- Sodium 250 mg
- Potassium 45 gm
- Total Carb 8 gm
- Dietary Fiber 1 gm
- Sugars 2 gm
- Protein 4 gm
- Phosphorus 110 gm

1. Mix baking mix, milk, and oil until soft
dough forms. Press into ungreased 9x13-inch
baking pan.

2. Top with sauerkraut and corned beef.

3. Mix mayonnaise, relish, and ketchup;
spread over corned beef. Sprinkle with
cheese.

4. Bake at 450°F until cheese is bubbly
and crust is golden brown, 12–15 minutes.

5. Cut into 2-inch squares.

Easy Turkey Roll-Ups

Rhoda Atzeff
Lancaster, PA

Makes 6 servings, 2 roll-ups per serving
Prep. Time: 10 minutes

3 6-inch flour tortillas

3 Tbsp. chive and onion cream cheese

12 slices deli shaved 97%-fat-free turkey breast, 6 oz. total

¾ cup shredded lettuce

1. Spread tortillas with cream cheese. Top with turkey. Place lettuce on bottom halves of tortillas; roll up.

2. Cut each into 4 pieces and lay flat to serve.

Exchange List Values
- Starch 0.5
- Lean Meat 1.0

Basic Nutritional Values
- Calories 90
  (Calories from Fat 20)
- Total Fat 2.5 gm
  (Saturated Fat 1.1 gm,
  Trans Fat 0.0 gm,
  Polyunsat Fat 0.5 gm,
  Monounsat Fat 0.8 gm)
- Cholesterol 15 mg
- Sodium 365 mg
- Potassium 125 gm
- Total Carb 8 gm
- Dietary Fiber 1 gm
- Sugars 1 gm
- Protein 9 gm
- Phosphorus 95 gm

Levi's Sesame Chicken Wings

Shirley Unternahrer Hinh
Wayland, IA

Makes 16 appetizer servings
Prep. Time: 40 minutes
Cooking Time: 2½–5 hours
Ideal slow-cooker size: 4-qt.

3 lbs. chicken wings

salt, to taste

pepper, to taste

1 cup honey

sugar substitute to equal 6 Tbsp. sugar

¾ cup light soy sauce

½ cup no-salt-added ketchup

2 Tbsp. canola oil

2 Tbsp. sesame oil

2 cloves garlic, minced

toasted sesame seeds

1. Rinse wings. Cut at joint. Sprinkle with salt and pepper. Place on broiler pan.

2. Broil 5 inches from top, 10 minutes on each side. Place chicken in slow cooker.

3. Combine remaining ingredients except sesame seeds. Pour over chicken.

4. Cover. Cook on Low 5 hours or High 2½ hours.

5. Sprinkle sesame seeds over top just before serving.

Exchange List Values
- Carbohydrate 1.5
- Meat, High Fat 1.0

Basic Nutritional Values
- Calories 192
  (Calories from Fat 77)
- Total Fat 9 gm
  (Saturated Fat 1.8 gm,
  Polyunsat Fat 2.3 gm,
  Monounsat Fat 3.7 gm)
- Cholesterol 22 mg
- Sodium 453 mg
- Total Carb 21 gm
- Dietary Fiber 0 gm
- Sugars 21 gm
- Protein 9 gm

Spinach Roll-Ups

Esther Gingerich
Kalona, IA

Makes 23 servings, 3 roll-ups per serving
Prep. Time: 30 minutes
Chilling Time: 12 hours

2 10-oz. boxes frozen spinach, thawed and drained

2 oz. bacon bits (half of a small jar)

¼ cup water chestnuts, chopped

1 pkg. ranch dressing mix

1 cup fat-free sour cream

6 green onions, chopped

1 cup light mayonnaise

7 10-inch tortillas

Warm Memories:
Our church often has "finger food" potlucks and this works well for that.

1. Mix together ingredients except tortillas.

2. Spread the mixture on the tortillas. Roll up and secure with toothpicks.

3. Refrigerate overnight. Slice into 1-inch pieces to serve.

Exchange List Values
- Starch 1.0
- Fat 1.0

Basic Nutritional Values
- Calories 120
  (Calories from Fat 45)
- Total Fat 5 gm
  (Saturated Fat 1.2 gm,
  Trans Fat 0.0 gm,
  Polyunsat Fat 1.8 gm,
  Monounsat Fat 1.7 gm)
- Cholesterol 5 mg
- Sodium 440 mg
- Potassium 160 gm
- Total Carb 15 gm
- Dietary Fiber 2 gm
- Sugars 1 gm
- Protein 4 gm
- Phosphorus 50 gm

TIP

Arrange on a pretty plate or tray to serve.

Party Kielbasa

**Mary C. Wirth
Lancaster, PA**

Makes 48 servings, 1 oz. per serving
Prep. Time: 15 minutes
Cooking/Baking Time: 2–2½ hours

3 lbs. 95%-fat free turkey kielbasa

1 cup ketchup

½ cup chili sauce

½ cup brown sugar, packed

2 Tbsp. Worcestershire sauce

1 Tbsp. lemon juice

¼ tsp. prepared mustard

Warm Memories:
I first tried this at a housewarming party and kept reminding the hostess about the recipe until she remembered to share it.

1. Cut kielbasa or smoked sausage into 6 or 9 large pieces. Lay it in a large pan of water. Simmer 20 minutes. Drain. Cool slightly. Cut into 1-oz. pieces.

2. Mix all other ingredients in 13x9-inch baking dish. Add kielbasa. Toss to coat with sauce.

3. Bake at 325°F for 1½–2 hours, stirring occasionally.

Exchange List Values
- Carbohydrate 0.5
- Lean Meat 1.0

Basic Nutritional Values
- Calories 65
  (Calories from Fat 15)
- Total Fat 2 gm
  (Saturated Fat 0.8 gm,
  Trans Fat 0.0 gm,
  Polyunsat Fat 0.3 gm,
  Monounsat Fat 0.5 gm)
- Cholesterol 20 mg
- Sodium 380 mg
- Potassium 95 gm
- Total Carb 5 gm
- Dietary Fiber 0 gm
- Sugars 3 gm
- Protein 5 gm
- Phosphorus 55 gm

TIP

You can keep this warm in a slow cooker or chafing dish.

Smoky Barbecue Meatballs

Carla Koslowsky
Hillsboro, KS
Sherry Kreider
Lancaster, PA

Jennie Martin
Richfield, PA

Makes 10 servings, 1 meatball per serving
Prep. Time: 30 minutes
Baking Time: 50–60 minutes

1½ lbs. 90%-lean ground beef

½ cup quick oats

½ cup fat-free evaporated milk or milk

¼ cup egg substitute

¼–½ cup finely chopped onion, *optional*

¼ tsp. garlic powder

¼ tsp. pepper

¼ tsp. chili powder

1 tsp. salt

Sauce:

1 cup ketchup

6 Tbsp. Splenda Brown Sugar Blend

¼ cup chopped onion

¼ tsp. liquid smoke

TIP

1. Bring the sauce to a boil and boil 2 minutes. Reserve a little before pouring over the meatballs. Then, at the end of baking and just before serving, brush on the reserved sauce.
   —Sherry Kreider, Lancaster, PA

1. Mix beef, oats, milk, egg substitute, onion, garlic powder, pepper, chili powder, and salt together. Form 10 balls, each weighing about 2 oz. Place in 9x13-oz baking dish.

2. Bake at 350°F for 40 minutes. Mix the sauce ingredients while the meatballs bake. Set aside.

3. Pour off any grease from the meatballs after they have baked for 40 minutes. Pour sauce over meatballs.

4. Bake meatballs and sauce an additional 10–20 minutes, until bubbling and heated through.

Exchange List Values
- Carbohydrate 1.0
- Lean Meat 2.0
- Fat 0.5

Basic Nutritional Values
- Calories 190
  (Calories from Fat 55)
- Total Fat 6 gm
  (Saturated Fat 2.3 gm,
  Trans Fat 0.3 gm,
  Polyunsat Fat 0.3 gm,
  Monounsat Fat 2.4 gm)
- Cholesterol 40 mg
- Sodium 450 mg
- Potassium 375 gm
- Total Carb 18 gm
- Dietary Fiber 1 gm
- Sugars 11 gm
- Protein 16 gm
- Phosphorus 170 gm

Tasty Barbecue Wings

Hope Comerford
Clinton Township, MI

Makes 8–10 servings
Prep. Time: 30 minutes
Broiling Time: 16 minutes
Cooking Time: 4–6 hours
Ideal slow-cooker size: 3-qt.

4 lbs. chicken wings, cut at the joint, tips removed and discarded

salt, to taste

pepper, to taste

12-oz. jar no sugar added or sugar-free grape jelly

2 Tbsp. Dijon mustard

½ cup barbecue sauce

1. Preheat your oven to a low broil.

2. Put your wing pieces onto a baking sheet and sprinkle both sides with salt and pepper. Put them under the broiler for 8 minutes on each side.

3. While the wings are broiling, mix together the remaining ingredients.

4. When your wings are done under the broiler, place them into a greased crock.

5. Pour the sauce you just mixed over the top, then use tongs to toss the wings around to make sure they're all coated with the sauce.

6. Cook on Low for 4–6 hours.

Exchange List Values
- Fruit 1.0
- Med-Fat Meat 4.0
- Fat 0

Basic Nutritional Values
- Calories 369
  (Calories from Fat 167)
  Total Fat 18.6 gm
  (Saturated Fat 9 gm,
  Trans Fat 0.2 gm,
  Polyunsat Fat 3.6 gm,
  Monounsat Fat 8.5 gm)
- Cholesterol 138 mg
- Sodium 544 mg
- Potassium 428 gm
- Total Carb 4.7 gm
- Dietary Fiber 0.4 gm
- Sugars 18.6gm
- Protein 30.9 gm
- Phosphorus 227 gm

Apricot-Glazed Wings

Hope Comerford
Clinton Township, MI

Makes 8–10 servings
Prep. Time: 30 minutes
Broiling Time: 16 minutes
Cooking Time: 4–6 hours
Ideal slow-cooker size: 3-qt.

4 lbs. chicken wings, cut at the joint, tips removed and discarded

salt, to taste

pepper, to taste

garlic powder, to taste

12-oz. jar no sugar added or sugar-free apricot preserves

¼ cup honey Catalina dressing

2 Tbsp. honey mustard

2 Tbsp. barbecue sauce

1 tsp. lime juice

4 dashes hot sauce

1 small onion, minced

1. Preheat your oven to a low broil.

2. Put your wing pieces onto a baking sheet and sprinkle both sides with salt, pepper, and garlic powder. Put them under the broiler for 8 minutes on each side.

3. While the wings are broiling, mix together the apricot preserves, honey Catalina dressing, honey mustard, barbecue sauce, lime juice, hot sauce, and onion.

4. When your wings are done under the broiler, place them into a greased crock.

5. Pour the sauce you just mixed over the top, then use tongs to toss the wings around to make sure they're all coated with the sauce.

6. Cook on Low for 4–6 hours.

Exchange List Values
- Fruit 1.0
- Med-Fat Meat 4.0

Basic Nutritional Values
- Calories 417
  (Calories from Fat 180)
  Total Fat 20 gm
  (Saturated Fat 5.4 gm,
  Trans Fat 0.5 gm,
  Polyunsat Fat 3.6 gm,
  Monounsat Fat 8.5 gm)
- Cholesterol 82 mg
- Sodium 589 mg
- Potassium 449 gm
- Total Carb 24 gm
- Dietary Fiber 1 gm
- Sugars 20.3gm
- Protein 31.2 gm
- Phosphorus 230 gm

Breakfast and Brunch

Breakfast and Brunch

California Egg Bake

Leona M. Slabaugh
Apple Creek, OH

Makes 2 servings
Prep. Time: 10–15 minutes
Baking Time: 25–30 minutes

¾ cup egg substitute

¼ cup fat-free sour cream

⅛ tsp. salt

1 medium tomato, chopped

1 green onion, sliced

¼ cup reduced-fat shredded cheddar cheese

1. In a small bowl, beat egg substitute, sour cream, and salt.

2. Stir in tomato, onion, and cheese.

3. Pour into greased 2-cup baking dish.

4. Bake at 350°F for 25–30 minutes, or until a knife inserted in center comes out clean.

Exchange List Values
- Carbohydrate 0.5
- Lean Meat 2.0

Basic Nutritional Values
- Calories 125
  (Calories from Fat 30)
- Total Fat 4 gm
  (Saturated Fat 1.9 gm,
  Trans Fat 0.0 gm,
  Polyunsat Fat 0.2 gm,
  Monounsat Fat 0.7 gm)
- Cholesterol 10 mg
- Sodium 480 mg
- Potassium 350 gm
- Total Carb 10 gm
- Dietary Fiber 1 gm
- Sugars 4 gm
- Protein 14 gm
- Phosphorus 140 gm

Eggs à la Shrimp

Willard E. Roth
Elkhart, IN

Makes 6 servings
Prep. Time: 15 minutes
Cooking Time: 15 minutes

1 Tbsp. canola oil

3 green onions with tops, sliced, or 1 small onion, chopped fine

¼ cup finely chopped celery with leaves

4 oz. shrimp, frozen or canned

3 Tbsp. plus ¼ cup white wine, *divided*

4 large eggs

1 cup egg substitute

4 oz. frozen peas, or fresh

¼ tsp. salt

¼ tsp. pepper

fresh parsley

Good Go-Alongs:
Freshly baked muffins
Fresh fruit in season

NOTES

A simple but special brunch—or supper—entrée.

1. Preheat electric skillet to 375°F, or cast-iron skillet to medium high.

2. Heat oil in skillet. Sauté onions, until limp.

3. Add celery and sauté until softened.

4. Add shrimp and 3 Tbsp. white wine. Cover and steam over low heat for 3 minutes.

5. In a medium-sized mixing bowl, toss eggs and egg substitute with ¼ cup white wine. Pour into skillet.

6. Stir in peas and seasonings.

7. Turn skillet to 300°F, or medium low. Stir gently as mixture cooks. Cook just until mixture sets according to your liking.

8. Serve on warm platter surrounded with fresh parsley.

Exchange List Values
- Lean Meat 2.0
- Fat 1.0

Basic Nutritional Values
- Calories 135 (Calories from Fat 55)
- Total Fat 6 gm (Saturated Fat 1.3 gm, Trans Fat 0.0 gm, Polyunsat Fat 1.4 gm, Monounsat Fat 2.8 gm)
- Cholesterol 165 mg
- Sodium 415 mg
- Potassium 195 gm
- Total Carb 4.5 gm
- Dietary Fiber 1 gm
- Sugars 2 gm
- Protein 14 gm
- Phosphorus 145 gm

Breakfast Soufflé

Freda Friesen
Hillsboro, KS

Makes 12 servings, 3-inch square per
  serving
Prep. Time: 20 minutes
Standing Time: 12 hours or overnight
Baking Time: 1 hour

½ lb. reduced-fat pork sausage

2¼ cups egg substitute

3 cups fat-free milk

1½ tsp. dry mustard

¾ tsp. salt

3 slices bread, cubed

¾ cup grated 75%-less-fat cheddar cheese

1. Brown pork sausage and drain excess fat. Set aside.

2. Combine egg substitute, milk, mustard, and salt. Add sausage, bread, and cheese.

3. Spoon into greased 9x13-inch pan. Cover and refrigerate overnight.

4. Bake, uncovered, at 350°F for 1 hour.

Exchange List Values
- Carbohydrate 0.5
- Lean Meat 2.0

Basic Nutritional Values
- Calories 115
  (Calories from Fat 35)
- Total Fat 4 gm
  (Saturated Fat 1.4 gm,
  Trans Fat 0.0 gm,
  Polyunsat Fat 0.5 gm,
  Monounsat Fat 1.5 gm)
- Cholesterol 15 mg
- Sodium 440 mg
- Potassium 220 gm
- Total Carb 7 gm
- Dietary Fiber 0 gm
- Sugars 4 gm
- Protein 12 gm
- Phosphorus 135 gm

Baked Eggs

Esther J. Mast
Lancaster, PA

Make 8 servings, 2¾x3½-inch rectangle per
  serving
Prep. Time: 15 minutes
Baking Time: 40–45 minutes

Breakfast and Brunch

2 Tbsp. trans-fat-free tub margarine

1 cup reduced-fat buttermilk baking mix

1½ cups fat-free cottage cheese

2 tsp. chopped onion

1 tsp. dried parsley

½ cup grated reduced-fat cheddar cheese

1 egg, slightly beaten

1¼ cups egg substitute

1 cup fat-free milk

1. Cut margarine into chunks and place in 7x11-inch baking dish. Turn oven to 350°F and put dish in oven to melt margarine.

2. Meanwhile, mix together buttermilk baking mix, cottage cheese, onion, parsley, cheese, egg, egg substitute, and milk in large mixing bowl.

3. Pour mixture over melted margarine. Stir slightly to distribute margarine.

4. Bake 40–45 minutes until firm but not drying out.

5. Allow to stand 10 minutes. Cut in rectangles and serve.

Exchange List Values

- Carbohydrate 1.0
- Lean Meat 2.0

Basic Nutritional Values

- Calories 155
  (Calories from Fat 45)
- Total Fat 5 gm
  (Saturated Fat 1.5 gm,
  Trans Fat 0.0 gm,
  Polyunsat Fat 1.2 gm,
  Monounsat Fat 1.8 gm)
- Cholesterol 30 mg
- Sodium 460 mg
- Potassium 195 gm
- Total Carb 15 gm
- Dietary Fiber 0 gm
- Sugars 4 gm
- Protein 12 gm
- Phosphorus 250 gm

Shredded Potato Omelet

Mary H. Nolt
East Earl, PA

Makes 6 servings
Prep. Time: 15 minutes
Cooking Time: 20 minutes

3 slices bacon

cooking spray

2 cups shredded cooked potatoes

¼ cup minced onion

¼ cup minced green bell pepper

1 cup egg substitute

¼ cup fat-free milk

¼ tsp. salt

⅛ tsp. black pepper

1 cup 75%-less-fat shredded cheddar cheese

1. In large skillet, fry bacon until crisp. Remove bacon and crumble. Wipe skillet, and spray lightly with cooking spray.

2. Mix potatoes, onion, and green pepper in bowl. Spoon into skillet. Cook over low heat—without stirring—until underside is crisp and brown.

3. Blend egg substitute, milk, salt, and pepper in mixing bowl. Pour over potato mixture.

4. Top with cheese and bacon.

5. Cover. Cook over low heat approximately 10 minutes, or until set. Loosen omelet and serve.

Exchange List Values
- Starch 1.0
- Lean Meat 1.0

Basic Nutritional Values
- Calories 130
  (Calories from Fat 25)
- Total Fat 3 gm
  (Saturated Fat 1.4 gm,
  Trans Fat 0.0 gm,
  Polyunsat Fat 0.2 gm,
  Monounsat Fat 0.9 gm)
- Cholesterol 10 mg
- Sodium 415 mg
- Potassium 280 gm
- Total Carb 13 gm
- Dietary Fiber 2 gm
- Sugars 2 gm
- Protein 12 gm
- Phosphorus 150 gm

Egg Scramble

Elva Bare
Lancaster, PA

Makes 6 servings, 4½–5½ oz. per serving
Prep. Time: 30–45 minutes
Cooking Time: 10 minutes

1 medium-large potato, enough to make 3/4 cup grated potatoes

1 Tbsp. canola oil

1/2 cup chopped red bell pepper

1/4 cup chopped green bell pepper

1/2 cup chopped onion

4 eggs

1 cup egg substitute

1/3 cup fat-free sour cream

1/4 cup fat-free milk

1/2 tsp. onion salt

1/4 tsp. garlic salt

1/8 tsp. pepper

1/2 cup real bacon bits

1/2 cup shredded 75%-less-fat cheddar, or Cooper sharp, cheese

1. Place the whole potato with skin on in a small pan. Add about ½ inch water, cover, and cook over low heat until fork-tender.

2. Remove and allow to reach room temperature.

3. Chill thoroughly. Grate.

4. Sauté peppers and onion in canola oil 3–5 minutes.

5. In a blender, combine eggs, egg substitute, sour cream, milk, onion salt, garlic salt, and pepper. Cover and process until smooth.

6. Stir grated potato and bacon into vegetables in skillet.

7. Pour egg mixture over vegetables.

8. Cook and stir over medium heat until eggs are set.

9. Sprinkle with cheese. Cover skillet with lid until cheese melts.

10. Cut in wedges in skillet and serve on heated dinner plates.

Good Go-Alongs:
Serve toasted bagels and fresh fruit. Add a broiled tomato, which you've cut in half and sprinkled with Parmesan cheese before running under the broiler.

TIP

1. You can do a lot of the prep for this dish the day or evening before serving it. Cook the potato in advance and chill it. Chop the vegetables ahead of time and refrigerate them. You can even blend the eggs, sour cream, milk, salts, and pepper the day before and then refrigerate the mixture. The morning of your breakfast you're ready to go.
2. I heat the dinner plates in my oven, turned on Low, for 5–10 minutes.

Exchange List Values

- Carbohydrate 1.0
- Lean Meat 2.0
- Fat 0.5

Basic Nutritional Values

- Calories 180
  (Calories from Fat 70)
- Total Fat 8 gm
  (Saturated Fat 2.5 gm,
  Trans Fat 0.0 gm,
  Polyunsat Fat 1.3 gm,
  Monounsat Fat 3.2 gm)
- Cholesterol 130 mg
- Sodium 485 mg
- Potassium 385 gm
- Total Carb 12 gm
- Dietary Fiber 1 gm
- Sugars 3 gm
- Protein 15 gm
- Phosphorus 175 gm

Egg Casserole

Marie Davis
Mineral Ridge, OH

Makes 6 servings
Prep. Time: 15 minutes
Baking Time: 35–40 minutes

4- or 6½-oz. jar marinated artichoke hearts

½ cup chopped green onions

2–3 cloves garlic, minced

1 Tbsp. vegetable oil

2 cups egg substitute

4½-oz. can sliced mushrooms, drained

1 cup 75%-less-fat shredded sharp cheddar cheese

⅔ cup butter-flavored cracker crumbs (about 16 crackers, crushed)

1. Drain artichokes. Cut artichokes into small pieces.

2. In small skillet, sauté green onions and garlic in oil until tender.

3. In large bowl, beat egg substitute.

4. Stir in artichokes, onion mixture, mushrooms, cheese, and cracker crumbs.

5. Bake at 350°F for 35–40 minutes.

TIP

You can use ¼ lb. fresh mushrooms, sliced, instead of canned mushrooms in this dish. If you use fresh ones, sauté with onion and garlic in Step 2.

Exchange List Values
- Carbohydrate 1.0
- Lean Meat 2.0
- Fat 0.5

Basic Nutritional Values
- Calories 165 (Calories from Fat 55)
- Total Fat 6 gm (Saturated Fat 1.3 gm, Trans Fat 0.0 gm, Polyunsat Fat 2.2 gm, Monounsat Fat 2.0 gm)
- Cholesterol 5 mg
- Sodium 480 mg
- Potassium 230 gm
- Total Carb 11 gm
- Dietary Fiber 1 gm
- Sugars 2 gm
- Protein 16 gm
- Phosphorus 150 gm

Cheese Soufflé Casserole

Iva Schmidt
Fergus Falls, MN

Makes 6 servings
Prep. Time: 20 minutes
Cooking Time: 3–4 hours
Ideal slow-cooker size: 3- or 4-qt.

8 slices bread (crusts removed), cubed or torn into squares

2 cups grated fat-free cheddar cheese

1 cup cooked, chopped extra-lean, lower-sodium ham

4 eggs

1 cup fat-free half-and-half

1 cup fat-free evaporated milk

1 Tbsp. parsley

paprika

Exchange List Values
- Starch 1.0
- Fat-Free Milk 0.5
- Lean Meat 2.0

Basic Nutritional Values
- Calories 233
  (Calories from Fat 46)
- Total Fat 5 gm
  (Saturated Fat 1.9 gm,
  Polyunsat Fat 0.9 gm,
  Monounsat Fat 1.6 gm)
- Cholesterol 159 mg
- Sodium 650 mg
- Total Carb 22 gm
- Dietary Fiber 0 gm
- Sugars 9 gm
- Protein 23 gm

1. Lightly grease slow cooker. Alternate layers of bread and cheese and ham.

2. Beat together eggs, half-and-half, milk, and parsley. Pour over bread in slow cooker.

3. Sprinkle with paprika.

4. Cover and cook on Low 3–4 hours. The longer cooking time yields a firmer, dryer dish.

5. About 30 minutes before finish, increase temperature to High and remove lid.

Egg and Broccoli Casserole

Joette Droz
Kalona, IA

Makes 8 servings
Prep. Time: 20 minutes
Cooking Time: 3½–4 hours
Ideal slow-cooker size: 4-qt.

24-oz. carton small-curd 1% milkfat cottage cheese

10-oz. pkg. frozen chopped broccoli, thawed and drained

1½ cups shredded cheddar cheese

6 eggs, beaten

⅓ cup flour

2 Tbsp. canola oil

3 Tbsp. finely chopped onion

shredded cheese, *optional*

1. Combine first 7 ingredients. Pour into greased slow cooker.

2. Cover and cook on High 1 hour. Stir. Reduce heat to Low. Cover and cook 2½–3 hours, or until temperature reaches 160°F and eggs are set.

3. Sprinkle with cheese, if using, and serve.

Exchange List Values
- Carbohydrate 0.5
- Lean Meat 3.0

Basic Nutritional Values
- Calories 211 (Calories from Fat 74)
- Total Fat 8 gm (Saturated Fat 2.3 gm, Polyunsat Fat 1.6 gm, Monounsat Fat 3.7 gm)
- Cholesterol 165 mg
- Sodium 550 mg
- Total Carb 10 gm
- Dietary Fiber 1 gm
- Sugars 5 gm
- Protein 23 gm

Peanut Butter Granola

Dawn Ranck
Harrisonburg, VA

Makes 26 servings
Prep. Time: 20 minutes
Cooking Time: 1½ hours
Ideal slow-cooker size: 5-qt.

6 cups dry oatmeal

½ cup wheat germ

¼ cup toasted coconut

½ cup sunflower seeds

½ cup raisins

8 Tbsp. light, soft tub margarine

¾ cup peanut butter

½ cup brown sugar substitute to equal 4
  Tbsp. sugar

1. Combine oatmeal, wheat germ, coconut, sunflower seeds, and raisins in large slow cooker.

2. Melt together margarine, peanut butter, and brown sugar. Pour over oatmeal in cooker. Mix well.

3. Cover. Cook on Low 1½ hours, stirring every 15 minutes.

4. Allow to cool in cooker, stirring every 30 minutes or so, or spread onto cookie sheet. When thoroughly cooled, break into chunks and store in airtight container.

Exchange List Values

- Starch 0.5
- Carbohydrate 1.0
- Fat 1.5

Basic Nutritional Values

- Calories 179
  (Calories from Fat 73)
- Total Fat 8 gm
  (Saturated Fat 1.5 gm,
  Polyunsat Fat 2.8 gm,
  Monounsat Fat 3.3 gm)
- Cholesterol 0 mg
- Sodium 70 mg
- Total Carb 22 gm
- Dietary Fiber 3 gm
- Sugars 7 gm
- Protein 6 gm

Southwestern Egg Casserole

Eileen Eash
Lafayette, CO

Makes 12 servings, approximately 3x3-inch
  square per serving
Prep. Time: 20–30 minutes
Baking Time: 35–45 minutes
Standing Time: 5–10 minutes

2½ cups egg substitute

½ cup flour

1 tsp. baking powder

⅛ tsp. salt

⅛ tsp. pepper

1½ cups shredded 75%-less-fat sharp
  cheddar cheese

2 cups fat-free cottage cheese

¼ cup trans-fat-free tub margarine

2 4-oz. cans chopped green chilies

1. Beat egg substitute in a large mixing
bowl.

2. In a smaller bowl, combine flour,
baking powder, salt, and pepper. Stir into egg
substitute. Batter will be lumpy.

3. Add cheeses, margarine, and chilies to
batter.

4. Pour into greased 9x13-inch baking dish.

5. Bake at 350°F for 35–45 minutes, or
until knife inserted near center comes out
clean.

6. Let stand 5–10 minutes before cutting.

TIP

1. This is a great recipe for brunch.
   I usually put it together the night
   before and then refrigerate it.
2. To take to a potluck after baking it,
   I transport it in an insulated carrier,
   which I wrap in an old mattress pad.
   It stays hot for at least an hour.

Exchange List Values
- Carbohydrate 0.5
- Lean Meat 2.0

Basic Nutritional Values
- Calories 130
  (Calories from Fat 35)
- Total Fat 4 gm
  (Saturated Fat 1.4 gm,
  Trans Fat 0.0 gm,
  Polyunsat Fat 1.2 gm,
  Monounsat Fat 1.2 gm)
- Cholesterol 10 mg
- Sodium 450 mg
- Potassium 180 gm
- Total Carb 9 gm
- Dietary Fiber 1 gm
- Sugars 1 gm
- Protein 14 gm
- Phosphorus 190 gm

Breakfast Pie

Darlene Bloom
San Antonio, TX

Makes 6 servings
Prep. Time: 20 minutes
Baking Time: 30 minutes

8 oz. lower-sodium ham

1 cup chopped onion

1 cup chopped bell pepper, red or green

1 cup 75%-less-fat shredded cheddar cheese

½ cup reduced-fat buttermilk baking mix

1 cup fat-free milk

2 eggs

1. Brown ham, onion, and bell pepper in skillet on stove until done. Drain off drippings.

2. Place cooked ingredients in a greased 9-inch pie plate.

3. Top with layer of shredded cheese.

4. In a mixing bowl, whisk baking mix, milk, and eggs together. Pour over ingredients in pie plate.

5. Bake at 400°F for 30 minutes.

6. Allow to stand 5–10 minutes before cutting and serving.

TIP

1. Double this recipe and prepare in a 9x13-inch baking pan. I take this to potlucks all the time (warm) out of the oven.
2. You can use ground turkey or beef as your choice of meats and add 1 envelope taco seasoning mix to the skillet as you cook. I call this version Taco Bake and often make it for dinner.

Exchange List Values
- Carbohydrate 1.0
- Lean Meat 2.0

Basic Nutritional Values
- Calories 170 (Calories from Fat 40)
- Total Fat 4.5 gm (Saturated Fat 1.8 gm, Trans Fat 0.0 gm, Polyunsat Fat 0.6 gm, Monounsat Fat 1.7 gm)
- Cholesterol 85 mg
- Sodium 595 mg
- Potassium 295 gm
- Total Carb 15 gm
- Dietary Fiber 1 gm
- Sugars 6 gm
- Protein 17 gm
- Phosphorus 310 gm

Easy Quiche

Becky Bontrager Horst
Goshen, IN

Makes 6 servings, 1 slice per serving
Prep. Time: 15 minutes
Baking Time: 45–55 minutes

¼ cup chopped onion

¼ cup chopped mushrooms, *optional*

1 tsp. canola oil

3 oz. 75%-less-fat cheddar cheese, shredded

2 Tbsp. bacon bits, chopped ham, or
 browned sausage

4 eggs

¼ tsp. salt

1½ cups fat-free milk

½ cup whole wheat flour

1 Tbsp. trans-fat-free tub margarine

Exchange List Values
• Carbohydrate 1.0
• Lean Meat 2.0

Basic Nutritional Values
• Calories 135
 (Calories from Fat 35)
• Total Fat 4 gm
 (Saturated Fat 1.5 gm,
 Trans Fat 0.0 gm,
 Polyunsat Fat 0.9 gm,
 Monounsat Fat 1.4 gm)
• Cholesterol 10 mg
• Sodium 400 mg
• Potassium 255 gm
• Total Carb 12 gm
• Dietary Fiber 1 gm
• Sugars 4 gm
• Protein 13 gm
• Phosphorus 170 gm

1. Sauté onion and mushrooms (if using) in oil.

2. Combine cheese, meat, and vegetables in greased 9-inch pie pan.

3. Combine remaining ingredients in medium bowl. Pour over meat and vegetables mixture.

4. Bake at 350°F for 45–55 minutes, or until the center is set. This quiche will make its own crust.

Quiche

Marjorie Weaver Nafziger
Harman, WV

Makes 6 servings, 1 slice of the pie per
  serving
Prep. Time: 25 minutes
Cooking/Baking Time: 55–65 minutes
Standing Time: 5–10 minutes

9-inch unbaked pie shell

2 cups chopped tomatoes, green beans,
  onions, or mushrooms

½ cup chopped chicken breast

½ tsp. basil, sage, thyme, or oregano

¾ tsp. salt

dash pepper

½ cup grated reduced-fat Swiss cheese

½ cup egg substitute

2 Tbsp. flour

1 cup fat-free evaporated milk

1. Bake pie shell for 10 minutes at 375°F.
Set aside.

2. Lightly sauté choice of vegetables and
chicken. Spoon into pie shell.

3. Sprinkle choice of seasonings over
vegetable mixture. Add salt and dash of
pepper. Cover with grated cheese.

4. Combine egg substitute, flour, and milk.
Pour over ingredients.

5. Bake at 375°F for 40–45 minutes or
until set. Let sit at least 5 minutes before
serving.

Variation:

Instead of using regular pie shell, combine
3 Tbsp. cooking oil with 3–4 cups grated
potatoes. Press mixture into 9-inch pie pan
and bake at 425°F for 15 minutes.

Exchange List Values

- Carbohydrate 1.0
- Lean Meat 2.0

Basic Nutritional Values

- Calories 160
  (Calories from Fat 45)
- Total Fat 5 gm
  (Saturated Fat 1.5 gm,
  Trans Fat 0.2 gm,
  Polyunsat Fat 0.8 gm,
  Monounsat Fat 1.8 gm)
- Cholesterol 20 mg
- Sodium 430 mg
- Potassium 365 gm
- Total Carb 16 gm
- Dietary Fiber 1 gm
- Sugars 7 gm
- Protein 13 gm
- Phosphorus 195 gm

Southwest Brunch Casserole

Janita Mellinger
Abbottstown, PA

Makes 4 servings, ½ an English muffin per serving
Prep. Time: 20–30 minutes
Chilling Time: 3–8 hours
Baking Time: 20–25 minutes

1 Tbsp. trans-fat-free tub margarine

2 English muffins, split

1 oz. reduced-fat bulk pork sausage

1 cup egg substitute

¼ cup fat-free sour cream

¼ cup grated 75%-less-fat cheddar cheese

¼ cup chopped chilies, *optional*

1. Spread margarine over cut sides of each muffin half. Place margarine-side up in 8-inch square baking pan coated with nonstick cooking spray.

2. In a small skillet, cook sausage. Drain off drippings.

3. Spoon sausage over muffin halves.

4. In a small mixing bowl, whisk egg substitute and sour cream together.

5. Pour over sausage.

6. Sprinkle with cheese, and chilies if you wish.

7. Cover and refrigerate 3 hours or overnight.

8. Remove from refrigerator 30 minutes before baking.

9. Bake uncovered at 350°F for 20–25 minutes, or until knife inserted near center comes out clean.

TIP

This is great for sleep-in mornings or overnight guests. You can avoid the morning rush.

Exchange List Values
- Starch 1.0
- Lean Meat 1.0
- Fat 0.5

Basic Nutritional Values
- Calories 160 (Calories from Fat 40)
- Total Fat 4.5 gm (Saturated Fat 1.5 gm, Trans Fat 0.0 gm, Polyunsat Fat 1.2 gm, Monounsat Fat 1.5 gm)
- Cholesterol 10 mg
- Sodium 365 mg
- Potassium 170 gm
- Total Carb 16 gm
- Dietary Fiber 1 gm
- Sugars 2 gm
- Protein 13 gm
- Phosphorus 95 gm

Brunch Delight

Jean Butzer
Batavia, NY

Makes 12 servings, 3-inch square per
 serving
Prep. Time: 15 minutes
Baking Time: 35–45 minutes

½ cup chopped onion

½ cup chopped green bell pepper

4 eggs

2 cups egg substitute

1 cup milk

½ lb. extra-lean 95%-fat-free cooked ham, cut
 into small cubes

16 oz. frozen shredded hash brown potatoes,
 thawed

1 cup shredded 75%-less-fat cheddar cheese

¼ tsp. salt

½ tsp. pepper

½ tsp. dill weed

1. Sauté onion and green pepper in small nonstick skillet. Or cook just until soft in microwave.

2. In large bowl whisk together eggs, egg substitute, and milk.

3. Stir in cooked vegetables, ham, potatoes, cheese, salt, pepper, and dill weed.

4. Spoon into well-greased 9x13-inch baking pan.

5. Bake at 350°F for 35–45 minutes, or until knife blade inserted in center comes out clean.

6. Allow to stand 10 minutes before cutting into squares to serve.

Variation:

Add ½ cup diced green chilies to Step 3.
 —Mamie Christopherson, Rio Rancho, NM

Exchange List Values
- Starch 0.5
- Lean Meat 2.0

Basic Nutritional Values
- Calories 135
 (Calories from Fat 30)
- Total Fat 4 gm
 (Saturated Fat 1.4 gm,
 Trans Fat 0.0 gm,
 Polyunsat Fat 0.5 gm,
 Monounsat Fat 1.3 gm)
- Cholesterol 75 mg
- Sodium 460 mg
- Potassium 335 gm
- Total Carb 10 gm
- Dietary Fiber 1 gm
- Sugars 2 gm
- Protein 15 gm
- Phosphorus 160 gm

Brunch Enchiladas

Ann Good
Perry, NY

Makes 16 servings, 1 filled tortilla per serving
Prep. Time: 20–35 minutes
Chilling Time: 8 hours, or overnight
Baking Time: 45–60 minutes
Standing Time: 5–10 minutes

¾ cup chopped bell peppers

¾ cup chopped onion

1 Tbsp. canola oil

2 cups extra-lean chopped cooked ham

16 6-inch flour tortillas

8-oz. container fat-free sour cream, *divided*

1½ cups shredded 75%-less-fat cheese, *divided*

2 cups egg substitute

8 eggs

1½ cups fat-free milk

2 Tbsp. flour

½ tsp. pepper

3 medium tomatoes, sliced

1. In saucepan, sauté peppers and onion in oil until soft.

2. Stir in meat and cook until heated through.

3. Spread 1 Tbsp. of sour cream in a strip through the center of each tortilla.

4. Spoon 2 Tbsp. meat mixture on top of sour cream on each tortilla.

5. Top with ½ Tbsp. cheese on each tortilla. (Reserve 1 cup cheese for topping enchiladas after baking.)

6. Roll up and place seams-down in two well-greased 9x13-inch baking pans.

7. In a large mixing bowl, beat together egg substitute, eggs, milk, flour, and pepper.

8. Pour over tortillas. Cover and refrigerate overnight.

9. Remove from refrigerator for 30 minutes before baking.

10. Bake uncovered at 350°F for 45–60 minutes, or until heated through.

11. Remove from oven. Top with tomato slices.

12. Let stand 5–10 minutes before serving.

Exchange List Values
- Starch 1.0
- Carbohydrate 0.5
- Lean Meat 2.0
- Fat 0.5

Basic Nutritional Values
- Calories 230
  (Calories from Fat 70)
- Total Fat 8 gm
  (Saturated Fat 2.4 gm,
  Trans Fat 0.0 gm,
  Polyunsat Fat 1.3 gm,
  Monounsat Fat 3.3 gm)
- Cholesterol 110 mg
- Sodium 595 mg
- Potassium 330 gm
- Total Carb 23 gm
- Dietary Fiber 2 gm
- Sugars 4 gm
- Protein 17 gm
- Phosphorus 225 gm

TIP

1. Serve with salsa and sour cream.
2. This dish freezes well.

Potato-Bacon Gratin

Valerie Drobel
Carlisle, PA

Makes 8 servings, about 5 oz. per serving
Prep. Time: 15 minutes
Baking Time: 1 hour
Standing Time: 10 minutes

6-oz. bag fresh spinach

1 clove garlic, minced

1 Tbsp. olive oil

4 large potatoes, peeled or unpeeled,
 divided

6-oz. Canadian bacon slices, *divided*

5-oz. reduced-fat grated Swiss cheddar,
 divided

1 cup lower-sodium, lower-fat chicken broth

1. In large skillet, sauté spinach and garlic in olive oil just until spinach is wilted.

2. Cut potatoes into thin slices.

3. In 2-qt. baking dish, layer ⅓ the potatoes, half the bacon, ⅓ the cheese, and half the wilted spinach.

4. Repeat layers ending with potatoes. Reserve ⅓ cheese for later.

5. Pour chicken broth over all.

6. Cover and bake at 350°F for 45 minutes.

7. Uncover and bake 15 more minutes. During last 5 minutes, top with cheese.

8. Allow to stand 10 minutes before serving.

TIP

Leftovers are delicious. Make two of these bakes at a time and freeze one.

Good Go-Alongs:
Baked apples or applesauce

Exchange List Values
- Carbohydrate 2.0
- Lean Meat 2.0

Basic Nutritional Values
- Calories 220
 (Calories from Fat 65)
- Total Fat 7 gm
 (Saturated Fat 2.4 gm,
 Trans Fat 0.0 gm,
 Polyunsat Fat 0.5 gm,
 Monounsat Fat 2.7 gm)
- Cholesterol 25 mg
- Sodium 415 mg
- Potassium 710 gm
- Total Carb 28 gm
- Dietary Fiber 3 gm
- Sugars 2 gm
- Protein 14 gm
- Phosphorus 285 gm

Brunch Pizza

Rachel King
Castile, NY

Makes 8 servings, 3¼x4½-inch rectangle
  per serving
Prep. Time: 1 hour
Baking Time: 15–18 minutes

8-oz. pkg. reduced-fat crescent rolls

2 Tbsp. chopped bacon

½ lb. fresh mushrooms, sliced

1 small onion, finely chopped

1 small green bell pepper, finely chopped

1 Tbsp. canola oil, *divided*

2 cups egg substitute

3 oz. fat-free cream cheese, softened to room
  temperature

⅓ cup fat-free sour cream

1 clove garlic, minced

¼ tsp. Italian seasoning

2 plum tomatoes, sliced thin

¾ cup shredded 75%-reduced-fat cheddar
  cheese

salsa and additional sour cream, *optional*

1. Open crescent dough tube and unroll. Press crescent dough over bottom and partway up sides of 9x13-inch baking pan.

2. Bake at 375°F for 6–8 minutes.

3. Meanwhile, cook bacon in large skillet until crispy. Remove bacon and allow to drain on a paper towel.

4. Sauté mushrooms, onions, and pepper in ½ Tbsp. oil until just tender.

5. Remove vegetables from pan and set aside.

6. Heat other ½ Tbsp. oil in skillet. Add egg substitute and cook, stirring, until almost set.

7. In a mixing bowl, beat together cream cheese, sour cream, garlic, and Italian seasoning. Spread over crescent-dough crust in baking pan.

8. Top with egg mixture, and then meat, and then sautéed vegetables.

9. Top with tomato slices and then cheese.

10. Bake at 375°F for 15–18 minutes, or until cheese is melted.

11. Serve with salsa and additional sour cream, if desired, for each person to add as they wish.

Exchange List Values
- Starch 1.0
- Vegetable 1.0
- Lean Meat 2.0
- Fat 0.5

Basic Nutritional Values
- Calories 200
  (Calories from Fat 70)
- Total Fat 8 gm
  (Saturated Fat 2.5 gm,
  Trans Fat 0.0 gm,
  Polyunsat Fat 1.6 gm,
  Monounsat Fat 1.9 gm)
- Cholesterol 5 mg
- Sodium 555 mg
- Potassium 380 gm
- Total Carb 19 gm
- Dietary Fiber 1 gm
- Sugars 6 gm
- Protein 15 gm
- Phosphorus 270 gm

Country Breakfast Pizza

Zoe Rohrer
Lancaster, PA

Makes 10 servings
Prep. Time: 25–30 minutes
Baking Time: 27 minutes

1½ Tbsp. olive oil

1 cup whole wheat pastry flour

⅔ cup, plus 2 Tbsp., all-purpose flour

1 Tbsp. flax meal, *optional*

2 tsp. baking powder

½ tsp. salt

¼ cup real maple syrup

scant ½ cup fat-free milk

¼ lb. lower-fat bulk pork sausage

½ green pepper, diced

2¼ cups egg substitute

1 cup shredded 75%-reduced-fat cheddar
  cheese, *divided*

maple syrup, or ketchup, for serving

1. Place oil in a 9x13-inch baking dish.

2. In a good-sized bowl, mix together flours, flax if you wish, baking powder, and salt.

3. Add maple syrup and milk. Stir to combine.

4. Knead a few minutes in bowl, or on countertop, to make a ball.

5. Press dough into oiled pan.

6. Bake 12 minutes at 425°F. Remove from the oven.

7. While crust is baking, brown sausage and pepper in skillet until pink is gone from meat and pepper is just tender. Stir frequently to break up meat. Place cooked meat and pepper on platter and keep warm. Discard drippings.

8. Beat egg substitute in mixing bowl. Pour into skillet used for sausage. Stir frequently. Add ⅔ cup cheese while eggs are cooking.

9. When crust is done, top with sausage, then eggs, and then remaining cheese.

10. Bake 10 more minutes or until cheese is melted.

11. Serve immediately with maple syrup or ketchup.

Exchange List Values
- Starch 1.0
- Carbohydrate 0.5
- Lean Meat 2.0

Basic Nutritional Values
- Calories 200
  (Calories from Fat 45)
- Total Fat 5 gm
  (Saturated Fat 1.5 gm,
  Trans Fat 0.0 gm,
  Polyunsat Fat 0.6 gm,
  Monounsat Fat 2.5 gm)
- Cholesterol 10 mg
- Sodium 435 mg
- Potassium 225 gm
- Total Carb 25 gm
- Dietary Fiber 2 gm
- Sugars 6 gm
- Protein 13 gm
- Phosphorus 235 gm

Bacon Cheese Squares

Katie Ebersol
Ronks, PA

Makes 12 servings, 3-inch square per
  serving
Prep. Time: 30 minutes
Baking Time: 18–24 minutes

2 cups reduced-fat buttermilk baking mix

1/2 cup cold water

4 oz. 75%-reduced-fat cheese, sliced

½ lb. 50–70% reduced-fat turkey bacon,
  sliced, cooked crisp, and crumbled

3 eggs

¾ cup egg substitute

½ cup fat-free milk

½ tsp. onion powder

1. In a bowl, combine the baking mix and
water. Stir 20 strokes.

2. Turn onto a floured surface. Knead 10
times.

3. Roll into a 10x14-inch rectangle. Fold
into quarters (without pressing down on the
folds) and place on the bottom and halfway
up the sides of a greased 9x13-inch baking
dish.

4. Lay cheese evenly over dough. Sprinkle
with bacon.

5. In the mixing bowl, beat together eggs,
egg substitute, milk, and onion powder.

6. Pour egg-milk mixture over bacon.

7. Bake at 425°F for 18–20 minutes, or
until a knife blade inserted in center comes
out clean. If it doesn't, continue baking
another 4 minutes. Test again. Continue
baking if needed, or remove from oven.

8. Allow to stand 10 minutes before cutting
into squares and serving.

Exchange List Values

- Starch 1.0
- Lean Meat 1.0
- Fat 0.5

Basic Nutritional Values

- Calories 140
  (Calories from Fat 45)
- Total Fat 5 gm
  (Saturated Fat 1.5 gm,
  Trans Fat 0.0 gm,
  Polyunsat Fat 0.9 gm,
  Monounsat Fat 2.0 gm)
- Cholesterol 60 mg
- Sodium 440 mg
- Potassium 110 gm
- Total Carb 15 gm
- Dietary Fiber 1 gm
- Sugars 2 gm
- Protein 9 gm
- Phosphorus 215 gm

Sausage and Eggs Baked in Mugs

Peggy C. Forsythe
Memphis, TN

Makes 10 servings
Prep. Time: 30 minutes
Baking Time: 25–30 minutes for mugs or
    ramekins; 1 hour for 9x13-inch baking
    dish

12 oz. sourdough bread, sliced and cut into
    ½-inch cubes

6 oz. 50%-reduced-fat pork bulk sausage

2½ cups fat-free milk

4 large eggs

1 Tbsp. Dijon mustard

½ cup fat-free buttermilk

10¾-oz. can cream of mushroom soup

¾ cup shredded 75%-less-fat sharp cheddar
    cheese

1. Spray insides of 10 ovenproof coffee mugs
or ramekins with nonstick cooking spray.

2. Divide bread cubes evenly among mugs
or ramekins.

3. Brown bulk sausage in skillet, breaking
up with wooden spoon and stirring until all
pink is gone. Drain off drippings.

4. Top bread cubes in each mug or
ramekin with crumbled sausage.

5. In a mixing bowl, whisk together milk,
eggs, and Dijon mustard. Pour evenly over
bread and sausage.

6. In same bowl, whisk together
buttermilk and cream of mushroom soup.
Spoon over bread mixture.

7. Sprinkle each mug or ramekin with
cheddar cheese.

8. Place coffee mugs or ramekins on
baking sheet.

9. Bake at 350°F for 25–30 minutes, or
until individual casseroles are set and puffed.
Serve immediately.

Exchange List Values
- Starch 1.0
- Carbohydrate 0.5
- Lean Meat 2.0
- Fat 0.5

Basic Nutritional Values
- Calories 225
  (Calories from Fat 55)
- Total Fat 6 gm
  (Saturated Fat 2.3 gm,
  Trans Fat 0.0 gm,
  Polyunsat Fat 1.3 gm,
  Monounsat Fat 2.4 gm)
- Cholesterol 90 mg
- Sodium 525 mg
- Potassium 435 gm
- Total Carb 26 gm
- Dietary Fiber 1 gm
- Sugars 5 gm
- Protein 15 gm
- Phosphorus 225 gm

Fast, Friendly French Toast

Donna Barnitz
Rio Rancho, NM

Makes 8 servings
Prep. Time: 15 minutes
Soaking Time: 1–24 hours
Baking Time: 15 minutes

1 lb. loaf French bread, cut into 1-inch-thick slices

1½ cups fat-free milk

4 eggs

½ cup orange juice

¼ cup sugar

1 Tbsp. vanilla extract

cinnamon, *optional*

1. Arrange bread slices in a 9x13-inch baking pan.

2. In a mixing bowl, beat milk, eggs, orange juice, sugar, and vanilla together until well blended.

3. Pour over bread.

4. Cover and refrigerate 1–24 hours, according to your schedule and how much time you have.

5. Heat oven to 400°F. Grease jelly-roll pan.

6. Transfer bread to pan, making sure slices don't touch. Dust with cinnamon, if you wish.

7. Bake 15 minutes, or until puffy and lightly browned.

Exchange List Values
- Starch 2.0
- Carbohydrate 1.0
- Lean Meat 1.0

Basic Nutritional Values
- Calories 250 (Calories from Fat 30)
- Total Fat 4 gm (Saturated Fat 1.1 gm, Trans Fat 0.0 gm, Polyunsat Fat 0.9 gm, Monounsat Fat 1.1 gm)
- Cholesterol 95 mg
- Sodium 345 mg
- Potassium 210 gm
- Total Carb 43 gm
- Dietary Fiber 1 gm
- Sugars 12 gm
- Protein 11 gm
- Phosphorus 165 gm

Overnight Apple French Toast

Eileen Eash
Lafayette, CO
Peggy C. Forsythe
Memphis, TN

Makes 9 servings, 1 slice per serving
Prep. Time: 40–45 minutes
Chilling Time: 8 hours, or overnight
Baking Time: 35–40 minutes

6 Tbsp. Splenda Brown Sugar Blend

3 Tbsp. trans-fat-free tub margarine

3–4 large tart apples, peeled and sliced ¼-inch thick

3 eggs

1 cup fat-free milk

1 tsp. vanilla extract

9 slices day-old French bread, ¾-inch thick, about 1 oz. each

Syrup:

½ cup unsweetened applesauce

¼ tsp. cinnamon

¼ cup apple jelly

1/16 tsp. ground cloves

sprinkle nutmeg, *optional*

maple syrup for serving, *optional*

whipped cream, *optional*

1. In a small saucepan, melt Splenda and margarine together about 3–4 minutes, stirring constantly, until slightly thick.

2. Pour into ungreased 9x13-inch baking pan.

3. Top with apple slices.

4. In a medium-sized mixing bowl, beat together eggs, milk, and vanilla.

5. Dip bread slices in egg mixture, one by one, and then lay over top of apples.

6. Cover and refrigerate overnight.

7. Remove from refrigerator 30 minutes before baking. Sprinkle with nutmeg if you wish.

8. Bake uncovered at 350°F for 35–40 minutes.

9. Meanwhile, prepare syrup by cooking applesauce, cinnamon, apple jelly, and ground cloves in small saucepan until hot.

10. Serve over toast.

11. Offer maple syrup and whipped cream as toppings, too.

Variation:
Crab apple jelly, instead of apple jelly, in the syrup is also delicious.

Exchange List Values
- Starch 1.0
- Fruit 1.0
- Carbohydrate 1.0
- Fat 1.0

Basic Nutritional Values
- Calories 245 (Calories from Fat 45)
- Total Fat 5 gm (Saturated Fat 1.3 gm, Trans Fat 0.0 gm, Polyunsat Fat 1.8 gm, Monounsat Fat 1.6 gm)
- Cholesterol 65 mg
- Sodium 220 mg
- Potassium 195 gm
- Total Carb 43 gm
- Dietary Fiber 2 gm
- Sugars 19 gm
- Protein 7 gm
- Phosphorus 105 gm

Baked French Toast with Cream Cheese

Blanche Nyce
Hatfield, PA

Makes 10 servings
Prep. Time: 15–20 minutes
Baking Time: 40–45 minutes

1-lb. loaf firm bread, *divided*

8-oz. pkg. fat-free cream cheese

2 cup berries of your choice—strawberries, blueberries, or raspberries

10 eggs

½ cup fat-free half-and-half

¼ cup maple syrup, or pancake syrup

¼ cup trans-fat-free tub margarine

TIP

Day-old bread works best for this toast.

1. Cube bread and layer half in well-greased 9x13-inch baking pan.

2. Cut cream cheese into small pieces and scatter across bread.

3. Sprinkle with berries.

4. Cover berries with remaining half of bread.

5. In mixing bowl, beat together eggs, half-and-half, syrup, and melted margarine.

6. Pour contents of baking pan over bread.

7. Press down until bread is submerged as much as possible.

8. Cover and refrigerate for 8 hours, or overnight.

9. Bake uncovered at 375°F for 40–45 minutes, or until lightly browned and puffy.

Exchange List Values
- Starch 1.5
- Carbohydrate 0.5
- Lean Meat 2.0
- Fat 0.5

Basic Nutritional Values
- Calories 270 (Calories from Fat 70)
- Total Fat 8 gm (Saturated Fat 2.4 gm, Trans Fat 0.0 gm, Polyunsat Fat 2.4 gm, Monounsat Fat 3.0 gm)
- Cholesterol 190 mg
- Sodium 485 mg
- Potassium 245 gm
- Total Carb 33 gm
- Dietary Fiber 1 gm
- Sugars 9 gm
- Protein 13 gm
- Phosphorus 285 gm

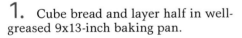

Blueberry French Toast

Stacie Skelly
Millersville, PA

Makes 12 servings
Prep. Time: 30 minutes
Chilling Time: 6–8 hours or overnight
Baking Time: 1 hour

12 slices day-old bread

4 oz. cream cheese

4 oz. Neufchâtel (1/3-less-fat) cream cheese

1 cup frozen blueberries

6 eggs

1½ cups egg substitute

2 cups fat-free milk

⅓ cup honey

Sauce:

¼ cup Splenda Sugar Blend

2 Tbsp. cornstarch

1 cup water

1 cup blueberries

1. Grease 9x13-inch baking pan.

2. Cube bread and spread in pan.

3. Cube cream cheese. Distribute evenly over bread.

4. Sprinkle blueberries on top.

5. In a mixing bowl, blend eggs, egg substitute, milk, and honey.

6. Pour over baking-pan contents.

7. Cover. Refrigerate 6–8 hours, or overnight.

8. Remove from refrigerator 30 minutes before baking.

9. Bake, covered, at 350°F for 30 minutes.

10. Uncover. Bake 30 more minutes. Serve with sauce.

11. Make Sauce: Mix Splenda, cornstarch, and water in a saucepan. Bring to a boil.

12. Stir in blueberries.

13. Reduce heat, cooking until blueberries burst.

14. Serve warm over French toast.

Exchange List Values
- Starch 1.0
- Carbohydrate 1.0
- Lean Meat 1.0
- Fat 0.5

Basic Nutritional Values
- Calories 225 (Calories from Fat 55)
- Total Fat 6 gm (Saturated Fat 2.2 gm, Trans Fat 0.0 gm, Polyunsat Fat 1.0 gm, Monounsat Fat 1.7 gm)
- Cholesterol 100 mg
- Sodium 380 mg
- Potassium 230 gm
- Total Carb 32 gm
- Dietary Fiber 1 gm
- Sugars 18 gm
- Protein 12 gm
- Phosphorus 185 gm

Breakfast and Brunch

Waffles with Cinnamon Apple Syrup

Betty L. Moore
Plano, IL

Makes 12 5-inch waffles and 1¾ cups syrup,
1 waffle and 2⅓ Tbsp. syrup per serving
Prep. Time: 15 minutes
Cooking Time: about 3 minutes per waffle

Waffles:

2 cups flour

2 Tbsp. sugar

3 tsp. baking powder

½ tsp. salt

2 eggs

1½ cups fat-free milk

4 Tbsp. canola oil

Cinnamon Apple Syrup:

2 Tbsp. cornstarch

½ tsp. cinnamon

⅛ tsp. salt

1 cup water

¾ cup unsweetened apple juice concentrate

½ tsp. vanilla extract

1. To make waffles, mix flour, sugar, baking powder, and salt together in large bowl.

2. In a separate bowl, beat eggs, milk, and oil together.

3. Add wet ingredients to dry ingredients. Beat just until mixed.

4. Pour scant ½ cup batter onto hot waffle iron. Cook according to your waffle iron's instructions.

5. To make syrup, combine cornstarch, cinnamon, and salt in saucepan.

6. Gradually stir in water and apple juice concentrate until smooth.

7. Over medium heat, and stirring continually, bring to boil.

8. Cook, stirring continually, for 2 minutes, or until thickened.

9. Remove from heat. Stir in vanilla.

10. Serve warm over waffles.

Exchange List Values

- Starch 1.0
- Carbohydrate 1.0
- Fat 1.0

Basic Nutritional Values

- Calories 180
  (Calories from Fat 55)
- Total Fat 6 gm
  (Saturated Fat 0.6 gm,
  Trans Fat 0.0 gm,
  Polyunsat Fat 1.6 gm,
  Monounsat Fat 3.3 gm)
- Cholesterol 30 mg
- Sodium 240 mg
- Potassium 145 gm
- Total Carb 28 gm
- Dietary Fiber 1 gm
- Sugars 11 gm
- Protein 4 gm
- Phosphorus 185 gm

Oatmeal Pancakes

Barbara J. Bey
Hillsboro, OH

Makes 6 servings, 1 pancake per serving
Prep. Time: 5 minutes
Cooking Time: 10 minutes

½ cup flour

½ cup dry oats, rolled or quick-cooking

1 Tbsp. Splenda

1 tsp. baking powder

½ tsp. baking soda

¾ cup fat-free buttermilk

¼ cup fat-free milk

2 Tbsp. canola oil

1 egg, beaten

1. Stir together flour, oats, Splenda, baking powder, and baking soda in a large mixing bowl.

2. In a separate bowl, blend buttermilk, milk, oil, and egg until smooth.

3. Stir wet ingredients into dry ingredients, just until moistened.

4. Drop by scant half-cupfuls into skillet or onto griddle.

5. Cook until small bubbles form on top.

6. Flip and cook until lightly browned.

Exchange List Values
- Starch 1.0
- Fat 1.0

Basic Nutritional Values
- Calories 140 (Calories from Fat 55)
- Total Fat 6 gm (Saturated Fat 0.7 gm, Trans Fat 0.0 gm, Polyunsat Fat 1.7 gm, Monounsat Fat 3.4 gm)
- Cholesterol 30 mg
- Sodium 215 mg
- Potassium 110 gm
- Total Carb 17 gm
- Dietary Fiber 1 gm
- Sugars 4 gm
- Protein 4 gm
- Phosphorus 170 gm

Breakfast and Brunch

Strawberry Muffins

Janessa Hochstedler
East Earl, PA

Makes 14 muffins, 1 muffin per serving
Prep. Time: 10–15 minutes
Standing Time: 30 minutes
Baking Time: 10–12 minutes

1½ cups mashed strawberries

6 Tbsp. Splenda Sugar Blend, *divided*

1¾ cups flour

¼ tsp. nutmeg

¼ tsp. salt

½ tsp. baking soda

2 eggs, beaten

¼ cup trans-fat-free tub margarine

1 tsp. vanilla extract

1. In a small mixing bowl, combine strawberries and 2 Tbsp. sweetener. Set aside for 30 minutes. Drain strawberries, reserving liquid.

2. In a large mixing bowl, combine flour, nutmeg, salt, and baking soda. Set aside.

3. In yet another bowl, mix together eggs, melted margarine, vanilla, 4 Tbsp. sweetener, and juice from berries.

4. Add to flour mixture, stirring just until combined.

5. Fold in berries.

6. Spoon batter into greased muffin tins.

7. Bake at 425°F for 10–12 minutes, or until toothpick inserted in centers of muffins comes out clean.

Exchange List Values
- Carbohydrate 1.5
- Fat 0.5

Basic Nutritional Values
- Calories 120
  (Calories from Fat 30)
- Total Fat 4 gm
  (Saturated Fat 0.8 gm,
  Trans Fat 0.0 gm,
  Polyunsat Fat 1.2 gm,
  Monounsat Fat 1.1 gm)
- Cholesterol 25 mg
- Sodium 120 mg
- Potassium 65 gm
- Total Carb 19 gm
- Dietary Fiber 1 gm
- Sugars 7 gm
- Protein 3 gm
- Phosphorus 40 gm

B & B Blueberry Coffee Cake

Kim Rapp
Longmont, CO

Makes 18 servings, 2 x3-inch rectangle per serving
Prep. Time: 15–20 minutes
Baking Time: 55–65 minutes

4 cups flour

¾ cup Splenda Sugar Blend

5 tsp. baking powder

1 tsp. salt

6 Tbsp. trans-fat-free tub margarine

1½ cups fat-free milk

2 eggs

4 cups fresh, or frozen, blueberries

Topping:
2 Tbsp. Splenda Sugar Blend

⅔ cup flour

1 tsp. cinnamon

½ tsp. nutmeg

6 Tbsp. trans-fat-free tub margarine

1. In an electric-mixer bowl, mix together flour, sweetener, baking powder, salt, margarine, milk, and eggs. Using mixer, beat vigorously for 30 seconds.

2. If using frozen blueberries, place in large bowl and stir in 3 Tbsp. flour until each blueberry is well coated. (If using fresh berries, no need to add flour.)

3. Carefully fold blueberries into batter.

4. Pour into lightly greased 9x13-inch baking pan.

5. For topping, combine sweetener, flour, cinnamon, and nutmeg in a bowl.

6. Using a pastry cutter, or two forks, cut in margarine until small crumbs form.

7. Sprinkle crumbs evenly over batter.

8. Bake at 350°F for 55–65 minutes, or until toothpick inserted in center of cake comes out clean.

Exchange List Values
- Starch 1.5
- Carbohydrate 1.0
- Fat 1.0

Basic Nutritional Values
- Calories 240 (Calories from Fat 55)
- Total Fat 6 gm (Saturated Fat 1.5 gm, Trans Fat 0.0 gm, Polyunsat Fat 2.6 gm, Monounsat Fat 2.1 gm)
- Cholesterol 20 mg
- Sodium 305 mg
- Potassium 105 gm
- Total Carb 40 gm
- Dietary Fiber 2 gm
- Sugars 14 gm
- Protein 5 gm
- Phosphorus 200 gm

Healthy Blueberry Muffins

Gloria Lehman
Singers Glen, VA

Makes 18 servings, 1 muffin per serving
Prep. Time: 20 minutes
Baking Time: 20 minutes

1 cup flour

½ cup whole wheat flour

6 Tbsp. Splenda Sugar Blend

¼ cup oat bran

¼ cup wheat germ

¼ cup quick, or old-fashioned, oats

1 tsp. baking powder

1 tsp. baking soda

½ tsp. cinnamon

¼ tsp. nutmeg

¼ tsp. allspice

¼ tsp. salt

1 cup blueberries, fresh or frozen and partially thawed

½ cup chopped walnuts

1 banana, mashed

1 cup buttermilk

1 egg

1 Tbsp. vegetable oil

1 tsp. vanilla extract

1. In large bowl, stir together all dry ingredients (through salt) until well blended.

2. Gently stir in blueberries and walnuts. (Adding the blueberries to dry ingredients first helps to prevent turning the batter blue from any juice.)

3. In a separate container, mix together mashed banana, buttermilk, egg, oil, and vanilla.

4. Make a well in dry ingredients. Pour wet ingredients into well. Mix just until blended.

5. Fill greased muffin cups almost to the top.

6. Bake at 350°F for approximately 20 minutes, or until toothpick inserted in centers of muffins comes out clean.

TIP

This moist muffin is made better and healthier by using a banana instead of more oil.

Exchange List Values
- Carbohydrate 1.0
- Fat 1.0

Basic Nutritional Values
- Calories 115 (Calories from Fat 30)
- Total Fat 4 gm (Saturated Fat 0.4 gm, Trans Fat 0.0 gm, Polyunsat Fat 2.1 gm, Monounsat Fat 1.0 gm)
- Cholesterol 10 mg
- Sodium 140 mg
- Potassium 120 gm
- Total Carb 18 gm
- Dietary Fiber 2 gm
- Sugars 7 gm
- Protein 3 gm
- Phosphorus 110 gm

Finnish Coffee Cake

Sharon Shank
Bridgewater, VA
Martha Ann Auker
Landisburg, PA

Makes 24 servings, 2-inch square bar per serving
Prep. Time: 10–20 minutes
Baking Time: 30–35 minutes

10 Tbsp. Splenda Sugar Blend

1 cup canola oil

2 eggs, beaten

1 cup fat-free buttermilk

1 tsp. vanilla extract

2 cups flour

¾ tsp. baking powder

½ tsp. salt

½ tsp. baking soda

2 Tbsp. Splenda Brown Sugar Blend

1-3 tsp. cinnamon, according to your taste preference

Glaze, *optional*

2 cups confectioners' sugar

1-2 tsp. vanilla extract, according to your taste preference

1-2 Tbsp. hot water, or a bit more

1. In good-sized mixing bowl, beat together Splenda, oil, eggs, buttermilk, and 1 tsp. vanilla.

2. In a separate bowl, sift together flour, baking powder, salt, and baking soda.

3. Stir dry ingredients into buttermilk mixture.

4. Pour half of batter into greased 9x13-inch baking dish.

5. Mix together brown sugar and cinnamon in bowl. Sprinkle half of mixture over batter.

6. Repeat layers.

7. Bake at 350°F for 30–35 minutes, or until toothpick inserted in center comes out clean.

8. If you're using glaze, poke holes in cake with fork while cake is still warm. In a medium-sized bowl, mix together confectioners' sugar, vanilla, and just enough water to make a thin glaze. Drizzle glaze over cake while still warm.

Variation:
Add ¾ cup chopped walnuts to brown sugar-cinnamon mixture in Step 5.
—Carrie Darby, Moreno Valley, CA

Exchange List Values
- Starch 0.5
- Carbohydrate 0.5
- Fat 2.0

Basic Nutritional Values
- Calories 155 (Calories from Fat 90)
- Total Fat 10 gm (Saturated Fat 0.8 gm, Trans Fat 0.0 gm, Polyunsat Fat 2.7 gm, Monounsat Fat 5.9 gm)
- Cholesterol 15 mg
- Sodium 105 mg
- Potassium 35 gm
- Total Carb 15 gm
- Dietary Fiber 0 gm
- Sugars 6 gm
- Protein 2 gm
- Phosphorus 45 gm

All-Bran Date Muffins

Mrs. Lewis L. Beachy
Sarasota, FL

Makes 16 servings, 1 muffin per serving
Prep. Time: 20 minutes
Standing Time: 20 minutes
Baking Time: 20–25 minutes

1 cup chopped dates

1 cup chopped nuts

1 tsp. baking soda

1 Tbsp. vegetable shortening

1 cup boiling water

¾ cup brown sugar

1 egg, well beaten

1 cup flour

1 cup All-Bran cereal

1 tsp. baking powder

1. Combine dates, nuts, baking soda, and shortening. Pour boiling water over mixture and let cool, 20 minutes.

2. Add sugar, egg, flour, All-Bran, and baking powder. Fold together until blended. Do not use mixer.

3. Spoon batter into well-greased muffin tins.

4. Bake at 350°F for 20–25 minutes.

Exchange List Values
- Carbohydrate 1.5
- Fat 1.0

Basic Nutritional Values
- Calories 150
  (Calories from Fat 55)
- Total Fat 6 gm
  (Saturated Fat 0.8 gm,
  Trans Fat 0.0 gm,
  Polyunsat Fat 4.0 gm,
  Monounsat Fat 1.1 gm)
- Cholesterol 10 mg
- Sodium 120 mg
- Potassium 160 gm
- Total Carb 24 gm
- Dietary Fiber 3 gm
- Sugars 14 gm
- Protein 3 gm
- Phosphorus 120 gm

Breakfast Apple Cobbler

Anona M. Teel
Bangor, PA

Makes 8 servings
Prep. Time: 25 minutes
Cooking Time: 2–9 hours
Ideal slow-cooker size: 4- or 5-qt.

8 medium apples, cored, peeled, sliced

2 Tbsp. sugar substitute to equal 1 Tbsp. sugar

dash cinnamon

juice of 1 lemon

2 Tbsp. light, soft tub margarine, melted

2 cups granola

1. Combine ingredients in slow cooker.

2. Cover. Cook on Low 7–9 hours (while you sleep!), or on High 2–3 hours (after you're up in the morning).

Exchange List Values
- Starch 1.5
- Fruit 1.5
- Fat 1.0

Basic Nutritional Values
- Calories 221
  (Calories from Fat 57)
- Total Fat 6 gm
  (Saturated Fat 2.1 gm,
  Polyunsat Fat 1.9 gm,
  Monounsat Fat 1.7 gm)
- Cholesterol 0 mg
- Sodium 102 mg
- Total Carb 42 gm
- Dietary Fiber 4 gm
- Sugars 29 gm
- Protein 2 gm

Banana Chocolate Chip Muffins

Jen Hoover
Akron, PA
Jane Steiner
Orrville, OH

Makes 24 servings, 1 muffin per serving
Prep. Time: 15 minutes
Baking Time: 12–18 minutes

4 large ripe bananas, mashed

6 Tbsp. Splenda Sugar Blend

1 egg

1½ cups flour

1 tsp. baking soda

1 tsp. baking powder

5⅓ Tbsp. trans-fat-free tub margarine, melted

½ cup chocolate chips

1. In a good-sized mixing bowl, blend together bananas, Splenda, egg, and flour.

2. Mix in baking soda, baking powder, and melted margarine.

3. Stir in chocolate chips.

4. Bake in lined muffin tins at 375°F for 12–18 minutes, or until toothpick inserted in center comes out clean. Check after 12 minutes to prevent muffins from overbaking.

Exchange List Values
- Carbohydrate 1.0
- Fat 0.5

Basic Nutritional Values
- Calories 100
  (Calories from Fat 25)
- Total Fat 3 gm
  (Saturated Fat 1.2 gm,
  Trans Fat 0.0 gm,
  Polyunsat Fat 0.9 gm,
  Monounsat Fat 1.1 gm)
- Cholesterol 10 mg
- Sodium 90 mg
- Potassium 105 gm
- Total Carb 17 gm
- Dietary Fiber 1 gm
- Sugars 8 gm
- Protein 1 gm
- Phosphorus 40 gm

Breakfast and Brunch

Zucchini Oatmeal Muffins

Donna Lantgen
Arvada, CO

Makes 30 muffins, 1 muffin per serving
Prep. Time: 15 minutes
Baking Time: 20–25 minutes

2½ cups flour

¾ cup Splenda Sugar Blend

½ cup dry oatmeal, quick or old-fashioned

1 Tbsp. baking powder

1 tsp. salt

1 tsp. cinnamon

1 cup chopped walnuts

4 eggs

10 oz. zucchini (1¼ cups shredded), peeled or unpeeled

¾ cup canola oil

TIP

Shredding zucchini in your food processor makes things easier.

1. Mix flour, sweetener, dry oatmeal, baking powder, salt, cinnamon, and walnuts together in a large mixing bowl.

2. In a separate bowl, combine eggs, zucchini, and oil.

3. Stir wet ingredients into dry ingredients, until just mixed. Do not over-stir.

4. Fill greased baking tins half-full. (Or use paper liners instead of greasing tins.)

5. Bake at 400°F for 20–25 minutes, or until toothpick inserted in centers of muffins comes out clean.

Exchange List Values
- Carbohydrate 1.0
- Fat 2.0

Basic Nutritional Values
- Calories 150
  (Calories from Fat 80)
- Total Fat 9 gm
  (Saturated Fat 0.9 gm,
  Trans Fat 0.0 gm,
  Polyunsat Fat 3.6 gm,
  Monounsat Fat 4.1 gm)
- Cholesterol 25 mg
- Sodium 125 mg
- Potassium 70 gm
- Total Carb 15 gm
- Dietary Fiber 1 gm
- Sugars 5 gm
- Protein 3 gm
- Phosphorus 95 gm

Morning Maple Muffins

Connie Lynn Miller
Shipshewana, IN

Makes 18 muffins, 1 muffin per serving
Prep. Time: 15 minutes
Baking Time: 15–20 minutes

Muffins:
2 cups flour

¼ cup Splenda Brown Sugar Blend

2 tsp. baking powder

½ tsp. salt

¾ cup fat-free milk

½ cup trans-fat-free tub margarine, melted

¼ cup maple syrup

¼ cup fat-free sour cream

1 egg

½ tsp. vanilla extract

Topping:
3 Tbsp. flour

3 Tbsp. sugar

2 Tbsp. chopped pecans

½ tsp. cinnamon

2 Tbsp. trans-fat-free tub margarine

1. To make muffins, combine flour, brown sugar blend, baking powder, and salt in a large bowl.

2. In another bowl, combine milk, melted margarine, maple syrup, sour cream, egg, and vanilla.

3. Stir wet ingredients into dry ingredients just until moistened.

4. Fill greased or paper-lined muffin cups ⅔ full.

5. For topping, combine flour, sugar, nuts, and cinnamon.

6. Cut in margarine, using a pastry cutter or two knives, until crumbly.

7. Sprinkle over batter in muffin cups.

8. Bake at 400°F for 15–20 minutes, or until a toothpick inserted near the center comes out clean.

9. Cool 5 minutes before removing from pans to wire racks. Serve warm.

TIP

The maple syrup gives these muffins the hint of a hearty pancake breakfast without all the fuss.

Exchange List Values
- Starch 1.0
- Carbohydrate 0.5
- Fat 1.0

Basic Nutritional Values
- Calories 140 (Calories from Fat 55)
- Total Fat 6 gm (Saturated Fat 1.2 gm, Trans Fat 0.0 gm, Polyunsat Fat 2.2 gm, Monounsat Fat 2.0 gm)
- Cholesterol 10 mg
- Sodium 165 mg
- Potassium 60 gm
- Total Carb 20 gm
- Dietary Fiber 1 gm
- Sugars 6 gm
- Protein 3 gm
- Phosphorus 90 gm

Cranberry Buttermilk Scones

Edwina Stoltzfus
Narvon, PA

Makes 16 servings, 1 scone per serving
Prep. Time: 20 minutes
Baking Time: 15–20 minutes

3 cups flour

2⅔ Tbsp. Splenda Sugar Blend

2½ tsp. baking powder

¾ tsp. salt

½ tsp. baking soda

12 Tbsp. cold trans-fat-free tub margarine

1 cup fat-free buttermilk

1 cup dried cranberries

1 tsp. grated orange peel

1 Tbsp. fat-free milk

2 Tbsp. sugar

¼ tsp. ground cinnamon

1. In a bowl, combine flour, Splenda, baking powder, salt, and baking soda.

2. Cut in margarine, using a pastry cutter or two knives, until mixture resembles small peas.

3. Stir in buttermilk, just until combined.

4. Fold in cranberries and orange peel.

5. Turn dough onto floured surface. Divide dough in half.

6. Shape each portion into a ball. Pat each into a 6-inch circle.

7. Cut each circle into six wedges.

8. Place on lightly greased baking sheet.

9. Brush tops with milk.

10. In a small bowl, combine 2 Tbsp. sugar with cinnamon. Sprinkle on top of wedges.

11. Bake at 400°F for 15–20 minutes, or until golden brown.

Exchange List Values
- Starch 1.5
- Fruit 0.5
- Fat 1.0

Basic Nutritional Values
- Calories 185
  (Calories from Fat 65)
- Total Fat 7 gm
  (Saturated Fat 1.4 gm,
  Trans Fat 0.0 gm,
  Polyunsat Fat 2.8 gm,
  Monounsat Fat 2.1 gm)
- Cholesterol 0 mg
- Sodium 290 mg
- Potassium 55 gm
- Total Carb 29 gm
- Dietary Fiber 1 gm
- Sugars 10 gm
- Protein 3 gm
- Phosphorus 115 gm

Glazed Cinnamon Biscuits

Virginia Graybill
Hershey, PA

Makes 12 servings, 1 biscuit per serving
Prep. Time: 30 minutes
Baking Time: 18–20 minutes

Biscuits:

2 cups flour

4 tsp. baking powder

½ tsp. salt

2 Tbsp. Splenda Sugar Blend

1 tsp. cinnamon

6 Tbsp. trans-fat-free tub margarine, *divided*

¾ cup fat-free milk

Glaze:

1 cup granulated Splenda

2⅔ Tbsp. cornstarch

¼ tsp. vanilla extract

1⅓ Tbsp. water

1. In a large bowl, combine flour, baking powder, salt, sweetener, and cinnamon.

2. Using a pastry cutter or two knives, cut in 4 Tbsp. margarine until mixture resembles coarse crumbs.

3. Stir in milk just until moistened.

4. Turn onto a lightly floured surface. Rub a bit of vegetable oil on your hands to keep dough from sticking to your fingers while kneading.

5. Knead gently 8–10 times.

6. Roll dough into an 8×11-inch rectangle, ½-inch thick.

7. Melt remaining 2 Tbs. margarine and brush 1 Tbsp. over dough.

8. Roll up jelly-roll style, starting with long end.

9. Cut roll into 12 equal slices.

10. Place slices cut-side down in greased 7×11-inch baking pan. Make 3 rows with 4 slices in each row.

11. Brush slices with remaining margarine.

12. Bake at 375°F for 18–20 minutes, or until golden brown.

13. While biscuits bake, make glaze. Blend Splenda and cornstarch in blender to a very fine powder.

14. In a small bowl, stir vanilla and water together and add Splenda mixture.

15. When biscuits finish baking, allow them to cool 5 minutes.

16. Spread with glaze. Serve immediately.

Exchange List Values
- Starch 1.0
- Carbohydrate 0.5
- Fat 0.5

Basic Nutritional Values
- Calories 140 (Calories from Fat 40)
- Total Fat 4.5 gm (Saturated Fat 0.9 gm, Trans Fat 0.0 gm, Polyunsat Fat 1.8 gm, Monounsat Fat 1.4 gm)
- Cholesterol 0 mg
- Sodium 270 mg
- Potassium 50 gm
- Total Carb 23 gm
- Dietary Fiber 1 gm
- Sugars 5 gm
- Protein 3 gm
- Phosphorus 190 gm

Sticky Buns

Dorothy Schrock
Arthur, IL

Makes 15 buns, 1 bun per serving
Prep. Time: 35 minutes
Rising Time: 30 minutes
Baking Time: 15 minutes

Dough:

½ cup warm water

1 Tbsp. yeast

¾ cup milk

2 Tbsp. trans-fat-free tub margarine

2 Tbsp. canola oil

1 tsp. salt

¼ cup sugar

1 egg, beaten

3 cups flour

Sauce:

6 Tbsp. trans-fat-free tub margarine

¾ tsp. cinnamon

½ cup Splenda Brown Sugar Blend

1 Tbsp. water

⅓ cup pecans

1. In a small bowl, stir yeast into warm water until dissolved. Set aside.

2. Heat milk, margarine, and oil in medium-sized saucepan over low heat until margarine melts. Remove pan from heat.

3. Stir salt and sugar into milk mixture until dissolved.

4. Stir yeast water, egg, and flour into other ingredients.

5. Set in warm place and let rise for 30 minutes.

6. Meanwhile, prepare sauce. In a medium-sized saucepan, heat margarine, cinnamon, Splenda, and water together. Make good and hot, but do not allow to boil.

7. Stir in pecans.

8. Pour sauce into well-greased 9×13-inch baking pan. Spread over bottom of pan.

9. Stir down batter. Drop by tablespoons over sauce. You should be able to make 12–15 batter "buns."

10. Bake at 350°F for 15 minutes.

11. Cool for 1 minute.

12. Cover baking pan with rimmed cookie sheet. Turn upside down carefully to release sticky buns onto cookie sheet.

Exchange List Values
- Starch 1.5
- Carbohydrate 0.5
- Fat 1.5

Basic Nutritional Values
- Calories 210 (Calories from Fat 70)
- Total Fat 8 gm (Saturated Fat 1.3 gm, Trans Fat 0.0 gm, Polyunsat Fat 2.9 gm, Monounsat Fat 3.8 gm)
- Cholesterol 15 mg
- Sodium 210 mg
- Potassium 85 gm
- Total Carb 30 gm
- Dietary Fiber 1 gm
- Sugars 7 gm
- Protein 4 gm
- Phosphorus 65 gm

Cinnamon Rolls—Easy Method

Betty L. Moore
Plano, IL

Makes 12 rolls, 1 roll per serving
Thawing Time: 8 hours or overnight
Prep. Time: 15–20 minutes
Rising Time: 4–5 hours, or overnight
Baking Time: 20–25 minutes

1 lb. loaf frozen bread dough

2 tsp. cinnamon

1½ cups granulated Splenda, *divided*

8 Tbsp. trans-fat-free tub margarine

2⅔ Tbsp. cornstarch

1½ Tbsp. fat-free milk

1. Thaw dough at room temperature.

2. Grease a 9×13-inch baking pan.

3. In a long, flat dish, mix together cinnamon and ½ cup sugar substitute.

4. Melt margarine.

5. Cut thawed bread dough diagonally into 12 pieces.

6. Roll each piece of dough between your hands until it forms a rope.

7. Brush each piece of dough with melted margarine, and then dip in cinnamon-sugar. Use a spoon to cover rope well with mixture.

8. Tie each buttered-sugared piece in a loose knot. Lay in greased 9×13-inch baking pan, keeping as much space as possible between knots to allow for rising.

9. Cover loosely and let set until knots double in size, or refrigerate overnight.

10. Set out in morning and allow to rise until doubled, if knots haven't risen fully.

11. Bake at 350°F for 20–25 minutes.

12. Meanwhile, prepare glaze. Blend remaining 1 cup Splenda in blender with cornstarch to a fine powder.

13. Mix the blended sugar and milk together in a bowl until smooth.

14. Drizzle glaze over cooled buns.

Exchange List Values

- Starch 1.5
- Fat 1.0

Basic Nutritional Values

- Calories 170
  (Calories from Fat 65)
- Total Fat 7 gm
  (Saturated Fat 1.5 gm,
  Trans Fat 0.0 gm,
  Polyunsat Fat 2.9 gm,
  Monounsat Fat 2.1 gm)
- Cholesterol 0 mg
- Sodium 280 mg
- Potassium 50 gm
- Total Carb 24 gm
- Dietary Fiber 1 gm
- Sugars 4 gm
- Protein 3 gm
- Phosphorus 45 gm

Grits—New Mexico Style

Karen Bryant
Corrales, NM

Makes 24 servings
Prep. Time: 20 minutes
Baking Time: 1 hour 20 minutes

1½ cups uncooked grits

¼ cup trans-fat-free tub margarine, at room temperature

4-oz. can chopped green chilies, drained

1 lb. 75%-less-fat shredded cheddar cheese

3 eggs, separated

2 tsp. salt

dash Tabasco sauce

¼ tsp. garlic powder

TIP

This dish is like a soufflé and makes a great brunch or light supper dish.

1. Cook grits in large pan according to package directions until thick.

2. Cut margarine into chunks and stir in, followed by chilies, cheese, beaten egg yolks, salt, Tabasco sauce, and garlic powder. Continue stirring until margarine is completely melted.

3. Beat egg whites until soft peaks form. Fold into hot ingredients.

4. Pour into well-greased 4-qt. baking dish.

5. Bake at 350°F for 1 hour and 20 minutes.

Exchange List Values
- Starch 0.5
- Lean Meat 1.0
- Fat 0.5

Basic Nutritional Values
- Calories 100 (Calories from Fat 35)
- Total Fat 4 gm (Saturated Fat 1.5 gm, Trans Fat 0.0 gm, Polyunsat Fat 0.8 gm, Monounsat Fat 1.0 gm)
- Cholesterol 30 mg
- Sodium 360 mg
- Potassium 50 gm
- Total Carb 9 gm
- Dietary Fiber 0 gm
- Sugars 0 gm
- Protein 8 gm
- Phosphorus 110 gm

Mexican-Style Grits

Mary Sommerfeld
Lancaster, PA

Makes 12 servings
Prep. Time: 25 minutes
Cooking Time: 2–6 hours
Ideal slow-cooker size: 4-qt.

1½ cups instant grits

4 oz. fat-free cheddar cheese, cubed

½ tsp. garlic powder

2 4-oz. cans diced chilies

2 Tbsp. light, soft tub margarine

1. Prepare grits according to package directions.

2. Stir in cheese, garlic powder, and chilies, until cheese is melted.

3. Stir in margarine. Pour into greased slow cooker.

4. Cover. Cook on High 2–3 hours or on Low 4–6 hours.

Exchange List Value
- Starch 1.0

Basic Nutritional Values
- Calories 91
  (Calories from Fat 9)
- Total Fat 1 gm
  (Saturated Fat 0.1 gm,
  Polyunsat Fat 0.3 gm,
  Monounsat Fat 0.5 gm)
- Cholesterol 1 mg
- Sodium 167 mg
- Total Carb 16 gm
- Dietary Fiber 2 gm
- Sugars 0 gm
- Protein 5 gm

Apple Breakfast Risotto

Hope Comerford
Clinton Township, MI

Makes 4 servings
Prep. Time: 10 minutes
Cooking Time: 8 hours
Ideal slow-cooker size: 3-qt.

4 Granny Smith apples, peeled, cored and sliced

2 cups no-added-sugar apple juice

2 cups water

2½ cups arborio rice

¼ cup brown sugar

1½ tsp. cinnamon

1/4 tsp. salt

1 tsp. vanilla extract

⅛ tsp. cloves

⅛ tsp. nutmeg

¼ cup butter, sliced

1. Add all ingredients to the crock and stir.

2. Cover and cook on Low for 8 hours.

Exchange List Values
- Bread/Starch 3.0
- Fruit 2.0
- Fat 1.0

Basic Nutritional Values
- Calories 221
- (Calories from Fat 54)
- Total Fat 6 gm
- (Saturated Fat 3.6 gm,
- Trans Fat 0.2 gm,
- Polyunsat Fat 0.27 gm,
- Monounsat Fat 1.7 gm)
- Cholesterol 15 mg
- Sodium 64 mg
- Potassium 153 gm
- Total Carb 69 gm
- Dietary Fiber 3.7 gm
- Sugars 19.6gm
- Protein 16.7 gm
- Phosphorus 4 gm

Oatmeal Morning

Barbara Forrester Landis
Lititz, PA

Makes 6 servings
Prep. Time: 10 minutes
Cooking Time: 2½–6 hours
Ideal slow-cooker size: 3-qt.

1 cup uncooked steel-cut oats

1 cup dried cranberries

1 cup walnuts

½ tsp. salt

1 Tbsp. cinnamon

2 cups fat-free milk

2 cups water

1. Combine all dry ingredients in slow cooker. Stir well.

2. Pour in milk and water. Mix together well.

3. Cover. Cook on High 2½ hours, or on Low 5–6 hours.

Exchange List Values

- Bread/Starch 3.0
- Fruit 2.0
- Fat 1.0

Basic Nutritional Values

- Calories 275
  (Calories from Fat 125)
- Total Fat 14 gm
  (Saturated Fat 1.5 gm,
  Polyunsat Fat 10.0 gm,
  Monounsat Fat 2.0 gm)
- Cholesterol 0 mg
- Sodium 235 mg
- Total Carb 34 gm
- Dietary Fiber 4 gm
- Sugars 18 gm
- Protein 8 gm

Baked Oatmeal

Esther Porter
Minneapolis, MN

Makes 12 servings, 3-inch square per
  serving
Prep. Time: 10 minutes
Baking Time: 20–25 minutes

3 Tbsp. Splenda Brown Sugar Blend

2 Tbsp. trans-fat-free tub margarine, melted

2 eggs, slightly beaten

3 cups quick oatmeal

2 tsp. baking powder

1 cup fat-free milk

1 tsp. salt

½ cup raisins or dried cranberries

TIP

Serve with hot milk, cinnamon, baked
apple slices, etc. You may cut leftover
baked oatmeal in pieces to freeze and
microwave for later. Great for brunch.

1. Combine brown sugar blend, margarine, and eggs in mixing bowl.

2. Mix oatmeal, baking powder, milk, and salt and add to bowl. Stir in raisins or cranberries.

3. Pour into 9x13-inch baking pan.

4. Bake at 350°F for 20–25 minutes.

Exchange List Values
- Starch 1.0
- Fruit 0.5
- Fat 0.5

Basic Nutritional Values
- Calories 140
  (Calories from Fat 30)
- Total Fat 4 gm
  (Saturated Fat 0.8 gm,
  Trans Fat 0.0 gm,
  Polyunsat Fat 1.2 gm,
  Monounsat Fat 1.2 gm)
- Cholesterol 30 mg
- Sodium 290 mg
- Potassium 165 gm
- Total Carb 23 gm
- Dietary Fiber 2 gm
- Sugars 6 gm
- Protein 5 gm
- Phosphorus 205 gm

Creamy Old-Fashioned Oatmeal

Mary Wheatley
Mashpee, MA

Makes 5 servings
Prep. Time: 5 minutes
Cooking Time: 6 hours
Ideal slow-cooker size: 3-qt.

1⅓ cups dry rolled oats

2½ cups, plus 1 Tbsp., water

dash salt

1. Mix together cereal, water, and salt in slow cooker.

2. Cook on Low 6 hours.

Variation:
Before cooking, stir in a few chopped dates or raisins for each serving, if you wish.
—Cathy Boshart, Lebanon, PA

NOTES

The formula is this: for one serving, use ⅓ cup dry oats and ⅔ cup water, plus a few grains salt. Multiply by the number of servings you need.

Exchange List Value
• Starch 1.0

Basic Nutritional Values
• Calories 83
  (Calories from Fat 12)
• Total Fat 1 gm
  (Saturated Fat 0.3 gm,
  Polyunsat Fat 0.5 gm,
  Monounsat Fat 0.4 gm)
• Cholesterol 0 mg
• Sodium 1 mg
• Total Carb 14 gm
• Dietary Fiber 2 gm
• Sugars 0 gm
• Protein 3 gm

Apple Oatmeal

Frances B. Musser
Newmanstown, PA

Makes 5 servings
Prep. Time: 20 minutes
Cooking Time: 5–6 hours
Ideal slow-cooker size: 3-qt.

2 cups fat-free milk

1 Tbsp. honey

1 Tbsp. light, soft tub margarine

¼ tsp. salt

½ tsp. cinnamon

1 cup dry rolled oats

1 cup chopped apples

½ cup chopped walnuts

1 Tbsp. brown sugar substitute to equal 1/2 Tbsp. sugar

1. Mix together all ingredients in greased slow cooker.

2. Cover. Cook on Low 5–6 hours.

Serving suggestion:
Serve with milk or ice cream.

Variation:
Add ½ cup light or dark raisins to mixture.
—Jeanette Oberholtzer, Manheim, PA

Exchange List Values
- Carbohydrate 2.0
- Fat 1.5

Basic Nutritional Values
- Calories 220
  (Calories from Fat 89)
- Total Fat 10 gm
  (Saturated Fat 1.1 gm,
  Polyunsat Fat 6.3 gm,
  Monounsat Fat 1.9 gm)
- Cholesterol 2 mg
- Sodium 180 mg
- Total Carb 28 gm
- Dietary Fiber 3 gm
- Sugars 15 gm
- Protein 8 gm

Berry Oatmeal

Hope Comerford
Clinton Township, MI

Makes 2–3 servings
Prep. Time: 5 minutes
Cooking Time: 7 hours
Ideal slow-cooker size: 2-qt.

½ cup steel-cut oats

2 cups unsweetened vanilla almond milk

1 cup mixed berries of your choice (if frozen, defrost first and drain juice)

½ tsp. vanilla extract

1. Spray crock with nonstick spray.

2. Place all ingredients into crock and stir lightly.

3. Cover and cook on Low for 7 hours.

Exchange List Values
- Bread/Starch 1.0
- Fruit 1.0
- Milk 0.5
- Fat 1.0

Basic Nutritional Values
- Calories 193
  (Calories from Fat 36)
  Total Fat 4 gm
  (Saturated Fat 0.2 gm,
  Trans Fat 0 gm,
  Polyunsat Fat 1.1 gm,
  Monounsat Fat 1.9 gm)
- Cholesterol 0 mg
- Sodium 153 mg
- Potassium 304 gm
- Total Carb 35 gm
- Dietary Fiber 4 gm
- Sugars 19gm
- Protein 4 gm
- Phosphorus 119 gm

Breads

Breads

Healthy Whole Wheat Bread

Esther Becker
Gordonville, PA

Makes 16 servings
Prep. Time: 20 minutes
Cooking Time: 2½–3 hours
Ideal slow-cooker size: 5- or 6-qt.

2 cups warm reconstituted fat-free powdered milk (⅔ cups powder to 1⅓ cup water)

2 Tbsp. canola oil

¼ cup honey or brown sugar

¾ tsp. salt

1 pkg. active dry yeast

2½ cups whole wheat flour

1¼ cups white flour

1. Mix together milk, oil, honey or brown sugar, salt, yeast, and half the flour in electric mixer bowl. Beat with mixer for 2 minutes. Add remaining flour. Mix well.

2. Place dough in well-greased bread or cake pan that will fit into your cooker. Cover with greased tinfoil. Let stand for 5 minutes. Place in slow cooker.

3. Cover cooker and bake on High 2½–3 hours. Remove pan and uncover. Let stand for 5 minutes. Serve warm.

Exchange List Value:
• Starch 2.0

Basic Nutritional Values
• Calories 140
  (Calories from Fat 20)
• Total Fat 2 gm
  (Saturated Fat 0.2 gm,
  Polyunsat Fat 0.7 gm,
  Monounsat Fat 1.1 gm)
• Cholesterol 0 mg
• Sodium 125 mg
• Total Carb 27 gm
• Dietary Fiber 3 gm
• Sugars 6 gm
• Protein 5 gm

Breads

Boston Brown Bread

Jean Butzer
Batavia, NY

Makes 3 loaves, 7 servings per loaf
Prep. Time: 45 minutes
Cooking Time: 4 hours
Ideal slow-cooker size: 6-qt.

3 16-oz. vegetable cans, emptied and cleaned, lids and labels discarded

½ cup rye flour

½ cup yellow cornmeal

½ cup whole wheat flour

3 Tbsp. sugar

1 tsp. baking soda

¾ tsp. salt

½ cup chopped walnuts

½ cup raisins

1 cup low-fat buttermilk

⅓ cup molasses

1. Spray insides of vegetable cans with nonstick cooking spray. Spray three 6-inch-square pieces of foil also with the cooking spray. Set aside.

2. Combine rye flour, cornmeal, whole wheat flour, sugar, baking soda, and salt in a large bowl.

3. Stir in walnuts and raisins.

4. Whisk together buttermilk and molasses. Add to dry ingredients. Stir until well mixed. Spoon into prepared cans.

5. Place one piece of foil, greased side down, on top of each can. Secure foil with rubber bands or cotton string. Place upright in slow cooker.

6. Pour boiling water into slow cooker to come halfway up sides of cans. Make sure foil tops do not touch boiling water.

7. Cover cooker. Cook on Low 4 hours, or until skewer inserted in center of bread comes out clean.

8. To remove bread, lay cans on their sides. Roll and tap gently on all sides until bread releases. Cool completely on wire racks.

Serving suggestion:
Serve with butter or cream cheese and bowls of soup.

Exchange List Values:
- Carbohydrate 1.0
- Fat 0.5

Basic Nutritional Values
- Calories 85 (Calories from Fat 20)
- Total Fat 2 gm (Saturated Fat 0.2 gm, Polyunsat Fat 1.4 gm, Monounsat Fat 0.3 gm)
- Cholesterol 0 mg
- Sodium 158 mg
- Total Carb 16 gm
- Dietary Fiber 2 gm
- Sugars 8 gm
- Protein 2 gm

Pumpernickel Bread

Helene Funk
Laird, SK

Makes 4 loaves, 16 slices per loaf, 1 slice per serving
Prep. Time: 35 minutes
Rising Time: 2 ¼ hours
Cooking/Baking Time: 1 hour

3 Tbsp. yeast

2 tsp. sugar

1 cup warm water

3¼ cups water

½ cup dark molasses

1 Tbsp. trans-fat-free tub margarine

1 tsp. salt

3½ cups whole wheat flour

4½ cups white flour

3½ cups rye flour

1 Tbsp. unsweetened cocoa, *optional*

1 cup bran

¾ cup yellow cornmeal

½ cup millet, *optional*

2 cups mashed potatoes

2 tsp. caraway seeds

½ cup flax

1. Dissolve yeast with sugar in 1 cup warm water. Let stand 10 minutes until bubbly. Stir well.

2. Combine 3¼ cups water, molasses, and margarine in saucepan. Heat over low heat until margarine is dissolved. When room temperature, add salt and yeast mixture.

3. Combine all flours and cocoa (if using) in large bowl.

4. Add bran, cornmeal, millet (if using), and mashed potatoes. Add to liquid yeast mixture and beat until thoroughly mixed. Stir in caraway seeds and flax and mix well.

5. Let dough rest 15 minutes. Knead until smooth.

6. Let rise until double in bulk, about 1 hour.

7. Punch down. Let rise again for 30 minutes.

8. Divide into 4 pieces and shape into loaves or balls and place in greased tins.

9. Cover and let rise in warm place, about 45 minutes.

10. Bake at 325°F for 45–50 minutes or until done.

Exchange List Value
- Starch 1.5

Basic Nutritional Values
- Calories 105
  (Calories from Fat 15)
- Total Fat 2 gm
  (Saturated Fat 0.2 gm,
  Trans Fat 0.0 gm,
  Polyunsat Fat 0.5 gm,
  Monounsat Fat 0.3 gm)
- Cholesterol 0 mg
- Sodium 60 mg
- Potassium 170 gm
- Total Carb 22 gm
- Dietary Fiber 4 gm
- Sugars 2 gm
- Protein 4 gm
- Phosphorus 100 gm

Breads

French Bread—No Knead

Naomi Ressler
Harrisonburg, VA

Makes 2 loaves, 19 slices per loaf, 1 slice per serving
Prep. Time: 1½ hours
Baking Time: 20 minutes

2 Tbsp. all-vegetable shortening

2 Tbsp. sugar

2 tsp. salt

1 cup boiling water

1 cup cold water

2 ¼-oz. pkgs. yeast

1 scant Tbsp. sugar

½ cup warm water

6 cups flour

1. Dissolve shortening, sugar, and salt in boiling water.

2. Add cold water to shortening mixture.

3. Dissolve yeast and sugar in warm water. Add to the shortening mixture.

4. Add flour. Do NOT beat. Stir with big spoon every 10 minutes, 4 or 5 times, for approximately an hour.

5. Divide dough in half. Flour dough board or counter and hands and pat each section into rectangle shape about ½-inch thick. Roll lengthwise in jelly roll fashion and tuck in ends. Cut slits diagonally 2–3 inches apart (shallow) on top of loaves.

6. Put on lightly greased baking sheet. Let rise until double, about 20–30 minutes depending on temperature of room.

7. Bake at 375–400°F for approximately 20 minutes.

Warm Memories:
A good friend shared this bread with us. I've made many loaves to donate to our Mennonite Relief Sale. It's so quick and easy as well as delicious and makes large loaves.

Exchange List Value
- Starch 1.0

Basic Nutritional Values
- Calories 85
  (Calories from Fat 10)
- Total Fat 1 gm
  (Saturated Fat 0.2 gm,
  Trans Fat 0.0 gm,
  Polyunsat Fat 0.3 gm,
  Monounsat Fat 0.3 gm)
- Cholesterol 0 mg
- Sodium 125 mg
- Potassium 30 gm
- Total Carb 16 gm
- Dietary Fiber 1 gm
- Sugars 1 gm
- Protein 2 gm
- Phosphorus 25 gm

TIP

1. You may wish to brush butter or margarine on top of loaf after baking.
2. Delicious with any meal but especially with pasta.
3. Dough will be stiff/thick so difficult to stir but do the best you can!

Breads

Oatmeal Herb Bread

Stacy Stoltzfus
Grantham, PA

Makes 1 loaf, 16 slices in the loaf, 1 slice per serving
Prep. Time: 20 minutes
Rising Time: 65–85 minutes
Baking Time: 30–35 minutes
Standing Time: 30–45 minutes

2 Tbsp. brown sugar

1 cup warm water (110-115°F)

1 Tbsp. yeast

1 egg, lightly beaten

3 Tbsp. olive oil

1 tsp. salt

½ cup dry quick oats

1 tsp. dried parsley

1 tsp. dried sage

1 tsp. dried oregano

1 tsp. dried basil

1 tsp. dried thyme

3½-4 cups unbleached bread flour, also called occident flour

1. Dissolve sugar in warm water in a large mixing bowl.

2. Sprinkle yeast over top.

3. Let rest 5–10 minutes until yeast begins to foam.

4. Stir in egg, olive oil, salt, oats, and herbs.

5. Gradually add in flour, one cup at a time, mixing until a ball forms that is not too dense. Dough should be soft but not sticky.

6. Knead about 5 minutes on floured surface.

7. Grease a large bowl. Place dough in bowl and cover with a tea towel.

8. Place in warm spot. Let rise until doubled, about 30–45 minutes.

9. Punch down. Form into a loaf.

10. Place in greased loaf pan. Let rise until dough comes to top of pan, about 35–40 minutes.

11. Meanwhile, preheat oven to 350°F. Place risen loaf in oven. Bake approximately 30–35 minutes. Loaf should be golden brown and should sound hollow when tapped.

12. Cool 10 minutes before removing from pan.

13. Let cool until lukewarm before slicing to keep moisture in the loaf. Slice the loaf just before serving.

Exchange List Values
- Starch 2.0
- Fat 0.5

Basic Nutritional Values
- Calories 175
  (Calories from Fat 45)
- Total Fat 5 gm
  (Saturated Fat 1.0 gm,
  Trans Fat 0.0 gm,
  Polyunsat Fat 0.9 gm,
  Monounsat Fat 2.7 gm)
- Cholesterol 70 mg
- Sodium 175 mg
- Potassium 85 gm
- Total Carb 26 gm
- Dietary Fiber 1 gm
- Sugars 2 gm
- Protein 7 gm
- Phosphorus 85 gm

Breads

Cheddar Biscuits

Jean Halloran
Green Bay, WI
Jessalyn Wantland
Napoleon, OH

Makes 12 servings, 1 biscuit per serving
Prep. Time: 10–20 minutes
Baking Time: 15–17 minutes

4 Tbsp. trans-fat-free tub margarine

2½ cups reduced-fat baking mix

1 cup 75%-less-fat shredded cheddar cheese

¾ cup fat-free milk

butter-flavored cooking spray

½ tsp. garlic powder, *divided*

¼ tsp. dried parsley flakes

1. In good-sized mixing bowl, cut margarine into baking mix using pastry cutter or 2 forks. Combine until mixture resembles small peas.

2. Stir in cheese, milk, and ¼ tsp. garlic powder until just combined. Do not over-mix.

3. Drop batter by ¼ cupfuls onto greased baking sheet. (An ice cream scoop works well.)

4. Bake 15–17 minutes at 400°F, or until tops are lightly browned.

5. Remove from oven. Spray tops lightly with cooking spray, 6 short sprays total. Sprinkle evenly with ¼ tsp. garlic powder and parsley flakes. Serve warm.

Exchange List Values
- Starch 1.0
- Fat 1.0

Basic Nutritional Values
- Calories 140
  (Calories from Fat 45)
- Total Fat 5 gm
  (Saturated Fat 1.3 gm,
  Trans Fat 0.0 gm,
  Polyunsat Fat 1.5 gm,
  Monounsat Fat 2.1 gm)
- Cholesterol 5 mg
- Sodium 370 mg
- Potassium 65 gm
- Total Carb 18 gm
- Dietary Fiber 1 gm
- Sugars 3 gm
- Protein 5 gm
- Phosphorus 210 gm

Cornbread from Scratch

Dorothy M. Van Deest
Memphis, TN

Makes 9 servings
Prep. Time: 15 minutes
Cooking Time: 2–3 hours
Ideal slow-cooker size: 6-qt.

1¼ cups flour

¾ cup yellow cornmeal

¼ cup sugar

4½ tsp. baking powder

½ tsp. salt

1 egg, slightly beaten

1 cup fat-free milk

¼ cup melted canola oil

1. In mixing bowl sift together flour, cornmeal, sugar, baking powder, and salt. Make a well in the center.

2. Pour egg, milk, and oil into well. Mix into the dry mixture until just moistened.

3. Pour mixture into a greased 2-qt. mold or casserole dish. Cover with a plate or lid. Place on a trivet or rack in the bottom of slow cooker.

4. Cover. Cook on High 2–3 hours.

Exchange List Values
- Starch 2.0
- Fat 1.0

Basic Nutritional Values
- Calories 200 (Calories from Fat 64)
- Total Fat 7 gm (Saturated Fat 0.7 gm, Polyunsat Fat 2.1 gm, Monounsat Fat 4.0 gm)
- Cholesterol 24 mg
- Sodium 330 mg
- Total Carb 29 gm
- Dietary Fiber 1 gm
- Sugars 7 gm
- Protein 4 gm

Breads

Cornbread

Rebecca B. Stoltzfus
Lititz, PA

Makes 16 servings, 2×2-inch square per
  serving
Prep. Time: 10 minutes
Baking Time: 35 minutes

6 Tbsp. Splenda Sugar Blend

5⅓ Tbsp. trans-fat-free tub margarine,
  softened

½ cup fat-free sour cream

½ cup buttermilk

2 eggs, beaten

1 cup flour

1 cup cornmeal

½ tsp. salt

1 tsp. baking soda

½ tsp. baking powder

1. Cream Splenda and margarine together well.

2. Mix in sour cream and buttermilk, and eggs. Mix well again.

3. In a separate bowl, combine flour, cornmeal, salt, baking soda, and baking powder.

4. Add dry ingredients to creamed mixture. Stir as little as possible.

5. Pour batter into greased 8×8-inch baking dish.

6. Bake at 350°F for 35 minutes, or until toothpick inserted in center comes out clean.

Exchange List Values
- Starch 1.0
- Fat 0.5

Basic Nutritional Values
- Calories 120
  (Calories from Fat 30)
- Total Fat 4 gm
  (Saturated Fat 0.9 gm,
  Trans Fat 0.0 gm,
  Polyunsat Fat 1.4 gm,
  Monounsat Fat 1.2 gm)
- Cholesterol 25 mg
- Sodium 210 mg
- Potassium 40 gm
- Total Carb 19 gm
- Dietary Fiber 1 gm
- Sugars 5 gm
- Protein 3 gm
- Phosphorus 50 gm

Breads

Lemon Bread

Ruth Ann Gingrich
New Holland, PA

Makes 12 servings
Prep. Time: 20 minutes
Cooking Time: 2–2¼ hours
Ideal slow-cooker size: 4-qt.

¼ cup canola oil

6 Tbsp. sugar substitute to equal 3 Tbsp.
   sugar

2 eggs, beaten

1⅔ cups flour

1⅔ tsp. baking powder

½ tsp. salt

½ cup fat-free milk

4 oz. chopped walnuts

grated peel from 1 lemon

Glaze:
¼ cup powdered sugar

juice of 1 lemon

1. Cream together oil and sugar. Add eggs. Mix well.

2. Sift together flour, baking powder, and salt. Add flour mixture and milk alternately to shortening mixture.

3. Stir in nuts and lemon peel.

4. Spoon batter into well-greased 2-lb. coffee can or 9×5-inch loaf pan and cover with well-greased foil. Place in cooker set on High for 2–2¼ hours, or until done. Remove bread from coffee can or pan.

5. For glaze: Mix together powdered sugar and lemon juice. Pour over loaf.

Exchange List Values
- Starch 1.5
- Fat 1.0

Basic Nutritional Values
- Calories 176
  (Calories from Fat 66)
- Total Fat 7 gm
  (Saturated Fat 0.9 gm,
  Polyunsat Fat 2.7 gm,
  Monounsat Fat 3.3 gm)
- Cholesterol 37 mg
- Sodium 168 mg
- Total Carb 24 gm
- Dietary Fiber 1 gm
- Sugars 10 gm

Breads

Old-Fashioned Gingerbread Loaf

Mary Ann Westerberg
Rosamond, CA

Makes 16 servings
Prep. Time: 25 minutes
Cooking Time: 2½–3 hours
Ideal slow-cooker size: 4-qt.

4 Tbsp. margarine, softened

4 Tbsp. sugar substitute to equal 2 Tbsp. sugar

1 egg

1 cup light molasses

2½ cups flour

1½ tsp. baking soda

1 tsp. ground cinnamon

2 tsp. ground ginger

½ tsp. ground cloves

½ tsp. salt

1 cup hot water

warm applesauce, *optional*

whipped cream, *optional*

nutmeg, *optional*

1. Cream together margarine and sugar substitute. Add egg and molasses. Mix well.

2. Stir in flour, baking soda, cinnamon, ginger, cloves, and salt. Mix well.

3. Add hot water. Beat well.

4. Pour batter into greased and floured 2-lb. coffee can.

5. Place can in cooker. Cover top of can with 8 paper towels. Cover cooker and bake on High 2½–3 hours.

6. Serve with applesauce, if desired. Top with whipped cream and sprinkle with nutmeg, if using.

Exchange List Values
- Carbohydrate 2.0
- Fat 0.5

Basic Nutritional Values
- Calories 168
  (Calories from Fat 30)
- Total Fat 3 gm
  (Saturated Fat 0.7 gm,
  Polyunsat Fat 1.0 gm,
  Monounsat Fat 1.4 gm)
- Cholesterol 13 mg
- Sodium 235 mg
- Total Carb 32 gm
- Dietary Fiber 1 gm
- Sugars 16 gm
- Protein 2 gm

Banana Loaf

Sue Hamilton
Minooka, IL

Makes 10 servings
Prep. Time: 20 minutes
Cooking Time: 2–2½ hours
Ideal slow-cooker size: 4- or 5-qt.

3 very ripe, medium bananas

¼ cup margarine, softened

2 eggs

1 tsp. vanilla

½ cup sugar substitute to equal ¼ cup sugar

1 cup flour

1 tsp. baking soda

1. Combine all ingredients in an electric mixing bowl. Beat 2 minutes or until well blended. Pour into well-greased 2-lb. coffee can or 9×5-inch loaf pan.

2. Place can/pan in slow cooker. Cover can/pan with 6 layers of paper towels between cooker lid and bread.

3. Cover cooker. Bake on High 2–2½ hours, or until toothpick inserted in center comes out clean. Cool 15 minutes before removing from pan.

Exchange List Values
- Carbohydrate 2.0
- Fat 1.0

Basic Nutritional Values
- Calories 177 (Calories from Fat 53)
- Total Fat 6 gm (Saturated Fat 1.3 gm, Polyunsat Fat 1.7 gm, Monounsat Fat 2.5 gm)
- Cholesterol 43 mg
- Sodium 192 mg
- Total Carb 29 gm
- Dietary Fiber 1 gm
- Sugars 16 gm
- Protein 3 gm

Breads

Beth's Banana Bread

Elizabeth Weaver Bonnar
Thorndale, ON

Makes 15 servings, 1 slice per serving
Prep. Time: 25 minutes
Baking Time: 50 minutes
Cooling Time: 30 minutes

⅓ cup canola oil

2 eggs, beaten

6 medium bananas, mashed

2 cups whole wheat flour

¼ tsp. salt

1¼ tsp. baking soda

¼ cup hot water

1 cup chopped walnuts

1. Beat oil and eggs and mix well. Stir in bananas.

2. Sift together all dry ingredients and add to batter, alternating with hot water. Mix until smooth. Fold in the walnuts.

3. Bake in greased loaf pan at 325°F for about 50 minutes.

4. Cool on wire rack for ½ hour before slicing.

Serving suggestion:
Serve with honey or maple syrup

Exchange List Values
- Carbohydrate 1.5
- Fat 2.0

Basic Nutritional Values
- Calories 205
  (Calories from Fat 100)
- Total Fat 11 gm
  (Saturated Fat 1.2 gm,
  Trans Fat 0.0 gm,
  Polyunsat Fat 5.4 gm,
  Monounsat Fat 4.0 gm)
- Cholesterol 25 mg
- Sodium 155 mg
- Potassium 290 gm
- Total Carb 24 gm
- Dietary Fiber 4 gm
- Sugars 6 gm
- Protein 5 gm
- Phosphorus 105 gm

Breads

Pumpkin Bread

Joanne Warfel
Lancaster, PA

Makes 2 larger loaves, or 8 small loaves, 32 slices total, 1 slice per serving
Prep. Time: 15–20 minutes
Baking Time: 25–70 minutes, depending on size of loaves
Cooling Time: 40 minutes

⅔ cup cooking oil

1⅓ cup Splenda Sugar Blend

4 eggs

16-oz. can pumpkin

⅔ cup water

3⅓ cups flour

2 tsp. baking soda

1 tsp. salt

½ tsp. baking powder

1 tsp. cinnamon

½ tsp. cloves

½ tsp. nutmeg

1 cup raisins

⅔ cup chopped nuts

1. In large bowl, cream oil and Splenda until fluffy.

2. Blend in eggs, and then pumpkin and water.

3. In a separate bowl, sift together flour, baking soda, salt, baking powder, cinnamon, cloves, and nutmeg.

4. Stir sifted dry ingredients into pumpkin mixture.

5. Stir in raisins and nuts.

6. Pour into two greased 5×9-inch loaf pans or eight 3×6-inch loaf pans. Bake at 350°F for 60–70 minutes for larger loaves; 25–30 minutes for small loaves. Test that bread is done by inserting toothpick into center of loaves. If pick comes out clean, bread is finished baking. If it doesn't, continue baking 3–5 minutes more. Test again.

7. Allow to cool in pans 10 minutes. Remove from pan and allow to cool another 30 minutes or so before slicing and serving.

Warm Memories:
I make the small loaves so I have them for gifts. They freeze well, and I've been told it's the best pumpkin bread they've ever had.

Exchange List Values
- Carbohydrate 1.5
- Fat 0.5

Basic Nutritional Values
- Calories 125 (Calories from Fat 20)
- Total Fat 2.5 gm (Saturated Fat 0.4 gm, Trans Fat 0.0 gm, Polyunsat Fat 1.4 gm, Monounsat Fat 0.7 gm)
- Cholesterol 25 mg
- Sodium 170 mg
- Potassium 95 gm
- Total Carb 23 gm
- Dietary Fiber 1 gm
- Sugars 11 gm
- Protein 3 gm
- Phosphorus 50 gm

John's Zucchini Bread

**Esther Yoder
Hartville, OH**

Makes 2 large loaves, or 7 small loaves, 30
 slices total, 1 slice per serving
Prep. Time: 20–30 minutes
Baking Time: 20–45 minutes

3 eggs

1 cup brown sugar

⅔ cup canola oil

1 tsp. vanilla extract

4 oz. fat-free cream cheese, cut in chunks

4 oz. Neufchâtel (⅓-less-fat) cream cheese,
 cut in chunks

1½ cups flour

½ cup dry quick, or old-fashioned, oats

1 tsp. baking powder

1 tsp. baking soda

1½ tsp. cinnamon

½ tsp. nutmeg

1 tsp. salt

1½ cups shredded zucchini

2 cups finely chopped walnuts

1. In an electric mixer bowl, beat eggs, sugar, oil, and vanilla 3 minutes.

2. Add cream cheese and beat 1 minute.

3. Mix flour, oats, baking powder, baking soda, cinnamon, nutmeg, and salt in another bowl.

4. Fold gently into egg mixture.

5. Fold in zucchini and nuts.

6. Pour into two 9×5-inch greased loaf pans. Bake at 350°F for 45 minutes. Or divide among seven small loaf pans, and then bake at 350°F for 20 minutes. Test that loaves are finished by inserting toothpick into center of loaves. If pick comes out clean, baking is complete. If not, bake another 3–5 minutes and test again with toothpick.

Exchange List Values
- Carbohydrate 1.0
- Fat 2.0

Basic Nutritional Values
- Calories 165
 (Calories from Fat 110)
- Total Fat 12 gm
 (Saturated Fat 1.5 gm,
 Trans Fat 0.0 gm,
 Polyunsat Fat 5.3 gm,
 Monounsat Fat 4.2 gm)
- Cholesterol 20 mg
- Sodium 180 mg
- Potassium 90 gm
- Total Carb 12 gm
- Dietary Fiber 1 gm
- Sugars 5 gm
- Protein 4 gm
- Phosphorus 95 gm

Date and Nut Loaf

Jean Butzer
Batavia, NY

Makes 20 servings
Prep. Time: 25 minutes
Cooking Time: 3½–4 hours
Ideal slow-cooker size: 6-qt.

1½ cups boiling water

1½ cups chopped dates

¾ cup sugar substitute to equal ¼ cup sugar

1 egg

2 tsp. baking soda

½ tsp. salt

1 tsp. vanilla extract

1 Tbsp. light, soft tub margarine, melted

2½ cups flour

1 cup walnuts, chopped

2 cups hot water

1. Pour 1½ cups boiling water over dates. Let stand 5–10 minutes.

2. Stir in sugar, egg, baking soda, salt, vanilla, and margarine.

3. In separate bowl, combine flour and nuts. Stir into date mixture.

4. Pour into two greased 11½-oz. coffee cans or one 8-cup baking insert. If using coffee cans, cover with foil and tie. If using baking insert, cover with its lid. Place cans or insert on rack in slow cooker. (If you don't have a rack, use rubber jar rings instead.)

5. Pour hot water around cans, up to half their height.

6. Cover slow cooker tightly. Cook on High 3½–4 hours.

7. Remove cans or insert from cooker. Let bread stand in coffee cans or baking insert 10 minutes. Turn out onto cooling rack. Slice.

Serving suggestion:
Spread with butter, cream cheese, or peanut butter.

Exchange List Values
- Carbohydrate 2.0
- Fat 0.5

Basic Nutritional Values
- Calories 168
  (Calories from Fat 41)
- Total Fat 5 gm
  (Saturated Fat 0.5 gm,
  Polyunsat Fat 3.0 gm,
  Monounsat Fat 0.8 gm)
- Cholesterol 11 mg
- Sodium 193 mg
- Total Carb 30 gm
- Dietary Fiber 2 gm
- Sugars 17 gm
- Protein 3 gm

Breads

Cocoa Zucchini Bread

Kathy Hertzler
Lancaster, PA
Katie Ebersol
Ronks, PA

Makes 2 loaves, 16 slices per loaf, 1 slice per serving
Prep. Time: 15 minutes
Baking Time: 1 hour
Cooling Time: 45–50 minutes

1 cup Splenda Sugar Blend

3 eggs

1 cup canola oil

2 cups grated zucchini

½ cup fat-free milk

1 tsp. vanilla extract

3 cups flour

1 tsp. cinnamon

1 tsp. baking soda

1 tsp. baking powder

½ tsp. salt

¼ cup cocoa powder, *optional*

½ cup mini-chocolate chips

½ cup chopped walnuts, or pecans

1. Blend Splenda, eggs, and oil in large mixing bowl.

2. Stir in zucchini.

3. Add milk and vanilla and stir well.

4. Mix flour, cinnamon, baking soda, baking powder, salt, and cocoa powder (if you wish) together in medium-sized mixing bowl.

5. Add dry ingredients to zucchini mixture. Stir thoroughly.

6. Add in chocolate chips and nuts. Stir.

7. Pour into two greased 9×5-inch loaf pans. Bake at 350°F for 1 hour. Test that bread is finished by inserting toothpick into center of each loaf. If pick comes out clean, bread is done. If it doesn't, continue baking 3–5 minutes. Test again.

8. Let cool in pans 15–20 minutes.

9. Remove from pans. Let stand 30 minutes or more before slicing and serving.

Warm Memories:

My sister first made this for me during a visit. I'm in Pennsylvania and she's in South Dakota, so it was special to share with her.
—Kathy Hertzler, Lancaster, PA

Exchange List Values
- Carbohydrate 1.0
- Fat 2.0

Basic Nutritional Values
- Calories 160 (Calories from Fat 80)
- Total Fat 9 gm (Saturated Fat 1.3 gm, Trans Fat 0.0 gm, Polyunsat Fat 3.0 gm, Monounsat Fat 4.9 gm)
- Cholesterol 20 mg
- Sodium 95 mg
- Potassium 60 gm
- Total Carb 18 gm
- Dietary Fiber 1 gm
- Sugars 8 gm
- Protein 2 gm
- Phosphorus 55 gm

Breads

Whole Wheat Rolls

Faye Pankratz
Inola, OK

Makes 2 dozen rolls, 1 roll per serving
Prep. Time: 25 minutes
Cooling Time: 20 minutes
Rising Time: about 2 hours
Baking Time: 20 minutes

2 pkgs. dry yeast

½ cup warm water

1 tsp. sugar

1¾ cups fat-free milk, scalded

¼ cup sugar

1 Tbsp. salt

3 Tbsp. all-vegetable shortening

2 cups whole wheat flour

3 egg whites

3 cups white flour, or more if needed

1. Combine yeast and warm water in small bowl. Sprinkle 1 tsp. sugar over yeast and water. Set aside.

2. Pour scalded milk over ¼ cup sugar, salt, and shortening in large bowl. Cool until lukewarm. Add yeast mixture and stir well.

3. Add whole wheat flour and egg whites. Beat well and gradually add white flour until you have soft dough.

4. Turn onto floured surface and knead until dough is elastic, about 5–7 minutes. Place in greased bowl, turning dough to grease top. Cover with clean cloth and let rise until doubled in bulk.

5. Punch down and shape into rolls. Place on greased cookie sheets until double.

6. Bake at 350° for 20 minutes or until lightly browned.

Exchange List Value
- Starch 1.5

Basic Nutritional Values
- Calories 125
  (Calories from Fat 20)
- Total Fat 2 gm
  (Saturated Fat 0.4 gm,
  Trans Fat 0.0 gm,
  Polyunsat Fat 0.6 gm,
  Monounsat Fat 0.7 gm)
- Cholesterol 0 mg
- Sodium 305 mg
- Potassium 105 gm
- Total Carb 23 gm
- Dietary Fiber 2 gm
- Sugars 3 gm
- Protein 4 gm
- Phosphorus 80 gm

Breads

Cheesy Garlic Bread

Loretta Krahn
Mountain Lake, MN

Makes 12 servings, 1 slice per serving
Prep. Time: 15 minutes
Baking Time: 10 minutes

4 Tbsp. trans-fat-free tub margarine

4 Tbsp. freshly grated Parmesan cheese

1 Tbsp. Italian seasoning

½ Tbsp. finely chopped onion

½ tsp. garlic powder

½ tsp. salt

16-oz. loaf French bread

1. Warm margarine until softened. Stir in all remaining ingredients except bread.

2. Slice bread and spread mixture thinly on each slice.

3. Warm in microwave or slow oven (200–300°F) until margarine melts immediately before serving.

Exchange List Values
- Starch 1.5
- Fat 0.5

Homemade Rolls

Ruth S. Weaver
Reinholds, PA

Makes 20 servings, 1 roll per serving
Prep. Time: 25 minutes
Rising Time: 2 hours
Baking Time: 15–20 minutes

5¾–6¾ cups bread flour, *divided*

⅓ cup instant nonfat dry milk solids

¼ cup sugar

1 Tbsp. salt

2 pkgs. dry yeast

5 Tbsp. margarine, softened

2 cups warm tap water, 120–130°F

1. In large bowl mix 2 cups flour, dry milk, sugar, salt, and yeast. Add margarine.

2. Gradually add water to dry ingredients and beat 2 minutes at medium speed with a mixer. Add 1 more cup flour and beat 2 minutes on high speed. Stir in enough flour to make a stiff dough.

3. Turn out onto a lightly floured board and knead about 8–10 minutes. Place in greased bowl, turning to grease top of dough.

4. Cover with a kitchen towel and let rise in warm place until doubled in bulk (about 45 minutes). Punch down and allow to rise again for 20 minutes.

5. Divide dough in half and cut each half into 10 equal pieces. Form into rolls and place on greased baking sheet about 2 inches apart. Cover and let rise again about 1 hour.

6. Bake at 375°F for 15–20 minutes. Remove from baking sheet and brush with melted margarine.

Exchange List Values
- Starch 2.0
- Fat 0.5

Basic Nutritional Values
- Calories 190 (Calories from Fat 25)
- Total Fat 3 gm (Saturated Fat 0.5 gm, Trans Fat 0.0 gm, Polyunsat Fat 1.2 gm, Monounsat Fat 0.8 gm)
- Cholesterol 0 mg
- Sodium 380 mg
- Potassium 75 gm
- Total Carb 34 gm
- Dietary Fiber 1 gm
- Sugars 4 gm
- Protein 6 gm
- Phosphorus 60 gm

TIP

Not many other people bring homemade bread or rolls to a church potluck, and I always bake them several days before the fellowship meal so I have no last-minute rush.

Icebox Butterhorns

Jolyn Nolt
Leola, PA

Makes 36 rolls, 1 roll per serving
Prep. Time: 15 minutes
Chilling Time: 8 hours or overnight
Rising Time: 1 hour
Baking Time: 15–20 minutes

2 cups fat-free milk

1 Tbsp. yeast

2 Tbsp. warm water, 110–115°F

½ cup sugar

1 egg

1 tsp. salt

6 cups flour

¾ cup butter-oil blend, such as Land O'Lakes tub butter with canola, at room temperature

1. Heat milk in small saucepan just until steaming.

2. Remove from heat and allow to cool to 110–115°F.

3. Meanwhile, in a large mixing bowl, dissolve yeast in warm water.

4. When milk has cooled, add it, plus sugar, egg, salt, and 3 cups flour to yeast mixture.

5. Beat until smooth.

6. Beat in butter spread and remaining flour. The dough will be sticky.

7. Cover bowl. Refrigerate 8 hours or overnight.

8. Then divide dough into three balls.

9. Roll each ball into a 12-inch circle on lightly floured surface.

10. Cut each circle into 12 wedges each.

11. Roll up each wedge crescent-style, starting with the wide end. Place rolls point-side down, 2 inches apart on wax paper–lined baking sheets. Curve ends, if you wish, to shape into crescents.

12. Cover and set in warm place. Let rise 1 hour.

13. Bake at 350°F for 15–20 minutes.

Exchange List Values
- Starch 1.5
- Fat 0.5

Basic Nutritional Values
- Calories 125 (Calories from Fat 35)
- Total Fat 4 gm (Saturated Fat 1.4 gm, Trans Fat 0.0 gm, Polyunsat Fat 0.8 gm, Monounsat Fat 1.8 gm)
- Cholesterol 10 mg
- Sodium 100 mg
- Potassium 50 gm
- Total Carb 19 gm
- Dietary Fiber 1 gm
- Sugars 4 gm
- Protein 3 gm
- Phosphorus 45 gm

Garlic Breadsticks

Sadie Mae Stoltzfus
Gordonville, PA

Makes 26 servings, 1×9-inch breadstick per
  serving
Prep. Time: 10 minutes
Rising Time: 20 minutes
Baking Time: 20 minutes

1½ cups warm water, 110–115°F

1 Tbsp. yeast

1 Tbsp. oil

1 Tbsp. sugar

1¼ tsp. salt

4 cups bread flour, also called unbleached
  occident flour

Topping:

3 Tbsp. olive oil, *divided*

½ cup trans-fat-free tub margarine, melted

1 tsp. coarsely ground salt

3 Tbsp. Parmesan cheese

1½ tsp. garlic powder

3 Tbsp. dried parsley flakes

1. Stir yeast into water in large bowl,
stirring until dissolved.

2. Add 1 Tbsp. oil, sugar, salt and flour.
Knead a little in the bowl to make sure
ingredients are fully incorporated.

3. Cover with tea towel. Let rise 5–8
minutes in warm spot.

4. Place 1 tsp. olive oil in each of two 9×13-
inch baking pans. Grease pans.

5. Divide dough between baking pans.
Spread to cover bottom of each pan. Set aside.

6. Prepare topping by placing melted
margarine in bowl.

7. Stir in remaining ingredients.

8. Pour topping mixture evenly over 2
pans of dough.

9. Bake at 350°F for 20 minutes, or until
golden brown.

10. Allow to cool slightly. Then using a
pizza cutter, start on the 13-inch side of the
pan and cut dough into 1-inch sticks.

Exchange List Values
- Starch 1.0
- Fat 1.0

Basic Nutritional Values
- Calories 125
  (Calories from Fat 45)
- Total Fat 5 gm
  (Saturated Fat 0.9 gm,
  Trans Fat 0.0 gm,
  Polyunsat Fat 1.6 gm,
  Monounsat Fat 2.4 gm)
- Cholesterol 0 mg
- Sodium 220 mg
- Potassium 35 gm
- Total Carb 16 gm
- Dietary Fiber 1 gm
- Sugars 1 gm
- Protein 3 gm
- Phosphorus 30 gm

Breads

Corn Sticks

Judith E. Bartel
North Newton, KS

Makes 20 servings
Prep. Time: 25 minutes
Baking Time: 10–12 minutes

2 cups reduced-fat baking mix

8½-oz. can cream-style corn

¼ cup freshly grated Parmesan cheese

1 tsp. powdered garlic

1 Tbsp. dill seed

4 Tbsp. trans-fat-free tub margarine, melted

1. Combine baking mix, corn, Parmesan cheese, garlic, and dill seed and mix well.

2. Knead 15–20 strokes on lightly floured on lightly floured board. Roll into large rectangle with rolling pin.

3. Cut into 1×3-inch strips. Place strips 1½ inches apart on ungreased cookie sheet. Brush with melted margarine.

4. Bake at 450°F for 10–12 minutes.

Exchange List Values
- Starch 0.5
- Fat 0.5

Basic Nutritional Values
- Calories 70 (Calories from Fat 20)
- Total Fat 2.5 gm (Saturated Fat 0.6 gm, Trans Fat 0.0 gm, Polyunsat Fat 0.9 gm, Monounsat Fat 1.1 gm)
- Cholesterol 0 mg
- Sodium 185 mg
- Potassium 35 gm
- Total Carb 10 gm
- Dietary Fiber 0 gm
- Sugars 2 gm
- Protein 1 gm
- Phosphorus 85 gm

Breads

Herbed Biscuit Knots

Melissa Wenger
Orrville, OH

Makes 20 servings
Prep. Time: 10 minutes
Baking Time: 9–12 minutes

12-oz. tube refrigerated buttermilk biscuits

¼ cup canola oil

½ tsp. salt

½ tsp. garlic powder

½ tsp. Italian seasoning

1. Cut each biscuit in half.

2. Roll each portion into a 6-inch-long rope.

3. Tie each in a loose knot. Place on greased baking sheet.

4. Bake at 400°F for 9–12 minutes, or until golden brown.

5. While knots bake, combine oil, salt, garlic powder, and Italian seasoning in small bowl.

6. Brush over warm knots immediately after baking.

Exchange List Values

- Starch 0.5
- Fat 1.0

Basic Nutritional Values

- Calories 75 (Calories from Fat 45)
- Total Fat 5 gm (Saturated Fat 1.0 gm, Trans Fat 0.0 gm, Polyunsat Fat 1.0 gm, Monounsat Fat 2.7 gm)
- Cholesterol 0 mg
- Sodium 245 mg
- Potassium 25 gm
- Total Carb 7 gm
- Dietary Fiber 0 gm
- Sugars 1 gm
- Protein 1 gm
- Phosphorus 60 gm

Breads

Garlic-Onion Bread

Loretta Krahn
Mountain Lake, MN

Makes 12 servings, 1 slice per serving
Prep. Time: 15 minutes
Baking Time: 10 minutes

4 Tbsp. trans-fat-free tub margarine

4 Tbsp. freshly grated Parmesan cheese

1 Tbsp. Italian seasoning

½ Tbsp. finely chopped onion

½ tsp. garlic powder

½ tsp. salt

16-oz. loaf French bread

1. Warm margarine until softened. Stir in all remaining ingredients except bread.

2. Slice bread and spread mixture thinly on each slice.

3. Warm in microwave or slow oven (200–300°F) until margarine melts immediately before serving.

Exchange List Values
- Starch 1.5
- Fat 0.5

Basic Nutritional Values
- Calories 140
  (Calories from Fat 35)
- Total Fat 4 gm
  (Saturated Fat 1.0 gm,
  Trans Fat 0.0 gm,
  Polyunsat Fat 1.5 gm,
  Monounsat Fat 1.1 gm)
- Cholesterol 0 mg
- Sodium 345 mg
- Potassium 55 gm
- Total Carb 22 gm
- Dietary Fiber 1 gm
- Sugars 1 gm
- Protein 5 gm
- Phosphorus 55 gm

Breads

Soups, Stews, Chilis, and Chowders

Soups, Stews, Chilis, and Chowders

Soups

Lilli's Vegetable Beef Soup

Lilli Peters
Dodge City, KS

Makes 12 servings
Prep. Time: 45 minutes
Cooking Time: 8–10 hours
Ideal slow-cooker size: 4- or 5-qt.

3 lbs. stewing meat, cut in 1-inch pieces

2 Tbsp. canola oil

4 potatoes, cubed

4 carrots, sliced

3 ribs celery, sliced

14-oz. can diced tomatoes

14-oz. can crushed Italian tomatoes

2 medium onions, chopped

2 wedges cabbage, sliced thinly

2 tsp. salt-free beef bouillon powder

2 Tbsp. fresh parsley

1 tsp. seasoned salt

1 tsp. garlic salt

½ tsp. pepper

water

1. Brown meat in oil in skillet. Drain.

2. Combine all ingredients in large slow cooker. Pour in enough water to cover the ingredients, plus half an inch or so.

3. Cover. Cook on Low 8–10 hours.

Exchange List Values
- Starch 0.5
- Vegetable 2.0
- Lean Meat 2.0
- Fat 0.5

Basic Nutritional Values
- Calories 223 (Calories from Fat 61)
- Total Fat 7 gm (Saturated Fat 1.5 gm, Polyunsat Fat 1.0 gm, Monounsat Fat 3.4 gm)
- Cholesterol 56 mg
- Sodium 465 mg
- Total Carb 20 gm
- Dietary Fiber 4 gm
- Sugars 7 gm
- Protein 21 gm

Vegetable Beef Borscht

Jeanne Heyerly
Chenoa, IL

Makes 8 servings
Prep. Time: 40 minutes
Cooking Time: 8–10 hours
Ideal slow-cooker size: 5-qt.

1 lb. beef roast, cooked and cubed

½ head of cabbage, sliced thin

3 medium potatoes, diced

4 carrots, sliced

1 large onion, diced

1 cup tomatoes, diced

1 cup corn

1 cup green beans

2 cups 98%-fat-free, lower-sodium beef broth

2 cups tomato juice

¼ tsp. garlic powder

¼ tsp. dill seed

½ tsp. pepper

sour cream

1.   Mix together all ingredients except sour cream. Add water to fill slow cooker three-quarters full.

2.   Cover. Cook on Low 8–10 hours.

3.   Top individual servings with sour cream.

Variation:
Add 1 cup diced cooked red beets during the last half hour of cooking.

Exchange List Values
- Starch 1.0
- Vegetable 3.0
- Lean Meat 1.0

Basic Nutritional Values
- Calories 185
  (Calories from Fat 25)
- Total Fat 3 gm
  (Saturated Fat 0.7 gm,
  Polyunsat Fat 0.4 gm,
  Monounsat Fat 1.1 gm)
- Cholesterol 28 mg
- Sodium 434 mg
- Total Carb 29 gm
- Dietary Fiber 6 gm
- Sugars 10 gm
- Protein 14 gm

Soups

Minestrone Soup

Lydia Konrad
Edmonton, AB

Makes 12 servings, about ¾ cup per serving
Prep. Time: 15 minutes
Cooking Time: about 2 hours

1½ lbs. 90%-lean ground beef

1 cup diced onions

1 cup diced zucchini

1 cup cubed potatoes

1 cup sliced carrots

½ cup diced celery

1 cup shredded cabbage

15-oz. can chopped tomatoes

1½ qts. water

1 bay leaf

½ tsp. dried thyme

2 tsp. salt

pepper, to taste

1 tsp. Worcestershire sauce

¼ cup uncooked brown rice

½ cup freshly grated Parmesan cheese

1. Brown ground beef in large soup kettle. Drain off grease.

2. Add vegetables, water, herbs, spices, and Worcestershire sauce and bring to a boil.

3. Sprinkle rice into mixture. Cover and simmer for at least 1 hour.

4. Sprinkle with Parmesan cheese.

Serving suggestion:
Serve with brown bread.

Exchange List Values
- Vegetable 2.0
- Lean Meat 1.0
- Fat 1.0

Basic Nutritional Values
- Calories 140 (Calories from Fat 55)
- Total Fat 6 gm (Saturated Fat 2.4 gm, Trans Fat 0.3 gm, Polyunsat Fat 0.2 gm, Monounsat Fat 2.2 gm)
- Cholesterol 35 mg
- Sodium 525 mg
- Potassium 360 gm
- Total Carb 9 gm
- Dietary Fiber 1 gm
- Sugars 2 gm
- Protein 13 gm
- Phosphorus 145 gm

Soups

Beef Dumpling Soup

Barbara Walker
Sturgis, SD

Makes 6 servings
Prep. Time: 35 minutes
Cooking Time: 4½–6½ hours
Ideal slow-cooker size: 4-qt.

1 lb. beef stewing meat, trimmed of visible fat, cubed

1 envelope dry, salt-free onion soup mix

6 cups hot water

2 carrots, shredded

1 celery rib, finely chopped

1 tomato, peeled and chopped

2 cloves garlic

½ tsp. dried basil

¼ tsp. dill weed

1 cup buttermilk biscuit mix

1 Tbsp. finely chopped parsley

6 Tbsp. fat-free milk

1. Place meat in slow cooker. Sprinkle with onion soup mix. Pour water over meat.

2. Add carrots, celery, tomato, garlic, basil, and dill weed.

3. Cover. Cook on Low 4–6 hours, or until meat is tender.

4. Combine biscuit mix and parsley. Stir in milk with fork until moistened. Drop dumplings by teaspoonfuls into pot.

5. Cover. Cook on High 30 minutes without lifting the lid.

Exchange List Values
- Starch 1.0
- Vegetable 1.0
- Lean Meat 1.0
- Fat 0.5

Basic Nutritional Values
- Calories 206 (Calories from Fat 57)
- Total Fat 6 gm (Saturated Fat 0.9 gm, Polyunsat Fat 1.4 gm, Monounsat Fat 2.6 gm)
- Cholesterol 38 mg
- Sodium 329 mg
- Total Carb 22 gm
- Dietary Fiber 2 gm
- Sugars 6 gm
- Protein 15 gm

Soups

Dottie's Creamy Steak Soup

Debbie Zeida
Mashpee, MA

Makes 8 servings
Prep. Time: 30 minutes
Cooking Time: 8–10 hours
Ideal slow-cooker size: 4-qt.

½ lb. 85%-lean ground beef

½ large onion, chopped

12-oz. can low-sodium V8 vegetable juice

3 medium potatoes, diced

10¾-oz. can 98%-fat-free, reduced-sodium cream of mushroom soup

10¾-oz. can cream of celery soup

16-oz. pkg. frozen mixed vegetables

½–¾ tsp. pepper

1. Sauté beef and onion in skillet. Drain.

2. Combine all ingredients in slow cooker.

3. Cover. Cook on Low 8–10 hours.

Exchange List Values
- Starch 1.0
- Vegetable 2.0
- Lean Meat 1.0
- Fat 0.5

Basic Nutritional Values
- Calories 202 (Calories from Fat 54)
- Total Fat 6 gm (Saturated Fat 2.2 gm, Polyunsat Fat 1.2 gm, Monounsat Fat 1.8 gm)
- Cholesterol 19 mg
- Sodium 506 mg
- Total Carb 28 gm
- Dietary Fiber 4 gm
- Sugars 7 gm
- Protein 10 gm

Soups

Hamburger Vegetable Soup

Donna Conto
Saylorsburg, PA

Makes 8 servings
Prep. Time: 35 minutes
Cooking Time: 5 hours
Ideal slow-cooker size: 4-qt.

½ lb. ground beef, browned, drained, and patted dry with a paper towel

1 beef bouillon cube, crushed

5 tsp. salt-free beef bouillon powder

16-oz. can diced tomatoes

1 large onion, diced

¾ cup sliced celery

1 medium carrot, diced

1 clove garlic, minced

1 bay leaf

½ tsp. salt

⅛ tsp. pepper

10-oz. pkg. frozen peas

3 Tbsp. chopped parsley

1. Combine all ingredients except peas and parsley in slow cooker.

2. Cover. Cook on Low 4 hours. Stir in peas. Cook on Low 1 more hour.

3. Garnish with parsley before serving.

Exchange List Values
- Vegetable 2.0
- Lean Meat 1.0

Basic Nutritional Values
- Calories 107 (Calories from Fat 28)
- Total Fat 3 gm (Saturated Fat 1.1 gm, Polyunsat Fat 0.2 gm, Monounsat Fat 1.3 gm)
- Cholesterol 17 mg
- Sodium 431 mg
- Total Carb 12 gm
- Dietary Fiber 3 gm
- Sugars 7 gm
- Protein 8 gm

Healthy Hamburger Soup

Chris Peterson
Green Bay, WI

Makes 8 servings
Prep. Time: 20 minutes
Cooking Time: 1–2 hours

1¾ lbs. 90%-lean ground beef

14½-oz. can stewed tomatoes

1 cup sliced mushrooms

2 cups sliced cabbage

1 cup sliced carrots

2 cups chopped celery

2 cups fresh or frozen green beans

4 cups tomato juice

2 cups no-added salt tomato juice

2 tsp. dried basil

2 tsp. dried oregano

1 Tbsp. Worcestershire sauce

TIP

1. Use canned mushrooms (pieces and stems) and a 14½-oz. can green or wax beans, no need to drain. I also sometimes add ¾ cup barley, quinoa, or broken spaghetti.
2. This is a great recipe for cleaning out your refrigerator. Whatever leftover veggies you have in there, throw them in the soup. I've added broccoli or rice and it's great.

1. In a soup pot, fry beef until brown and drain.

2. Add rest of ingredients.

3. Simmer 1–2 hours.

Exchange List Values
- Vegetable 3.0
- Med.-Fat Meat 2.0

Basic Nutritional Values
- Calories 230 (Calories from Fat 80)
- Total Fat 9 gm (Saturated Fat 3.3 gm, Trans Fat 0.5 gm, Polyunsat Fat 0.5 gm, Monounsat Fat 3.5 gm)
- Cholesterol 60 mg
- Sodium 560 mg
- Potassium 1055 gm
- Total Carb 18 gm
- Dietary Fiber 4 gm
- Sugars 11 gm
- Protein 22 gm
- Phosphorus 245 gm

Cheeseburger Soup

Rebecca B. Stoltzfus
Lititz, PA

Makes 6 servings
Prep. Time: 35 minutes
Cooking Time: 1 hour

½ lb. extra-lean 90%-fat-free ground beef

1 cup chopped onion

¾ cup grated carrots

¾ cup chopped celery

1 tsp. dried basil

1 tsp. parsley flakes

3 cups no-added-salt chicken broth

4 cups diced potatoes

2 Tbsp. trans-fat-free tub margarine

¼ cup flour

1½ cups fat-free milk

4 oz. reduced-fat American cheese, sliced or cubed

¼ cup fat-free sour cream

¼ tsp. salt

¼ tsp. pepper

1. In a soup pot, fry the beef until almost browned.

2. Add onion, carrots, celery, basil, and parsley. Sauté for a few minutes.

3. Add broth, potatoes.

4. Simmer until tender, 20 minutes.

5. In another pot, melt margarine; add flour. Whisk vigorously.

6. Add milk, whisking constantly. Cook over low heat until thickened.

7. Add cheese, sour cream, salt, and pepper.

8. Pour the cheese sauce into the beef soup. Stir gently to combine.

Variation:
Put the recipe in the slow cooker on Low 5 hours.

Exchange List Values
- Starch 1.5
- Fat-Free Milk 0.5
- Vegetable 1.0
- Med-Fat Meat 1.0
- Fat 0.5

Basic Nutritional Values
- Calories 295 (Calories from Fat 80)
- Total Fat 9 gm (Saturated Fat 3.4 gm, Trans Fat 0.2 gm, Polyunsat Fat 1.5 gm, Monounsat Fat 3.0 gm)
- Cholesterol 35 mg
- Sodium 515 mg
- Potassium 850 gm
- Total Carb 36 gm
- Dietary Fiber 3 gm
- Sugars 8 gm
- Protein 18 gm
- Phosphorus 375 gm

Soups

Springtime Soup

Clara L. Hershberger
Goshen, IN

Makes 12 servings, about ¾ cup per serving
Prep. Time: 15 minutes
Cooking Time: about 1 hour

1 lb. 90%-lean ground beef

1 cup chopped onion

4 cups water

1 cup diced carrots

1 cup diced celery

1 cup diced potatoes

2 tsp. salt, or less

1 tsp. Worcestershire sauce

¼ tsp. pepper

1 bay leaf

⅛ tsp. dried basil

6 tomatoes, chopped

fresh parsley, to garnish

1. In large saucepan, cook and stir ground beef until browned. Drain excess fat.

2. In large, heavy soup pot, cook and stir onion with meat until onion pieces are clear and tender, about 5 minutes.

3. Stir in all remaining ingredients except parsley. Bring to a boil.

4. Reduce heat, cover, and simmer until vegetables are just tender, about 1 hour.

5. Immediately before serving, add fresh parsley.

Exchange List Values
- Vegetable 1.0
- Lean Meat 1.0
- Fat 0.5

Basic Nutritional Values
- Calories 95
  (Calories from Fat 30)
- Total Fat 4 gm
  (Saturated Fat 1.3 gm,
  Trans Fat 0.2 gm,
  Polyunsat Fat 0.2 gm,
  Monounsat Fat 1.3 gm)
- Cholesterol 25 mg
- Sodium 435 mg
- Potassium 385 gm
- Total Carb 8 gm
- Dietary Fiber 2 gm
- Sugars 3 gm
- Protein 8 gm
- Phosphorus 95 gm

Taco Soup with Black Beans

Alexa Slonin
Harrisonburg, VA

Makes 8 servings
Prep. Time: 25 minutes
Cooking Time: 4–6 hours
Ideal slow-cooker size: 4-qt.

¾ lb. 90%-lean ground beef, browned and drained

28-oz. can crushed tomatoes

1 small onion, chopped

¼–½ cup water

15¼-oz. can corn, drained and rinsed

15-oz. can no-salt-added black beans, undrained

15½-oz. can no-salt-added red kidney beans, undrained

1 envelope dry Hidden Valley Ranch Dressing mix

2 Tbsp. low-sodium taco seasoning mix

tortilla chips, for garnish

grated cheese, for garnish

fat-free sour cream, for garnish

1. Combine all ingredients except chips, shredded cheese, and sour cream in slow cooker.

2. Cover. Cook on Low 4–6 hours.

3. Garnish individual servings with chips, cheese, and sour cream.

Exchange List Values
- Starch 1.5
- Vegetable 2.0
- Meat, Very Lean 2.0

Basic Nutritional Values
- Calories 247 (Calories from Fat 41)
- Total Fat 5 gm (Saturated Fat 1.5 gm, Polyunsat Fat 0.6 gm, Monounsat Fat 1.7 gm)
- Cholesterol 26 mg
- Sodium 652 mg
- Total Carb 35 gm
- Dietary Fiber 9 gm
- Sugars 9 gm
- Protein 17 gm

Hamburger Soup with Barley

Becky Oswald
Broadway, VA

Makes 10 servings
Prep. Time: 30 minutes
Cooking Time: 3–8 hours
Ideal slow-cooker size: 4-qt.

¾ lb. 85%-lean ground beef

1 medium onion, chopped

2 14½-oz. cans beef consommé

1¾ cup water

2 tsp. sodium-free beef bouillon powder

28-oz. can no-added-salt diced, tomatoes

3 carrots, sliced

3 celery ribs, sliced

8 Tbsp. barley

1 bay leaf

1 tsp. dried thyme

1 Tbsp. dried parsley

½ tsp. pepper

1. Brown beef and onion in skillet. Drain.

2. Combine all ingredients in slow cooker.

3. Cover. Cook on High 3 hours, or Low 6–8 hours.

Exchange List Values
- Starch 1.0
- Vegetable 1.0
- Lean Meat 1.0

Basic Nutritional Values
- Calories 154 (Calories from Fat 34)
- Total Fat 4 gm (Saturated Fat 1.4 gm, Polyunsat Fat 0.3 gm, Monounsat Fat 1.5 gm)
- Cholesterol 22 mg
- Sodium 623 mg
- Total Carb 20 gm
- Dietary Fiber 4 gm
- Sugars 6 gm
- Protein 11 gm

Soups

Taco Soup with Whole Tomatoes

Marla Folkerts
Holland, OH

Makes 8 servings
Prep. Time: 15 minutes
Cooking Time: 4–6 hours
Ideal slow-cooker size: 4-qt.

⅔ lb. 85%-lean ground beef

½ cup chopped onion

28-oz. can whole tomatoes with juice

14-oz. can kidney beans with juice

7-oz. can corn with juice

8-oz. can no-salt-added tomato sauce

2 Tbsp. low-sodium dry taco seasoning

1–2 cups water

pepper, to taste

1 cup fat-free grated cheddar cheese

tortilla chips, for garnish

1. Brown beef and onion in skillet. Drain.

2. Combine all ingredients except cheese and chips in slow cooker.

3. Cover. Cook on Low 4–6 hours.

4. Ladle into bowls. Top with cheese and serve with tortilla chips.

Exchange List Values
- Starch 1.0
- Vegetable 1.0
- Lean Meat 1.0
- Fat 0.5

Basic Nutritional Values
- Calories 191 (Calories from Fat 44)
- Total Fat 5 gm (Saturated Fat 1.6 gm, Polyunsat Fat 0.5 gm, Monounsat Fat 1.9 gm)
- Cholesterol 24 mg
- Sodium 612 mg
- Total Carb 22 gm
- Dietary Fiber 5 gm
- Sugars 10 gm
- Protein 16 gm

Hearty Beef and Cabbage Soup

Carolyn Mathias
Williamsville, NY

Makes 8 servings
Prep. Time: 30 minutes
Cooking Time: 4 hours
Ideal slow-cooker size: 4-qt.

⅔ lb. (about 11 oz.) ground beef

1 medium onion, chopped

40-oz. can tomatoes

2 cups water

15-oz. can kidney beans

½ tsp. pepper

1 Tbsp. chili powder

½ cup chopped celery

2 cups thinly sliced cabbage

1. Sauté beef in skillet. Drain.

2. Combine all ingredients except cabbage in slow cooker.

3. Cover. Cook on Low 3 hours. Add cabbage. Cook on High 30–60 minutes longer.

Exchange List Values
- Starch 0.5
- Vegetable 2.0
- Lean Meat 1.0

Basic Nutritional Values
- Calories 150
  (Calories from Fat 40)
- Total Fat 4 gm
  (Saturated Fat 1.5 gm,
  Polyunsat Fat 0.4 gm,
  Monounsat Fat 1.7 gm)
- Cholesterol 22 mg
- Sodium 507 mg
- Total Carb 18 gm
- Dietary Fiber 5 gm
- Sugars 8 gm
- Protein 12 gm

Soups

Shredded Pork Tortilla Soup

Hope Comerford
Clinton Township, MI

Makes 6–8 servings
Prep. Time: 10 minutes
Cooking Time: 8–10 hours
Ideal slow-cooker size: 5-qt.

3 large tomatoes, chopped

1 cup chopped red onion

1 jalapeño, seeded and minced

1 lb. pork loin

2 tsp. cumin

2 tsp. chili powder

2 tsp. onion powder

2 tsp. garlic powder

2 tsp. lime juice

8 cups chicken broth

Garnish, *optional*:

fresh chopped cilantro

tortilla chips

avocado slices

freshly grated Mexican cheese

1. In your crock, place the tomatoes, onion, and jalapeño.

2. Place the pork loin on top.

3. Add all the seasonings and lime juice, and pour in the chicken broth.

4. Cover and cook on Low for 8–10 hours.

5. Remove the pork and shred it between two forks. Place it back into the soup and stir.

6. Serve each bowl of soup with fresh chopped cilantro, tortilla chips, avocado slices and freshly grated Mexican cheese, if desired . . . or any other garnishes you would like!

TIP

If you don't have any fresh tomatoes, you can use canned.

Exchange List Values
- Vegetable 0.5
- Lean Meat 1.0
- Fat 0.5

Basic Nutritional Values
- Calories 145
  (Calories from Fat 45)
  Total Fat 5 gm
  (Saturated Fat 1.6 gm,
  Trans Fat 0 gm,
  Polyunsat Fat 0.7 gm,
  Monounsat Fat 2.1 gm)
- Cholesterol 34 mg
- Sodium 788 mg
- Potassium 602 gm
- Total Carb 6 gm
- Dietary Fiber 1.4 gm
- Sugars 3gm
- Protein 17.9 gm
- Phosphorus 215 gm

Soups

Tortellini Soup

Kim Rapp
Longmont, CO

Makes 8 servings
Prep. Time: 20 minutes
Cooking Time: 1 hour

12 oz. beef sausage, chopped or broken up

1 cup chopped onions

2 cloves garlic, chopped

2 cups chopped, peeled tomatoes

1 cup sliced carrots

8-oz. no-salt-added tomato sauce

5 cups lower-sodium, fat-free beef broth

½ cup water

½ cup dry red wine

1 tsp. dried basil

1 tsp. dried oregano

1½ cups sliced zucchini

8-oz. cheese tortellini

1 medium green pepper, chopped

3 Tbsp. chopped parsley

1. Combine sausage, onions, garlic, tomatoes, carrots, tomato sauce, broth, water, wine, basil, and oregano in a pot.

2. Bring to a boil, then turn down to a simmer.

3. Simmer uncovered, 30 minutes. Skim fat.

4. Stir in zucchini, tortellini, and pepper.

5. Simmer 30 minutes. Stir in chopped parsley.

Exchange List Values

- Starch 1.0
- Vegetable 2.0
- High-Fat Meat 1.0

Basic Nutritional Values

- Calories 225
  (Calories from Fat 90)
- Total Fat 10 gm
  (Saturated Fat 3.6 gm,
  Trans Fat 0.0 gm,
  Polyunsat Fat 1.0 gm,
  Monounsat Fat 3.9 gm)
- Cholesterol 30 mg
- Sodium 565 mg
- Potassium 560 gm
- Total Carb 22 gm
- Dietary Fiber 4 gm
- Sugars 6 gm
- Protein 12 gm
- Phosphorus 160 gm

Soups

Italian Sausage Soup

Mary Puskar
Forest Hill, MI

Makes 8 servings
Prep. Time: 30 minutes
Cooking Time: 1 hour

1 lb. lean sweet Italian turkey sausage

2 large onions, chopped

2 cloves garlic, minced

16-oz. can diced tomatoes and liquid

42-oz. low-sodium fat-free beef broth

1½ cups dry red wine

½ tsp. dried basil leaves

2 medium zucchini, cut in ¼-inch slices

2 cups shell pasta

1 medium green pepper, chopped

3 Tbsp. fresh parsley

grated Parmesan cheese, *optional*

1. Sauté sausage in large soup pot. Drain.

2. Add onions and garlic; sauté.

3. Stir in tomatoes, breaking them up.

4. Add broth, wine, and basil. Simmer 30 minutes.

5. Add zucchini, pasta, pepper, and parsley. Simmer 15 minutes.

6. Top bowls with lots of grated Parmesan cheese if you wish.

Exchange List Values
- Starch 1.5
- Vegetable 2.0
- Med-Fat Meat 1.0

Basic Nutritional Values
- Calories 250
  (Calories from Fat 55)
- Total Fat 6 gm
  (Saturated Fat 1.5 gm,
  Trans Fat 0.2 gm,
  Polyunsat Fat 1.6 gm,
  Monounsat Fat 1.9 gm)
- Cholesterol 30 mg
- Sodium 595 mg
- Potassium 595 gm
- Total Carb 31 gm
- Dietary Fiber 4 gm
- Sugars 6 gm
- Protein 16 gm
- Phosphorus 185 gm

Soups

German Potato Soup

Lee Ann Hazlett
Freeport, IL

Makes 8 servings
Prep. Time: 35 minutes
Cooking Time: 4–10 hours
Ideal slow-cooker size: 4-qt.

1 onion, chopped

1 leek, trimmed and diced

2 carrots, diced

1 cup chopped cabbage

¼ cup chopped fresh parsley

4 cups 99%-fat-free, lower-sodium beef broth

1 lb. potatoes, diced

1 bay leaf

1–2 tsp. black pepper

¼ tsp. nutmeg

1 tsp. salt, *optional*

½ tsp. caraway seeds, *optional*

½ lb. bacon, cooked and crumbled

½ cup fat-free sour cream

1. Combine all ingredients except bacon and sour cream.

2. Cover. Cook on Low 8–10 hours, or High 4–5 hours.

3. Remove bay leaf. Use a slotted spoon to remove potatoes. Mash potatoes and mix with sour cream. Return to slow cooker. Stir in. Add bacon and mix together thoroughly.

Exchange List Values
- Starch 1.0
- Vegetable 1.0
- Fat 0.5

Basic Nutritional Values
- Calories 130 (Calories from Fat 37)
- Total Fat 4 gm (Saturated Fat 1.3 gm, Polyunsat Fat 0.5 gm, Monounsat Fat 1.9 gm)
- Cholesterol 8 mg
- Sodium 384 mg
- Total Carb 17 gm
- Dietary Fiber 2 gm
- Sugars 4 gm
- Protein 6 gm

Soups

French Market Soup

Ethel Mumaw
Berlin, OH

Makes 8 servings (about 9 oz. per serving)
Prep. Time: 20 minutes
Cooking Time: 10 hours
Ideal slow-cooker size: 4-qt.

2 cups mixed dry beans, washed with stones removed

2 qts. water

1 ham hock, all visible fat removed

1 tsp. salt

¼ tsp. pepper

16-oz. can chopped tomatoes

1 large onion, chopped

1 clove garlic, minced

1 chili pepper, chopped, or 1 tsp. chili powder

¼ cup lemon juice

1. Combine all ingredients in slow cooker.

2. Cover. Cook on Low 8 hours. Turn to High and cook an additional 2 hours, or until beans are tender.

3. Debone ham, cut meat into bite-sized pieces, and stir back into soup.

Exchange List Values
- Starch 1.5
- Vegetable 1.0
- Lean Meat 1.0

Basic Nutritional Values
- Calories 191 (Calories from Fat 34)
- Total Fat 4 gm (Saturated Fat 1.3 gm, Polyunsat Fat 0.6 gm, Monounsat Fat 1.5 gm)
- Cholesterol 9 mg
- Sodium 488 mg
- Total Carb 29 gm
- Dietary Fiber 7 gm
- Sugars 5 gm
- Protein 12 gm

Soups

Calico Ham and Bean Soup

**Esther Martin
Ephrata, PA**

Makes 8 servings
Prep. Time: 25 minutes
Cooking Time: 4–10 hours
Ideal slow-cooker size: 5- or 6-qt.

1 lb. mixed dry beans, rinsed and drained, with stones removed

6 cups water

2 cups extra-lean, lower-sodium, cubed, cooked ham

1 cup chopped onions

1 cup chopped carrots

1 tsp. dried basil

1 tsp. dried oregano

¾ tsp. salt

¼ tsp. pepper

2 bay leaves

6 cups water

1 tsp. liquid smoke, *optional*

1. Combine beans and 6 cups water in large saucepan. Bring to boil, reduce heat, and simmer uncovered for 10 minutes. Drain, discarding cooking water, and rinse beans.

2. Combine all ingredients in slow cooker.

3. Cover. Cook on Low 8–10 hours, or High 4–5 hours. Discard bay leaves before serving.

Exchange List Values
- Starch 2.0
- Vegetable 1.0
- Meat, Very Lean 1.0

Basic Nutritional Values
- Calories 228
  (Calories from Fat 12)
- Total Fat 1 gm
  (Saturated Fat 0.4 gm,
  Polyunsat Fat 0.5 gm,
  Monounsat Fat 0.3 gm)
- Cholesterol 13 mg
- Sodium 462 mg
- Total Carb 38 gm
- Dietary Fiber 10 gm
- Sugars 6 gm
- Protein 17 gm

Soups

Dorothy's Split Pea Soup

Dorothy M. Van Deest
Memphis, TN

Makes 8 servings
Prep. Time: 25 minutes
Cooking Time: 8–10 hours
Ideal slow-cooker size: 5-qt.

2 Tbsp. canola oil

1 cup minced onions

8 cups water

2 cups (1 lb.) green split peas, washed and stone removed

4 whole cloves

1 bay leaf

¼ tsp. pepper

6 oz. extra-lean lower-sodium ham, cubed

1 cup finely minced celery

1 cup diced carrots

⅛ tsp. dried marjoram

¾ tsp. salt

⅛ tsp. dried savory

1. Combine all ingredients in slow cooker.

2. Cover. Cook on Low 8–10 hours.

Variation:

For a thick soup, uncover soup after 8–10 hours and turn heat to High. Simmer, stirring occasionally, until the desired consistency is reached.

Exchange List Values
- Starch 2.0
- Vegetable 1.0
- Lean Meat 1.0

Basic Nutritional Values
- Calories 239 (Calories from Fat 40)
- Total Fat 4 gm (Saturated Fat 0.5 gm, Polyunsat Fat 1.4 gm, Monounsat Fat 2.3 gm)
- Cholesterol 10 mg
- Sodium 419 mg
- Total Carb 35 gm
- Dietary Fiber 13 gm
- Sugars 7 gm
- Protein 16 gm

Soups

Gazpacho

Maxine Hershberger
Dalton, OH

Makes 6 servings, about 5 oz. per serving
Prep. Time: 30 minutes
Chilling Time: 4 hours or more

1 cup finely chopped tomato

½ cup chopped green pepper

½ cup chopped celery

½ cup chopped cucumber

¼ cup finely chopped onion

2 tsp. snipped parsley

1 tsp. snipped chives

1 small clove garlic, minced

2-3 Tbsp. tarragon wine vinegar

2 Tbsp. olive oil

½ tsp. salt

¼ tsp. black pepper

½ tsp. Worcestershire sauce

2 cups tomato juice

1 cup croutons

1. Combine all ingredients except croutons in a glass bowl. Toss to mix well.

2. Cover and chill at least 4 hours before serving.

3. Sprinkle croutons on top and serve. Serve as a salad or soup.

Exchange List Values
- Vegetable 2.0
- Fat 1.0

Basic Nutritional Values
- Calories 90
  (Calories from Fat 45)
- Total Fat 5 gm
  (Saturated Fat 0.7 gm,
  Trans Fat 0.0 gm,
  Polyunsat Fat 0.6 gm,
  Monounsat Fat 3.5 gm)
- Cholesterol 0 mg
- Sodium 365 mg
- Potassium 335 gm
- Total Carb 10 gm
- Dietary Fiber 1 gm
- Sugars 5 gm
- Protein 2 gm
- Phosphorus 35 gm

Soups

Chicken Noodle Soup

Beth Shank
Wellman, IA

Makes 8 servings
Prep. Time: 15 minutes
Cooking Time: 4–6 hours
Ideal slow-cooker size: 4-qt.

5 cups hot water

2 tsp. sodium-free chicken bouillon powder

46-oz. can fat-free, lower-sodium chicken broth

2 cups cooked, chopped chicken

4 cups "homestyle" noodles, uncooked

⅓ cup thinly sliced celery, lightly precooked in microwave

⅓ cup shredded carrots

1. Dissolve bouillon in water. Pour into slow cooker.

2. Add remaining ingredients. Mix well.

3. Cover. Cook on Low 4–6 hours.

Exchange List Values
- Starch 1.0
- Lean Meat 1.0

Basic Nutritional Values
- Calories 155 (Calories from Fat 31)
- Total Fat 3 gm (Saturated Fat 1.0 gm, Polyunsat Fat 0.8 gm, Monounsat Fat 1.2 gm)
- Cholesterol 49 mg
- Sodium 382 mg
- Total Carb 15 gm
- Dietary Fiber 1 gm
- Sugars 2 gm
- Protein 14 gm

Soups

Chicken Rice Soup

Karen Ceneviva
Seymour, CT

Makes 8 servings
Prep. Time: 15 minutes
Cooking Time: 4–8 hours
Ideal slow-cooker size: 3½-qt.

½ cup wild rice, uncooked

½ cup long-grain rice, uncooked

1 tsp. vegetable oil

1 lb. boneless skinless chicken breasts, cut into ¾-inch cubes

5¼ cups fat-free, low-sodium chicken broth

1 cup celery (about 2 ribs), chopped in ½-inch-thick pieces

1 medium onion, chopped

2 tsp. dried thyme leaves

¼ tsp. red pepper flakes

1. Mix wild and white rice with oil in slow cooker.

2. Cover. Cook on High 15 minutes.

3. Add chicken, broth, vegetables, and seasonings.

4. Cover. Cook 4–5 hours on High or 7–8 hours on Low.

TIP

A dollop of sour cream sprinkled with finely chopped green onions on top of each individual serving bowl makes a nice finishing touch.

Exchange List Values
- Starch 1.0
- Lean Meat 2.0

Basic Nutritional Values
- Calories 160 (Calories from Fat 20)
- Total Fat 2 gm (Saturated Fat 0 gm, Polyunsat Fat 0.5 gm, Monounsat Fat 1.0 gm)
- Cholesterol 35 mg
- Sodium 375 mg
- Total Carb 18 gm
- Dietary Fiber 1 gm
- Sugars 2 gm
- Protein 16 gm

Soups

Mexican Rice and Bean Soup

Esther J. Mast
East Petersburg, PA

Makes 6 servings
Prep. Time: 25 minutes
Cooking Time: 6 hours
Ideal slow-cooker size: 4-qt.

½ cup chopped onion

⅓ cup chopped green bell pepper

1 clove garlic, minced

1 Tbsp. oil

4-oz. pkg. sliced or chipped dried beef

18-oz. can no-added-salt tomato juice

15½-oz. can red kidney beans, undrained

1½ cups water

½ cup long-grain rice, uncooked

1 tsp. paprika

½–1 tsp. chili powder

dash pepper

1. Cook onion, green pepper, and garlic in oil in skillet until vegetables are tender but not brown. Transfer to slow cooker.

2. Tear beef into small pieces and add to slow cooker.

3. Add remaining ingredients. Mix well.

4. Cover. Cook on Low 6 hours. Stir before serving.

Exchange List Values
- Starch 1.5
- Vegetable 2.0
- Fat 0.5

Basic Nutritional Values
- Calories 190
  (Calories from Fat 28)
- Total Fat 3 gm
  (Saturated Fat 0.4 gm,
  Polyunsat Fat 0.9 gm,
  Monounsat Fat 1.6 gm)
- Cholesterol 15 mg
- Sodium 796 mg
- Total Carb 30 gm
- Dietary Fiber 4 gm
- Sugars 7 gm
- Protein 12 gm

Soups

Chicken Tortilla Soup

Becky Harder
Monument, CO

Makes 8 servings
Prep. Time: 15 minutes
Cooking Time: 8 hours
Ideal slow-cooker size: 4- or 5-qt.

4 boneless skinless chicken breast halves

2 15-oz. cans no-salt-added black beans, undrained

2 15-oz. cans Mexican stewed tomatoes, or Ro*Tel tomatoes

1 cup salsa of your choice

4-oz. can chopped green chilies

14½-oz. can no-added-salt tomato sauce

2 oz. (about 24 chips) tortilla chips

1 cup fat-free cheddar cheese

1. Combine all ingredients except chips and cheese in large slow cooker.

2. Cover. Cook on Low 8 hours.

3. Just before serving, remove chicken breasts and slice into bite-sized pieces. Stir into soup.

4. To serve, put a handful of chips in each individual soup bowl. Ladle soup over chips. Top with cheese.

Exchange List Values
- Starch 1.0
- Vegetable 2.0
- Meat, Very Lean 3.0
- Fat 0.5

Basic Nutritional Values
- Calories 263 (Calories from Fat 36)
- Total Fat 4 gm (Saturated Fat 0.9 gm, Polyunsat Fat 0.8 gm, Monounsat Fat 1.7 gm)
- Cholesterol 43 mg
- Sodium 793 mg
- Total Carb 29 gm
- Dietary Fiber 7 gm
- Sugars 9 gm
- Protein 28 gm

Soups

Southwest Chicken and White Bean Soup

**Karen Ceneviva
Seymour, CT**

Makes 6 servings
Prep. Time: 15 minutes
Cooking Time: 4–10 hours
Ideal slow-cooker size: 3½-qt.

1 Tbsp. vegetable oil

1 lb. boneless skinless chicken breasts, cut into 1-inch cubes

1¾ cups fat-free, low-sodium chicken broth

1 cup chunky salsa

3 cloves garlic, minced

2 Tbsp. cumin

15½-oz. can small white beans, drained and rinsed

1 cup frozen corn

1 large onion, chopped

1. Heat oil in 10-inch skillet over medium to high heat. Add chicken and cook until it is well browned on all sides. Stir frequently to prevent sticking.

2. Mix broth, salsa, garlic, cumin, beans, corn, and onion in slow cooker. Add chicken. Stir well.

3. Cover. Cook 8–10 hours on Low or 4–5 hours on High.

Exchange List Values
- Starch 1.0
- Vegetable 1.0
- Lean Meat 2.0
- Fat 0.5

Basic Nutritional Values
- Calories 220
  (Calories from Fat 45)
- Total Fat 5 gm
  (Saturated Fat 1.0 gm,
  Polyunsat Fat 1.5 gm,
  Monounsat Fat 2.5 gm)
- Cholesterol 45 mg
- Sodium 535 mg
- Total Carb 23 gm
- Dietary Fiber 6 gm
- Sugars 4 gm
- Protein 22 gm

Broccoli-Cheese Soup

Darla Sathre
Baxter, MN

Makes 8 servings
Prep. Time: 20 minutes
Cooking Time: 8–10 hours
Ideal slow-cooker size: 4-qt.

2 16-oz. pkgs. frozen chopped broccoli

10¾-oz. can cheddar cheese soup

12-oz. can fat-free evaporated milk

2½ cups fat-free half-and-half

¼ cup finely chopped onion

1 Tbsp. Italian seasoning

¼ tsp. pepper

2 oz. fat-free cheddar cheese

sunflower seeds, *optional*

crumbled bacon, *optional*

1. Combine all ingredients except sunflower seeds and bacon in slow cooker.

2. Cover. Cook on Low 8–10 hours.

3. Garnish with sunflower seeds and bacon, if using.

Exchange List Values
- Fat-Free Milk 1.0
- Vegetable 2.0
- Fat 0.5

Basic Nutritional Values
- Calories 171
  (Calories from Fat 36)
- Total Fat 4 gm
  (Saturated Fat 1.6 gm,
  Polyunsat Fat 0.9 gm,
  Monounsat Fat 0.9 gm)
- Cholesterol 12 mg
- Sodium 581 mg
- Total Carb 22 gm
- Dietary Fiber 4 gm
- Sugars 12 gm
- Protein 12 gm

Soups

French Onion Soup

Jenny R. Unternahrer
Wayland, IA
Janice Yoskovich
Carmichaels, PA

Makes 10 servings
Prep. Time: 30 minutes
Cooking Time: 5–7 hours
Ideal slow-cooker size: 4-qt.

8–10 large onions, sliced

½ cup light, soft tub margarine

3 14-oz. cans 98%-fat-free, lower-sodium beef broth

2½ cups water

3 tsp. sodium-free chicken bouillon powder

1½ tsp. Worcestershire sauce

3 bay leaves

10 (1 oz.) slices French bread, toasted

shredded cheese for serving, optional (not included in nutritional analysis)

NOTES

For a more intense beef flavor, add one beef bouillon cube, or use home-cooked beef broth instead of canned broth.

1. Sauté onions in margarine until crisp-tender. Transfer to slow cooker.

2. Add beef broth, water, and bouillon powder. Mix well. Add Worcestershire sauce and bay leaves.

3. Cover. Cook on Low 5–7 hours, or until onions are tender. Discard bay leaves.

4. Ladle into bowls. Top each with a slice of bread and some cheese.

Exchange List Values
- Starch 1.0
- Vegetable 3.0
- Fat 0.5

Basic Nutritional Values
- Calories 178 (Calories from Fat 35)
- Total Fat 4 gm (Saturated Fat 0.3 gm, Polyunsat Fat 0.9 gm, Monounsat Fat 2.0 gm)
- Cholesterol 0 mg
- Sodium 476 mg
- Total Carb 31 gm
- Dietary Fiber 4 gm
- Sugars 12 gm
- Protein 6 gm

Soups

Tomato Soup

Hope Comerford
Clinton Township, MI

Makes 6–8 servings
Prep. Time: 10 minutes
Cooking Time: 6–9 hours
Ideal slow-cooker size: 5-qt.

1 small onion, chopped

1½ tsp. diced garlic

2 tsp. oregano

⅛ tsp. pepper

¾ tsp. salt

28-oz. can stewed tomatoes

28-oz. can crushed tomatoes

1 tsp. sugar

2 cups vegetable broth

2 cups heavy cream

1. Place onion, garlic, oregano, pepper, salt, stewed tomatoes, crushed tomatoes, sugar, and vegetable broth in crock.

2. Cover and cook on Low for 6–9 hours.

3. Using an immersion blender, blend the soup until as smooth as you like it.

4. Remove half a cup of the tomato soup and mix briskly with the 2 cups of heavy cream.

5. Whisk the mixture of soup and cream very slowly into the rest of the soup in the crock.

Exchange List Values
- Bread/Starch 1.0
- Vegetable 1.0
- Fat 5.0

Basic Nutritional Values
- Calories 340 (Calories from Fat 219)
  Total Fat 24.3 gm
  (Saturated Fat 0.2 gm,
  Trans Fat 0.7 gm,
  Polyunsat Fat 1.8 gm,
  Monounsat Fat 6.5 gm)
- Cholesterol 68 mg
- Sodium 1053 mg
- Potassium 737 gm
- Total Carb 24 gm
- Dietary Fiber 3.8 gm
- Sugars 10gm
- Protein 6 gm
- Phosphorus 177 gm

Tomato Basil Soup

Barbara Kuhns
Millersburg, OH

Makes 8 servings
Prep. Time: 15 minutes
Cooking Time: 25 minutes

1 Tbsp. canola oil

¼ cup finely chopped onion

2 10¾-oz. cans lower-sodium, lower-fat
condensed tomato soup

2 cups no-added-salt tomato sauce

6-oz. can no-added-salt tomato paste

2⅔ cups low-sodium chicken broth

1 Tbsp. dried basil

2 Tbsp. Splenda Brown Sugar Blend

2–3 cloves garlic, minced, *optional*

1 cup fat-free half-and-half

⅓ cup flour

1. Heat oil in soup pot.

2. Add and sauté onion.

3. Add condensed soup, sauce, paste,
broth, basil, Brown Sugar Blend, and garlic.

4. Cook, covered, until hot.

5. Whisk together half-and-half and flour.
Add and heat gently, stirring, until soup is
steaming and thick. Do not boil.

Exchange List Values
- Carbohydrate 1.5
- Vegetable 2.0
- Fat 0.5

Basic Nutritional Values
- Calories 170
  (Calories from Fat 30)
- Total Fat 4 gm
  (Saturated Fat 0.8 gm,
  Trans Fat 0.0 gm,
  Polyunsat Fat 0.9 gm,
  Monounsat Fat 1.3 gm)
- Cholesterol 5 mg
- Sodium 365 mg
- Potassium 1025 gm
- Total Carb 30 gm
- Dietary Fiber 4 gm
- Sugars 15 gm
- Protein 6 gm
- Phosphorus 125 gm

Soups

Vegetarian Minestrone Soup

Connie Johnson
Loudon, NH

Makes 8 servings
Prep. Time: 35 minutes
Cooking Time: 6–8 hours
Ideal slow-cooker size: 4-qt.

6 cups fat-free, 60%-less sodium vegetable broth

2 carrots, chopped

2 large onions, chopped

3 ribs celery, chopped

2 cloves garlic, minced

1 small zucchini, cubed

1 handful fresh kale, chopped

½ cup dry barley

15-oz. can chickpeas, or white kidney beans, rinsed and drained

1 Tbsp. parsley

½ tsp. dried thyme

1 tsp. dried oregano

28-oz. can crushed Italian tomatoes

¼ tsp. pepper

Exchange List Values
- Starch 1.5
- Vegetable 4.0

Basic Nutritional Values
- Calories 200 (Calories from Fat 13)
- Total Fat 1 gm (Saturated Fat 0.1 gm, Polyunsat Fat 0.6 gm, Monounsat Fat 0.3 gm)
- Cholesterol 0 mg
- Sodium 641 mg
- Total Carb 41 gm
- Dietary Fiber 9 gm
- Sugars 12 gm
- Protein 7 gm

1. Combine all ingredients in slow cooker.

2. Cover. Cook on Low 6–8 hours, or until vegetables are tender.

Soups

Super Healthy Cabbage Soup

Hope Comerford
Clinton Township, MI

Makes 8–10 servings
Prep. Time: 20 minutes
Cooking Time: 8 hours
Ideal slow-cooker size: 5- to 6-qt.

3 cups chopped cabbage

1½ cups chopped onion

2 large tomatoes, chopped

3 carrots, halved and sliced

2 stalks celery, halved and sliced

1 jalapeño, seeded and diced

1 Tbsp. garlic powder

2–3 tsp. salt

1 tsp. basil

1 tsp. oregano

¼ tsp. pepper

46 oz. no-salt-added tomato juice

5 cups water

1. Place all ingredients into crock.

2. Cover and cook on Low for 8 hours.

Exchange List Value
- Bread/Starch 1.0
- Vegetable 0.5

Basic Nutritional Values
- Calories 56
  (Calories from Fat 2)
  Total Fat 0.2 gm
  (Saturated Fat 0.1 gm,
  Trans Fat 0 gm,
  Polyunsat Fat 0.1 gm,
  Monounsat Fat 0.03 gm)
- Cholesterol 0 mg
- Sodium 426 mg
- Potassium 567 gm
- Total Carb 13 gm
- Dietary Fiber 2.8 gm
- Sugars 8gm
- Protein 4 gm
- Phosphorus 2.2 gm

Soups

Lentil Vegetable Soup

Mary C. Jungerman
Boulder, CO

Makes 10 servings, about ⅔ cup per serving
Prep. Time: 15 minutes
Cooking Time: 2 hours

2 cups lentils

8 cups water

2 slices cooked bacon, diced

½ cup chopped onion

½ cup chopped celery

¼ cup chopped carrots

3 Tbsp. snipped fresh parsley

1 clove garlic, minced

2 tsp. salt

¼ tsp. pepper

½ tsp. dried oregano

2 cups chopped tomatoes

2 Tbsp. wine vinegar

1. Rinse lentils. Drain and place in large soup kettle. Add water and all remaining ingredients except tomatoes and vinegar.

2. Cover and simmer 1½ hours.

3. Add tomatoes and vinegar. Cover and simmer for 30 minutes longer.

4. Adjust seasoning and serve.

Exchange List Values
- Starch 1.5
- Lean Meat 1.0

Basic Nutritional Values
- Calories 165
  (Calories from Fat 25)
- Total Fat 3 gm
  (Saturated Fat 1.1 gm,
  Trans Fat 0.0 gm,
  Polyunsat Fat 0.6 gm,
  Monounsat Fat 1.3 gm)
- Cholesterol 5 mg
- Sodium 510 mg
- Potassium 535 gm
- Total Carb 25 gm
- Dietary Fiber 9 gm
- Sugars 3 gm
- Protein 11 gm
- Phosphorus 215 gm

Soups

Russian Red-Lentil Soup

**Naomi E. Fast
Hesston, KS**

Makes 8 servings
Prep. Time: 25 minutes
Cooking Time: 4–5 hours
Ideal slow-cooker size: 5- or 6-qt.

1 Tbsp. canola oil

1 large onion, chopped

3 cloves garlic, minced

½ cup diced, dried apricots

1½ cups dried red lentils

½ tsp. cumin

½ tsp. dried thyme

3 cups water

2 14½-oz. cans chicken or vegetable broth

14½-oz. can diced tomatoes

1 Tbsp. honey

½ tsp. coarsely ground black pepper

2 Tbsp. chopped fresh mint

1½ cups plain yogurt

1. Combine all ingredients except mint and yogurt in slow cooker.

2. Cover. Heat on High until soup starts to simmer, then turn to Low and cook 3–4 hours.

3. Add mint and dollop of yogurt to each bowl of soup.

Exchange List Values
- Starch 1.5
- Fruit 1.0
- Vegetable 1.0
- Meat, Very Lean 1.0

Basic Nutritional Values
- Calories 244
  (Calories from Fat 37)
- Total Fat 4 gm
  (Saturated Fat 1.2 gm,
  Polyunsat Fat 0.8 gm,
  Monounsat Fat 1.5 gm)
- Cholesterol 8 mg
- Sodium 587 mg
- Total Carb 42 gm
- Dietary Fiber 10 gm
- Sugars 21 gm
- Protein 13 gm

Soups

Potato Soup

Dale Peterson
Rapid City, SD

Makes 6 servings, about 9 oz. per serving
Prep. Time: 20 minutes
Cooking Time: 30 minutes

2 Tbsp. trans-fat-free tub margarine

¼ cup diced onion

4 cups diced potatoes

1–2 carrots, grated

2 cups water

1 tsp. salt

½ tsp. pepper

1 tsp. dried dill weed

3 cups fat-free milk

2 Tbsp. fresh parsley, chopped

1. In a soup pot, sauté onion in margarine until golden.

2. Bring potatoes, carrots, water, salt, pepper, and dill weed to boil.

3. Reduce heat to low and simmer with lid cocked until potatoes are tender.

4. Stir in milk and parsley and heat until hot.

TIP

If you like thicker soup, add in some instant potatoes.

Exchange List Values
- Starch 1.5
- Fat-Free Milk 0.5

Basic Nutritional Values
- Calories 165 (Calories from Fat 25)
- Total Fat 3 gm (Saturated Fat 0.7 gm, Trans Fat 0.0 gm, Polyunsat Fat 1.2 gm, Monounsat Fat 1.0 gm)
- Cholesterol 0 mg
- Sodium 480 mg
- Potassium 590 gm
- Total Carb 29 gm
- Dietary Fiber 2 gm
- Sugars 8 gm
- Protein 6 gm
- Phosphorus 175 gm

Soups

Stews

Meatball Stew

**Barbara Hershey
Lititz, PA**

Makes 8 servings

Prep. Time: 1 hour (includes preparing and baking meatballs)

Cooking Time: 4–5 hours

Ideal slow-cooker size: 4- or 6-qt.

Meatballs:

2 lbs. 90%-lean ground beef

2 eggs, beaten

2 Tbsp. dried onion

⅔ cup bread crumbs

½ cup milk

½ tsp. salt

¼ tsp. pepper

1 tsp. Dijon mustard

2 tsp. Worcestershire sauce

Stew

6 medium potatoes, unpeeled if you wish, and diced fine

1 large onion, sliced

8 medium carrots, sliced

4 cups vegetable juice

1 tsp. dried basil

1 tsp. dried oregano

½ tsp. pepper

1. In a bowl, thoroughly mix meatball ingredients together. Form into 1-inch balls.

2. Place meatballs on a lightly greased rimmed baking sheet. Bake at 400°F for 20 minutes.

3. Meanwhile, to make stew, prepare potatoes, onion, and carrots. Place in slow cooker.

4. When finished baking, remove meatballs from pan. Blot dry with paper towels to remove excess fat.

5. Place meatballs on top of vegetables in slow cooker.

6. In a large bowl, combine vegetable juice and seasonings. Pour over meatballs and vegetables in slow cooker.

7. Cover cooker. Cook on High 4–5 hours, or until vegetables are tender.

Exchange List Values
- Starch 2.0
- Vegetable 3.0
- Lean Meat 3.0
- Fat 1.0

Basic Nutritional Values
- Calories 405 (Calories from Fat 100)
- Total Fat 11 gm (Saturated Fat 4.0 gm, Polyunsat Fat 1.0 gm, Monounsat Fat 4.5 gm)
- Cholesterol 115 mg
- Sodium 595 mg
- Total Carb 45 gm
- Dietary Fiber 6 gm
- Sugars 12 gm
- Protein 30 gm

Pirate Stew

Nancy Graves
Manhattan, KS

Makes 6 servings
Prep. Time: 20 minutes
Cooking Time: 6 hours
Ideal slow-cooker size: 4-qt.

¾ cup sliced onion

1 lb. ground beef

¼ cup uncooked, long-grain rice

3 cups diced raw potatoes

1 cup diced celery

2 cups canned kidney beans, drained

½ tsp. salt

⅛ tsp. pepper

¼ tsp. chili powder

¼ tsp. Worcestershire sauce

1 cup tomato sauce

½ cup water

1. Brown onion and ground beef in skillet. Drain.

2. Layer ingredients in slow cooker in order given.

3. Cover. Cook on Low 6 hours, or until potatoes and rice are cooked.

Variation:

Add a layer of 2 cups sliced carrots between potatoes and celery.

—Katrine Rose, Woodbridge, VA

Exchange List Values
- Starch 2.0
- Vegetable 1.0
- Lean Meat 2.0
- Fat 0.5

Basic Nutritional Values
- Calories 310
  (Calories from Fat 73)
- Total Fat 8 gm
  (Saturated Fat 3.0 gm,
  Polyunsat Fat 0.5 gm,
  Monounsat Fat 3.4 gm)
- Cholesterol 45 mg
- Sodium 611 mg
- Total Carb 38 gm
- Dietary Fiber 7 gm
- Sugars 6 gm
- Protein 22 gm

Stews

Easy Southern Brunswick Stew

Barbara Sparks
Glen Burnie, MD

Makes 12 servings
Prep. Time: 20 minutes
Cooking Time: 7–9 hours
Ideal slow-cooker size: 4-qt.

2 lbs. pork butt, visible fat removed

15.25-oz. can white corn

1¼ cup ketchup

2 cups diced, cooked potatoes

10-oz. pkg. frozen peas

2 10¾-oz. cans reduced-sodium tomato soup

hot sauce, to taste, *optional*

1. Place pork in slow cooker.

2. Cover. Cook on Low 6–8 hours. Remove meat from bone and shred, removing and discarding all visible fat.

3. Combine all ingredients in slow cooker.

4. Cover. Bring to boil on High. Reduce heat to Low and simmer 30 minutes. Add hot sauce if you wish.

Exchange List Values
- Starch 1.0
- Vegetable 2.0
- Lean Meat 1.0
- Fat 0.5

Basic Nutritional Values
- Calories 213
  (Calories from Fat 61)
- Total Fat 7 gm
  (Saturated Fat 2.3 gm,
  Polyunsat Fat 0.9 gm,
  Monounsat Fat 2.6 gm)
- Cholesterol 34 mg
- Sodium 584 mg
- Total Carb 27 gm
- Dietary Fiber 3 gm
- Sugars 9 gm
- Protein 13 gm

Stews

Chili

Texican Chili

Becky Oswald
Broadway, VA

Makes 15 servings
Prep. Time: 35 minutes
Cooking Time: 9–10 hours
Ideal slow-cooker size: 5- or 6-qt.

8 bacon strips, diced

2½ lbs. beef stewing meat, cubed

28-oz. can stewed tomatoes

14½-oz. can stewed tomatoes

8-oz. can tomato sauce

8-oz. can no-added-salt tomato sauce

16-oz. can kidney beans, rinsed and drained

2 cups sliced carrots

1 medium onion, chopped

1 cup chopped celery

½ cup chopped green pepper

¼ cup minced fresh parsley

1 Tbsp. chili powder

½ tsp. ground cumin

¼ tsp. pepper

1. Cook bacon in skillet until crisp. Drain on paper towel.

2. Brown beef in bacon drippings in skillet.

3. Combine all ingredients in slow cooker.

4. Cover. Cook on Low 9–10 hours, or until meat is tender. Stir occasionally.

Exchange List Values
- Starch 0.5
- Vegetable 2.0
- Lean Meat 1.0
- Fat 0.5

Basic Nutritional Values
- Calories 165
  (Calories from Fat 44)
- Total Fat 5 gm
  (Saturated Fat 1.5 gm,
  Polyunsat Fat 0.5 gm,
  Monounsat Fat 2.2 gm)
- Cholesterol 40 mg
- Sodium 434 mg
- Total Carb 15 gm
- Dietary Fiber 3 gm
- Sugars 6 gm
- Protein 16 gm

Chili

Three-Bean Chili

**Chris Kaczynski
Schenectady, NY**

Makes 12 servings
Prep. Time: 30 minutes
Cooking Time: 8–10 hours
Ideal slow-cooker size: 6-qt.

2 lbs. ground beef

2 medium onions, diced

16-oz. jar medium salsa

2 pkgs. dry chili seasoning

2 16-oz. cans red kidney beans, drained

2 16-oz. cans black beans, drained

2 16-oz. cans white kidney, or garbanzo, beans drained

28-oz. can crushed tomatoes

16-oz. can diced tomatoes

2 tsp. sugar

1. Brown beef and onions in skillet.

2. Combine all ingredients in 6-qt. slow cooker, or in two 4- or 5-qt. cookers.

3. Cover. Cook on Low 8–10 hours.

NOTES

If you don't have a cooker large enough to handle the full amount, this recipe can be cut in half without sacrificing flavor.

Exchange List Values

- Starch 2.5
- Vegetable 2.0
- Lean Meat 2.0
- Fat 0.5

Basic Nutritional Values

- Calories 381
  (Calories from Fat 80)
- Total Fat 9 gm
  (Saturated Fat 3.1 gm,
  Polyunsat Fat 0.7 gm,
  Monounsat Fat 3.4 gm)
- Cholesterol 45 mg
- Sodium 717 mg
- Total Carb 47 gm
- Dietary Fiber 14 gm
- Sugars 9 gm
- Protein 29 gm

Chili

Easy Chili

Sheryl Shenk
Harrisonburg, VA

Makes 12 servings
Prep. Time: 20 minutes
Cooking Time: 3–8 hours
Ideal slow-cooker size: 5-qt.

1 lb. ground beef

1 onion, chopped

1 medium green pepper, chopped

½ tsp. salt

1 Tbsp. chili powder

2 tsp. Worcestershire sauce

29-oz. can no-added-salt tomato sauce

3 16-oz. cans kidney beans, drained

14½-oz. can crushed, or stewed, tomatoes

6-oz. can tomato paste

4 oz. fat-free grated cheddar cheese

1. Brown meat in skillet. Add onion and green pepper halfway through browning process. Drain. Pour into slow cooker.

2. Stir in remaining ingredients except cheese.

3. Cover. Cook on High 3 hours, or Low 7–8 hours.

4. Serve in bowls topped with cheddar cheese.

Serving suggestion:
Serve over cooked rice.

Exchange List Values
- Starch 1.0
- Vegetable 3.0
- Lean Meat 1.0
- Fat 0.5

Basic Nutritional Values
- Calories 232 (Calories from Fat 41)
- Total Fat 5 gm (Saturated Fat 1.5 gm, Polyunsat Fat 0.5 gm, Monounsat Fat 1.8 gm)
- Cholesterol 23 mg
- Sodium 456 mg
- Total Carb 30 gm
- Dietary Fiber 8 gm
- Sugars 9 gm
- Protein 18 gm

Chili

Pumpkin Black-Bean Turkey Chili

Rhoda Atzeff
Harrisburg, PA

Makes 10 servings
Prep. Time: 25 minutes
Cooking Time: 7–8 hours
Ideal slow-cooker size: 4- or 5-qt.

1 cup chopped onions

1 cup chopped yellow bell pepper

3 cloves garlic, minced

2 Tbsp. canola oil

1½ tsp. dried oregano

1½–2 tsp. ground cumin

2 tsp. chili powder

2 15-oz. cans black beans, rinsed and drained

2½ cups chopped cooked turkey

16-oz. can pumpkin

14½-oz. can diced tomatoes

3 cups 98%-fat-free, lower-sodium chicken broth

1. Sauté onions, yellow pepper, and garlic in oil for 8 minutes, or until soft.

2. Stir in oregano, cumin, and chili powder. Cook 1 minute. Transfer to slow cooker.

3. Add remaining ingredients.

4. Cover. Cook on Low 7–8 hours.

Exchange List Values
- Starch 1.0
- Vegetable 1.0
- Lean Meat 1.0
- Fat 0.5

Basic Nutritional Values
- Calories 189 (Calories from Fat 46)
- Total Fat 5 gm (Saturated Fat 0.9 gm, Polyunsat Fat 1.5 gm, Monounsat Fat 2.1 gm)
- Cholesterol 27 mg
- Sodium 327 mg
- Total Carb 20 gm
- Dietary Fiber 7 gm
- Sugars 6 gm
- Protein 17 gm

White Bean Chili

Tracey Stenger
Gretna, LA

Makes 12 servings
Prep. Time: 25 minutes
Cooking Time: 8–10 hours
Ideal slow-cooker size: 6-qt.

1 lb. ground beef, browned and drained

1 lb. ground turkey, browned and drained

3 bell peppers, chopped

2 onions, chopped

4 cloves garlic, minced

2 14½-oz. cans 98%-fat-free, lower-sodium chicken, or vegetable, broth

15½-oz. can butter beans, rinsed and drained

15-oz. can black-eyed peas, rinsed and drained

15-oz. can garbanzo beans, rinsed and drained

15-oz. can navy beans, rinsed and drained

4-oz. can chopped green chilies

2 Tbsp. chili powder

3 tsp. ground cumin

2 tsp. dried oregano

2 tsp. paprika

½ tsp. salt

½ tsp. pepper

Exchange List Values
- Starch 1.5
- Vegetable 1.0
- Lean Meat 2.0
- Fat 0.5

Basic Nutritional Values
- Calories 282 (Calories from Fat 79)
- Total Fat 9 gm (Saturated Fat 2.5 gm, Polyunsat Fat 1.6 gm, Monounsat Fat 3.3 gm)
- Cholesterol 50 mg
- Sodium 570 mg
- Total Carb 28 gm
- Dietary Fiber 8 gm
- Sugars 6 gm
- Protein 24 gm

1. Combine all ingredients in slow cooker.

2. Cover. Cook on Low 8–10 hours.

Chili

White Chili

Esther Martin
Ephrata, PA

Makes 8 servings
Prep. Time: 20 minutes
Cooking Time: 4–10 hours
Ideal slow-cooker size: 5-qt.

3 15-oz. cans great northern beans, rinsed
and drained

8 oz. cooked and shredded chicken breasts

1 cup chopped onions

1½ cups chopped yellow, red, or green bell
peppers

2 cloves garlic, minced

2 tsp. ground cumin

½ tsp. salt

½ tsp. dried oregano

3½ cups chicken broth

suggested garnishes:
reduced-fat sour cream

reduced-fat cheddar cheese

tortilla chips

1. Combine all ingredients except sour cream, cheddar cheese, and chips in slow cooker.

2. Cover. Cook on Low 8–10 hours, or High 4–5 hours.

Exchange List Values
- Starch 1.5
- Vegetable 1.0
- Meat, Very Lean 1.0

Basic Nutritional Values
- Calories 189
  (Calories from Fat 15)
- Total Fat 2 gm
  (Saturated Fat 0.4 gm,
  Polyunsat Fat 0.5 gm,
  Monounsat Fat 0.5 gm)
- Cholesterol 24 mg
- Sodium 561 mg
- Total Carb 25 gm
- Dietary Fiber 8 gm
- Sugars 5 gm
- Protein 19 gm

Chili

Chicken Three-Bean Chili

Deb Kepiro
Strasburg, PA

Makes 8 servings
Prep. Time: 15 minutes
Cooking Time: 1 hour

1 large onion, chopped

2 Tbsp. oil

2 cups diced cooked chicken

15½-oz. can kidney beans, rinsed and drained

15½-oz. can pinto beans, rinsed and drained

15½-oz. can black beans, rinsed and drained

2 14½-oz. cans diced tomatoes

1 cup no-added-salt chicken broth

¾ cup salsa

1 tsp. cumin

shredded cheese, *optional*

green onions, *optional*

sour cream, *optional*

Go-Alongs:
Great with warm cornbread.

Exchange List Values
- Starch 1.5
- Vegetable 1.0
- Lean Meat 2.0
- Fat 0.5

Basic Nutritional Values
- Calories 270 (Calories from Fat 65)
- Total Fat 7 gm (Saturated Fat 1.1 gm, Trans Fat 0.0 gm, Polyunsat Fat 1.9 gm, Monounsat Fat 3.3 gm)
- Cholesterol 30 mg
- Sodium 545 mg
- Potassium 820 gm
- Total Carb 33 gm
- Dietary Fiber 10 gm
- Sugars 5 gm
- Protein 21 gm
- Phosphorus 250 gm

1. In a soup pot, sauté onion in oil until tender.

2. Add chicken, beans, tomatoes, broth, salsa, and cumin.

3. Bring to a boil. Reduce heat and let simmer for 30–60 minutes.

4. If desired, garnish with shredded cheese, green onions, and sour cream.

Chili

Chicken Barley Chili

Colleen Heatwole
Burton, MI

Makes 10 servings
Prep. Time: 20 minutes
Cooking Time: 6–8 hours
Ideal slow-cooker size: 6-qt.

2 14½-oz. cans diced tomatoes

16-oz. jar salsa

1 cup quick-cooking barley, uncooked

3 cups water

14½-oz. can fat-free, low-sodium chicken broth

15½-oz. can black beans, rinsed and drained

3 cups cooked chicken, or turkey, cubed

15¼-oz. can whole-kernel corn, undrained

1–3 tsp. chili powder

1 tsp. ground cumin

sour cream, *optional*

shredded cheese, *optional*

1. Combine all ingredients except sour cream and cheese in slow cooker.

2. Cover. Cook on Low 6–8 hours, or until barley is tender.

3. Serve in individual soup bowls topped with sour cream and shredded cheese, if desired.

Exchange List Values
- Starch 1.5
- Vegetable 1.0
- Lean Meat 2.0

Basic Nutritional Values
- Calories 210
  (Calories from Fat 20)
- Total Fat 2.5 gm
  (Saturated Fat 0.5 gm,
  Polyunsat Fat 1.0 gm,
  Monounsat Fat 0.5 gm)
- Cholesterol 35 mg
- Sodium 565 mg
- Total Carb 30 gm
- Dietary Fiber 6 gm
- Sugars 5 gm
- Protein 19 gm

Vegetarian Tex-Mex Chili

Joleen Albrecht
Gladstone, MI

Makes 8 servings
Prep. Time: 10–15 minutes
Cooking Time: 2–4 hours
Ideal slow-cooker size: 5-qt.

15½-oz. can kidney beans, rinsed and drained

15½-oz. can garbanzo beans, rinsed and drained

16-oz. can vegetarian baked beans

19-oz. can black bean soup

15-oz. can whole-kernel corn, drained

14½-oz. can chopped tomatoes

1 green bell pepper, chopped

1 onion, chopped

2 ribs celery, chopped

2 cloves garlic, chopped

1 Tbsp. chili powder

1 Tbsp. dried oregano

1 Tbsp. dried parsley

1 Tbsp. dried basil

1½ tsp. Tabasco sauce, *optional*

sour cream, *optional*

shredded cheddar cheese, *optional*

tortilla chips, *optional*

1. Combine all beans, soup, and all vegetables in slow cooker.

2. Stir in chili powder, oregano, parsley, basil, and optional Tabasco.

3. Cover. Cook on High 2–3 hours, or on Low 4 hours.

4. If you wish, garnish individual servings of chili with sour cream, shredded cheese, and tortilla chips.

Exchange List Values
- Starch 2.5
- Vegetable 1.0
- Lean Meat (Protein) 1.0

Basic Nutritional Values
- Calories 260 (Calories from Fat 20)
- Total Fat 2 gm (Saturated Fat 0 gm, Polyunsat Fat 1.0 gm, Monounsat Fat 0 gm)
- Cholesterol 0 mg
- Sodium 530 mg
- Total Carb 49 gm
- Dietary Fiber 13 gm
- Sugars 9 gm
- Protein 14 gm

Chili

Chowders

Ham and Potato Chowder

Penny Blosser
Beavercreek, OH

Makes 5 servings
Prep. Time: 25 minutes
Cooking Time: 8 hours
Ideal slow-cooker size: 4-qt.

5-oz. pkg. scalloped potatoes

sauce mix from potato pkg.

1 cup extra-lean, reduced sodium, cooked
    ham, cut into narrow strips

4 tsp. sodium-free bouillon powder

4 cups water

1 cup chopped celery

⅓ cup chopped onions

pepper, to taste

2 cups fat-free half-and-half

⅓ cup flour

1. Combine potatoes, sauce mix, ham, bouillon powder, water, celery, onions, and pepper in slow cooker.

2. Cover. Cook on Low 7 hours.

3. Combine half-and-half and flour. Gradually add to slow cooker, blending well.

4. Cover. Cook on Low up to 1 hour, stirring occasionally until thickened.

Exchange List Values
- Starch 1.5
- Carbohydrate 1.0
- Lean Meat 1.0

Basic Nutritional Values
- Calories 241
  (Calories from Fat 29)
- Total Fat 3 gm
  (Saturated Fat 1.2 gm,
  Polyunsat Fat 0.7 gm,
  Monounsat Fat 0.2 gm)
- Cholesterol 21 mg
- Sodium 836 mg
- Total Carb 41 gm
- Dietary Fiber 3 gm
- Sugars 8 gm
- Protein 11 gm

Chowders

Corn and Shrimp Chowder

Naomi E. Fast
Hesston, KS

Makes 6 servings
Prep. Time: 20 minutes
Cooking Time: 3–4 hours
Ideal slow-cooker size: 4- or 5-qt.

4 slices bacon, diced

1 cup chopped onions

2 cups diced, unpeeled red potatoes

2 10-oz. pkgs. frozen corn

1 tsp. Worcestershire sauce

½ tsp. paprika

½ tsp. salt

⅛ tsp. pepper

2 6-oz. cans shrimp

2 cups water

2 Tbsp. light, soft tub margarine

12-oz. can fat-free evaporated milk

chopped chives

1. Fry bacon in skillet until lightly crisp. Add onions to drippings and sauté until transparent. Using slotted spoon, transfer bacon and onions to slow cooker.

2. Add remaining ingredients to cooker except milk and chives.

3. Cover. Cook on Low 3–4 hours, adding milk and chives 30 minutes before end of cooking time.

TIP

Delicious served with broccoli salad.

Exchange List Values
- Starch 3.0
- Fat-Free Milk 0.5
- Meat, Very Lean 1.0
- Fat 0.5

Basic Nutritional Values
- Calories 331
  (Calories from Fat 50)
- Total Fat 6 gm
  (Saturated Fat 0.9 gm,
  Polyunsat Fat 1.2 gm,
  Monounsat Fat 2.1 gm)
- Cholesterol 102 mg
- Sodium 488 mg
- Total Carb 49 gm
- Dietary Fiber 5 gm
- Sugars 11 gm
- Protein 24 gm

Manhattan Clam Chowder

Joyce Slaymaker
Strasburg, PA
Louise Stackhouse
Benton, PA

Makes 8 servings
Prep. Time: 25 minutes
Cooking Time: 8–10 hours
Ideal slow-cooker size: 4-qt.

¼ lb. bacon, diced and fried

1 large onion, chopped

2 carrots, thinly sliced

3 ribs celery, sliced

1 Tbsp. dried parsley flakes

28-oz. can chopped tomatoes

⅛ tsp. salt

2 8-oz. cans clams with liquid

2 whole peppercorns

1 bay leaf

1½ tsp. dried crushed thyme

3 medium potatoes, cubed

1. Combine all ingredients in slow cooker.

2. Cover. Cook on Low 8–10 hours.

Exchange List Values
- Starch 0.5
- Vegetable 2.0
- Lean Meat 1.0

Basic Nutritional Values
- Calories 151
  (Calories from Fat 25)
- Total Fat 3 gm
  (Saturated Fat 0.8 gm,
  Polyunsat Fat 0.6 gm,
  Monounsat Fat 0.9 gm)
- Cholesterol 21 mg
- Sodium 427 mg
- Total Carb 22 gm
- Dietary Fiber 4 gm
- Sugars 8 gm
- Protein 11 gm

Chowders

Harvest Corn Chowder

Flossie Sultzaberger
Mechanicsburg, PA

Makes 10 servings
Prep. Time: 20 minutes
Cooking Time: 40 minutes

1 medium onion, chopped

1 Tbsp. trans-fat-free tub margarine

2 14½-oz. cans no-salt-added cream-style corn

4 cups no-salt-added whole kernel corn

4 cups diced peeled potatoes

6-oz. jar sliced mushrooms, drained

½ medium green pepper, chopped

½–1 medium sweet red pepper, chopped

10¾-oz. can lower-sodium, lower-fat mushroom soup

3 cups fat-free milk

pepper, to taste

½ lb. bacon, cooked and crumbled

1. In a large saucepan, sauté onion in margarine until tender.

2. Add cream-style corn, kernel corn, potatoes, mushrooms, green and red peppers, soup, milk, and pepper.

3. Simmer 30 minutes or until vegetables are tender.

4. To serve, garnish with bacon.

Exchange List Values
- Starch 2.5
- Carbohydrate 0.5
- Fat 0.5

Basic Nutritional Values
- Calories 265 (Calories from Fat 45)
- Total Fat 5 gm (Saturated Fat 1.4 gm, Trans Fat 0.0 gm, Polyunsat Fat 1.5 gm, Monounsat Fat 2.0 gm)
- Cholesterol 10 mg
- Sodium 360 mg
- Potassium 850 gm
- Total Carb 46 gm
- Dietary Fiber 6 gm
- Sugars 14 gm
- Protein 11 gm
- Phosphorus 245 gm

Chowders

Main Dishes

Beef

Pot Roast

Carole Whaling
New Tripoli, PA

Makes 8 servings
Prep. Time: 30 minutes
Cooking Time: 10–12 hours
Ideal slow-cooker size: 4-qt.

4 medium potatoes, cubed

4 medium carrots, sliced

1 medium onion, sliced

3–4-lb. rump roast, or pot roast, bone
    removed, and cut into serving-size pieces,
    trimmed of fat

1 tsp. salt

½ tsp. pepper

1 bouillon cube

½ cup boiling water

1. Put vegetables and meat in slow cooker. Stir in salt and pepper.

2. Dissolve bouillon cube in water, then pour over other ingredients.

3. Cover. Cook on Low 10–12 hours.

Exchange List Values

- Starch 1.0
- Vegetable 1.0
- Lean Meat 3.0

Basic Nutritional Values

- Calories 246
  (Calories from Fat 56)
- Total Fat 6 gm
  (Saturated Fat 2.2 gm,
  Polyunsat Fat 0.3 gm,
  Monounsat Fat 2.5 gm)
- Cholesterol 73 mg
- Sodium 485 mg
- Total Carb 20 gm
- Dietary Fiber 3 gm
- Sugars 4 gm
- Protein 27 gm

Easy Pot Roast and Veggies

Tina Houk
Clinton, MO
Arlene Wines
Newton, KS

Makes 6 servings
Prep. Time: 20 minutes
Cooking Time: 6–8 hours
Ideal slow-cooker size: 4- or 5-qt.

3–4-lb. chuck roast, trimmed of fat

4 medium potatoes, cubed, unpeeled

4 medium carrots, sliced, or 1 lb. baby carrots

2 celery ribs, sliced thin

1 envelope dry onion soup mix

3 cups water

1. Put roast, potatoes, carrots, and celery in slow cooker.

2. Add onion soup mix and water.

3. Cover. Cook on Low 6–8 hours.

Variations:

1. To add flavor to the broth, stir 1 tsp. Kitchen Bouquet Browning & Seasoning Sauce, ½ tsp. salt, ½ tsp. black pepper, and ½ tsp. garlic powder into water before pouring over meat and vegetables.

—Bonita Ensenberger, Albuquerque, NM

2. Before putting roast in cooker, sprinkle it with the dry soup mix, patting it on so it adheres.

—Betty Lahman, Elkton, VA

Exchange List Values
- Starch 1.5
- Vegetable 1.0
- Lean Meat 3.0

Basic Nutritional Values
- Calories 325 (Calories from Fat 76)
- Total Fat 8 gm (Saturated Fat 2.9 gm, Polyunsat Fat 0.5 gm, Monounsat Fat 3.6 gm)
- Cholesterol 98 mg
- Sodium 560 mg
- Total Carb 26 gm
- Dietary Fiber 4 gm
- Sugars 6 gm
- Protein 35 gm

Beef

Hearty Pot Roast

Colleen Heatwole
Burton, MI

Makes 12 servings, about 1 cup per serving
Prep. Time: 30 minutes
Cooking Time: 2–2½ hours

4-lb. beef roast, ideally rump roast

4 medium red potatoes, cut in thirds

3 medium carrots, quartered

2 ribs celery, chopped

2 medium onions, sliced

½ cup flour

6-oz. can tomato paste

¼ cup water

1 tsp. instant beef bouillon, or 1 beef bouillon cube

¼ tsp. pepper

1. Place roast in 9×13-inch baking pan or roasting pan.

2. Arrange vegetables around roast.

3. Combine flour, tomato paste, water, bouillon, and pepper in small bowl.

4. Pour over meat and vegetables.

5. Cover. Roast at 325°F for 2–2½ hours, or until meat thermometer registers 170°F.

6. Allow meat to stand for 10 minutes.

7. Slice and place on platter surrounded by vegetables.

8. Pour gravy over top. Place additional gravy in bowl and serve along with platter.

Variation:

You can make this in a large oven cooking bag. Combine flour, tomato paste, water, bouillon, and pepper in a bowl. Pour into cooking bag. Place in 9×13-inch baking pan. Add roast to bag in pan. Add vegetables around roast in bag. Close bag with its tie. Make six ½-inch slits on top of bag. Roast according to instructions in Step 5 and following.

Exchange List Values

- Starch 1.0
- Vegetable 1.0
- Lean Meat 4.0

Basic Nutritional Values

- Calories 305 (Calories from Fat 70)
- Total Fat 8 gm (Saturated Fat 2.7 gm, Trans Fat 0.0 gm, Polyunsat Fat 0.4 gm, Monounsat Fat 3.2 gm)
- Cholesterol 100 mg
- Sodium 255 mg
- Potassium 840 gm
- Total Carb 22 gm
- Dietary Fiber 3 gm
- Sugars 5 gm
- Protein 36 gm
- Phosphorus 280 gm

French Dip Roast

Patti Boston
Newark, OH

Makes 8 servings
Prep. Time: 15 minutes
Cooking Time: 5–12 hours
Ideal slow-cooker size: 4-qt.

1 large onion, sliced

3-lb. beef bottom roast, trimmed of fat

½ cup dry white wine, or water

½ of 1-oz. pkg. dry au jus gravy mix

2 cups lower-sodium fat-free beef broth

1. Place onion in slow cooker. Add roast.

2. Combine wine and gravy mix. Pour over roast.

3. Add enough broth to cover roast.

4. Cover. Cook on High 5–6 hours, or Low 10–12 hours.

5. Remove meat from liquid. Let stand 5 minutes before slicing thinly across grain.

Exchange List Value
• Lean Meat 3.0

Basic Nutritional Values
• Calories 177
  (Calories from Fat 55)
• Total Fat 6 gm
  (Saturated Fat 2.2 gm,
  Polyunsat Fat 0.3 gm,
  Monounsat Fat 2.5 gm)
• Cholesterol 74 mg
• Sodium 376 mg
• Total Carb 3 gm
• Dietary Fiber 1 gm
• Sugars 2 gm
• Protein 25 gm

Beef

Shredded Beef for Tacos

Dawn Day
Westminster, CA

Makes 8 servings
Prep. Time: 20 minutes
Cooking Time: 6–8 hours
Ideal slow-cooker size: 4-qt.

2-lb. round roast, cut into large chunks, trimmed of fat

1 large onion, chopped

2 Tbsp. canola oil

2 serrano chilies, chopped

3 cloves garlic, minced

1 tsp. salt

1 cup water

1. Brown meat and onion in oil. Transfer to slow cooker.

2. Add chilies, garlic, salt, and water.

3. Cover. Cook on High 6–8 hours.

4. Pull meat apart with two forks until shredded.

Serving suggestion:

Serve with fresh tortillas, lettuce, tomatoes, cheese, and guacamole.

Exchange List Value
- Lean Meat 3.0

Basic Nutritional Values
- Calories 184
  (Calories from Fat 79)
- Total Fat 9 gm
  (Saturated Fat 2.1 gm,
  Polyunsat Fat 1.2 gm,
  Monounsat Fat 4.2 gm)
- Cholesterol 64 mg
- Sodium 335 mg
- Total Carb 4 gm
- Dietary Fiber 1 gm
- Sugars 3 gm
- Protein 22 gm

Beef

Beef Burgundy

Rosemarie Fitzgerald
Gibsonia, PA

Makes 6 servings, about 6 oz. each
Prep. Time: 20 minutes
Cooking Time: 2¾–3 hours

2 lbs. lean stewing beef cubes, trimmed of visible fat

1 cup chopped green onions

2 cloves garlic

2 cups burgundy

½ tsp. marjoram

½ lb. fresh mushrooms, sliced, or canned and drained

6-oz. can tomato paste

½ tsp. sugar

1. Brown beef in nonstick Dutch oven with chopped green onions and garlic.

2. Pour in burgundy. Cover and simmer 2 hours, or until tender but not dry.

3. Stir in marjoram and sliced mushrooms.

4. Cover and simmer ½ hour longer.

5. Add tomato paste and sugar.

6. Simmer uncovered until slightly thickened.

Serving suggestion:
This is good served over noodles or potatoes (mashed, browned, steamed, or baked).

Exchange List Values
- Vegetable 1.0
- Lean Meat 4.0

Basic Nutritional Values
- Calories 220 (Calories from Fat 55)
- Total Fat 6 gm (Saturated Fat 2.6 gm, Trans Fat 0.3 gm, Polyunsat Fat 0.5 gm, Monounsat Fat 3.1 gm)
- Cholesterol 80 mg
- Sodium 300 mg
- Potassium 835 gm
- Total Carb 8 gm
- Dietary Fiber 2 gm
- Sugars 5 gm
- Protein 32 gm
- Phosphorus 315 gm

Beef

Beef Burgundy and Bacon

Joyce Kaut
Rochester, NY

Makes 6 servings
Prep. Time: 25 minutes
Cooking Time: 6¼–8¼ hours
Ideal slow-cooker size: 3- or 4-qt.

1 slice bacon, cut in squares

2 lbs. sirloin tip or round steak, cubed, trimmed of fat

1 tsp. canola oil

¼ cup flour

⅛ tsp. salt

½ tsp. seasoning salt

¼ tsp. dried marjoram

¼ tsp. dried thyme

¼ tsp. pepper

1 clove garlic, minced

1 beef bouillon cube, crushed

1 cup burgundy wine

¼ lb. fresh mushrooms, sliced

2 Tbsp. cornstarch

2 Tbsp. cold water

1. Cook bacon in skillet until browned. Remove bacon.

2. Coat beef with flour and brown on all sides in canola oil.

3. Combine steak, bacon drippings, bacon, seasonings, garlic, bouillon, and wine in slow cooker.

4. Cover. Cook on Low 6–8 hours.

5. Add mushrooms.

6. Dissolve cornstarch in water. Add to slow cooker.

7. Cover. Cook on High 15 minutes.

Serving suggestion:
Serve over noodles.

Exchange List Values
- Starch 0.5
- Lean Meat 3.0

Basic Nutritional Values
- Calories 202 (Calories from Fat 63)
- Total Fat 7 gm (Saturated Fat 2.0 gm, Polyunsat Fat 0.6 gm, Monounsat Fat 3.5 gm)
- Cholesterol 76 mg
- Sodium 389 mg
- Total Carb 8 gm
- Dietary Fiber 0 gm
- Sugars 1 gm
- Protein 25 gm

Beef

Aunt Iris's Barbecue Brisket

Carolyn Spohn
Shawnee, KS

Makes 10 servings, 2 oz. meat with a little
 sauce
Prep. Time: 20–30 minutes
Marinating Time: 8 hours, or overnight
Cooking Time: 3–4 hours
Standing Time: 30 minutes

2 lb. lean beef brisket

¼ tsp. garlic powder

¼ tsp. onion powder

¼ tsp. celery salt

2 oz. liquid smoke

2 tsp. Worcestershire sauce

Barbecue Sauce:

⅓ cup honey

¼ cup light soy sauce

⅔ cup ketchup

½ tsp. Tabasco sauce

1 tsp. dry mustard

1 tsp. paprika

1 cup apple cider vinegar

1 cup orange juice

1 tsp. salt

1. Sprinkle both sides of brisket with garlic powder, onion powder, and celery salt. Sprinkle liquid smoke on both sides.

2. Place in large bowl or roaster. Refrigerate overnight, tightly covered.

3. In morning, drain meat. Return meat to pan.

4. Sprinkle with Worcestershire sauce.

5. Bake covered at 225°F for 3–4 hours, or until meat thermometer registers 175°F.

6. Turn off oven, but keep meat in oven for 30 more minutes.

7. While brisket is roasting, prepare barbecue sauce by combining all ingredients in saucepan.

8. Cook uncovered, stirring occasionally, until sauce comes to a boil.

9. Continue simmering for 30 minutes, or until sauce thickens and reduces down.

10. Serve alongside, or spooned over, sliced brisket.

Exchange List Values
- Carbohydrate 1.0
- Lean Meat 3.0

Basic Nutritional Values
- Calories 190
  (Calories from Fat 55)
- Total Fat 6 gm
  (Saturated Fat 1.9 gm,
  Trans Fat 0.0 gm,
  Polyunsat Fat 0.2 gm,
  Monounsat Fat 2.5 gm)
- Cholesterol 50 mg
- Sodium 475 mg
- Potassium 315 gm
- Total Carb 17 gm
- Dietary Fiber 0 gm
- Sugars 15 gm
- Protein 17 gm
- Phosphorus 150 gm

Beef

Swiss Steak

Wanda S. Curtin
Bradenton, FL
Jeanne Hertzog
Bethlehem, PA

Makes 6 servings
Prep. Time: 25 minutes
Cooking Time: 3–10 hours
Ideal slow-cooker size: 4-qt.

1½ lbs. round steak, about ¾ inches thick, trimmed of fat

2–4 tsp. flour

½–1 tsp. salt

¼ tsp. pepper

1 medium onion, sliced

1 medium carrot, chopped

1 rib celery, chopped

14½-oz. can diced tomatoes, or 15-oz. can tomato sauce

Serving suggestion:
Serve over noodles or rice.

Exchange List Values
- Vegetable 2.0
- Lean Meat 2.0

Basic Nutritional Values
- Calories 172 (Calories from Fat 48)
- Total Fat 5 gm (Saturated Fat 1.7 gm, Polyunsat Fat 0.3 gm, Monounsat Fat 2.2 gm)
- Cholesterol 64 mg
- Sodium 381 mg
- Total Carb 8 gm
- Dietary Fiber 2 gm
- Sugars 4 gm
- Protein 22 gm

1. Cut steak into serving pieces.

2. Combine flour, salt, and pepper. Dredge meat in seasoned flour.

3. Place onion in bottom of slow cooker. Add meat. Top with carrot and celery and cover with tomatoes.

4. Cover. Cook on Low 8–10 hours, or High 3–5 hours.

Steak Stroganoff

Marie Morucci
Glen Lyon, PA

Makes 6 servings
Prep. Time: 15 minutes
Cooking Time: 3¼–7¼ hours
Ideal slow-cooker size: 4-qt.

2 Tbsp. flour

½ tsp. garlic powder

½ tsp. pepper

¼ tsp. paprika

1¾-lb. boneless beef round steak, trimmed of fat

10¾-oz. can reduced-sodium 98%-fat-free cream of mushroom soup

½ cup water

1 envelope sodium-free dried onion soup mix

9-oz. jar sliced mushrooms, drained

½ cup fat-free sour cream

1 Tbsp. minced fresh parsley

1. Combine flour, garlic powder, pepper, and paprika in slow cooker.

2. Cut meat into 1½×½-inch strips. Place in flour mixture and toss until meat is well coated.

3. Add mushroom soup, water, and soup mix. Stir until well blended.

4. Cover. Cook on High 3–3½ hours, or Low 6–7 hours.

5. Stir in mushrooms, sour cream, and parsley. Cover and cook on High 10–15 minutes, or until heated through.

Exchange List Values
- Carbohydrate 1.0
- Lean Meat 3.0

Basic Nutritional Values
- Calories 256
  (Calories from Fat 66)
- Total Fat 7 gm
  (Saturated Fat 2.4 gm,
  Polyunsat Fat 0.5 gm,
  Monounsat Fat 2.8 gm)
- Cholesterol 77 mg
- Sodium 390 mg
- Total Carb 17 gm
- Dietary Fiber 2 gm
- Sugars 5 gm
- Protein 29 gm

Beef

Slow-Cooked Pepper Steak

Carolyn Baer
Conrath, WI
Ann Driscoll
Albuquerque, NM

Makes 8 servings
Prep. Time: 25 minutes
Cooking Time: 6¼–7¼ hours
Ideal slow-cooker size: 4-qt.

1½–2 lbs. beef round steak, cut in 3×1-inch strips, trimmed of fat

2 Tbsp. canola oil

¼ cup soy sauce

1 clove garlic, minced

1 cup chopped onions

1 tsp. sugar

¼ tsp. pepper

¼ tsp. ground ginger

2 large green peppers, cut in strips

4 medium tomatoes cut in eighths, or 16-oz. can diced tomatoes

½ cup cold water

1 Tbsp. cornstarch

1. Brown beef in oil in saucepan. Transfer to slow cooker.

2. Combine soy sauce, garlic, onions, sugar, pepper, and ginger. Pour over meat.

3. Cover. Cook on Low 5–6 hours.

4. Add green peppers and tomatoes. Cook 1 hour longer.

5. Combine water and cornstarch to make paste. Stir into slow cooker. Cook on High until thickened, about 10 minutes.

Serving suggestion:
Serve over rice or noodles.

Exchange List Values
- Vegetable 2.0
- Lean Meat 2.0

Basic Nutritional Values
- Calories 174
  (Calories from Fat 68)
- Total Fat 8 gm
  (Saturated Fat 1.5 gm,
  Polyunsat Fat 1.3 gm,
  Monounsat Fat 3.7 gm)
- Cholesterol 48 mg
- Sodium 546 mg
- Total Carb 10 gm
- Dietary Fiber 2 gm
- Sugars 6 gm
- Protein 17 gm

Tender Flank Steak

Kayla Snyder
North East, PA

Makes 6 servings
Prep. Time: 15 minutes
Marinating Time: 6–8 hours, or overnight
Grilling Time: 20 minutes

1 cup light soy sauce

¼ cup lemon juice

¼ cup honey

6 cloves garlic cloves, minced (or fewer cloves if you prefer)

1½ lbs. beef flank steak

1. In a large resealable plastic bag, combine soy sauce, lemon juice, honey, and garlic.

2. Add steak. Seal bag and turn to coat. Place in shallow dish with sides to catch any leaks.

3. Refrigerate 6–8 hours or overnight to marinate in sauce.

4. When ready to grill, drain meat and discard marinade.

5. Grill over medium heat 8–10 minutes on each side, or until meat reaches desired doneness (for medium-rare, a meat thermometer should read 145°F; medium 160°F; well-done 170°F).

6. Allow to stand off heat 10 minutes before slicing.

7. Slice steak into thin slices across the grain.

Exchange List Values
- Lean Meat 3.0
- Fat 0.5

Basic Nutritional Values
- Calories 170 (Calories from Fat 55)
- Total Fat 6 gm (Saturated Fat 2.5 gm, Trans Fat 0.0 gm, Polyunsat Fat 0.2 gm, Monounsat Fat 2.3 gm)
- Cholesterol 40 mg
- Sodium 410 mg
- Potassium 305 gm
- Total Carb 4 gm
- Dietary Fiber 0 gm
- Sugars 3 gm
- Protein 23 gm
- Phosphorus 185 gm

Beef

Hungarian Goulash

Audrey Romonosky
Austin, TX

Makes 6 servings
Prep. Time: 20 minutes
Cooking Time: 8¼ hours
Ideal slow-cooker size: 4-qt.

2 lbs. beef chuck, cubed, trimmed of fat

1 medium onion, sliced

½ tsp. garlic powder

½ cup ketchup

2 Tbsp. Worcestershire sauce

1 Tbsp. brown sugar

¼ tsp. salt

2 tsp. paprika

½ tsp. dry mustard

1 cup cold water

¼ cup flour

½ cup water

1. Place meat in slow cooker. Add onion.

2. Combine garlic powder, ketchup, Worcestershire sauce, brown sugar, salt, paprika, mustard, and 1 cup water. Pour over meat.

3. Cover. Cook on Low 8 hours.

4. Dissolve flour in ½ cup water. Stir into meat mixture. Cook on High until thickened, about 10 minutes.

Serving suggestion:
Serve over noodles.

Exchange List Values
- Carbohydrate 1.0
- Lean Meat 2.0

Basic Nutritional Values
- Calories 207
  (Calories from Fat 52)
- Total Fat 6 gm
  (Saturated Fat 2.0 gm,
  Polyunsat Fat 0.3 gm,
  Monounsat Fat 2.3 gm)
- Cholesterol 65 mg
- Sodium 444 mg
- Total Carb 15 gm
- Dietary Fiber 1 gm
- Sugars 7 gm
- Protein 23 gm

Cowboy Casserole

Lori Berezovsky
Salina, KS

Makes 6 servings
Prep. Time: 25 minutes
Cooking Time: 5–6 hours
Ideal slow-cooker size: 4-qt.

1 medium onion, chopped

1¼ lbs. 90%-lean ground beef, browned, drained, and patted dry

6 medium potatoes, sliced, unpeeled

1 clove garlic, minced

16-oz. can kidney beans

15-oz. can diced tomatoes mixed with 2 Tbsp. flour, or 10¾-oz. can tomato soup

¼ tsp. salt

¼ tsp. pepper

1. Layer onion, ground beef, potatoes, garlic, and beans in slow cooker.

2. Spread tomatoes or soup over all. Sprinkle with salt and pepper.

3. Cover. Cook on Low 5–6 hours, or until potatoes are tender.

Exchange List Values
- Starch 2.5
- Vegetable 2.0
- Lean Meat 2.0

Basic Nutritional Values
- Calories 373 (Calories from Fat 73)
- Total Fat 8 gm (Saturated Fat 3.2 gm, Polyunsat Fat 0.6 gm, Monounsat Fat 3.4 gm)
- Cholesterol 57 mg
- Sodium 567 mg
- Total Carb 48 gm
- Dietary Fiber 7 gm
- Sugars 8 gm
- Protein 27 gm

Beef

Stuffed Cabbage

Barbara Nolan
Pleasant Valley, NY

Makes 6 servings
Prep. Time: 35 minutes
Cooking Time: 6–8 hours
Ideal slow-cooker size: 4- or 5-qt.

4 cups water

12 large cabbage leaves

1 lb. ground beef, lamb, or turkey

½ cup cooked rice

½ tsp. salt

⅛ tsp. pepper

¼ tsp. dried thyme

¼ tsp. nutmeg

¼ tsp. cinnamon

6-oz. can tomato paste

¾ cup water

Exchange List Values
- Vegetable 2.0
- Lean Meat 2.0
- Fat 0.5

Basic Nutritional Values
- Calories 186
  (Calories from Fat 73)
- Total Fat 8 gm
  (Saturated Fat 3.0 gm,
  Polyunsat Fat 0.4 gm,
  Monounsat Fat 3.4 gm)
- Cholesterol 45 mg
- Sodium 269 mg
- Total Carb 13 gm
- Dietary Fiber 3 gm
- Sugars 3 gm
- Protein 16 gm

1. Boil 4 cups water in deep kettle. Remove kettle from heat. Soak cabbage leaves in hot water 5 minutes, or just until softened. Remove. Drain. Cool.

2. Combine ground meat, rice, salt, pepper, thyme, nutmeg, and cinnamon. Place 2 Tbsp. of mixture on each leaf.

3. Roll up firmly. Stack stuffed leaves in slow cooker.

4. Combine tomato paste and ¾ cup water until smooth. Pour over cabbage rolls.

5. Cover. Cook on Low 6–8 hours.

Easy Taco Casserole

Orpha M. Herr
Andover, NY
Lori Lehman
Ephrata, PA
Gretchen Maust
Keezletown, VA

Makes 8 servings, 2×4-inch rectangle per
serving
Prep. Time: 20 minutes
Baking Time: 20–25 minutes

10 oz. 95%-lean ground beef

15-oz. can red beans, rinsed and drained

1 cup salsa, your choice of heat

½ cup fat-free mayonnaise

2 tsp. chili powder

2 cups crushed baked low-fat tortilla chips,
divided

¾ cup shredded reduced-fat Colby cheese

3 medium tomatoes, chopped

3 cups shredded lettuce

1. Brown beef in nonstick skillet, stirring
often with wooden spoon to break up
clumps. Keep stirring and cooking until pink
disappears. Drain off any drippings.

2. Combine beef, beans, salsa,
mayonnaise, and chili powder in skillet. Mix
well.

3. In greased 8×8-inch baking dish, layer
in half of meat mixture, topped by half of
chips.

4. Repeat layers of meat mixture, followed
by remaining chips.

5. Bake uncovered at 350°F for 20–25
minutes or until heated through.

6. Five minutes before end of baking time,
top with cheese.

7. Just before serving, top with tomato and
lettuce.

Variation:
Reduce ground beef to 1 cup. Add 15-oz. can
black pinto beans, drained, or 2 cups cooked
rice, to Step 2.
—Juanita Weaver, Johnsonville, IL

Exchange List Values
- Starch 1.5
- Vegetable 1.0
- Lean Meat 1.0
- Fat 0.5

Basic Nutritional Values
- Calories 200
  (Calories from Fat 45)
- Total Fat 5 gm
  (Saturated Fat 2.4 gm,
  Trans Fat 0.0 gm,
  Polyunsat Fat 0.5 gm,
  Monounsat Fat 1.4 gm)
- Cholesterol 30 mg
- Sodium 550 mg
- Potassium 545 gm
- Total Carb 25 gm
- Dietary Fiber 5 gm
- Sugars 4 gm
- Protein 15 gm
- Phosphorus 225 gm

Whole Enchilada Pie

Cova Rexroad
Baltimore, MD

Makes 10 servings
Prep. Time: 20–25 minutes
Baking Time: 30–40 minutes

1 lb. 95%-lean ground beef

1 medium onion, chopped

2 cloves garlic, minced fine

½ cup picante sauce

1¼ cup fat-free refried beans

10- or 12-oz. can enchilada sauce

1 cup sliced black olives

9 torn corn tortillas, *divided*

1½ cups freshly grated light (75% less fat) cheddar cheese

garnishes: chopped fresh tomatoes, green peppers, chopped lettuce, sliced green onions, *optional*

1. Brown ground beef and onion with garlic in large nonstick skillet until beef is no longer pink and onion is soft. Stir frequently to break up chunks of meat.

2. Lower heat and stir in picante sauce, beans, enchilada sauce, olives, and salt. Cook until bubbly. Remove from heat.

3. Line bottom of well-greased glass 9×13-inch pan with ⅓ of torn tortillas.

4. Layer half of beef mixture on top.

5. Top with half the remaining tortillas.

6. Top with remaining meat mixture.

7. Top with remaining tortillas and cheese.

8. Bake 30–40 minutes at 350°F, or until bubbly and heated through.

TIP

1. Serve hot with serving bowls of garnishes.
2. Sometimes I add one 8-oz. can whole white beans, drained, to Step 2. They add good texture and nutrition.

Exchange List Values
- Starch 1.0
- Vegetable 1.0
- Lean Meat 2.0
- Fat 0.5

Basic Nutritional Values
- Calories 210 (Calories from Fat 65)
- Total Fat 7 gm (Saturated Fat 2.3 gm, Trans Fat 0.1 gm, Polyunsat Fat 0.8 gm, Monounsat Fat 2.7 gm)
- Cholesterol 35 mg
- Sodium 595 mg
- Potassium 455 gm
- Total Carb 19 gm
- Dietary Fiber 4 gm
- Sugars 2 gm
- Protein 18 gm
- Phosphorus 280 gm

Beef

Shepherd's Pie

Judi Manos
West Islip, NY

Makes 6 servings
Prep. Time: 15 minutes
Cooking/Baking Time: 50 minutes

1¼ lb. red potatoes, unpeeled and cut in chunks

3 cloves garlic

1 lb. 95%-lean ground beef

2 Tbsp. flour

4 cups fresh vegetables of your choice (for example, carrots, corn, green beans, peas)

¾ cup beef broth (canned, or boxed, or your own homemade)

2 Tbsp. ketchup

¾ cup fat-free sour cream

½ cup shredded reduced-fat sharp cheddar cheese, *divided*

1. In saucepan, cook potatoes and garlic in 1½-inch boiling water for 20 minutes, or until potatoes are tender.

2. Meanwhile, brown beef in large nonstick skillet.

3. Stir in flour. Cook 1 minute.

4. Stir in vegetables, broth, and ketchup. Cover. Cook 10 minutes, stirring frequently.

5. Drain cooked potatoes and garlic. Return to their pan.

6. Stir in sour cream. Mash until potatoes are smooth and mixture is well blended.

7. Stir ¼ cup cheddar cheese into mashed potatoes.

8. Spoon meat mixture into well-greased 8×8-inch baking dish.

9. Cover with mashed potatoes.

10. Bake at 375°F for 18 minutes.

11. Top with remaining cheddar cheese. Bake 2 minutes more, or until cheese is melted.

Variation:
If you don't have access to fresh vegetables, use leftovers from your fridge or frozen ones.

Exchange List Values
- Starch 2.0
- Fat-Free Milk 0.5
- Vegetable 1.0
- Lean Meat 2.0

Basic Nutritional Values
- Calories 310 (Calories from Fat 65)
- Total Fat 7 gm (Saturated Fat 3.1 gm, Trans Fat 0.1 gm, Polyunsat Fat 0.5 gm, Monounsat Fat 2.1 gm)
- Cholesterol 55 mg
- Sodium 360 mg
- Potassium 890 gm
- Total Carb 41 gm
- Dietary Fiber 5 gm
- Sugars 7 gm
- Protein 24 gm
- Phosphorus 370 gm

Grandma's Best Meatloaf

Nanci Keatley
Salem, OR

Makes 10 servings, 1 slice per serving
Prep. Time: 15–25 minutes
Baking Time: 1 hour and 5 minutes

2 lbs. 90%-lean ground beef

2 Tbsp. fresh Italian parsley, chopped

1 tsp. dried oregano

1 small onion, chopped fine

4 cloves garlic, minced

¼ cup, plus 2 Tbsp., Romano cheese, *optional*

½ cup dry bread crumbs

½ cup ketchup

½ cup egg substitute

1 tsp. black pepper

1 tsp. kosher salt

1. In a large mixing bowl, mix together ground beef, parsley, oregano, onion, garlic, optional cheese, bread crumbs, ketchup, egg substitute, pepper, and salt.

2. Roll mixture into a large ball.

3. Place in well-greased 9×13-inch baking dish or roaster, flattening slightly.

4. Bake at 375°F for 1 hour. Keep in oven 5 more minutes with oven off and door closed.

5. Remove meatloaf from oven. Let stand 10 minutes before slicing to allow meatloaf to gather its juices and firm up.

TIP

This is great for meatloaf sandwiches the next day—if you have any left!

Exchange List Values
- Carbohydrate 0.5
- Lean Meat 3.0
- Fat 0.5

Basic Nutritional Values
- Calories 185 (Calories from Fat 70)
- Total Fat 8 gm (Saturated Fat 3.0 gm, Trans Fat 0.5 gm, Polyunsat Fat 0.4 gm, Monounsat Fat 3.2 gm)
- Cholesterol 55 mg
- Sodium 445 mg
- Potassium 365 gm
- Total Carb 9 gm
- Dietary Fiber 1 gm
- Sugars 4 gm
- Protein 20 gm
- Phosphorus 175 gm

Beef

Applesauce Meatloaf

Dale Peterson
Rapid City, SD

Makes 8 servings
Prep. Time: 15 minutes
Baking Time: 40–60 minutes

2 lbs. 95%-lean ground beef

¾ cup dry oatmeal

¼ cup egg substitute

½ cup unsweetened applesauce

¼ cup chopped onion

1 tsp. salt

dash pepper

1½ Tbsp. chili powder

1. Combine ground beef, dry oatmeal, egg substitute, applesauce, onion, salt, pepper, and chili powder in a good-sized mixing bowl.

2. Shape into a loaf. Place in 5×9-inch greased loaf pan.

3. Bake at 350°F for 40–60 minutes, or until meat thermometer registers 160°F in center of loaf.

4. Allow to stand 10 minutes before slicing to allow meat to gather its juices and firm up.

Variations:
1. You can use bread crumbs instead of oatmeal in this recipe.
2. You can make meatballs with this mixture.

Exchange List Values
- Carbohydrate 0.5
- Lean Meat 4.0

Basic Nutritional Values
- Calories 200
  (Calories from Fat 55)
- Total Fat 6 gm
  (Saturated Fat 2.7 gm,
  Trans Fat 0.4 gm,
  Polyunsat Fat 0.6 gm,
  Monounsat Fat 2.6 gm)
- Cholesterol 70 mg
- Sodium 395 mg
- Potassium 480 gm
- Total Carb 8 gm
- Dietary Fiber 2 gm
- Sugars 2 gm
- Protein 26 gm
- Phosphorus 265 gm

Beef

Easy Meatballs

Cindy Krestynick
Glen Lyon, PA

Makes 8 servings, 1 meatball per serving
Prep. Time: 15 minutes
Cooking Time: 7–15 minutes

1 lb. 95%-lean ground beef

3 slices white bread, torn or cubed

1 small onion, chopped

4 sprigs fresh parsley, finely chopped

1½ Tbsp. freshly grated Parmesan cheese

¼ cup egg substitute

1 tsp. salt

¼ tsp. pepper

¾ cup water

1. Combine beef, bread pieces, onion, parsley, cheese, egg substitute, salt, pepper, and water in a large mixing bowl until well mixed.

2. Form into 8 meatballs.

3. Brown in nonstick skillet until golden brown on each side.

TIP

Serve with spaghetti sauce in hoagie rolls or over cooked spaghetti.

Exchange List Values
- Starch 0.5
- Lean Meat 2.0

Basic Nutritional Values
- Calories 110
  (Calories from Fat 30)
- Total Fat 4 gm
  (Saturated Fat 1.5 gm,
  Trans Fat 0.1 gm,
  Polyunsat Fat 0.3 gm,
  Monounsat Fat 1.3 gm)
- Cholesterol 35 mg
- Sodium 415 mg
- Potassium 220 gm
- Total Carb 6 gm
- Dietary Fiber 0 gm
- Sugars 1 gm
- Protein 13 gm
- Phosphorus 120 gm

Beef

Homemade Hamburgers

Janet Derstine
Telford, PA

Makes 6 servings, 1 burger per serving
Prep. Time: 30–35 minutes
Baking Time: 60 minutes

1 cup dry bread crumbs

½ cup fat-free milk

1 lb. 90%-lean ground beef

¼ cup chopped onion

¼ tsp. pepper

Sauce:
3 Tbsp. brown sugar

1 Tbsp. vinegar

¼ cup ketchup

1 Tbsp. Worcestershire sauce

¼ cup barbecue sauce

½ cup water

1. In good-sized mixing bowl, moisten bread crumbs with milk.

2. Add ground beef, onion, and pepper. Mix well. Set aside.

3. In a mixing bowl, make sauce by mixing together thoroughly brown sugar, vinegar, ketchup, Worcestershire sauce, barbecue sauce, and water.

4. Shape hamburger mixture into 6 patties.

5. Place in single layer in baking dish.

6. Pour barbecue sauce over patties.

7. Cover and bake at 375°F for 30 minutes.

8. Remove cover and bake another 30 minutes, basting occasionally with sauce.

TIP

You can double or triple this recipe and freeze the patties for a later meal. I make the sauce then, when I bake them.

Exchange List Values
- Starch 1.0
- Carbohydrate 1.0
- Lean Meat 2.0
- Fat 0.5

Basic Nutritional Values
- Calories 255
  (Calories from Fat 65)
- Total Fat 7 gm
  (Saturated Fat 2.7 gm,
  Trans Fat 0.4 gm,
  Polyunsat Fat 0.6 gm,
  Monounsat Fat 2.8 gm)
- Cholesterol 45 mg
- Sodium 445 mg
- Potassium 395 gm
- Total Carb 28 gm
- Dietary Fiber 1 gm
- Sugars 14 gm
- Protein 18 gm
- Phosphorus 190 gm

Beef

So-Good Sloppy Joes

Judy Diller
Bluffton, OH

Makes 18 servings, 1 sandwich per serving
Prep. Time: 15–20 minutes
Cooking or Baking Time: 1–2 hours

3 lbs. 90%-lean ground beef

1 medium onion, chopped

1 green bell pepper, chopped fine

10¾-oz. can lower-sodium, lower-fat tomato soup

¾ cup + 2 Tbsp. ketchup

2 Tbsp. prepared mustard

2 Tbsp. vinegar

1 Tbsp. brown sugar

2 Tbsp. Worcestershire sauce

18 whole wheat hamburger buns

1. Brown ground beef in large skillet or saucepan. Stir frequently to break up clumps and to brown thoroughly. Drain off drippings.

2. Stir onion, pepper, soup, ketchup, mustard, vinegar, brown sugar, and Worcestershire sauce into beef.

3. Simmer slowly on stovetop for 2 hours, or spoon into a Dutch oven or baking dish and bake at 325°F for 1 hour.

4. Divide evenly among the buns. Serve.

Exchange List Values
- Starch 2.0
- Lean Meat 2.0
- Fat 0.5

Basic Nutritional Values
- Calories 265 (Calories from Fat 80)
- Total Fat 9 gm (Saturated Fat 2.9 gm, Trans Fat 0.4 gm, Polyunsat Fat 1.3 gm, Monounsat Fat 3.2 gm)
- Cholesterol 45 mg
- Sodium 475 mg
- Potassium 525 gm
- Total Carb 30 gm
- Dietary Fiber 4 gm
- Sugars 9 gm
- Protein 19 gm
- Phosphorus 240 gm

Beef

Creamy Baked Ziti

Judi Manos
West Islip, NY

Makes 12 servings, 3-inch square per
  serving
Prep. Time: 20 minutes
Baking Time: 20 minutes

4 cups uncooked ziti pasta

24½-oz. jar lower-sodium marinara sauce

14½-oz. can diced tomatoes, undrained

2 3-oz. pkgs. fat-free cream cheese, cubed

¾ cup fat-free sour cream

8 oz. shredded part-skim mozzarella cheese,
  divided

⅓ cup freshly grated Parmesan cheese

1. Cook pasta as directed on package, but omit salt. Drain cooked pasta well.

2. While pasta drains, add marinara sauce, tomatoes, and cream cheese to cooking pot.

3. Cook on medium heat 5 minutes, or until cream cheese is melted and mixture is well blended. Stir frequently.

4. Return pasta to pan. Mix well.

5. Layer half the pasta mixture in greased 9×13-inch baking dish.

6. Cover with layer of sour cream.

7. Top with half of the mozzarella.

8. Spoon over remaining pasta mixture.

9. Top with remaining mozzarella.

10. Sprinkle with Parmesan cheese.

11. Bake 20 minutes, or until bubbly and heated through.

Exchange List Values

- Starch 2.0
- Med.-Fat Meat 1.0

Basic Nutritional Values

- Calories 230
  (Calories from Fat 55)
- Total Fat 6 gm
  (Saturated Fat 2.5 gm,
  Trans Fat 0.0 gm,
  Polyunsat Fat 1.1 gm,
  Monounsat Fat 1.6 gm)
- Cholesterol 15 mg
- Sodium 440 mg
- Potassium 350 gm
- Total Carb 31 gm
- Dietary Fiber 2 gm
- Sugars 6 gm
- Protein 12 gm
- Phosphorus 255 gm

Lasagna

**Hope Comerford
Clinton Township, MI**

Makes 8 servings
Prep. Time: 30 minutes
Cooking Time: 3 hours
Ideal slow-cooker size: 6-qt.

1 lb. lean ground beef

1 medium onion, chopped

salt and pepper, to taste

28-oz. can crushed tomatoes

15-oz. can tomato sauce

2 tsp. Italian seasoning

1 tsp. garlic powder

1 tsp. onion powder

1 cup skim cottage cheese

1½ cups shredded mozzarella cheese, *divided*

6–8 lasagna noodles, uncooked, *divided*

½ cup shredded Parmesan cheese

1. Spray crock well with nonstick spray.

2. Brown ground beef with onion. Season with salt and pepper.

3. Add the crushed tomatoes, tomato sauce, Italian seasoning, garlic powder, and onion powder to the browned beef/onion mixture and simmer on Low for about 5 minutes.

4. While the sauce is simmering, mix together the 1 cup cottage cheese and 1 cup of the shredded mozzarella cheese. Set aside.

5. In the bottom of your crock, add ⅓ of the sauce.

6. Line the bottom of the crock with about 3 noodles.

7. Spread half of the cottage cheese/ mozzarella mixture over the noodles and add ⅓ of the sauce again.

8. Add another layer of noodles, cottage cheese/mozzarella mixture, and remaining sauce.

9. Cook on Low for about 3 hours.

10. About 20 minutes before serving, sprinkle the top with remaining ½ cup mozzarella cheese and the Parmesan cheese.

Exchange List Values
- Carbohydrate 2.0
- Lean Meat 1.0
- Fat 2.5

Basic Nutritional Values
- Calories 306 (Calories from Fat 86)
- Total Fat 10 gm (Saturated Fat 4.5 gm, Trans Fat 2.5 gm, Polyunsat Fat 0.3 gm, Monounsat Fat 3.4 gm)
- Cholesterol 51 mg
- Sodium 936 mg
- Potassium 397 gm
- Total Carb 29 gm
- Dietary Fiber 3.7 gm
- Sugars 7gm
- Protein 24 gm
- Phosphorus 260 gm

Beef

Pizza Cups

Alice Miller
Stuarts Draft, VA

Makes 8 servings, 1 pizza cup per serving
Prep. Time: 20–25 minutes
Baking Time: 10–12 minutes

8 oz. 95%-lean ground beef

6-oz. can no-salt-added tomato paste

1 Tbsp. instant minced onion

½ tsp. dried oregano

½ tsp. dried basil

¼ tsp. salt

Biscuits:
2 cups flour

3 tsp. baking powder

½ tsp. salt

¾ cup fat-free milk

¼ cup canola oil

2⅔ Tbsp. shredded part-skim mozzarella
   cheese, *divided*

1. Cook ground beef in large skillet, stirring frequently to break up clumps, until no pink remains. Drain off drippings.

2. Stir in tomato paste, onion, and seasonings.

3. Cook over medium heat an additional 5 minutes, stirring frequently.

4. Prepare biscuits by sifting flour, baking powder, and salt together in large bowl.

5. Add milk and oil together. Add to flour mixture and stir with fork until a ball forms.

6. Roll ball onto lightly floured counter. Knead lightly, about 20 turns.

7. Divide ball into 8 pieces.

8. Place a ball in each of 8 muffin cups, pressing to cover bottom and sides as evenly as you can.

9. Spoon meat mixture into cups, distributing evenly.

10. Sprinkle each cup with 1 tsp. cheese.

11. Bake at 400°F for 10–12 minutes.

Exchange List Values
- Starch 1.5
- Vegetable 1.0
- Lean Meat 1.0
- Fat 1.5

Basic Nutritional Values
- Calories 250
  (Calories from Fat 80)
- Total Fat 9 gm
  (Saturated Fat 1.5 gm,
  Trans Fat 0.1 gm,
  Polyunsat Fat 2.2 gm,
  Monounsat Fat 5.2 gm)
- Cholesterol 20 mg
- Sodium 415 mg
- Potassium 390 gm
- Total Carb 30 gm
- Dietary Fiber 2 gm
- Sugars 5 gm
- Protein 11 gm
- Phosphorus 310 gm

Meat Pasties (Turnovers)

Jeanette Zacharias
Morden, MB

Makes 12 pasties, 1 per serving
Prep. Time: 30 minutes
Cooking/Baking Time: 1 hour

Dough:

2 cups all-purpose flour

½ cup trans-fat-free shortening

½ tsp. salt

7 Tbsp. fat-free milk, or more

Filling:

¾ lb. 90%-lean ground beef

2 Tbsp. chopped onion

1 Tbsp. chopped bell pepper

1 Tbsp. chopped celery

1 tsp. dried oregano

1 tsp. dried basil

2 Tbsp. barbecue sauce, lowest sodium available

1. Combine all ingredients for dough and mix well. Add as much milk as needed to make a soft dough.

2. Divide dough into four parts. Roll each part out thin and cut into three 6-inch circles for a total of 12.

3. Combine all filling ingredients in a skillet and cook until meat has browned.

4. Place 1 Tbsp. meat on each circle. Moisten edges of dough with water and fold in half to make a turnover. Seal edges will with fork. Prick top to allow steam to escape. Place on ungreased cookie sheet.

5. Bake at 375°F for 40 minutes. Serve hot or cold.

Exchange List Values
- Starch 1.0
- Lean Meat 1.0

Basic Nutritional Values
- Calories 135
  (Calories from Fat 25)
- Total Fat 3 gm
  (Saturated Fat 1.1 gm,
  Trans Fat 0.1 gm,
  Polyunsat Fat 0.4 gm,
  Monounsat Fat 1.2 gm)
- Cholesterol 15 mg
- Sodium 140 mg
- Potassium 145 gm
- Total Carb 18 gm
- Dietary Fiber 1 gm
- Sugars 2 gm
- Protein 8 gm
- Phosphorus 80 gm

Beef

Pork

Cranberry Pork Roast

Barbara Aston
Ashdown, AR

Makes 9 servings
Prep. Time: 20 minutes
Cooking Time: 8–10 hours
Ideal slow-cooker size: 4-qt.

2¾-lb. boneless pork roast, trimmed of fat

1 cup ground, or finely chopped, cranberries

3 Tbsp. honey

1 tsp. grated orange peel

⅛ tsp. ground cloves

⅛ tsp. ground nutmeg

TIP

You may want to add a little salt and pepper to this recipe if you generally use them in your diet.

1. Place roast in slow cooker.

2. Combine remaining ingredients. Pour over roast.

3. Cover. Cook on Low 8–10 hours.

Exchange List Values
- Carbohydrate 0.5
- Lean Meat 3.0

Basic Nutritional Values
- Calories 214
  (Calories from Fat 81)
- Total Fat 9 gm
  (Saturated Fat 3.5 gm,
  Polyunsat Fat 0.6 gm,
  Monounsat Fat 4.3 gm)
- Cholesterol 63 mg
- Sodium 37 mg
- Total Carb 7 gm
- Dietary Fiber 1 gm
- Sugars 7 gm
- Protein 25 gm

Pork

Zesty Pulled Pork

Sheila Plock
Boalsburg, PA

Makes 10 servings
Prep. Time: 20 minutes
Cooking Time: 4½–10¾ hours
Ideal slow-cooker size: 4-qt.

2½-lb. boneless pork shoulder roast, or pork sirloin roast

salt and pepper, to taste

½ cup water

3 Tbsp. cider vinegar

2 Tbsp. Worcestershire sauce

1 tsp. cumin

1 cup barbecue sauce of your choice

1. Trim fat from roast. Fit roast into slow cooker.

2. Season meat with salt and pepper.

3. In a small bowl, combine water, vinegar, Worcestershire sauce, and cumin. Spoon over roast, being careful not to wash off the seasonings.

4. Cover. Cook on Low 8–10 hours, or on High 4–5 hours, just until pork is very tender but not dry.

5. Remove meat onto a platter. Discard liquid.

6. Shred meat using 2 forks. Return to slow cooker.

7. Stir in barbecue sauce.

8. Cover. Cook on High 30–45 minutes

Serving suggestion:
Serve on split hamburger buns.

Exchange List Values
- Carbohydrate 1.0
- Lean Meat 3.0

Basic Nutritional Values
- Calories 190 (Calories from Fat 25)
- Total Fat 3 gm (Saturated Fat 1.0 gm, Polyunsat Fat 0.5 gm, Monounsat Fat 1.5 gm)
- Cholesterol 70 mg
- Sodium 280 mg
- Total Carb 12 gm
- Dietary Fiber 0 gm
- Sugars 10 gm
- Protein 26 gm

Pork

Blackberry Pulled Pork Shoulder

Hope Comerford
Clinton Township, MI

Makes 10–12 servings
Prep. Time: 15 minutes
Cooking Time: 8–10 hours
Ideal slow-cooker size: 5-qt.

2–3-lb. pork shoulder

1 large onion, chopped

2 pints fresh blackberries

¼ cup brown sugar

1 tsp. salt

2 tsp. garlic powder

½ tsp. red pepper

1 tsp. apple cider vinegar

1. Place the pork shoulder in the crock and place the onion on top.

2. Puree the blackberries and pass them through a sieve or strainer to separate the puree from the seeds.

3. Mix the remaining ingredients with the blackberry puree.

4. Pour the blackberry puree over the contents of the crock.

5. Cover and cook on Low for 8–10 hours.

6. Remove the roast and pull between two forks to shred. Stir back through the liquid in the crock.

Serving suggestion:
Serve on buns.

Exchange List Values

- Fruit 0.5
- Medium-Fat Meat 3.0
- Fat 1.5

Basic Nutritional Values

- Calories 218
  (Calories from Fat 108)
- Total Fat 12 gm
  (Saturated Fat 3.9 gm,
  Trans Fat 0.1 gm,
  Polyunsat Fat 2.4 gm,
  Monounsat Fat 5 gm)
- Cholesterol 60 mg
- Sodium 241 mg
- Potassium 485 gm
- Total Carb 8 gm
- Dietary Fiber 2.7 gm
- Sugars 5.6 gm
- Protein 6 gm
- Phosphorus 202 gm

Pork

Slow-Cooker Pork Tenderloin

**Kathy Hertzler
Lancaster, PA**

Makes 6 servings
Prep. Time: 5–15 minutes
Cooking Time: 4 hours
Ideal slow-cooker size: 4-qt.

2-lb. pork tenderloin, cut in half lengthwise,
  visible fat removed

1 cup water

¾ cup red wine

3 Tbsp. light soy sauce

1 envelope salt-free onion soup mix

6 cloves garlic, peeled and chopped

freshly ground pepper

1. Place pork tenderloin pieces in slow cooker. Pour water, wine, and soy sauce over pork.

2. Turn pork over in liquid several times to completely moisten.

3. Sprinkle with dry onion soup mix. Top with chopped garlic and pepper.

4. Cover. Cook on Low 4 hours.

Exchange List Values
- Carbohydrate 0.5
  Lean Meat 4.0

Basic Nutritional Values
- Calories 220
  (Calories from Fat 35)
- Total Fat 4 gm
  (Saturated Fat 1.0 gm,
  Polyunsat Fat 0.5 gm,
  Monounsat Fat 1.5 gm)
- Cholesterol 115 mg
- Sodium 370 mg
- Total Carb 6 gm
- Dietary Fiber 0 gm
- Sugars 2 gm
- Protein 37 gm

TIP

I mix ½ cup uncooked long-grain white rice and ½ cup uncooked brown rice in a microwavable bowl. Stir in 2½ cups water and ¾ tsp. salt. Cover. Microwave 5 minutes on high, and then 20 minutes on medium. Place finished pork on a large platter and the finished rice alongside, topped with the au jus from the meat. A green salad goes well with this to make a meal.

Perfect Pork Chops

Brenda Pope
Dundee, OH

Makes 2 servings
Prep. Time: 20 minutes
Cooking Time: 3–4 hours
Ideal slow-cooker size: 4-qt.

2 small onions

½ lb. boneless, center loin pork chops, frozen, trimmed of fat

fresh ground pepper, to taste

¾ tsp. reduced-sodium bouillon granules

¼ cup hot water

2 Tbsp. prepared mustard with white wine

fresh parsley sprigs, or lemon slices, *optional*

1. Cut off ends of onions and peel. Cut onions in half crosswise to make 4 thick wheels. Place in bottom of slow cooker.

2. Sear both sides of frozen chops in heavy skillet. Place in cooker on top of onions. Sprinkle with pepper.

3. Dissolve bouillon in hot water. Stir in mustard. Pour into slow cooker.

4. Cover. Cook on High 3–4 hours.

5. Serve topped with fresh parsley sprigs or lemon slices, if desired.

Exchange List Values
- Carbohydrate 0.5
  Lean Meat 3.0

Basic Nutritional Values
- Calories 204
  (Calories from Fat 72)
- Total Fat 8 gm
  (Saturated Fat 2.9 gm,
  Polyunsat Fat 0.7 gm,
  Monounsat Fat 3.9 gm)
- Cholesterol 51 mg
- Sodium 392 mg
- Total Carb 11 gm
- Dietary Fiber 2 gm
- Sugars 7 gm
- Protein 22 gm

Pork

Gourmet Pork Chops

Elsie R. Russett
Fairbank, IA

Makes 6 servings, 1 pork chop per serving
Prep. Time: 15-20 minutes
Baking Time: 60-75 minutes

2 Tbsp. vegetable oil

2 Tbsp. flour

¼ tsp. salt

dash pepper

6 loin pork chops, ½-inch thick

10½-oz. can lower-sodium, lower-fat cream of chicken soup

¾ cup water

1 tsp. ground ginger

1 tsp. dried rosemary, crushed

½ cup whole wheat panko bread crumbs

1. Place oil in good-sized skillet.

2. Combine flour, salt, and pepper in shallow but wide dish.

3. Dredge chops in mixture one at a time.

4. Place 2 or 3 chops in oil in skillet at a time, being careful not to crowd skillet. Brown chops over medium to high heat, 3–4 minutes on each side, until a browned crust forms.

5. As chops brown, place in well-greased 7×11-inch baking dish.

6. In bowl, combine soup, water, ginger, and rosemary.

7. Pour over chops.

8. Sprinkle with half the panko bread crumbs.

9. Cover. Bake at 350°F for 50–60 minutes, or until chops are tender but not dry.

10. Uncover. Sprinkle with remaining panko bread crumbs.

11. Bake uncovered 10–15 minutes. Remove from oven and serve.

Exchange List Values

- Starch 1.0
- Lean Meat 2.0
- Fat 1.0

Basic Nutritional Values

- Calories 215 (Calories from Fat 90)
- Total Fat 10 gm (Saturated Fat 2.3 gm, Trans Fat 0.0 gm, Polyunsat Fat 2.1 gm, Monounsat Fat 5.2 gm)
- Cholesterol 50 mg
- Sodium 315 mg
- Potassium 465 gm
- Total Carb 11 gm
- Dietary Fiber 1 gm
- Sugars 1 gm
- Protein 18 gm
- Phosphorus 130 gm

Pork Chops with Apple Stuffing

Arlene Yoder
Hartville, OH

Makes 6 servings, 1 pork chop per serving
Prep. Time: 20 minutes
Cooking Time: 45–60 minutes

6 bone-in pork chops, at least 1-inch thick, about 2 lbs. total

1 Tbsp. canola oil

¼ cup chopped celery

¼ cup chopped onion

3 apples, peeled, cored, and diced

¼ cup sugar

½ cup bread crumbs, or cracker crumbs

¼ tsp. salt

¼ tsp. pepper

2 tsp. chopped parsley

1. Cut a pocket about 1½-inch deep into the side of each chop for stuffing.

2. Heat oil in skillet.

3. Stir celery and onion into oil in skillet. Cook over medium until tender, stirring frequently.

4. Stir in diced apples. Sprinkle with sugar.

5. Cover skillet. Cook apples over low heat until tender and glazed.

6. Stir in bread crumbs.

7. Stir in salt, pepper, and parsley.

8. Spreading open the pocket in each chop with your fingers, stuff with mixture.

9. Place half of stuffed chops in skillet. Brown on both sides over medium to high heat.

10. Remove browned chops to platter. Cover to keep warm.

11. Repeat Step 9 with remaining chops.

12. Return other chops to skillet.

13. Reduce heat. Add a few tablespoons of water.

14. Cover. Cook slowly over low heat until done, about 20–25 minutes.

Exchange List Values
- Carbohydrate 1.5
- Lean Meat 3.0
- Fat 0.5

Basic Nutritional Values
- Calories 270 (Calories from Fat 80)
- Total Fat 9 gm (Saturated Fat 2.6 gm, Trans Fat 0.0 gm, Polyunsat Fat 1.3 gm, Monounsat Fat 4.3 gm)
- Cholesterol 65 mg
- Sodium 210 mg
- Potassium 370 gm
- Total Carb 24 gm
- Dietary Fiber 1 gm
- Sugars 16 gm
- Protein 24 gm
- Phosphorus 160 gm

Pork

Simple Barbecue Pork Chops

Hope Comerford
Clinton Township, MI

Makes 4 servings
Prep. Time: 5 minutes
Cooking Time: 5 hours
Ideal slow-cooker size: 3-qt.

3 lbs. bone-in thick cut pork chops

2–3 Tbsp. barbecue seasoning

¼ cup water

1. Coat each side of each pork chop with the barbecue seasoning. Place them in the crock.

2. Pour the water around the outside of the pork chops.

3. Cover and cook on Low for 5 hours.

Serving suggestion:
Top with additional barbecue sauce and canned pears.

Exchange List Values
- Lean Meat 3.0
- Fat 0.5

Basic Nutritional Values
- Calories 507
  (Calories from Fat 180)
- Total Fat 20 gm
  (Saturated Fat 7 gm,
  Trans Fat 0.1 gm,
  Polyunsat Fat 2.7 gm,
  Monounsat Fat 7.8 gm)
- Cholesterol 200 mg
- Sodium 450 mg
- Potassium 1062 gm
- Total Carb 3.7 gm
- Dietary Fiber 0 gm
- Sugars 0 gm
- Protein 72 gm
- Phosphorus 766 gm

Pork

Pork and Cabbage Dinner

Mrs. Paul Gray
Beatrice, NE

Makes 8 servings
Prep. Time: 25 minutes
Cooking Time: 5–6 hours
Ideal slow-cooker size: 4- or 5-qt.

2 lbs. pork steaks, or chops, or shoulder, bone-in, trimmed of fat

¾ cup chopped onions

¼ cup chopped fresh parsley, or 2 Tbsp. dried parsley

4 cups shredded cabbage

1 tsp. salt

⅛ tsp. pepper

½ tsp. caraway seeds

⅛ tsp. allspice

½ cup beef broth

2 medium cooking apples, cored and sliced ¼-inch thick

Exchange List Values
- Fruit 0.5
- Vegetable 1.0
- Lean Meat 2.0

Basic Nutritional Values
- Calories 149 (Calories from Fat 44)
- Total Fat 5 gm (Saturated Fat 1.7 gm, Polyunsat Fat 0.4 gm, Monounsat Fat 2.1 gm)
- Cholesterol 47 mg
- Sodium 382 mg
- Total Carb 9 gm
- Dietary Fiber 2 gm
- Sugars 6 gm
- Protein 18 gm

1. Place pork in slow cooker. Layer onions, parsley, and cabbage over pork.

2. Combine salt, pepper, caraway seeds, and allspice. Sprinkle over cabbage. Pour broth over cabbage.

3. Cover. Cook on Low 5–6 hours.

4. Add apple slices 30 minutes before serving.

Pork

Ham in Cider

Dorothy M. Van Deest
Memphis, TN

Makes 8 servings
Prep. Time: 20 minutes
Cooking Time: 8½–10½ hours
Ideal slow-cooker size: 4- or 5-qt.

3-lb. boneless, precooked extra-lean, lower-sodium ham, trimmed of fat

4 cups sweet cider, or apple juice

¼ cup brown sugar substitute to equal ¼ cup sugar

2 tsp. dry mustard

1 tsp. ground cloves

1 cup golden raisins

1. Place ham and cider in slow cooker.

2. Cover. Cook on Low 8–10 hours.

3. Remove ham from cider and place in baking pan.

4. Make a paste of sugar, mustard, cloves, and a little hot cider. Brush over ham. Pour ½ cup of juice from slow cooker into baking pan. Stir in raisins.

5. Bake at 375°F for 30 minutes, until the paste has turned into a glaze.

Exchange List Values
- Carbohydrate 2.0
- Meat, Very Lean 3.0

Basic Nutritional Values
- Calories 255 (Calories from Fat 26)
- Total Fat 3 gm (Saturated Fat 1.0 gm, Polyunsat Fat 0.6 gm, Monounsat Fat 1.0 gm)
- Cholesterol 67 mg
- Sodium 1194 mg
- Total Carb 31 gm
- Dietary Fiber 1 gm
- Sugars 28 gm
- Protein 27 gm

Glazed Ham Balls

Teresa Koenig
Leola, PA
Dorothy Schrock
Arthur, IL

Makes 20 servings, 1 ball per serving
Prep. Time: 20 minutes
Baking Time: 50 minutes

8-oz. can (1 cup) crushed pineapple, undrained

2⅔ Tbsp. Splenda Brown Sugar Blend

1 Tbsp. vinegar

2–3 Tbsp. prepared mustard

1 lb. 50%-reduced-fat bulk sausage

½ cup cooked lower-sodium ground ham

¾ cup bread crumbs, or crushed saltine crackers

½ cup egg substitute

½ cup ketchup, or milk

⅛ cup chopped onion

¼ tsp. pepper, *optional*

1. In a mixing bowl, mix together pineapple, Splenda, vinegar, and mustard. Set aside.

2. In a large mixing bowl, thoroughly combine sausage, ham, bread crumbs, egg substitute, ketchup, and onion.

3. Shape into 20 1½-inch balls. Place in well-greased shallow baking dish.

4. Spoon pineapple mixture over ham balls.

5. Cover. Bake at 350°F for 25 minutes.

6. Uncover. Continue baking for 25 more minutes.

Exchange List Values

- Carbohydrate 0.5
- Lean Meat 1.0
- Fat 0.5

Basic Nutritional Values

- Calories 100
  (Calories from Fat 35)
- Total Fat 4 gm
  (Saturated Fat 1.4 gm,
  Trans Fat 0.0 gm,
  Polyunsat Fat 0.6 gm,
  Monounsat Fat 2.0 gm)
- Cholesterol 15 mg
- Sodium 335 mg
- Potassium 145 gm
- Total Carb 8 gm
- Dietary Fiber 0 gm
- Sugars 4 gm
- Protein 7 gm
- Phosphorus 65 gm

Pork

Ham-Potatoes Green Bean Casserole

Sarah Miller
Harrisonburg, VA

Makes 12 servings, 3-inch square per serving
Prep. Time: 45 minutes
Baking Time: 30 minutes

3 Tbsp. trans-fat-free tub margarine

½ cup flour

3 cups fat-free milk

1¼ cups grated 50%-reduced fat cheddar cheese

5 medium-sized potatoes, cooked and sliced thin

2 lbs. fresh green beans with ends nipped off, or 2 16-oz. pkgs. frozen green beans, steamed or microwaved until just-tender

3 cups diced lower-sodium cooked ham

1 cup panko bread crumbs

1. Melt margarine in saucepan.

2. Stir in flour.

3. Gradually stir in milk. Stir continually while cooking over low heat until mixture thickens.

4. Add cheese and stir until it melts.

5. Arrange potatoes in well-greased 9×13-inch baking dish.

6. Drain any liquid off green beans. Spread beans over potatoes.

7. Pour half of cheese sauce over beans.

8. Spread ham over sauce.

9. Pour remaining sauce over all.

10. Scatter panko crumbs over casserole.

11. Bake at 350°F for 30 minutes, or until heated through.

TIP

1. Instead of cooking potatoes, you can use frozen shredded potatoes, thawed.
2. To save more time, you can use 2 15½-oz. cans green beans, drained, instead of fresh or frozen beans.

Exchange List Values
- Starch 1.5
- Vegetable 1.0
- Lean Meat 2.0

Basic Nutritional Values
- Calories 235 (Calories from Fat 55)
- Total Fat 6 gm (Saturated Fat 2.4 gm, Trans Fat 0.0 gm, Polyunsat Fat 1.3 gm, Monounsat Fat 2.1 gm)
- Cholesterol 25 mg
- Sodium 455 mg
- Potassium 565 gm
- Total Carb 31 gm
- Dietary Fiber 4 gm
- Sugars 5 gm
- Protein 16 gm
- Phosphorus 275 gm

Pork

Sweet-Sour Pork

Mary W. Stauffer
Ephrata, PA

Makes 6 servings
Prep. Time: 30 minutes
Cooking Time: 5–7 hours
Ideal slow-cooker size: 4-qt.

2 lbs. boneless pork shoulder, cut in strips, trimmed of fat

1 green bell pepper, cut in strips

½ medium onion, thinly sliced

¾ cup shredded carrots

2 Tbsp. coarsely chopped sweet pickles

2 Tbsp. brown sugar substitute to equal 1 Tbsp. sugar

2 Tbsp. cornstarch

¼ cup water

1 cup pineapple juice (reserved from pineapple chunks)

¼ cup cider vinegar

1 Tbsp. soy sauce

20-oz. can pineapple chunks canned in juice

1. Place pork strips in slow cooker.

2. Add green pepper, onion, carrots, and pickles.

3. In bowl, mix together brown sugar and cornstarch. Add water, pineapple juice, vinegar, and soy sauce. Stir until smooth.

4. Pour over ingredients in slow cooker.

5. Cover. Cook on Low 5–7 hours. One hour before serving, add pineapple chunks. Stir.

Serving suggestion:
Serve over buttered noodles with an additional dash of vinegar or garlic, to taste.

Exchange List Values
- Fruit 1.0
- Carbohydrate 0.5
- Vegetable 1.0
- Lean Meat 3.0

Basic Nutritional Values
- Calories 270 (Calories from Fat 74)
- Total Fat 8 gm (Saturated Fat 2.8 gm, Polyunsat Fat 0.8 gm, Monounsat Fat 3.8 gm)
- Cholesterol 75 mg
- Sodium 285 mg
- Total Carb 27 gm
- Dietary Fiber 2 gm
- Sugars 21 gm
- Protein 22 gm

Pork

Bubble and Squeak

Mrs. Anna Gingerich
Apple Creek, OH

Makes 8 servings
Prep. Time: 15–20 minutes
Cooking Time: 45 minutes

1 onion, diced

12 oz. reduced-fat bulk sausage

4 medium potatoes, sliced thin

½ head cabbage, sliced thin

⅓ cup vinegar, *optional*

cheese of your choice, sliced or grated,
    optional

Good Go-Alongs:
Applesauce, coleslaw, or salad.

1. Sauté onion and sausage together in a deep iron skillet until no pink remains in meat. Stir frequently to break up clumps of meat.

2. Stir in potatoes. Continue cooking over low heat until potatoes begin to become tender. Stir often to prevent sticking and burning, but let potatoes brown.

3. Stir in cut cabbage. Continue cooking until cabbage wilts and potatoes are tender.

4. Stir in vinegar if you wish. Cook a few minutes to blend flavors.

5. Cover contents of skillet with cheese if you wish. Let stand a few minutes until cheese melts.

Exchange List Values
- Starch 1.0
- Vegetable 1.0
- Med-Fat Meat 1.0

Basic Nutritional Values
- Calories 185
  (Calories from Fat 55)
- Total Fat 6 gm
  (Saturated Fat 2.3 gm,
  Trans Fat 0.1 gm,
  Polyunsat Fat 0.9 gm,
  Monounsat Fat 3.0 gm)
- Cholesterol 20 mg
- Sodium 225 mg
- Potassium 540 gm
- Total Carb 22 gm
- Dietary Fiber 3 gm
- Sugars 4 gm
- Protein 9 gm
- Phosphorus 150 gm

Pork

Polish Kraut 'n' Apples

Lori Berezovsky
Salina, KS
Marie Morucci
Glen Lyon, PA

Makes 6 servings
Prep. Time: 25 minutes
Cooking Time: 3–7 hours
Ideal slow-cooker size: 4-qt.

1 lb. fresh, or canned, sauerkraut, *divided*

1 lb. lean low-fat, smoked Polish sausage

3 tart cooking apples, unpeeled, thinly sliced

2 Tbsp. brown sugar substitute to equal 3 Tbsp. sugar

⅛ tsp. pepper

½ tsp. caraway seeds, *optional*

¾ cup apple juice, or cider

1. Rinse sauerkraut and squeeze dry. Place half in slow cooker.

2. Cut sausage into 2-inch lengths and add to cooker.

3. Continue to layer remaining ingredients in slow cooker in order given. Top with remaining sauerkraut. Do not stir.

4. Cover. Cook on High 3–3½ hours, or Low 6–7 hours. Stir before serving.

Exchange List Values
- Fruit 1.0
- Carbohydrate 1.0
- Lean Meat 1.0

Basic Nutritional Values
- Calories 195 (Calories from Fat 33)
- Total Fat 4 gm (Saturated Fat 1.4 gm, Polyunsat Fat 0.3 gm, Monounsat Fat 1.9 gm)
- Cholesterol 35 mg
- Sodium 945 mg
- Total Carb 31 gm
- Dietary Fiber 4 gm
- Sugars 20 gm
- Protein 10 gm

Pork

Kielbasa and Cabbage

Barbara McGinnis
Jupiter, FL

Makes 6 servings
Prep. Time: 35 minutes
Cooking Time: 7–8 hours
Ideal slow-cooker size: 4- or 5-qt.

1½-lb. head green cabbage, shredded

2 medium onions, chopped

3 medium red potatoes, peeled and cubed

1 red bell pepper, chopped

2 cloves garlic, minced

⅔ cup dry white wine

1 lb. low-fat Polish kielbasa, cut into 3-inch
pieces

28-oz. can diced no-added-salt tomatoes
with juice

1 Tbsp. Dijon mustard

¾ tsp. caraway seeds

½ tsp. pepper

1. Combine all ingredients in slow cooker.

2. Cover. Cook on Low 7–8 hours, or until cabbage is tender.

Exchange List Values
- Starch 0.5
- Carbohydrate 0.5
- Vegetable 3.0
- Lean Meat 1.0

Basic Nutritional Values
- Calories 226
  (Calories from Fat 39)
- Total Fat 4 gm
  (Saturated Fat 1.4 gm,
  Polyunsat Fat 0.6 gm,
  Monounsat Fat 2.0 gm)
- Cholesterol 35 mg
- Sodium 781 mg
- Total Carb 34 gm
- Dietary Fiber 7 gm
- Sugars 15 gm
- Protein 14 gm

Chicken

Grilled Chicken Breasts

Gloria Mumbauer
Singers Glen, VA
Thelma F. Good
Harrisonburg, VA

Makes 2½–2¾ cups marinade; 12 chicken
breast halves, 1 breast half per serving
Prep. Time: 5 minutes
Marinating Time: 6–8 hours or overnight
Grilling Time: 15–18 minutes

12 boneless skinless chicken breast halves, 5 oz. each

¾ cup vegetable oil

¾ cup light soy sauce

¼ cup Worcestershire sauce

2 tsp. prepared mustard

1 tsp. black pepper

½ cup apple cider vinegar

2 cloves garlic, minced, or 1½ tsp. garlic powder

⅓ cup lemon juice

1. Place chicken breasts in a single layer in a nonmetallic dish.

2. In a bowl, mix together oil, soy sauce, Worcestershire sauce, mustard, black pepper, vinegar, garlic, and lemon juice.

3. When well blended, pour over chicken.

4. Cover. Marinate 6–8 hours or overnight. Turn chicken over about half-way through, if it's not the middle of the night and you're able to, to coat both sides.

5. Remove from marinade. Grill over medium heat until cooked through, about 15–18 minutes. Do not overcook or meat will dry out!

Warm Memories:
Our children are delighted when this recipe is on our menu at home. They love to slice it over a big salad for a delicious meal that is both healthy and tasty!
—Thelma F. Good, Harrisonburg, VA

TIP

To serve at a potluck, slice grilled chicken into strips about ¾-inch wide so lots of people get a taste. Do not expect to bring any of this chicken home from a potluck!
—Thelma F. Good, Harrisonburg, VA

Exchange List Value
• Lean Meat 4.0

Basic Nutritional Values
• Calories 210
  (Calories from Fat 70)
• Total Fat 8 gm
  (Saturated Fat 1.3 gm,
  Trans Fat 0.0 gm,
  Polyunsat Fat 2.0 gm,
  Monounsat Fat 4.1 gm)
• Cholesterol 80 mg
• Sodium 275 mg
• Potassium 280 gm
• Total Carb 1 gm
• Dietary Fiber 0 gm
• Sugars 0 gm
• Protein 31 gm
• Phosphorus 230 gm

Chicken

Herb-Roasted Chicken

Hope Comerford
Clinton Township, MI

Makes 4–5 servings
Prep. Time: 10 minutes
Cooking Time: 7 hours
Ideal slow-cooker size: 7-qt.

3–4-lb. whole roasting chicken (or smaller depending on the size of your slow cooker), gizzards removed

2–3 Tbsp. olive oil

2 tsp. rosemary

1 tsp. thyme

1 tsp. sage

2–3 Tbsp. poultry seasoning

1. Truss the legs/wings of your bird. Rub it all over with olive oil.

2. Place balled-up foil in the bottom of your crock to keep the bird from floating in the juices. Place the chicken on top, breast-side down.

3. Mix together the rosemary, thyme, sage, and poultry seasoning. Pat this all over the bird.

4. Cover and cook on Low for 7 hours.

Exchange List Values
- Lean Meat 3.0
- Fat 1.0

Basic Nutritional Values
- Calories 361 (Calories from Fat 117)
- Total Fat 13 gm (Saturated Fat 2.7 gm, Trans Fat 0 gm, Polyunsat Fat 2.4 gm, Monounsat Fat 6.2 gm)
- Cholesterol 176 mg
- Sodium 205 mg
- Potassium 677 gm
- Total Carb 1.7 gm
- Dietary Fiber 0.5 gm
- Sugars 0.04 gm
- Protein 56 gm
- Phosphorus 543 gm

Chicken

Baked Chicken Breasts

Janice Crist
Quinter, KS
Tracy Supcoe
Barclay, MD

Makes 6 servings
Prep. Time: 15 minutes
Cooking Time: 8–10 hours
Ideal slow-cooker size: 4-qt.

3 whole chicken breasts, halved

10¾-oz. can 98%-fat-free, reduced sodium
   cream of chicken soup

½ cup dry sherry

1 tsp. dried tarragon, or rosemary

1 tsp. Worcestershire sauce

¼ tsp. garlic powder

4-oz. can sliced mushrooms, drained

1. Place chicken breasts in slow cooker.

2. In saucepan, combine remaining ingredients. Heat until smooth and hot. Pour over chicken.

3. Cover. Cook on Low 8–10 hours.

Exchange List Values
- Carbohydrate 0.5
- Meat, Very Lean 4.0
- Fat 0.5

Basic Nutritional Values
- Calories 214
  (Calories from Fat 40)
- Total Fat 4 gm
  (Saturated Fat 1.3 gm,
  Polyunsat Fat 1.2 gm,
  Monounsat Fat 1.3 gm)
- Cholesterol 88 mg
- Sodium 339 mg
- Total Carb 7 gm
- Dietary Fiber 1 gm
- Sugars 2 gm
- Protein 34 gm

Chicken

Oven Barbecued Chicken

Carol Eberly
Harrisonburg, VA

Makes 12 servings, 1 thigh per serving
Prep. Time: 10 minutes
Baking Time: 1¼ hours

3 Tbsp. ketchup

2 Tbsp. Worcestershire sauce

2 Tbsp. vinegar

2 Tbsp. light soy sauce

3 Tbsp. brown sugar

1 tsp. spicy brown mustard

1 tsp. salt

1 tsp. pepper

12 boneless, skinless chicken thighs, 2 lbs. total

TIP

You can use chicken legs or chicken breasts, too. Check the legs after they've baked for a total of 50 minutes to be sure they're not drying out. Check breasts after they've baked for a total of 30 minutes to be sure they're not becoming dry.

1. In a mixing bowl, combine ketchup, Worcestershire sauce, vinegar, soy sauce, brown sugar, mustard, salt, and pepper. Blend well.

2. Lay chicken pieces in one layer in well-greased baking dish.

3. Pour sauce over top.

4. Bake at 350°F for 40 minutes.

5. Turn pieces over. Bake 35 more minutes.

Exchange List Values
- Carbohydrate 0.5
- Lean Meat 2.0

Basic Nutritional Values
- Calories 130 (Calories from Fat 55)
- Total Fat 6 gm (Saturated Fat 1.5 gm, Trans Fat 0.0 gm, Polyunsat Fat 1.3 gm, Monounsat Fat 2.1 gm)
- Cholesterol 50 mg
- Sodium 410 mg
- Potassium 170 gm
- Total Carb 5 gm
- Dietary Fiber 0 gm
- Sugars 5 gm
- Protein 13 gm
- Phosphorus 100 gm

Chicken

Barbecue Chicken for Buns

Linda Sluiter
Schererville, IN

Makes 20 servings
Prep. Time: 25 minutes
Cooking Time: 8 hours
Ideal slow-cooker size: 4-qt.

6 cups diced cooked chicken

2 cups chopped celery

1 cup chopped onions

1 cup chopped green peppers

2 Tbsp. canola oil

2 cups ketchup

2 cups water

2 Tbsp. brown sugar

4 Tbsp. vinegar

2 tsp. dry mustard

1 tsp. pepper

½ tsp. salt

20 steak rolls or buns

Exchange List Values
- Carbohydrate 0.5
- Lean Meat 2.0

Basic Nutritional Values
- Calories 131
  (Calories from Fat 43)
- Total Fat 5 gm
  (Saturated Fat 1.0 gm,
  Polyunsat Fat 1.1 gm,
  Monounsat Fat 1.9 gm)
- Cholesterol 37 mg
- Sodium 391 mg
- Total Carb 10 gm
- Dietary Fiber 1 gm
- Sugars 5 gm
- Protein 13 gm

1. Combine all ingredients except rolls in slow cooker.

2. Cover. Cook on Low 8 hours.

3. Stir chicken until it shreds.

4. Pile into steak rolls and serve.

Oven-Fried Chicken Legs

Hazel N. Hassan
Goshen, IN

Makes 12 servings, 1 leg (thigh and
  drumstick) per serving
Prep. Time: 25 minutes
Baking Time: 1 hour

1 cup bread crumbs

¼ tsp. salt, or less

1 tsp. paprika

1 tsp. poultry seasoning

½ tsp. onion salt

¼ tsp. pepper

2 Tbsp. canola oil

12 chicken legs (thigh and drumstick), skin
  removed

1. Mix bread crumbs, seasonings, and oil.

2. Rinse chicken legs under running water
and roll each leg in crumb mixture, shaking
off excess.

3. Place legs in two rows in greased
9×13-inch baking pan, alternating thick and
thin side of legs.

4. Bake at 350°F for 1 hour. Remove from
oven and place in clean, hot casserole dish.
Wrap well in newspaper for transporting to
church.

Warm Memories
I first made this dish for the benefit of the
children, and was amused to see adults put
one leg on a child's plate and take one for
themselves.

Exchange List Values
- Starch 0.5
- Lean Meat 4.0
- Fat 0.5

Basic Nutritional Values
- Calories 240
  (Calories from Fat 100)
- Total Fat 11 gm
  (Saturated Fat 2.5 gm,
  Trans Fat 0.0 gm,
  Polyunsat Fat 2.7 gm,
  Monounsat Fat 4.5 gm)
- Cholesterol 90 mg
- Sodium 255 mg
- Potassium 255 gm
- Total Carb 7 gm
- Dietary Fiber 0 gm
- Sugars 1 gm
- Protein 27 gm
- Phosphorus 190 gm

Chicken

Chicken and Broccoli Bake

Jan Rankin
Millersville, PA

Makes 12 servings, each a 3-inch square
Prep. Time: 15 minutes
Baking Time: 30 minutes

2 10¾-oz. cans lower-sodium, lower-fat cream of chicken soup

2½ cups fat-free milk, *divided*

16-oz. bag frozen chopped broccoli, thawed and drained

3 cups cooked and chopped chicken breast

2 cups reduced-fat buttermilk baking mix

1. Mix soup and 1 cup milk together in large mixing bowl until smooth.

2. Stir in broccoli and chicken.

3. Pour into well-greased 9×13-inch baking dish.

4. Mix together 1½ cups milk and baking mix in mixing bowl.

5. Spoon evenly over top of chicken-broccoli mixture.

6. Bake at 450°F for 30 minutes.

Exchange List Values
- Starch 1.0
- Carbohydrate 0.5
- Lean Meat 2.0

Basic Nutritional Values
- Calories 180 (Calories from Fat 30)
- Total Fat 4 gm (Saturated Fat 0.7 gm, Trans Fat 0.0 gm, Polyunsat Fat 1.0 gm, Monounsat Fat 1.4 gm)
- Cholesterol 35 mg
- Sodium 445 mg
- Potassium 485 gm
- Total Carb 22 gm
- Dietary Fiber 2 gm
- Sugars 5 gm
- Protein 16 gm
- Phosphorus 280 gm

Coq au Vin

Hope Comerford
Clinton Township, MI

Makes 4–6 servings
Prep. Time: 30 minutes
Cooking Time: 7 hours, 20 minutes
Ideal slow-cooker size: 4- to 5-qt.

2 Tbsp. olive oil

salt and pepper, to taste

6 chicken thighs, skin removed

1 cup red wine

1 onion, sliced into rings

8 oz. baby bella mushrooms, sliced

2 tsp. Italian seasoning

1. Heat the olive oil in a skillet.

2. Salt and pepper one side of your chicken thighs and place them seasoned-side down in the skillet. While that side is cooking, season the second side with salt and pepper as well. Once the first side is browned, flip it and brown the other side. Once both sides are browned, arrange them in bottom of your slow cooker.

3. In the same skillet in which you browned the chicken, add the wine, onion, and mushrooms. Cook until just softened, about 5 minutes. Pour this mixture over the top of the chicken in the crock and sprinkle with the Italian seasoning.

4. Cover and cook on Low for 7 hours.

Serving suggestion:
Serve over rice or noodles.

TIP

Buy presliced mushrooms to cut down on time.

Exchange List Values
- Vegetable 0.5
- Medium-Fat Meat 2.0
- Fat 0.5

Basic Nutritional Values
- Calories 175 (Calories from Fat 68)
- Total Fat 7.5 gm (Saturated Fat 1.4 gm, Trans Fat 0.0 gm, Polyunsat Fat 1.2 gm, Monounsat Fat 4.3 gm)
- Cholesterol 65 mg
- Sodium 150 mg
- Potassium 344 gm
- Total Carb 5.3 gm
- Dietary Fiber 1 gm
- Sugars 1.7 gm
- Protein 15 gm Phosphorus 175 gm

Chicken

Chicken Parmesan

Jessalyn Wantland
Napoleon, OH

Makes 4 servings, 1 breast half per serving
Prep. Time: 10 minutes
Baking Time: 45 minutes

1 egg, beaten

½ cup Italian-seasoned bread crumbs

4 boneless, skinless chicken breast halves, about 5 oz. each

12 oz. low-sodium, fat-free pasta sauce with basil

¾ cup shredded Parmesan cheese

1. Grease 7×11-inch baking dish.

2. Place egg in shallow bowl.

3. Place bread crumbs in another shallow bowl.

4. Dip each piece of chicken in egg, and then in bread crumbs.

5. Place coated chicken in baking dish.

6. Bake at 400°F for 30 minutes.

7. Spoon pasta sauce over chicken.

8. Top evenly with cheese.

9. Bake another 15 minutes, or until heated through and cheese is melted.

Exchange List Values
- Starch 1.0
- Lean Meat 5.0

Basic Nutritional Values
- Calories 280 (Calories from Fat 55)
- Total Fat 6 gm (Saturated Fat 2.4 gm, Trans Fat 0.0 gm, Polyunsat Fat 0.9 gm, Monounsat Fat 2.0 gm)
- Cholesterol 85 mg
- Sodium 450 mg
- Potassium 575 gm
- Total Carb 17 gm
- Dietary Fiber 1 gm
- Sugars 6 gm
- Protein 37 gm
- Phosphorus 320 gm

Chicken Cacciatore

Donna Lantgen
Arvada, CO

Makes 6 servings, 1 breast half per serving
Prep. Time: 10 minutes
Cooking/Baking Time: 65–70 minutes,
    depending on thickness of chicken

6 boneless skinless chicken breast halves,
    each about 5 oz. in weight

1 medium green bell pepper, chopped

1 medium onion, chopped

15½-oz. can tomatoes, chopped, or 2 cups
    fresh tomatoes, diced and peeled

1 Tbsp. Italian seasoning

sprinkle of mozzarella or Parmesan cheese,
    shredded

1. Place chicken in well-greased 9×13-inch baking pan.

2. In mixing bowl, stir together green pepper, onion, tomatoes, and seasoning.

3. Spoon vegetables evenly over chicken.

4. Cover. Bake at 350°F for 45 minutes.

5. With a sharp knife make 2–3 vertical slashes in thickest part of each chicken breast. (Do not cut the whole way through.) Baste with pan juices.

6. Cover. Return to oven and continue baking 15 more minutes, or until thermometer inserted in center of chicken registers 165°F.

7. Top chicken with cheese.

8. Return to oven for 5–10 minutes, or until cheese melts.

Exchange List Values
- Vegetable 1.0
- Lean Meat 4.0

Basic Nutritional Values
- Calories 185
  (Calories from Fat 30)
- Total Fat 4 gm
  (Saturated Fat 1.0 gm,
  Trans Fat 0.0 gm,
  Polyunsat Fat 0.8 gm,
  Monounsat Fat 1.2 gm)
- Cholesterol 80 mg
- Sodium 175 mg
- Potassium 465 gm
- Total Carb 7 gm
- Dietary Fiber 2 gm
- Sugars 3 gm
- Protein 31 gm
- Phosphorus 245 gm

Chicken

Easy Chicken Enchiladas

Lois Peterson
Huron, SD

Makes 6 servings, 1 enchilada per serving
Prep. Time: 35–45 minutes
Baking Time: 40 minutes

10¾-oz. can lower-sodium, lower-fat cream of chicken soup

½ cup fat-free sour cream

¼ cup picante sauce

¾ cup no-salt-added tomato sauce

2 tsp. chili powder

2 cups chopped cooked chicken

1 oz. reduced-fat pepper Jack cheese

6 6-inch flour, or whole wheat, tortillas

1 large tomato, chopped

1 green onion, sliced

1. Stir soup, sour cream, picante sauce, tomato sauce, and chili powder in a medium bowl.

2. In a large bowl, combine 1 cup sauce mixture, chicken, and cheese.

3. Grease 9×13-inch baking dish.

4. Divide mixture among tortillas.

5. Roll up each tortilla. Place in baking dish, seam side down.

6. Pour remaining sauce mixture over filled tortillas.

7. Cover. Bake at 350°F for 40 minutes or until enchiladas are hot and bubbling.

8. Top with chopped tomato and onion and serve.

Exchange List Values
- Starch 1.0
- Carbohydrate 0.5
- Vegetable 1.0
- Lean Meat 2.0
- Fat 1.0

Basic Nutritional Values
- Calories 260 (Calories from Fat 70)
- Total Fat 8 gm (Saturated Fat 2.5 gm, Trans Fat 0.0 gm, Polyunsat Fat 1.8 gm, Monounsat Fat 3.0 gm)
- Cholesterol 50 mg
- Sodium 565 mg
- Potassium 650 gm
- Total Carb 28 gm
- Dietary Fiber 3 gm
- Sugars 4 gm
- Protein 19 gm
- Phosphorus 200 gm

Easy Chicken Cordon Bleu

Sharon Miller
Holmesville, OH

Makes 8 servings, half a roll-up per serving
Prep. Time: 35 minutes
Cooking Time: 45 minutes

4 large boneless, skinless chicken breast
   halves, each about 8 oz. in weight
½ cup Italian-seasoned dry bread crumbs
2 slices ultra-thin Swiss cheese, cut in half
2 oz. lean lower-sodium deli ham
8 sturdy toothpicks

1. Grease a 9×13-inch baking dish.

2. Pound each chicken breast to about
¼–½-inch thickness.

3. Place bread crumbs in shallow bowl.

4. Dredge each chicken piece in bread
crumbs, coating each side.

5. Lay slice of Swiss cheese and slice of
ham on each chicken breast.

6. Tightly roll up each layered breast.

7. Holding roll firmly, re-roll in crumbs.

8. Stick 2 toothpicks through each roll to
maintain its shape.

9. Place in baking dish. Cover with foil.

10. Bake at 350°F for 30 minutes.

11. Remove foil. Bake an additional 15
minutes.

12. Cut each roll in half before serving.

TIP

If the cheese is too "exposed" instead
of being enclosed in the bundle, it
melts outside the bundle.

Exchange List Values
- Starch 0.5
- Lean Meat 3.0

Basic Nutritional Values
- Calories 170
  (Calories from Fat 35)
- Total Fat 4 gm
  (Saturated Fat 1.3 gm,
  Trans Fat 0.0 gm,
  Polyunsat Fat 0.7 gm,
  Monounsat Fat 1.3 gm)
- Cholesterol 70 mg
- Sodium 225 mg
- Potassium 240 gm
- Total Carb 5 gm
- Dietary Fiber 0 gm
- Sugars 0 gm
- Protein 27 gm
- Phosphorus 215 gm

Chicken

Chicken and Stuffing

Janice Yoskovich
Carmichaels, PA
Jo Ellen Moore
Pendleton, IN

Makes 16 servings
Prep. Time: 35 minutes
Cooking Time: 4½–5 hours
Ideal slow-cooker size: 6-qt.

2½ tsp. salt-free chicken bouillon powder

2½ cups water

¼ cup canola oil

½ cup chopped onions

½ cup chopped celery

4-oz. can mushrooms, stems and pieces, drained

¼ cup dried parsley flakes

1½ tsp. rubbed sage

1 tsp. poultry seasoning

½ tsp. salt

½ tsp. pepper

12 cups day-old bread cubes (½-inch pieces)

2 eggs

10¾-oz. can 98%-fat-free, reduced-sodium cream of chicken soup

5 cups cubed cooked chicken

1. Combine all ingredients except bread, eggs, soup, and chicken in saucepan. Simmer for 10 minutes.

2. Place bread cubes in large bowl.

3. Combine eggs and soup. Stir into broth mixture until smooth. Pour over bread and toss well.

4. Layer half of stuffing and then half of chicken into very large slow cooker (or two medium-sized cookers). Repeat layers.

5. Cover. Cook on low 4½–5 hours.

Exchange List Values
- Starch 1.0
- Lean Meat 2.0
- Fat 0.5

Basic Nutritional Values
- Calories 215
  (Calories from Fat 78)
- Total Fat 9 gm
  (Saturated Fat 1.6 gm,
  Polyunsat Fat 2.5 gm,
  Monounsat Fat 3.7 gm)
- Cholesterol 67 mg
- Sodium 362 mg
- Total Carb 16 gm
- Dietary Fiber 1 gm
- Sugars 2 gm
- Protein 16 gm

Chicken Baked with Red Onions, Potatoes, and Rosemary

Kristine Stalter
Iowa City, IA

Makes 8 servings
Prep. Time: 10–15 minutes
Baking Time: 45–60 minutes

2 red onions, each cut into 10 wedges

1¼ lbs. new potatoes, unpeeled and cut into chunks

2 garlic bulbs, separated into cloves, unpeeled

salt

pepper

3 tsp. extra-virgin olive oil

2 Tbsp. balsamic vinegar

approximately 5 sprigs rosemary

8 chicken thighs, skin removed

1. Spread onions, potatoes, and garlic in single layer over bottom of large roasting pan so that they will crisp and brown.

2. Season with salt and pepper.

3. Pour over the oil and balsamic vinegar and add rosemary, leaving some sprigs whole and stripping the leaves off the rest.

4. Toss vegetables and seasonings together.

5. Tuck chicken pieces among vegetables.

6. Bake at 400°F for 45–60 minutes, or until chicken and vegetables are cooked through.

7. Transfer to a big platter, or take to the table in the roasting pan.

Warm Memories:
A neighbor and friend shared this simple recipe with me when my family and I were on sabbatical in the UK.

Exchange List Values
- Starch 1.0
- Lean Meat 2.0
- Fat 1.5

Basic Nutritional Values
- Calories 235 (Calories from Fat 100)
- Total Fat 11 gm (Saturated Fat 2.3 gm, Trans Fat 0.0 gm, Polyunsat Fat 1.9 gm, Monounsat Fat 5.9 gm)
- Cholesterol 50 mg
- Sodium 55 mg
- Potassium 485 gm
- Total Carb 18 gm
- Dietary Fiber 2 gm
- Sugars 3 gm
- Protein 16 gm
- Phosphorus 155 gm

Mushroom Chicken in Sour Cream Sauce

Lavina Hochstedler
Grand Blanc, MI
Joyce Shackelford
Green Bay, WI

Makes 6 servings
Prep. Time: 15 minutes
Cooking Time: 5–8 hours
Ideal slow-cooker size: 4-qt.

¼ tsp. salt

¼ tsp. pepper

½ tsp. paprika

¼ tsp. lemon pepper

1 tsp. garlic powder

6 skinless, bone-in chicken breast halves

10¾-oz. can 98%-fat-free, reduced-sodium cream of mushroom soup

8-oz. container fat-free sour cream

½ cup dry white wine or chicken broth

½ lb. fresh mushrooms, sliced

NOTES

Serve over potatoes, rice, or couscous. Delicious accompanied with broccoli-cauliflower salad and applesauce.

1. Combine salt, pepper, paprika, lemon pepper, and garlic powder. Rub over chicken. Place in slow cooker.

2. Combine soup, sour cream, and wine or broth. Stir in mushrooms. Pour over chicken.

3. Cover. Cook on Low 6–8 hours or High 5 hours.

Exchange List Values
- Carbohydrate 1.0
  Meat, Very Lean 4.0

Basic Nutritional Values
- Calories 217
  (Calories from Fat 37)
- Total Fat 4 gm
  (Saturated Fat 1.2 gm,
  Polyunsat Fat 0.9 gm,
  Monounsat Fat 1.2 gm)
- Cholesterol 76 mg
- Sodium 407 mg
- Total Carb 12 gm
- Dietary Fiber 1 gm
- Sugars 4 gm
- Protein 30 gm

Chicken

Sweet-and-Sour Chicken

Bernice A. Esau
North Newton, KS

Makes 6 servings
Prep. Time: 20 minutes
Cooking Time: 8–10 hours
Ideal slow-cooker size: 4-qt.

1½ cups sliced carrots

1 large green pepper, chopped

1 medium onion, chopped

2 Tbsp. quick-cooking tapioca

2½ lbs. chicken, cut into serving-size pieces, skin removed, trimmed of fat

8-oz. can pineapple chunks in juice

3 Tbsp. brown sugar substitute to equal 1½ Tbsp. sugar

⅓ cup vinegar

1 Tbsp. soy sauce

½ tsp. instant chicken bouillon

¼ tsp. garlic powder

½ tsp. freshly grated ginger

⅛ tsp. salt

1. Place vegetables in bottom of slow cooker. Sprinkle with tapioca. Add chicken.

2. In separate bowl, combine pineapple, brown sugar, vinegar, soy sauce, bouillon, garlic powder, ginger, and salt. Pour over chicken.

3. Cover. Cook on Low 8–10 hours.

Exchange List Values
- Fruit 0.5
- Carbohydrate 0.5
- Vegetable 1.0
- Lean Meat 2.0

Basic Nutritional Values
- Calories 208 (Calories from Fat 41)
- Total Fat 5 gm (Saturated Fat 1.2 gm, Polyunsat Fat 1.1 gm, Monounsat Fat 1.6 gm)
- Cholesterol 54 mg
- Sodium 365 mg
- Total Carb 23 gm
- Dietary Fiber 2 gm
- Sugars 16 gm
- Protein 19 gm

Chicken

Cheesy Mexican Chicken

Lori Newswanger
Lancaster, PA

Makes 8 servings, 3¼×4½-inch rectangle
per serving
Prep. Time: 15 minutes
Baking Time: 35–45 minutes

2 lbs. boneless, skinless chicken breasts

10¾-oz. can lower-fat, lower-sodium cream of chicken soup

1¾ cups shredded 75%-less-fat cheddar cheese, *divided*

½ cup fat-free milk

7 tsp. salt-free taco seasoning

3 cups baked low-fat corn chips, or tortilla chips, coarsely crushed

1. Grease 9×13-inch baking dish.

2. Slice chicken in 1-inch-wide strips. Spread chicken in baking dish.

3. Combine soup, 1¼ cups cheese, milk, and taco seasoning in mixing bowl. Spoon over chicken.

4. Top with chips.

5. Cover dish.

6. Bake at 375°F for 30–40 minutes, or until chicken is cooked through and no pink remains. (Fish out a piece from middle of dish and check.)

7. Remove cover. Top with remaining ½ cup cheese.

8. Bake uncovered until cheese is melted, about 5 minutes.

Serving suggestion:
Serve over rice.

Basic Nutritional Values
- Calories 275 (Calories from Fat 55)
- Total Fat 6 gm

(Saturated Fat 2.4 gm, Trans Fat 0.0 gm, Polyunsat Fat 1.3 gm, Monounsat Fat 1.8 gm)
- Cholesterol 75 mg
- Sodium 495 mg
- Potassium 505 gm
- Total Carb 20 gm
- Dietary Fiber 2 gm
- Sugars 1 gm
- Protein 35 gm
- Phosphorus 380 gm

Chicken

Tex-Mex Chicken and Rice

Kelly Amos
Pittsboro, NC

Makes 8 servings
Prep. Time: 25 minutes
Cooking Time: 4–4½ hours
Ideal slow-cooker size: 4- or 5-qt.

1 cup converted uncooked white rice

28-oz. can diced tomatoes

6-oz. can tomato paste

3 cups hot water

1 pkg. dry taco seasoning mix

4 whole boneless, skinless chicken breasts,
  uncooked and cut into ½-inch cubes

2 medium onions, chopped

1 green pepper, chopped

4-oz. can diced green chilies

1 tsp. garlic powder

½ tsp. pepper

1. Combine all ingredients in a large slow cooker.

2. Cover. Cook on Low 4–4½ hours, or until rice is tender and chicken is cooked.

Exchange List Values
- Starch 1.5
- Vegetable 3.0
- Meat, Very Lean 3.0

Basic Nutritional Values
- Calories 300
  (Calories from Fat 32)
- Total Fat 4 gm
  (Saturated Fat 0.8 gm,
  Polyunsat Fat 0.9 gm,
  Monounsat Fat 1.1 gm)
- Cholesterol 73 mg
- Sodium 656 mg
- Total Carb 34 gm
- Dietary Fiber 4 gm
- Sugars 7 gm
- Protein 32 gm

Chicken Strata Casserole

Mrs. Lewis L. Beachy
Sarasota, FL
Mary Vaughn Warye
West Liberty, OH

Makes 8 servings, about ¾ cup per serving
Prep. Time: 20 minutes
Baking Time: 1 hour

2 cups cubed, cooked chicken

½ cup chopped celery

½ cup chopped onion

½ cup chopped green pepper

⅓ cup reduced-fat light mayonnaise

½ tsp. salt

¼ tsp. pepper

4 slices bread, cubed

1½ cups fat-free milk

2 eggs, beaten

14½-oz. can lower-sodium, lower-fat cream of mushroom soup

½ cup reduced-fat freshly grated yellow cheddar cheese

Exchange List Values
- Carbohydrate 1.0
- Lean Meat 2.0
- Fat 1.0

Basic Nutritional Values
- Calories 200
  (Calories from Fat 70)
- Total Fat 8 gm
  (Saturated Fat 2.4 gm,
  Trans Fat 0.0 gm,
  Polyunsat Fat 2.7 gm,
  Monounsat Fat 2.6 gm)
- Cholesterol 85 mg
- Sodium 560 mg
- Potassium 490 gm
- Total Carb 14 gm
- Dietary Fiber 1 gm
- Sugars 5 gm
- Protein 16 gm
- Phosphorus 205 gm

1. Combine chicken, celery, onion, green pepper, mayonnaise, salt, and pepper.

2. Put half of bread into well-greased casserole. Top with chicken mixture and remaining bread.

3. Combine milk and eggs and pour over other ingredients. Top with mushroom soup and cheese.

4. Bake at 350°F for 1 hour.

Chicken Pie

Lavina Ebersol
Ronks, PA

Makes 8 servings, 2¾×3½-inch rectangle
   per serving
Prep. Time: 45 minutes
Baking Time: 45 minutes

Filling:

2 Tbsp. canola oil

3 Tbsp. flour

¼ tsp. salt

⅛ tsp. pepper

1 sodium-free chicken bouillon cube

2 cups fat-free milk

12-oz. pkg. frozen vegetables, including non-
   starchy veggies like broccoli and peppers

1 cup chopped cooked chicken

Biscuit Topping:

2 cups flour

3 tsp. baking powder

¾ tsp. salt

1 tsp. paprika

⅓ cup trans-fat-free tub margarine

⅔ cup fat-free milk

1. Heat oil in saucepan. Stir in flour, salt, pepper, and bouillon cube.

2. Remove from heat and gradually stir in milk.

3. Return to heat. Cook, stirring constantly, until smooth and slightly thickened.

4. Add vegetables and chicken to sauce.

5. In good-sized mixing bowl, stir together flour, baking powder, salt, and paprika.

6. Cut in margarine with pastry cutter, or 2 forks, until mixture resembles small peas.

7. Stir in milk until mixture forms ball.

8. Roll out dough on lightly floured surface into 8×12-inch rectangle.

9. Fold dough lightly into quarters. Lift onto top of chicken mixture.

10. Unfold dough and center over greased 7×11-inch baking dish. Pinch dough around edges of baking dish. Cut slits in dough to allow steam to escape.

11. Bake at 350°F for 45 minutes, or until pie is bubbly and crust is browned.

Exchange List Values
- Starch 2.5
- Lean Meat 1.0
- Fat 1.5

Basic Nutritional Values
- Calories 295
  (Calories from Fat 100)
- Total Fat 11 gm
  (Saturated Fat 1.9 gm,
  Trans Fat 0.0 gm,
  Polyunsat Fat 3.8 gm,
  Monounsat Fat 4.5 gm)
- Cholesterol 15 mg
- Sodium 545 mg
- Potassium 350 gm
- Total Carb 36 gm
- Dietary Fiber 3 gm
- Sugars 6 gm
- Protein 13 gm
- Phosphorus 350 gm

Chicken and Dumplings

Barbara Nolan
Pleasant Valley, NY

Makes 8 servings, about 9 oz. per serving
Prep. Time: 15 minutes
Cooking Time: 30 minutes

4 carrots, cut into ½-inch-thick slices

2 medium onions, cut into eighths

1 clove garlic, sliced thin

3 celery ribs, cut into ½-inch-thick slices

2 Tbsp. canola oil

3 Tbsp. flour

2 14-oz. cans lower-sodium, fat-free chicken broth

1 lb. uncooked chicken cutlets, cut into 1-inch cubes

2 Tbsp. grated carrots

½ tsp. poultry seasoning

¼ tsp. garlic powder

⅛ tsp. black pepper

¼ cup half-and-half

fresh parsley, snipped, for garnish

Dumplings:

1½ cups flour

2 tsp. baking powder

½ tsp. salt

1 cup milk

1 egg

2 Tbsp. vegetable oil

1. Sauté carrot pieces, onions, garlic, and celery in oil in medium saucepan for 3 minutes, or until vegetables soften.

2. Sprinkle with flour.

3. Stir to combine. Cook 1–2 minutes.

4. Stir in chicken broth, chicken, grated carrots, poultry seasoning, garlic powder, and pepper until smooth.

5. Bring to boil. Simmer 5 minutes, or until thickened, stirring constantly.

6. To prepare dumplings, mix together flour, baking powder, and salt in mixing bowl.

7. In a separate bowl, combine milk, egg, and oil.

8. Add egg-milk mixture to dry ingredients, barely mixing.

9. Drop dumpling batter by tablespoonfuls onto simmering chicken.

10. Cook 10 minutes uncovered.

11. Then cover and cook an additional 10 minutes.

12. Pour half-and-half between dumplings into broth.

13. Scatter fresh parsley over top. Serve immediately.

Exchange List Values
- Starch 1.5
- Vegetable 1.0
- Lean Meat 1.0
- Fat 1.5

Basic Nutritional Values
- Calories 260 (Calories from Fat 90)
- Total Fat 10 gm (Saturated Fat 1.7 gm, Trans Fat 0.0 gm, Polyunsat Fat 2.6 gm, Monounsat Fat 5.4 gm)
- Cholesterol 45 mg
- Sodium 565 mg
- Potassium 430 gm
- Total Carb 30 gm
- Dietary Fiber 3 gm
- Sugars 6 gm
- Protein 12 gm
- Phosphorus 270 gm

Chicken Noodle Casserole

Leesa DeMartyn
Enola, PA

Makes 6 servings, 7–8 oz. per serving
Prep. Time: 15–20 minutes
Baking Time: 30 minutes

1 Tbsp. canola oil

¼ cup chopped onion

¼ cup chopped green bell pepper

8-oz. pkg. egg noodles, cooked and drained

2 cups cooked and cubed chicken

1 medium tomato, peeled and chopped

1 Tbsp. lemon juice

¼ tsp. salt

¼ tsp. pepper

½ cup fat-free mayonnaise

⅓ cup fat-free milk

⅓ cup shredded reduced-fat cheddar cheese

bread crumbs, *optional*

1. Warm canola oil in small skillet over medium heat.

2. Sauté onion and pepper about 5 minutes.

3. In large mixing bowl, combine sautéed vegetables with cooked noodles, chicken, tomato, lemon juice, salt, pepper, mayonnaise, and milk.

4. Turn into greased 2-qt. casserole.

5. Top with cheese, and with bread crumbs, if you wish.

6. Cover with foil. Bake at 400°F for 20–25 minutes, until heated through.

7. Let baked dish stand 10 minutes before serving to allow sauce to thicken.

Exchange List Values
- Starch 2.0
- Lean Meat 2.0
- Fat 1.0

Basic Nutritional Values
- Calories 290 (Calories from Fat 90)
- Total Fat 10 gm (Saturated Fat 2.4 gm, Trans Fat 0.0 gm, Polyunsat Fat 2.1 gm, Monounsat Fat 3.6 gm)
- Cholesterol 75 mg
- Sodium 360 mg
- Potassium 260 gm
- Total Carb 30 gm
- Dietary Fiber 2 gm
- Sugars 4 gm
- Protein 20 gm
- Phosphorus 230 gm

Creamy Chicken and Noodles

Rhonda Burgoon
Collingswood, NJ

Makes 6 servings
Prep. Time: 25 minutes
Cooking Time: 4¼–9¼ hours
Ideal slow-cooker size: 4-qt.

2 cups sliced carrots

1½ cups chopped onions

1 cup sliced celery

2 Tbsp. snipped fresh parsley

bay leaf

3 medium-sized chicken legs and thighs (about 2 lbs.), skin removed

2 10¾-oz. cans 98%-fat-free, reduced-sodium cream of chicken soup

½ cup water

1 tsp. dried thyme

¼ tsp. salt

¼ tsp. pepper

1 cup frozen peas

8 oz. dry wide noodles, cooked

1. Place carrots, onions, celery, parsley, and bay leaf in bottom of slow cooker.

2. Place chicken on top of vegetables.

3. Combine soup, water, thyme, salt, and pepper. Pour over chicken and vegetables.

4. Cover. Cook on Low 8–9 hours or High 4–4½ hours.

5. Remove chicken from slow cooker. Cool slightly. Remove from bones, cut into bite-sized pieces, and return to slow cooker.

6. Remove and discard bay leaf.

7. Stir peas into mixture in slow cooker. Allow to cook for 5–10 more minutes.

8. Pour over cooked noodles. Toss gently to combine.

Serving suggestion:
Serve with crusty bread and a salad.

Exchange List Values
- Starch 2.0
- Carbohydrate 0.5
- Vegetable 2.0
- Lean Meat 2.0

Basic Nutritional Values
- Calories 357 (Calories from Fat 71)
- Total Fat 8 gm (Saturated Fat 2.4 gm, Polyunsat Fat 2.3 gm, Monounsat Fat 2.3 gm)
- Cholesterol 87 mg
- Sodium 614 mg
- Total Carb 48 gm
- Dietary Fiber 5 gm
- Sugars 9 gm
- Protein 22 gm

Turkey

Traditional Turkey Breast

Hope Comerford
Clinton Township, MI

Makes 10–12 servings
Prep. Time: 10 minutes
Cooking Time: 8 hours
Ideal slow-cooker size: 7-qt.

7-lb. or less turkey breast

olive oil

4 Tbsp. (½ stick) butter

Rub:

2 tsp. garlic powder

1 tsp. onion powder

1 tsp. salt

¼ tsp. pepper

1 tsp. poultry seasoning

1. Remove gizzards from turkey breast, rinse it, and pat dry. Place breast into crock.

2. Rub turkey breast all over with olive oil.

3. Cut the butter into 8 pieces. Mix together all rub ingredients. Rub this mixture all over turkey breast and press it in.

4. Place the pieces of butter all over top of the breast.

5. Cover and cook on Low for 8 hours.

Exchange List Values
- Lean Meat 2.5
- Fat 1.0

Basic Nutritional Values
- Calories 347
  (Calories from Fat 108)
- Total Fat 12 gm
  (Saturated Fat 5 gm,
  Trans Fat 0.2 gm,
  Polyunsat Fat 2.2 gm,
  Monounsat Fat 4.3 gm)
- Cholesterol 200 mg
- Sodium 351 mg
- Potassium 466 gm
- Total Carb 1 gm
- Dietary Fiber 0 gm
- Sugars 0 gm
- Protein 6 gm
- Phosphorus 55 gm

Turkey

Hope's Meatloaf

Hope Comerford
Clinton Township, MI

Makes 10 servings
Prep. Time: 20 minutes
Cooking Time: 8 hours
Ideal slow-cooker size: 6-qt.

3 lbs. ground turkey

2 eggs

¾ cups gluten-free panko bread crumbs

¼ cup minced onion

1 Tbsp. onion powder

1 Tbsp. garlic powder

1 ½ tsp. salt

1 tsp. Italian seasoning

¼ tsp. pepper

1 tsp. Worchestershire sauce

1. Mix together all ingredients well.

2. Line crock with parchment paper.

3. Dump turkey mixture into crock and form into the shape of a loaf.

4. Cover and cook on Low for 8 hours.

5. Turn off the heat, remove lid, and let it sit for about 20 miutes. Remove from crock by holding the edges of the parchment paper. Slice and serve.

Exchange List Values
- Bread/Starch 0.5
- Lean Meat 1.0
- Fat 1.0

Basic Nutritional Values
- Calories 207 (Calories from Fat 90)
- Total Fat 10 gm (Saturated Fat 4 gm, Trans Fat 0.0 gm, Polyunsat Fat 0.0 gm, Monounsat Fat 0.0 gm)
- Cholesterol 96 mg
- Sodium 458 mg
- Potassium 49 gm
- Total Carb 4.7 gm
- Dietary Fiber 0.5 gm
- Sugars 0.4 gm
- Protein 28 gm
- Phosphorus 12 gm

Spinach Meatloaf

Ellie Oberholtzer
Ronks, PA

Makes 6 servings, 1 slice per serving
Prep. Time: 25 minutes
Baking Time: 60 minutes
Standing Time: 10 minutes

1 lb. 93%-lean ground turkey

10-oz. box frozen chopped spinach, thawed
and squeezed dry

¼ cup chopped fresh cilantro, or fresh
parsley

2 oz. crumbled fat-free feta cheese

2 Tbsp. molasses

¼ cup egg substitute

3 pieces millet, or other whole-grain, bread,
toasted and crumbled

1–2 tsp. poultry seasoning

¼ tsp. salt

¼ tsp. pepper

TIP

Instead of mixing the spinach into the
loaf, sometimes I pat the meat mixture
into a rectangular shape, about ½ inch
thick, onto a piece of wax paper. I spread
the spinach on top, in about ½ inch from
all the edges. I press the spinach down
to make it adhere. Then, using the wax
paper to lift the meat, I roll it into a loaf,
taking care to keep the spinach from
falling out. Remove wax paper. Then
bake as directed above.

1. In a large bowl, mix together turkey,
spinach, cilantro, cheese, molasses, egg
substitute, bread crumbs, poultry seasoning,
salt, and pepper.

2. Form mixture into a loaf.

3. Place in greased loaf pan.

4. Bake at 350°F for 60 minutes.

5. Allow to stand 10 minutes before slicing
and serving.

Exchange List Values
- Carbohydrate 1.0
- Lean Meat 3.0

Basic Nutritional Values
- Calories 195
  (Calories from Fat 65)
- Total Fat 7 gm
  (Saturated Fat 1.7 gm,
  Trans Fat 0.1 gm,
  Polyunsat Fat 2.2 gm,
  Monounsat Fat 2.2 gm)
- Cholesterol 55 mg
- Sodium 405 mg
- Potassium 430 gm
- Total Carb 14 gm
- Dietary Fiber 2 gm
- Sugars 5 gm
- Protein 21 gm
- Phosphorus 225 gm

Turkey Sloppy Joes

Marla Folkerts
Holland, OH

Makes 6 servings
Prep. Time: 20 minutes
Cooking Time: 4½–6 hours
Ideal slow-cooker size: 4-qt.

1 red onion, chopped

1 bell pepper, chopped

1½ lbs. boneless turkey, finely chopped

1 cup no-salt-added ketchup

½ tsp. salt

1 clove garlic, minced

1 tsp. Dijon-style mustard

⅛ tsp. pepper

6 (1½ oz. each) multigrain sandwich rolls

1. Place onion, bell pepper, and turkey in slow cooker.

2. Combine ketchup, salt, garlic, mustard, and pepper. Pour over turkey mixture. Mix well.

3. Cover. Cook on Low 4½–6 hours.

4. Serve on sandwich rolls.

Exchange List Values

- Starch 1.5
- Vegetable 3.0
- Lean Meat 1.0
- Fat 0.5

Basic Nutritional Values

- Calories 271 (Calories from Fat 49)
- Total Fat 5 gm (Saturated Fat 1.6 gm, Polyunsat Fat 1.3 gm, Monounsat Fat 1.8 gm)
- Cholesterol 40 mg
- Sodium 457 mg
- Total Carb 36 gm
- Dietary Fiber 3 gm
- Sugars 16 gm
- Protein 21 gm

Turkey

Turkey Supreme

Janet Suderman
Indianapolis, IN

Makes 6 servings, about 1 cup per serving
Prep. Time: 15 minutes
Cooking Time: about 20 minutes

2 cups sliced fresh mushrooms

1 small onion, chopped

1 cup thinly sliced celery

10¾-oz. can lower-sodium, lower-fat cream of chicken soup

1 cup fat-free milk

2 cups cubed, cooked turkey

2 cups herb-flavored stuffing

½ cup fat-free sour cream

¼–½ tsp. pepper

¼ cup sliced almonds

1. Combine mushrooms, onion, and celery in 2-qt. microwave-safe casserole dish.

2. Microwave on High, uncovered, 5–6 minutes or until vegetables are tender, stirring once.

3. Remove from microwave and add soup, milk, turkey, stuffing, sour cream, and pepper. Top with sliced almonds.

4. Cover and microwave on High 10–12 minutes or until heated through. Let stand about 5 minutes before serving.

Exchange List Values

- Starch 1.0
- Carbohydrate 1.0
- Lean Meat 2.0

Basic Nutritional Values

- Calories 250 (Calories from Fat 55)
- Total Fat 6 gm (Saturated Fat 1.5 gm, Trans Fat 0.0 gm, Polyunsat Fat 1.7 gm, Monounsat Fat 2.2 gm)
- Cholesterol 40 mg
- Sodium 530 mg
- Potassium 690 gm
- Total Carb 28 gm
- Dietary Fiber 3 gm
- Sugars 6 gm
- Protein 20 gm
- Phosphorus 245 gm

Favorite Enchilada Casserole

Janice Muller
Derwood, MD

Makes 8 servings, 3¼×4½-inch rectangle
  per serving
Prep. Time: 20 minutes
Baking Time: 30 minutes

1 lb. 93%-lean ground turkey

2 onions, chopped

1 red, or green, bell pepper, chopped

¾ cup beef gravy

1 cup water

1 tsp. reduced-sodium beef bouillon granules

10½-oz. can mild enchilada sauce

7-oz. can pitted black olives, *divided*

12 corn tortillas, *divided*

1 cup 75%-less-fat shredded cheddar cheese,
  divided

Exchange List Values
- Starch 1.0
- Vegetable 2.0
- Lean Meat 2.0
- Fat 1.0

Basic Nutritional Values
- Calories 260
  (Calories from Fat 80)
- Total Fat 9 gm
  (Saturated Fat 2.5 gm,
  Trans Fat 0.1 gm,
  Polyunsat Fat 2.2 gm,
  Monounsat Fat 3.3 gm)
- Cholesterol 50 mg
- Sodium 590 mg
- Potassium 465 gm
- Total Carb 26 gm
- Dietary Fiber 4 gm
- Sugars 3 gm
- Protein 19 gm
- Phosphorus 320 gm

1. In large nonstick skillet, brown ground turkey with onions and bell pepper, until meat is no longer pink and vegetables are just tender. Drain off any drippings.

2. In saucepan, heat gravy, water, beef bouillon granules, and enchilada sauce together.

3. Into a well-greased 9×13-inch baking pan layer 6 of the tortillas, half the turkey mixture, half the olives, half the sauce, and half the cheese.

4. Repeat layers.

5. Bake at 350°F for 30 minutes.

Polish Reuben Casserole

Jean Heyerly
Shipshewana, IN

Makes 12 servings, 3-inch square per
   serving
Prep. Time: 25–30 minutes
Baking Time: 1 hour

2 10¾-oz. cans lower-sodium, lower-fat
   cream of mushroom soup

1⅓ cups milk

1 Tbsp. prepared mustard

½ cup chopped onion

8 oz. sauerkraut (half of a 16-oz. can), rinsed
   and drained

2 cups shredded green cabbage

8-oz. pkg. uncooked medium-width noodles

12 oz. 95%-fat-free turkey kielbasa, cut in
   ½-inch-thick slices

1 cup shredded reduced-fat Swiss cheese

¾ cup whole wheat panko bread crumbs

1. Mix soup, milk, mustard, and onion in a bowl. Set aside.

2. Mix sauerkraut and cabbage. Spread mixture in well-greased 9×13-inch baking dish.

3. Top with uncooked noodles.

4. Spoon soup mixture evenly over noodles.

5. Top with sliced kielbasa.

6. Sprinkle with shredded cheese.

7. Sprinkle panko on top of cheese.

8. Cover with foil and bake at 350°F for 1 hour, or until noodles are tender.

Exchange List Values

- Starch 1.0
- Carbohydrate 1.0
- Med-Fat Meat 1.0

Basic Nutritional Values

- Calories 220
  (Calories from Fat 45)
- Total Fat 5 gm
  (Saturated Fat 2.2 gm,
  Trans Fat 0.0 gm,
  Polyunsat Fat 1.0 gm,
  Monounsat Fat 1.4 gm)
- Cholesterol 50 mg
- Sodium 580 mg
- Potassium 555 gm
- Total Carb 27 gm
- Dietary Fiber 2 gm
- Sugars 5 gm
- Protein 13 gm
- Phosphorus 220 gm

Smoked Sausage and Sauerkraut

Joan Terwilliger
Lebanon, PA

Makes 8 servings
Prep. Time: 20 minutes
Baking Time: 1¾–2 hours

2 Tbsp. trans-fat-free tub margarine

3 apples, peeled, halved, thickly sliced

1 large sweet onion, halved, thickly sliced

1½ lbs. (about 4) Yukon Gold potatoes, peeled, cut in ½-inch cubes

¼ cup Splenda Brown Sugar Blend

1½ Tbsp. Dijon mustard

½ lb. 95%-fat-free turkey kielbasa, sliced ½-inch thick

1 cup apple cider, or Riesling

1 lb. sauerkraut, rinsed and drained

1. Melt margarine in large ovenproof Dutch oven over medium-high heat.

2. Sauté apples and onion 10 minutes in margarine, stirring occasionally.

3. Add potatoes.

4. In small bowl, mix together Splenda and mustard. Add to onion-potato mixture.

5. Place kielbasa slices on top of onion-potato mixture.

6. Pour in cider or wine.

7. Place sauerkraut on top of sausage.

8. Bake, covered, at 350°F for 1¾–2 hours, or until potatoes are tender.

Exchange List Values
- Starch 1.0
- Fruit 0.5
- Vegetable 1.0
- Lean Meat 1.0
- Fat 0.5

Basic Nutritional Values
- Calories 200 (Calories from Fat 35)
- Total Fat 4 gm (Saturated Fat 1.3 gm, Trans Fat 0.0 gm, Polyunsat Fat 1.2 gm, Monounsat Fat 1.3 gm)
- Cholesterol 20 mg
- Sodium 600 mg
- Potassium 435 gm
- Total Carb 32 gm
- Dietary Fiber 3 gm
- Sugars 12 gm
- Protein 7 gm
- Phosphorus 105 gm

Italian Sausage and White Beans

Lucille Amos
Greensboro, NC

Makes 8 servings, about 6½ oz. per serving
Prep. Time: 15 minutes
Cooking/Baking Time: 3 hours

1 cup chopped onion

1 Tbsp. olive oil

12-oz. pkg. 95%-fat-free turkey kielbasa
  sausage

4½ cups cooked great northern beans (from
  approximately 2 cups dry beans)

14½-oz. can diced tomatoes

1 cup red wine or beef broth

1 tsp. Italian seasoning, salt-free

1 tsp. chopped garlic

½ tsp. black pepper

⅓ cup cooked, crumbled bacon

1. Sauté onion in olive oil in skillet until softened. Set aside.

2. Cut sausages in ½-inch slices.

3. Put onions and sausages in casserole dish or Dutch oven.

4. Add beans, tomatoes, wine or broth, Italian seasoning, garlic, and black pepper. Mix gently.

5. Bake covered at 325°F for 2 hours.

6. Remove lid. Stir. Return to oven, uncovered, for 20–40 minutes, until liquid is reduced to your preference.

7. Sprinkle top with bacon. Check seasonings. Serve.

Exchange List Values

- Starch 1.5
- Vegetable 1.0
- Lean Meat 2.0
- Fat 0.5

Basic Nutritional Values

- Calories 265
  (Calories from Fat 55)
- Total Fat 6 gm
  (Saturated Fat 2.0 gm,
  Trans Fat 0.0 gm,
  Polyunsat Fat 0.9 gm,
  Monounsat Fat 2.7 gm)
- Cholesterol 35 mg
- Sodium 580 mg
- Potassium 650 gm
- Total Carb 28 gm
- Dietary Fiber 8 gm
- Sugars 5 gm
- Protein 17 gm
- Phosphorus 280 gm

Seafood

Shrimp Creole

**Ethel Camardelle
Des Allemands, LA**

Makes 8 servings, about 1 cup per serving
Prep. Time: 20 minutes
Cooking Time: 1½ hours

1¾ lbs. raw shrimp, peeled

pepper, to taste

2 Tbsp. canola oil

1 cup chopped onion

1 cup chopped celery

½ cup chopped bell pepper

8-oz. can no-salt-added tomato paste

8-oz. can no-salt-added tomato sauce

1 Tbsp. Louisiana hot sauce

2½ cups water

3 cloves garlic, minced

1 cup chopped green onions

parsley

rice

1. Peel shrimp. Pepper to taste and set aside.

2. In a heavy saucepan, heat oil. Sauté onion, celery, and pepper until wilted.

3. Add tomato paste and cook 5 minutes over low heat, stirring constantly.

4. Add tomato sauce, hot sauce, and water. Cook for 1 hour, stirring occasionally.

5. Stir in shrimp and garlic. Cook another 15 minutes.

6. Sprinkle with green onions and parsley. Cook 2–3 more minutes.

7. Serve with rice.

Exchange List Values
- Vegetable 3.0
- Lean Meat 1.0
- Fat 0.5

Basic Nutritional Values
- Calories 150
  (Calories from Fat 40)
- Total Fat 4.5 gm
  (Saturated Fat 0.6 gm,
  Trans Fat 0.0 gm,
  Polyunsat Fat 1.4 gm,
  Monounsat Fat 2.5 gm)
- Cholesterol 120 mg
- Sodium 600 mg
- Potassium 600 gm
- Total Carb 13 gm
- Dietary Fiber 3 gm
- Sugars 6 gm
- Protein 15 gm
- Phosphorus 220 gm

Shrimp Jambalaya

Karen Ashworth
Duenweg, MO

Makes 8 servings
Prep. Time: 25 minutes
Cooking Time: 2¼ hours
Ideal slow-cooker size: 4-qt.

2 Tbsp. margarine

2 medium onions, chopped

2 green bell peppers, chopped

3 ribs celery, chopped

1 cup chopped extra-lean, lower-sodium
   cooked ham

2 cloves garlic, chopped

1½ cups instant rice

1½ cups 99%-fat-free, lower-sodium beef
   broth

28-oz. can chopped tomatoes

2 Tbsp. chopped parsley

1 tsp. dried basil

½ tsp. dried thyme

¼ tsp. pepper

⅛ tsp. cayenne pepper

1 lb. shelled, deveined, medium-sized shrimp

1 Tbsp. chopped fresh parsley

1. Melt margarine in slow cooker set on High. Add onions, peppers, celery, ham, and garlic. Cook 30 minutes.

2. Add rice. Cover and cook 15 minutes.

3. Add broth, tomatoes, 2 Tbsp. parsley, and remaining seasonings. Cover and cook on High 1 hour.

4. Add shrimp. Cook on High 30 minutes, or until liquid is absorbed.

5. Garnish with parsley.

Exchange List Values
- Starch 1.0
- Vegetable 2.0
- Lean Meat 1.0
- Fat 0.5

Basic Nutritional Values
- Calories 205
  (Calories from Fat 36)
- Total Fat 4 gm
  (Saturated Fat 0.8 gm,
  Polyunsat Fat 1.3 gm,
  Monounsat Fat 1.5 gm)
- Cholesterol 95 mg
- Sodium 529 mg
- Total Carb 26 gm
- Dietary Fiber 3 gm
- Sugars 7 gm
- Protein 16 gm

Seafood

Curried Shrimp

Charlotte Shaffer
East Earl, PA

Makes 5 servings
Prep. Time: 10 minutes
Cooking Time: 4–6 hours
Ideal slow-cooker size: 3- or 4-qt.

1 small onion, chopped

2 cups cooked shrimp

1½ tsp. curry powder

10¾-oz. can 98%-fat-free, lower-sodium cream of mushroom soup

1 cup fat-free sour cream

Serving suggestion:
Serve over rice or puff pastry.

1. Combine all ingredients except sour cream in slow cooker.

2. Cover. Cook on Low 4–6 hours.

3. Ten minutes before serving, stir in sour cream.

Exchange List Values
- Vegetable 1.5
- Fat 1.5

Basic Nutritional Values
- Calories 130
  (Calories from Fat 16)
- Total Fat 2 gm
  (Saturated Fat 0.6 gm,
  Polyunsat Fat 0.5 gm,
  Monounsat Fat 0.4 gm)
- Cholesterol 92 mg
- Sodium 390 mg
- Total Carb 15 gm
- Dietary Fiber 1 gm
- Sugars 5 gm
- Protein 12 gm

Scalloped Scallops

Flossie Sultzaberger
Mechanicsburg, PA

Makes 6 servings, about 2 oz. per serving
Prep. Time: 15 minutes
Baking Time: 25 minutes

2 Tbsp. trans-fat-free tub margarine

2 Tbsp. canola oil

½ cup snack-cracker crumbs (preferably Wheat Thins)

¼ cup soft bread crumbs

1 lb. scallops (if large, cut in half)

cooking spray

dash salt

dash pepper

TIP

Add a few shrimp to the scallops for a very special dish.

1. Melt margarine and oil together in saucepan.

2. Stir in cracker crumbs and bread crumbs.

3. Spray a 1½–2-qt. casserole lightly with cooking spray.

4. Place half the scallops in bottom of baking dish.

5. Sprinkle with salt and pepper.

6. Cover with half of crumbs.

7. Repeat layers.

8. Bake at 400°F for 25 minutes.

Exchange List Values
- Starch 0.5
- Lean Meat 1.0
- Fat 1.5

Basic Nutritional Values
- Calories 155 (Calories from Fat 80)
- Total Fat 9 gm (Saturated Fat 1.2 gm, Trans Fat 0.1 gm, Polyunsat Fat 3.2 gm, Monounsat Fat 4.2 gm)
- Cholesterol 20 mg
- Sodium 450 mg
- Potassium 170 gm
- Total Carb 8 gm
- Dietary Fiber 0 gm
- Sugars 1 gm
- Protein 11 gm
- Phosphorus 225 gm

Seafood

Herbed Potato Fish Bake

Barbara Sparks
Glen Burnie, MD

Makes 4 servings
Prep. Time: 25 minutes
Cooking Time: 1–2 hours
Ideal slow-cooker size: 4-qt.

10¾-oz. can cream of celery soup

½ cup water

1-lb. perch fillet, fresh or thawed

2 cups cooked, diced potatoes

¼ cup freshly grated Parmesan cheese

1 Tbsp. chopped parsley

½ tsp. dried basil

¼ tsp. dried oregano

1. Combine soup and water. Pour half in slow cooker.

2. Lay fillet on top. Place potatoes on fillet. Pour remaining soup mix over top.

3. Combine cheese and herbs. Sprinkle over ingredients in slow cooker.

4. Cover. Cook on High 1–2 hours, being careful not to overcook fish.

Exchange List Values
- Starch 1.0
- Carbohydrate 0.5
- Lean Meat 3.0

Basic Nutritional Values
- Calories 269
  (Calories from Fat 73)
- Total Fat 8 gm
  (Saturated Fat 2.8 gm,
  Polyunsat Fat 2.3 gm,
  Monounsat Fat 2.2 gm)
- Cholesterol 56 mg
- Sodium 696 mg
- Total Carb 22 gm
- Dietary Fiber 2 gm
- Sugars 2 gm
- Protein 26 gm

Spanish Paella

Melodie Davis
Harrisonburg, VA

Makes 10 servings, about 11 oz. per serving
Prep. Time: 20 minutes
Cooking Time: 50 minutes

1¼ lbs. boneless skinless chicken thighs, cut in 5 pieces

1¼ lbs. boneless skinless chicken breasts, cut in 5 pieces

¼ cup olive oil

¼ lb. lean boneless pork chop, cubed

¼ lb. bulk lean Italian turkey sweet sausage

8 slices onion

4 medium tomatoes, diced

1 green pepper, chopped

2 cups uncooked rice

3 cups lower-sodium, fat-free chicken broth

2 Tbsp. paprika

½ tsp. pepper

¼ tsp. red pepper

⅛ tsp. saffron

pinch minced garlic

1¾ cups shrimp, shelled and deveined

10-oz. pkg. frozen green peas

4-oz. jar sliced pimento, drained

1. Wash chicken pieces and dry. In Dutch oven or heavy kettle, brown chicken in oil. Remove chicken and drain excess fat.

2. Brown pork and sausage. Remove and drain excess fat.

3. Sauté onions, tomatoes, and green pepper, stirring until onion is tender. Stir in rice, chicken broth, and seasonings. Add chicken.

4. Cover tightly and simmer for 20 minutes.

5. Gently fold in shrimp, pork, sausage, and peas. Cover and simmer another 15 minutes.

6. Add pimento, heat through, and serve.

Exchange List Values
- Starch 2.0
- Vegetable 1.0
- Lean Meat 4.0
- Fat 1.5

Basic Nutritional Values
- Calories 435 (Calories from Fat 125)
- Total Fat 14 gm (Saturated Fat 3.1 gm, Trans Fat 0.0 gm, Polyunsat Fat 2.5 gm, Monounsat Fat 6.9 gm)
- Cholesterol 135 mg
- Sodium 575 mg
- Potassium 610 gm
- Total Carb 39 gm
- Dietary Fiber 4 gm
- Sugars 4 gm
- Protein 37 gm
- Phosphorus 365 gm

Company Seafood Pasta

Jennifer Yoder Sommers
Harrisonburg, VA

Makes 8 servings
Prep. Time: 35 minutes
Cooking Time: 1–2 hours
Ideal slow-cooker size: 4-qt.

2 cups fat-free sour cream

1¼ cups shredded reduced-fat Monterey Jack cheese

1 Tbsp. light, soft tub margarine, melted

½ lb. fresh crabmeat

⅛ tsp. pepper

½ lb. bay scallops, lightly cooked

1 lb. medium shrimp, cooked and peeled

4 cups cooked linguine

fresh parsley, for garnish

1. Combine sour cream, cheese, and margarine in slow cooker.

2. Stir in remaining ingredients, except linguine and parsley.

3. Cover. Cook on Low 1–2 hours.

4. Serve immediately over linguine. Garnish with fresh parsley.

Exchange List Values
- Starch 2.0
- Lean Meat 3.0

Basic Nutritional Values
- Calories 308 (Calories from Fat 59)
- Total Fat 7 gm (Saturated Fat 3.1 gm, Polyunsat Fat 1.1 gm, Monounsat Fat 2.1 gm)
- Cholesterol 127 mg
- Sodium 449 mg
- Total Carb 31 gm
- Dietary Fiber 1 gm
- Sugars 5 gm
- Protein 29 gm

Seafood

Seafood Gumbo

Barbara Katrine Rose
Woodbridge, VA

Makes 6 servings
Prep. Time: 40 minutes
Cooking Time: 2½–3 hours
Ideal slow-cooker size: 4- or 5-qt.

1 lb. okra, sliced

3 Tbsp. canola oil, *divided*

¼ cup flour

1 bunch green onions, sliced

½ cup chopped celery

2 cloves garlic, minced

16-oz. can diced tomatoes and juice

1 bay leaf

1 Tbsp. chopped fresh parsley

1 fresh thyme sprig

½ tsp. salt

½–1 tsp. red pepper

3–5 cups water, depending upon the
 consistency you like

1 lb. peeled, deveined fresh shrimp

½ lb. fresh crabmeat

1. Sauté okra in 1 Tbsp. canola oil until okra is lightly browned. Transfer to slow cooker.

2. Combine remaining 2 Tbsp. canola oil and flour in skillet. Cook over medium heat, stirring constantly until roux is the color of chocolate, 20–25 minutes.

3. Stir in green onions, celery, and garlic. Cook until vegetables are tender. Add to slow cooker.

4. Gently stir in tomatoes with juice, bay leaf, parsley, thyme, salt, red pepper, and water.

5. Cover. Cook on High 2 hours.

6. Add shrimp, crab, and additional water if you wish. Cover. Cook an additional 30–60 minutes on high, until shrimp is cooked and crab is heated.

Exchange List Values
- Vegetable 3.0
- Meat, Very Lean 2.0
- Fat 1.5

Basic Nutritional Values
- Calories 221
 (Calories from Fat 75)
- Total Fat 8 gm
 (Saturated Fat 0.7 gm,
 Polyunsat Fat 2.6 gm,
 Monounsat Fat 4.3 gm)
- Cholesterol 148 mg
- Sodium 548 mg
- Total Carb 15 gm
- Dietary Fiber 3 gm
- Sugars 5 gm
- Protein 22 gm

Tuna Bake with Cheese Swirls

Mary Ann Lefever
Lancaster, PA

Makes 8 servings, 3¼×4½-inch rectangle
  per serving
Prep. Time: 30 minutes
Baking Time: 25 minutes

½ cup diced green bell pepper

½ cup chopped onion

2 Tbsp. canola oil

6 Tbsp. flour

2 cups fat-free milk

6½- or 7-oz. can or pouch tuna

Cheese Swirls:

1½ cups reduced-fat buttermilk biscuit mix

¾ cup grated 50%-less fat cheddar cheese

½ cup fat-free milk

2 chopped pimentos (from jar)

1. In saucepan, sauté green pepper and onion in oil until soft but not brown.

2. Blend in flour and cook over low heat a few minutes to get rid of raw flour taste.

3. Gradually stir in milk. Cook over low heat, stirring continually until smooth.

4. Add tuna.

5. Spoon into greased 9×13-inch baking pan. Set aside.

6. To make cheese swirls, prepare biscuits with milk according to package directions.

7. On lightly floured board, roll out to 8×13-inch rectangle.

8. Sprinkle with cheese and chopped pimento. Press into dough to help adhere.

9. Roll up jelly-roll fashion.

10. Cut roll into 8 slices.

11. Flatten slightly and place on top of tuna mixture.

12. Bake at 450°F for 25 minutes, or until tuna mix is bubbly and biscuits are browned.

Exchange List Values
- Starch 1.5
- Lean Meat 2.0

Basic Nutritional Values
- Calories 215
  (Calories from Fat 65)
- Total Fat 7 gm
  (Saturated Fat 1.7 gm,
  Trans Fat 0.0 gm,
  Polyunsat Fat 1.5 gm,
  Monounsat Fat 3.6 gm)
- Cholesterol 15 mg
- Sodium 440 mg
- Potassium 270 gm
- Total Carb 26 gm
- Dietary Fiber 1 gm
- Sugars 7 gm
- Protein 13 gm
- Phosphorus 310 gm

Seafood

Tuna Noodle Casserole

Leona Miller
Millersburg, OH

Makes 6 servings
Prep. Time: 20 minutes
Cooking Time: 3–9 hours
Ideal slow-cooker size: 4-qt.

2 6½-oz. cans water-packed tuna, drained

2 10½-oz. cans 98%-fat-free, lower-sodium cream of mushroom soup

1 cup milk

2 Tbsp. dried parsley

10-oz. pkg. frozen mixed vegetables, thawed

8-oz. pkg. noodles, cooked and drained

½ cup toasted sliced almonds

1. Combine tuna, soup, milk, parsley, and vegetables. Fold in noodles. Pour into greased slow cooker. Top with almonds.

2. Cover. Cook on Low 7–9 hours, or High 3–4 hours.

Exchange List Values
- Starch 2.0
- Carbohydrate 1.0
- Lean Meat 3.0

Basic Nutritional Values
- Calories 395 (Calories from Fat 101)
- Total Fat 11 gm (Saturated Fat 1.9 gm, Polyunsat Fat 2.5 gm, Monounsat Fat 5.7 gm)
- Cholesterol 21 mg
- Sodium 637 mg
- Total Carb 46 gm
- Dietary Fiber 5 gm
- Sugars 8 gm
- Protein 27 gm

Meatless

Creamy Crunchy Mac and Cheese

Kathy Hertzler
Lancaster, PA

Makes 10 servings, a 2⅗×4½-inch rectangle per serving
Prep. Time: 25 minutes
Cooking/Baking Time: 30 minutes

1 lb. uncooked macaroni

2 cups fat-free milk

1½ Tbsp. canola oil

3 Tbsp. flour

3½ cups shredded 75%-less-fat cheddar cheese, *divided*

½ tsp. seasoned salt

½ tsp. ground black pepper

1 tsp. dry mustard

1 tsp. garlic powder, or 2 cloves garlic, minced

1 tsp. onion powder, or ¼ cup chopped onions

¾ cup crushed cornflakes

1. Cook macaroni until al dente in unsalted water, according to package directions, about 7 minutes. Drain well.

2. While pasta is cooking, warm milk until steamy but not boiling.

3. In another medium-sized saucepan, warm oil. Add flour, and whisk until smooth.

4. Add warm milk to oil/flour mixture. Whisk until smooth.

5. Cook, stirring constantly, on low heat for 2 minutes.

6. Add 3 cups shredded cheddar. Stir well, and then remove from heat. Set aside.

7. Stir salt, pepper, mustard, minced garlic or garlic powder, and chopped onions or onion powder into creamy sauce.

8. Place cooked macaroni in large mixing bowl.

9. Stir in cheese sauce.

10. Transfer mixture to greased 9×13-inch baking dish.

11. Sprinkle with cornflakes, and then remaining shredded cheddar.

12. Bake at 400°F for 10–12 minutes, or until hot and bubbly.

Exchange List Values
- Starch 3.0
- Lean Meat 2.0

Basic Nutritional Values
- Calories 320 (Calories from Fat 65)
- Total Fat 7 gm (Saturated Fat 2.4 gm, Trans Fat 0.0 gm, Polyunsat Fat 1.0 gm, Monounsat Fat 2.2 gm)
- Cholesterol 15 mg
- Sodium 400 mg
- Potassium 185 gm
- Total Carb 43 gm
- Dietary Fiber 2 gm
- Sugars 4 gm
- Protein 21 gm
- Phosphorus 310 gm

Meatless

Slow Cooker Macaraoni

Lisa F. Good
Harrisonburg, VA

Makes 6 servings
Prep. Time: 10 minutes
Cooking Time: 3–4 hours
Ideal slow-cooker size: 4-qt.

1½ cups dry macaroni

1½ Tbsp. light, soft tub margarine

6 oz. reduced-fat Velveeta cheese, sliced

2 cups fat-free milk

1 cup fat-free half-and-half

1. Combine macaroni and margarine.

2. Layer cheese over top.

3. Pour in milk and half-and-half.

4. Cover. Cook on High 3–4 hours, or until macaroni is soft.

Exchange List Values
- Starch 1.0
- Fat-Free Milk 1.0
- Fat 1.0

Basic Nutritional Values
- Calories 208
  (Calories from Fat 45)
- Total Fat 5 gm
  (Saturated Fat 2.5 gm,
  Polyunsat Fat 0.5 gm,
  Monounsat Fat 1.6 gm)
- Cholesterol 15 mg
- Sodium 555 mg
- Total Carb 27 gm
- Dietary Fiber 0 gm
- Sugars 12 gm
- Protein 14 gm

Spinach Cheese Manicotti

Kimberly Richard
Mars, PA

Makes 7 servings, 2 stuffed shells and about
⅔ cup sauce per serving
Prep. Time: 35 minutes
Baking Time: 45 minutes

15-oz. container fat-free ricotta cheese

10-oz. pkg. frozen chopped spinach, thawed
and squeezed dry

½ cup minced onion

¼ cup egg substitute

2 tsp. parsley

½ tsp. black pepper

½ tsp. garlic powder

2 tsp. dried basil

1¼ cups part-skim shredded mozzarella,
divided

½ cup freshly grated Parmesan, *divided*

24½-oz. jar marinara pasta sauce, light in
sodium

1½ cups water

1 cup diced fresh tomatoes

8-oz. pkg. manicotti shells

1. In large bowl combine ricotta, spinach,
onion, and egg substitute.

2. Stir in parsley, black pepper, garlic, and
basil.

3. Mix in 1 cup mozzarella and ¼ cup
Parmesan cheese.

4. In separate bowl, mix together sauce,
water, and tomatoes.

5. Grease 9×13-inch baking pan. Spread 1
cup spaghetti sauce in bottom of pan.

6. Stuff uncooked manicotti with ricotta
mixture. Arrange in single layer in baking
pan.

7. Cover stuffed manicotti with remaining
sauce.

8. Sprinkle with remaining cheeses.

9. Cover. Bake at 350 degrees for 45
minutes, or until bubbly.

Exchange List Values

- Starch 2.0
- Vegetable 1.0
- Lean Meat 2.0
- Fat 1.0

Basic Nutritional Values

- Calories 325
  (Calories from Fat 80)
- Total Fat 9 gm
  (Saturated Fat 3.4 gm,
  Trans Fat 0.0 gm,
  Polyunsat Fat 1.8 gm,
  Monounsat Fat 2.3 gm)
- Cholesterol 35 mg
- Sodium 555 mg
- Potassium 640 gm
- Total Carb 40 gm
- Dietary Fiber 5 gm
- Sugars 9 gm
- Protein 22 gm
- Phosphorus 350 gm

Meatless

Garden Lasagna

Deb Martin
Gap, PA

Makes 12 servings, 3-inch square per
serving
Prep. Time: 30 minutes
Baking Time: 70–75 minutes

8 oz. lasagna noodles, *divided*

1 lb. bag frozen broccoli, cauliflower, and
carrots, *divided*

2 10¾-oz. cans lower-sodium, fat-free cream
of chicken soup

1 cup fat-free sour cream

¾ cup lower-sodium, lower-fat chicken broth

½ cup egg substitute

3 cups cooked chopped chicken, *divided*

½ cup freshly grated Parmesan cheese,
divided

1 cup part-skim mozzarella cheese, shredded

1. Cook noodles according to package
directions. Drain well.

2. Steam vegetables until lightly cooked.
Drain well.

3. In large bowl, mix soup, sour cream,
broth, and egg substitute.

4. Place small amount of sauce on bottom
of greased 9×13-inch baking pan. Swirl to
cover bottom.

5. Layer 3 lasagna noodles on top of sauce.

6. Add half of soup mixture.

7. Top with half of chicken.

8. Top with half of vegetables.

9. Sprinkle with half of Parmesan cheese.

10. Repeat layers, using all remaining
amounts of ingredients.

11. Top with mozzarella cheese.

12. Bake, covered, at 350°F for 1 hour.

13. Uncover. Bake another 10–15 minutes.

Exchange List Values
- Starch 1.0
- Carbohydrate 0.5
- Lean Meat 2.0
- Fat 0.5

Basic Nutritional Values
- Calories 235
  (Calories from Fat 55)
- Total Fat 6 gm
  (Saturated Fat 2.5 gm,
  Trans Fat 0.0 gm,
  Polyunsat Fat 1.3 gm,
  Monounsat Fat 1.8 gm)
- Cholesterol 45 mg
- Sodium 395 mg
- Potassium 460 gm
- Total Carb 24 gm
- Dietary Fiber 2 gm
- Sugars 3 gm
- Protein 19 gm
- Phosphorus 215 gm

Meatless Lasagna Roll-Ups

Judy Buller
Bluffton, OH

Makes 12 servings, 1 roll per serving
Prep. Time: 30 minutes
Baking Time: 25–30 minutes

12 uncooked whole-grain lasagna noodles

2 eggs, slightly beaten

2½ cups fat-free ricotta cheese

2½ cups shredded part-skim mozzarella cheese, *divided*

½ cup freshly grated Parmesan cheese

1 pkg. frozen, chopped spinach, thawed and squeezed dry, or 4 cups chopped fresh spinach that has been microwaved on High 1–2 minutes and squeezed dry

¼ tsp. salt

¼ tsp. pepper

1–2 cups cooked black beans, rinsed and drained

24½-oz. jar marinara pasta sauce, light in sodium, *divided*

1. Cook lasagna noodles according to box directions in unsalted water. Drain and rinse well. Lay flat.

2. In a good-sized mixing bowl, mix together eggs, ricotta cheese, 1½ cups mozzarella cheese, Parmesan cheese, spinach, salt, and pepper.

3. Spread about ⅓ cup mixture on each noodle.

4. Sprinkle each noodle with black beans. Press down to make beans adhere.

5. Spread 1 cup marinara sauce in bottom of well greased 9×13-inch baking pan.

6. Roll up noodles and place seam side down in baking pan.

7. Top rolls with remaining sauce. Sprinkle with 1 cup mozzarella cheese.

8. Bake uncovered at 350°F for 25–30 minutes, or until heated through.

Exchange List Values

- Starch 2.0
- Lean Meat 2.0

Basic Nutritional Values

- Calories 250 (Calories from Fat 65)
- Total Fat 7 gm (Saturated Fat 2.5 gm, Trans Fat 0.0 gm, Polyunsat Fat 1.2 gm, Monounsat Fat 1.8 gm)
- Cholesterol 60 mg
- Sodium 420 mg
- Potassium 405 gm
- Total Carb 29 gm
- Dietary Fiber 5 gm
- Sugars 5 gm
- Protein 19 gm
- Phosphorus 285 gm

TIP

You can assemble this dish ahead of time, and then freeze or refrigerate it until you're ready to use it. Allow more time to bake if the dish is cold, probably 45–50 minutes. But check while baking so as not to have it dry out or be over-baked.

Meatless

Spinach in Phyllo

Jeanette Zacharias
Morden, MB

Makes 20 slices, 1 slice per serving
Prep. Time: 25 minutes
Cooling Time: 20 minutes
Cooking/Baking Time: 45 minutes

1 medium onion, finely chopped

10-oz. pkg. frozen spinach, thawed and drained

1 cup finely chopped mushrooms

1 clove garlic, crushed

1 Tbsp. dried oregano

2 Tbsp. white wine

1 cup low-fat 1% milkfat cottage cheese

1 egg

salt and pepper, to taste

12 14×18-inch sheets phyllo dough

¼ cup trans-fat-free tub margarine, melted

1. Sauté onion in nonstick skillet until transparent.

2. Chop spinach into fine pieces.

3. To onions in skillet add spinach, mushrooms, garlic, oregano, and wine. Cook until most of moisture has evaporated. Cool at least 20 minutes.

4. Combine cottage cheese and egg. Add cooled spinach mixture. Add salt and pepper.

5. Spread phyllo sheets out and layer one on top of the other, brushing melted margarine over each sheet.

6. On last phyllo sheet put spinach filling. Roll up, being careful to fold in ends.

7. Lay seam-side down on greased cookie sheet. Brush phyllo roll with melted margarine.

8. Bake at 350°F for 30–35 minutes or until golden brown and crisp.

9. Slice in 20 slices and serve either hot or cold.

Exchange List Values
- Starch 0.5
- Fat 0.5

Basic Nutritional Values
- Calories 75 (Calories from Fat 20)
- Total Fat 2.5 gm (Saturated Fat 0.5 gm, Trans Fat 0.0 gm, Polyunsat Fat 0.9 gm, Monounsat Fat 0.7 gm)
- Cholesterol 10 mg
- Sodium 130 mg
- Potassium 80 gm
- Total Carb 10 gm
- Dietary Fiber 1 gm
- Sugars 1 gm
- Protein 3 gm
- Phosphorus 40 gm

Zucchini Supper

Susan Kastings
Jenks, OK

Makes 8 servings, 3¼×4½-inch rectangle
  per serving
Prep. Time: 15 minutes
Baking Time: 25–30 minutes

4 cups thinly sliced zucchini

1 cup reduced-fat buttermilk baking mix

½ cup chopped green onions

½ cup freshly grated Parmesan cheese

2 Tbsp. chopped parsley, fresh or dried

½ tsp. dried oregano

½ tsp. pepper

½ tsp. garlic powder

½ tsp. seasoned salt

¼ cup canola oil

½ cup fat-free milk

1 cup egg substitute

Exchange List Values
- Starch 1.0
- Lean Meat 1.0
- Fat 1.0

Basic Nutritional Values
- Calories 165
  (Calories from Fat 80)
- Total Fat 9 gm
  (Saturated Fat 1.4 gm,
  Trans Fat 0.0 gm,
  Polyunsat Fat 2.2 gm,
  Monounsat Fat 5.2 gm)
- Cholesterol 5 mg
- Sodium 400 mg
- Potassium 265 gm
- Total Carb 14 gm
- Dietary Fiber 1 gm
- Sugars 3 gm
- Protein 7 gm
- Phosphorus 165 gm

1. In a large mixing bowl, mix together zucchini, baking mix, green onions, cheese, parsley, oregano, pepper, garlic powder, seasoned salt, oil, milk, and egg substitute.

2. Pour into well-greased 9×13-inch baking pan.

3. Bake at 350°F for 25–30 minutes, or until firm.

4. Serve warm or at room temperature.

Meatless

Stuffed Eggplant

Jean Harris Robinson
Pemberton, NJ

Makes 8 servings, ¼ eggplant per serving
Prep. Time: 30 minutes
Baking Time: 30–45 minutes

2 large eggplants

1 medium onion, chopped

4 tomatoes, chopped

3 medium green bell peppers, chopped

1 rib celery, chopped

2 Tbsp. olive oil

½ cup egg substitute

1 tsp. salt

1 tsp. pepper

½ cup freshly grated Parmesan cheese

¼ tsp. cayenne pepper, *optional*

½ tsp. grated garlic, *optional*

1. Cut eggplants in half and scrape out seeds. Parboil* 15 minutes.

2. After eggplant halves have drained, remove pulp within ½-inch of outer "shell." Chop pulp. Set aside.

3. Place eggplant shells, cut-side up, in 12×24-inch baking dish.

4. Empty stockpot of water. Place onion, tomatoes, peppers, and celery, and olive oil in stockpot. Cook until soft and almost a purée. Remove from heat.

5. Stir in eggplant pulp, egg substitute, salt, and pepper.

6. Fill eggplant halves with the mixture. Sprinkle with cheese.

7. Distribute any leftover stuffing in baking dish around eggplant halves.

8. Bake at 350°F for 30 minutes, or until eggplant is tender and cheese is brown.

*To parboil eggplants, submerge unpeeled halves in a stockpot of boiling water with a shake of salt added. Cook in boiling water for 15 minutes. Remove and drain.

TIP

I have used 4–5 whole canned tomatoes when I haven't been able to find fresh tomatoes. Before adding them to the mixture (Step 4), I've chopped them, and drained off as much of their liquid as I could.

Exchange List Values
- Vegetable 4.0
- Fat 1.0

Basic Nutritional Values
- Calories 145 (Calories from Fat 45)
- Total Fat 5 gm (Saturated Fat 1.3 gm, Trans Fat 0.0 gm, Polyunsat Fat 0.6 gm, Monounsat Fat 2.9 gm)
- Cholesterol 5 mg
- Sodium 405 mg
- Potassium 515 gm
- Total Carb 22 gm
- Dietary Fiber 6 gm
- Sugars 9 gm
- Protein 6 gm
- Phosphorus 90 gm

Tempeh-Stuffed Peppers

Sara Harter Fredette
Williamsburg, MA

Makes 4 servings
Prep. Time: 35 minutes
Cooking Time: 3–8 hours
Ideal slow-cooker size: 6-qt. oval, so the
   peppers can each sit on the bottom of
   slow cooker

4 oz. tempeh, cubed

1 clove garlic, minced

2 14½-oz. cans diced no-salt-added
   tomatoes, *divided*

2 tsp. soy sauce

¼ cup chopped onion

1½ cups cooked rice

1 cup shredded fat-free cheddar cheese,
   divided

Tabasco sauce, *optional*

4 green, red, or yellow, bell peppers, with
   tops sliced off and seeds removed

1. Steam tempeh 10 minutes in saucepan.
Mash in bowl with the garlic, half the
tomatoes, and soy sauce.

2. Stir in onion, rice, ½ cup cheese, and
Tabasco sauce (if using). Stuff into peppers.

3. Place peppers in slow cooker. Pour
remaining half of tomatoes over peppers.

4. Cover. Cook on Low 6–8 hours, or High
3–4 hours. Top with remaining cheese in last
30 minutes.

Exchange List Values
- Starch 2.0
- Vegetable 3.0
- Lean Meat 1.0

Basic Nutritional Values
- Calories 266
  (Calories from Fat 26)
- Total Fat 3 gm
  (Saturated Fat 0.1 gm,
  Polyunsat Fat 1.5 gm,
  Monounsat Fat 0.6 gm)
- Cholesterol 4 mg
- Sodium 510 mg
- Total Carb 42 gm
- Dietary Fiber 6 gm
- Sugars 17 gm
- Protein 21 gm

Meatless

Middle Eastern Lentils

Judith Houser
Hershey, PA

Makes 8 servings (a serving of lentils is about 6 oz. with ⅛ of the salad)
Prep. Time: 20 minutes
Cooking Time: 50–60 minutes

Lentils:
2 large onions, chopped

1 Tbsp. olive oil

¾ cup brown rice, uncooked

1½ tsp. salt

1½ cups lentils, rinsed

4 cups water

Salad:
1 bunch (about ½ lb.) leaf lettuce

2 medium tomatoes, diced

1 medium cucumber, peeled and sliced

2 green onions, chopped

1 red bell pepper, diced

Dressing:
2 Tbsp. olive oil

2 Tbsp. lemon juice

½ tsp. paprika

¼ tsp. dry mustard

1 clove garlic, finely minced

¼ tsp. salt

½ tsp. sugar

1. In a large kettle, prepare lentils by sautéing onions in olive oil until soft and golden.

2. Add rice and salt. Continue cooking over medium heat for 3 minutes.

3. Stir in lentils and water. Bring to a simmer.

4. Cover and cook until rice and lentils are tender, 50–60 minutes.

5. While the lentil mixture cooks, prepare salad by tossing together lettuce, tomatoes, cucumber, onions, and pepper in a good-sized mixing bowl.

6. Place all dressing ingredients in a jar with a tight-fitting lid. Shake vigorously until well mixed.

7. Just before serving, shake dressing again to make sure it's thoroughly mixed. Then toss salad with dressing.

8. To serve each individual, place serving of lentil mixture on dinner plate and top with a generous serving of salad.

Exchange List Values
- Starch 2.0
- Vegetable 1.0
- Lean Meat 1.0
- Fat 1.0

Basic Nutritional Values
- Calories 270 (Calories from Fat 55)
- Total Fat 6 gm (Saturated Fat 0.9 gm, Trans Fat 0.0 gm, Polyunsat Fat 1.0 gm, Monounsat Fat 4.0 gm)
- Cholesterol 0 mg
- Sodium 525 mg
- Potassium 685 gm
- Total Carb 43 gm
- Dietary Fiber 11 gm
- Sugars 7 gm
- Protein 12 gm
- Phosphorus 275 gm

Lentil, Rice, and Veggie Bake

Andrea Zuercher
Lawrence, KS

Makes 12 servings, 3-inch square per serving
Prep. Time: 20 minutes
Baking Time: 65–70 minutes

1 cup uncooked long-grain rice

5 cups water, *divided*

2 cups red lentils

2 tsp. vegetable oil

2 small onions, chopped

6 cloves garlic, minced

2 fresh tomatoes, chopped

2/3 cup chopped celery

2/3 cup chopped carrots

2/3 cup chopped summer squash

16-oz. can tomato sauce, *divided*

2 tsp. dried, or 2 Tbsp. fresh basil, *divided*

2 tsp. dried, or 2 Tbsp. fresh oregano, *divided*

2 tsp. ground cumin, *divided*

3/4 tsp. salt, *divided*

1/2 tsp. pepper, *divided*

1. Cook rice according to package directions, using 2 cups water and cooking about 20 minutes. Set aside.

2. Cook lentils with remaining 3 cups water until tender, about 15 minutes. Set aside.

3. Heat oil in good-sized skillet over medium heat. Stir in onions and garlic. Sauté 5 minutes, or until just tender.

4. Stir in tomatoes, celery, carrots, squash, and half the tomato sauce.

5. Season with half the herbs, salt, and pepper.

6. Cook until vegetables are tender. Add water if too dry.

7. Place cooked, rice, lentils and vegetables in well-greased 9×13-inch baking pan, or equivalent-size casserole dish. Layer, or mix together, whichever you prefer.

8. Top with remaining tomato sauce and seasonings.

9. Bake at 350°F for 30 minutes, or until bubbly.

Exchange List Values

- Starch 2.0
- Vegetable 1.0

Basic Nutritional Values

- Calories 200 (Calories from Fat 15)
- Total Fat 2 gm (Saturated Fat 0.2 gm, Trans Fat 0.0 gm, Polyunsat Fat 0.5 gm, Monounsat Fat 0.6 gm)
- Cholesterol 0 mg
- Sodium 355 mg
- Potassium 620 gm
- Total Carb 38 gm
- Dietary Fiber 9 gm
- Sugars 5 gm
- Protein 11 gm
- Phosphorus 215 gm

Meatless

Minestra Di Ceci

Jeanette Oberholtzer
Manheim, PA

Makes 8 servings
Soaking Time: 8 hours
Prep. Time: 20 minutes
Cooking Time: 5½–6 hours
Ideal slow-cooker size: 4-qt.

1 lb. dry chickpeas

1 sprig fresh rosemary

10 leaves fresh sage

1 Tbsp. salt

1–2 large cloves garlic, minced

1 tsp. olive oil

1 cup small dry pasta, your choice of shape

1. Wash chickpeas. Place in slow cooker. Soak for 8 hours in full pot of water, along with rosemary, sage, and salt.

2. Drain water. Remove herbs.

3. Refill slow cooker with water to 1-inch above peas.

4. Cover. Cook on Low 5 hours.

5. Sauté garlic in olive oil in skillet until clear.

6. Purée half of chick peas, along with several cups of broth from cooker, in blender. Return purée to slow cooker. Add garlic and oil.

7. Boil pasta in saucepan until al dente, about 5 minutes. Drain. Add to beans.

8. Cover. Cook on High 30–60 minutes, or until pasta is tender and heated through, but not mushy.

Variation:
Add ½ tsp. black pepper to Step 1, if you like.

Exchange List Values
- Starch 2.5
- Meat, Very Lean 1.0

Basic Nutritional Values
- Calories 236 (Calories from Fat 34)
- Total Fat 4 gm (Saturated Fat 0.4 gm, Polyunsat Fat 1.5 gm, Monounsat Fat 1.1 gm)
- Cholesterol 0 mg
- Sodium 445 mg
- Total Carb 40 gm
- Dietary Fiber 9 gm
- Sugars 7 gm
- Protein 12 gm

Vegetables and Side Dishes

Asparagus Bake

Leona M. Slabaugh
Apple Creek, OH

Makes 6 servings
Prep. Time: 20 minutes
Baking Time: 45–60 minutes

5 medium potatoes, sliced

2 medium onions, diced

2 cups fresh, chopped asparagus

salt and pepper

2 Tbsp. trans-fat free tub margarine

3 oz. 75%-less-fat cheddar cheese slices

1. Lay potatoes in greased 2-qt. casserole dish. Sprinkle with salt and pepper.

2. Sprinkle diced onions over potatoes.

3. Add asparagus.

4. Add salt and pepper, to taste.

5. Dot top with pieces of margarine.

6. Cover tightly.

7. Bake at 325°F for 45–60 minutes, or until potatoes are tender when poked with a fork.

8. Remove from oven and lay sliced cheese over hot vegetables to melt.

Good Go-Alongs:
Meatloaf, corn, apple crisp—a meal made entirely in the oven.

Exchange List Values
- Starch 1.5
- Vegetable 1.0
- Lean Meat 1.0
- Fat 0.5

Basic Nutritional Values
- Calories 195
  (Calories from Fat 40)
- Total Fat 4.5 gm,
  (Saturated Fat 1.4 gm,
  Trans Fat 0.0 gm,
  Polyunsat Fat 1.3 gm,
  Monounsat Fat 1.2 gm)
- Cholesterol 5 mg
- Sodium 150 mg
- Potassium 820 gm
- Total Carb 32 gm
- Dietary Fiber 5 gm
- Sugars 4 gm
- Protein 9 gm
- Phosphorus 195 gm

Baked Asparagus Roll-Ups

Peggy C. Forsythe
Memphis, TN

Makes 12 servings, 1 roll-up per serving
Prep. Time: 20 minutes
Baking Time: 15 minutes

12 slices white bread, crusts removed

½ cup reduced-fat crumbled blue cheese

1–2 Tbsp. mayonnaise

12 asparagus spears, canned and patted dry, or fresh and lightly steamed, dried, and cooled

2 Tbsp. trans-fat-free tub margarine, melted

paprika

4 Tbsp. freshly grated Parmesan cheese

1. Flatten bread with a rolling pin. Set aside.

2. In a small bowl, mix blue cheese and mayonnaise to a spreading consistency, starting with 1 Tbsp. mayonnaise and adding by teaspoons as needed. Set aside.

3. Divide cheese mixture among bread slices and spread evenly.

4. Place an asparagus spear on one end of a bread slice. Starting with the spear end, roll up with the bread with the spear inside. Pinch seam a little bit to hold in place.

5. Place roll-up seam side down on greased cookie sheet. Roll up remaining bread and asparagus.

6. Brush each roll-up with melted margarine. Sprinkle each roll-up with 1 tsp. Parmesan cheese and a sprinkle of paprika.

7. Bake for 15 minutes at 375°F or until golden brown.

Exchange List Values
- Starch 0.5
- Fat 0.5

Basic Nutritional Values
- Calories 85
  (Calories from Fat 30)
- Total Fat 4 gm
  (Saturated Fat 1.3 gm,
  Trans Fat 0.0 gm,
  Polyunsat Fat 0.9 gm,
  Monounsat Fat 1.0 gm)
- Cholesterol 5 mg
- Sodium 240 mg
- Potassium 65 gm
- Total Carb 10 gm
- Dietary Fiber 1 gm
- Sugars 1 gm
- Protein 3 gm
- Phosphorus 55 gm

Glazed Carrots

Dorothy Lingerfelt
Stonyford, CA

Makes 6 servings, about 4 oz. per serving
Prep. Time: 20 minutes
Cooking Time: 30 minutes

12 medium carrots, cut into 1-inch pieces

¼ cup Splenda Brown Sugar Blend

2 Tbsp. trans-fat-free margarine

1 Tbsp. grated lemon peel

¼ tsp. vanilla extract

1. In saucepan, cook carrots in a small amount of water until crisp-tender; drain. Remove and keep warm.

2. In the same pan, heat Splenda and margarine until bubbly. Stir in lemon peel.

3. Return carrots to pan; cook and stir over low heat for 10 minutes or until glazed.

4. Remove from heat; stir in vanilla.

Variation:
Substitute 2 Tbsp. Dijon mustard for the lemon peel and vanilla.

—Joette Droz, Kalona, IA

Exchange List Values
- Carbohydrate 0.5
- Vegetable 2.0
- Fat 0.5

Basic Nutritional Values
- Calories 105 (Calories from Fat 25)
- Total Fat 3 gm (Saturated Fat 0.6 gm, Trans Fat 0.0 gm, Polyunsat Fat 1.3 gm, Monounsat Fat 0.9 gm)
- Cholesterol 0 mg
- Sodium 115 mg
- Potassium 405 gm
- Total Carb 20 gm
- Dietary Fiber 4 gm
- Sugars 9 gm
- Protein 1 gm
- Phosphorus 45 gm

Orange Glazed Carrots

**Cyndie Marrara
Port Matilda, PA**

Makes 8 servings
Prep. Time: 10 minutes
Cooking Time: 3–4 hours
Ideal slow-cooker size: 4-qt.

32-oz. (2 lbs.) pkg. baby carrots

3 Tbsp. brown sugar substitute to equal 2
Tbsp. sugar

½ cup orange juice

2 Tbsp. margarine

¾ tsp. cinnamon

¼ tsp. nutmeg

2 Tbsp. cornstarch

¼ cup water

1. Combine all ingredients except cornstarch and water in slow cooker.

2. Cover. Cook on Low 3–4 hours until carrots are tender crisp.

3. Put carrots in serving dish and keep warm, reserving cooking juices. Put reserved juices in small saucepan. Bring to boil.

4. Mix cornstarch and water in small bowl until blended. Add to juices. Boil one minute or until thickened, stirring constantly.

5. Pour over carrots and serve.

Exchange List Values
- Carbohydrate 0.5
- Vegetable 2.0
- Fat 0.5

Basic Nutritional Values
- Calories 108
  (Calories from Fat 29)
- Total Fat 3 gm
  (Saturated Fat 0.6 gm,
  Polyunsat Fat 1.0 gm,
  Monounsat Fat 1.3 gm)
- Cholesterol 0 mg
- Sodium 115 mg
- Total Carb 20 gm
- Dietary Fiber 4 gm
- Sugars 12 gm
- Protein 1 gm

Crisp Carrot Casserole

**Jan McDowell
New Holland, PA**

Makes 8 serving, 3¼×4½-inch rectangle per
  serving
Prep. Time: 30 minutes
Baking Time: 50 minutes

6 cups sliced carrots

1 large onion, chopped

2 Tbsp. trans-fat-free tub margarine

1 cup shredded 75%-reduced-fat cheddar
  cheese

1 oz. lightly crumbled baked potato chips

Warm Memories:
I always have an empty dish to take home
from potlucks!

1. In a covered saucepan, cook carrots and
onion in small amount of water until barely
crisp-tender. Drain.

2. Place carrots and onion in a greased
9×13-inch baking dish.

3. Slice margarine into pieces and layer
over top of carrots and onion in dish.

4. Sprinkle with cheese. Top with potato
chips.

5. Bake at 350°F for 30–40 minutes, until
casserole is hot through and bubbling at
edges.

Exchange List Values
- Starch 0.5
- Vegetable 2.0
- Fat 0.5

Basic Nutritional Values
- Calories 115
  (Calories from Fat 35)
- Total Fat 4 gm
  (Saturated Fat 1.2 gm,
  Trans Fat 0.0 gm,
  Polyunsat Fat 1.1 gm,
  Monounsat Fat 1.0 gm)
- Cholesterol 5 mg
- Sodium 210 mg
- Potassium 385 gm
- Total Carb 15 gm
- Dietary Fiber 3 gm
- Sugars 6 gm
- Protein 6 gm
- Phosphorus 115 gm

Creamed Peas and Mushrooms

Diena Schmidt
Henderson, NE

Makes 8 servings, about 4 oz. per serving
Prep. Time: 15 minutes
Cooking Time: 25 minutes

20-oz. pkg. frozen peas

½ cup mushroom caps

1 Tbsp. onion, minced

2 Tbsp. trans-fat-free tub margarine

2 Tbsp. flour

1½ cups fat-free half-and-half

3 Tbsp. reduced-fat Velveeta cheese

¼ tsp. salt

1. Cook peas in boiling salted water until tender.

2. Sauté mushroom caps and onion in oil until lightly browned. Add to peas.

3. Stir flour into remaining drippings. Add half-and-half gradually, cooking and stirring until slightly thickened.

4. Turn heat to low and add cheese. Stir until dissolved. Combine with peas and mushrooms.

Exchange List Values
- Starch 1.0
- Fat 0.5

Basic Nutritional Values
- Calories 115
  (Calories from Fat 30)
- Total Fat 4 gm
  (Saturated Fat 1.2 gm,
  Trans Fat 0.0 gm,
  Polyunsat Fat 1.0 gm,
  Monounsat Fat 1.0 gm)
- Cholesterol 5 mg
- Sodium 280 mg
- Potassium 195 gm
- Total Carb 15 gm
- Dietary Fiber 4 gm
- Sugars 6 gm
- Protein 6 gm
- Phosphorus 185 gm

Wild Mushrooms Italian

Connie Johnson
Loudon, NH

Makes 10 servings
Prep. Time: 45 minutes
Cooking Time: 6–8 hours
Ideal slow-cooker size: 4-qt.

2 large onions, chopped

3 large red bell peppers, chopped

3 large green bell peppers, chopped

2 Tbsp. canola oil

12-oz. pkg. oyster mushrooms, cleaned and chopped

4 cloves garlic, minced

3 fresh bay leaves

10 fresh basil leaves, chopped

1 tsp. salt

1½ tsp. pepper

28-oz. can Italian plum tomatoes, crushed or chopped

1. Sauté onions and peppers in oil in skillet until soft. Stir in mushrooms and garlic. Sauté just until mushrooms begin to turn brown. Pour into slow cooker.

2. Add remaining ingredients. Stir well.

3. Cover. Cook on Low 6–8 hours.

NOTES

Good as an appetizer or on pita bread, or serve over rice or pasta for main dish.

Exchange List Values
- Vegetable 3.0
- Fat 0.5

Basic Nutritional Values
- Calories 82
  (Calories from Fat 29)
- Total Fat 3 gm
  (Saturated Fat 0.2 gm,
  Polyunsat Fat 1.0 gm,
  Monounsat Fat 1.7 gm)
- Cholesterol 0 mg
- Sodium 356 mg
- Total Carb 13 gm
- Dietary Fiber 4 gm
- Sugars 8 gm
- Protein 3 gm

Garlic Mushrooms

Lizzie Ann Yoder
Hartville, OH

Makes 4 servings, about ½ cup per serving
Prep. Time: 20 minutes
Cooking Time: 15–20 minutes

3 Tbsp. trans-fat-free tub margarine

2 cloves garlic, minced

1 lb. mushrooms, sliced

4 green onions, chopped

1 tsp. lemon juice

1. In a skillet, melt the margarine and sauté the garlic briefly.

2. Add mushrooms, green onions, and lemon juice and cook, stirring, about 10 minutes.

Good Go-Alongs:
A nice side dish for meat.

Exchange List Values
- Vegetable 1.0
- Fat 1.5

Basic Nutritional Values
- Calories 90
  (Calories from Fat 65)
- Total Fat 7 gm
  (Saturated Fat 1.4 gm,
  Trans Fat 0.0 gm,
  Polyunsat Fat 2.8 gm,
  Monounsat Fat 2.0 gm)
- Cholesterol 0 mg
- Sodium 75 mg
- Potassium 400 gm
- Total Carb 5 gm
- Dietary Fiber 2 gm
- Sugars 2 gm
- Protein 4 gm
- Phosphorus 105 gm

Stuffed Mushrooms

Melanie L. Thrower
McPherson, KS

Makes 6 servings
Prep. Time: 25 minutes
Cooking Time: 2–4 hours
Ideal slow-cooker size: 3- or 4-qt.

12 large mushrooms

1 Tbsp. canola oil

¼ tsp. minced garlic

dash salt

dash pepper

dash cayenne pepper

¼ cup grated reduced-fat Monterey Jack
   cheese

1. Remove stems from mushrooms and dice.

2. Heat oil in skillet. Sauté diced stems with garlic until softened. Remove skillet from heat.

3. Stir in seasonings and cheese. Stuff into mushroom shells. Place in slow cooker.

4. Cover. Heat on Low 2–4 hours.

Variations:
1. Add 1 Tbsp. minced onion to Step 2.
2. Use Monterey Jack cheese with jalapeños.

Exchange List Values
- Vegetable 1.0
- Fat 0.5

Basic Nutritional Values
- Calories 46
  (Calories from Fat 30)
- Total Fat 3 gm
  (Saturated Fat 0.8 gm,
  Polyunsat Fat 0.8 gm,
  Monounsat Fat 1.6 gm)
- Cholesterol 3 mg
- Sodium 39 mg
- Total Carb 2 gm
- Dietary Fiber 1 gm
- Sugars 1 gm
- Protein 3 gm

Golden Cauliflower

Carol Peachey
Lancaster, PA

Makes 6 servings
Prep. Time: 15 minutes
Cooking Time: 3½–5 hours
Ideal slow-cooker size: 4-qt.

2 10-oz. pkgs. frozen cauliflower, thawed

2 Tbsp. light soft tub margarine, melted

1 Tbsp. flour

1 cup evaporated fat-free milk

1 oz. (¼ cup) fat-free cheddar cheese

2 Tbsp. 1% milkfat cottage cheese

2 tsp. Parmesan cheese

4 slices bacon, crisply browned and
    crumbled

1. Place cauliflower in slow cooker.

2. Melt margarine in saucepan on stove.
Add flour and evaporated milk. Heat till
thickened. Add cheeses.

3. Pour sauce over cauliflower. Top with
bacon.

4. Cover. Cook on High 1½ hours and then
reduce to low for an additional 2 hours. Or
cook only on Low 4–5 hours.

Exchange List Values
- Carbohydrate 0.5
- Lean Meat 1.0

Basic Nutritional Values
- Calories 106
  (Calories from Fat 37)
- Total Fat 4 gm
  (Saturated Fat 0.8 gm,
  Polyunsat Fat 0.6 gm,
  Monounsat Fat 1.9 gm)
- Cholesterol 5 mg
- Sodium 228 mg
- Total Carb 10 gm
- Dietary Fiber 2 gm
- Sugars 6 gm
- Protein 8 gm

Julia's Broccoli and Cauliflower with Cheese

Julia Lapp
New Holland, PA

Makes 6 servings
Prep. Time: 25 minutes
Cooking Time: 1½ hours
Ideal slow-cooker size: 4-qt.

5 cups chopped broccoli and cauliflower

¼ cup water

2 Tbsp. margarine

2 Tbsp. flour

½ tsp. salt

1 cup fat-free milk

1 cup fat-free shredded cheddar cheese

1. Cook broccoli and cauliflower in saucepan in water, until just crisp-tender. Set aside.

2. Make white sauce by melting the margarine in another pan over low heat. Blend in flour and salt. Add milk all at once. Cook quickly, stirring constantly, until mixture thickens and bubbles. Add cheese. Stir until melted and smooth.

3. Combine vegetables and sauce in slow cooker. Mix well.

4. Cook on Low 1½ hours.

Variation:
Substitute green beans and carrots or other vegetables for broccoli and cauliflower.

Exchange List Values
- Carbohydrate 0.5
- Vegetable 1.0
- Lean Meat 1.0

Basic Nutritional Values
- Calories 108 (Calories from Fat 37)
- Total Fat 4 gm (Saturated Fat 0.8 gm, Polyunsat Fat 1.3 gm, Monounsat Fat 1.7 gm)
- Cholesterol 3 mg
- Sodium 412 mg
- Total Carb 9 gm
- Dietary Fiber 2 gm
- Sugars 5 gm
- Protein 10 gm

Quick Broccoli Fix

Willard E. Roth
Elkhart, IN

Makes 6 servings
Prep. Time: 20 minutes
Cooking Time: 5–6 hours
Ideal slow-cooker size: 4-qt.

1 lb. fresh or frozen broccoli, cut up

10¾-oz. can 98%-fat-free, reduced-sodium
   cream of mushroom soup

¼ cup fat-free mayonnaise

½ cup fat-free plain yogurt

½ lb. sliced fresh mushrooms

1 cup shredded fat-free cheddar cheese,
   divided

1 cup crushed saltine crackers with unsalted
   tops

sliced almonds, *optional*

Exchange List Values
- Carbohydrate 1.0
- Vegetable 1.0
- Lean Meat 1.0

Basic Nutritional Values
- Calories 158
  (Calories from Fat 28)
- Total Fat 3 gm
  (Saturated Fat 0.4 gm,
  Polyunsat Fat 0.8 gm,
  Monounsat Fat 1.0 gm)
- Cholesterol 3 mg
- Sodium 523 mg
- Total Carb 22 gm
- Dietary Fiber 3 gm
- Sugars 5 gm
- Protein 12 gm

1. Microwave broccoli for 3 minutes. Place
in greased slow cooker.

2. Combine soup, mayonnaise, yogurt,
mushrooms, and ½ cup cheese. Pour over
broccoli.

3. Cover. Cook on Low 5–6 hours.

4. Top with remaining cheese and crackers
for last half hour of cooking time.

5. Top with sliced almonds, for a special
touch, before serving.

Broccoli and Rice Casserole

Deborah Swartz
Grottoes, VA

Makes 6 servings
Prep. Time: 20 minutes
Cooking Time: 3–4 hours
Ideal slow-cooker size: 4-qt.

1 lb. chopped broccoli, fresh or frozen, thawed

1 medium onion, chopped

1 Tbsp. canola oil

1 cup instant rice, or 1½ cups cooked rice

10¾-oz. can 98%-fat-free, reduced-sodium cream of chicken or mushroom soup

¼ cup fat-free milk

1⅓ cups fat-free cheddar cheese, shredded

1. Cook broccoli for 5 minutes in saucepan in boiling water. Drain and set aside.

2. Sauté onion in canola oil in saucepan until tender. Add to broccoli.

3. Combine remaining ingredients. Add to broccoli mixture. Pour into greased slow cooker.

4. Cover. Cook on Low 3–4 hours.

Exchange List Values
- Starch 1.5
- Vegetable 1.0
- Lean Meat 1.0

Basic Nutritional Values
- Calories 188
  (Calories from Fat 33)
- Total Fat 4 gm
  (Saturated Fat 0.5 gm,
  Polyunsat Fat 1.2 gm,
  Monounsat Fat 1.6 gm)
- Cholesterol 7 mg
- Sodium 404 mg
- Total Carb 26 gm
- Dietary Fiber 3 gm
- Sugars 5 gm
- Protein 13 gm

Very Special Spinach

Jeanette Oberholtzer
Manheim, PA

Makes 8 servings
Prep. Time: 10 minutes
Cooking Time: 5 hours
Ideal slow-cooker size: 4-qt.

3 10-oz. boxes frozen spinach, thawed and drained

2 cups 1% milkfat cottage cheese

1½ cups grated fat-free cheddar cheese

3 eggs

¼ cup flour

4 Tbsp. (¼ cup) light, soft tub margarine, melted

1. Mix together all ingredients.

2. Pour into slow cooker.

3. Cook on High 1 hour. Reduce heat to Low and cook 4 more hours.

Exchange List Values
- Starch 0.5
- Vegetable 1.0
- Lean Meat 2.0

Basic Nutritional Values
- Calories 160
  (Calories from Fat 44)
- Total Fat 5 gm
  (Saturated Fat 1.3 gm,
  Polyunsat Fat 0.9 gm,
  Monounsat Fat 2.1 gm)
- Cholesterol 84 mg
- Sodium 520 mg
- Total Carb 11 gm
- Dietary Fiber 3 gm
- Sugars 3 gm
- Protein 19 gm

Green Beans Caesar

Carol Shirk
Leola, PA

Makes 8 servings, 3 oz. per serving, a
  generous ½ cup
Prep. Time: 10 minutes
Baking Time: 20 minutes

1½ lbs. green beans, trimmed

2 Tbsp. oil

1 Tbsp. vinegar

1 Tbsp. minced onion

salt and pepper, to taste

2 Tbsp. bread crumbs

2 Tbsp. freshly grated Parmesan cheese

1 Tbsp. trans-fat-free tub margarine, melted

1. Cook the green beans until barely tender. Drain.

2. Toss with oil, vinegar, onion, salt, and pepper.

3. Pour into an ungreased 2-qt. casserole.

4. Mix bread crumbs, Parmesan cheese, and margarine. Sprinkle over beans.

5. Bake at 350°F for 20 minutes.

Exchange List Values
- Vegetable 1.0
- Fat 1.0

Basic Nutritional Values
- Calories 80
  (Calories from Fat 45)
- Total Fat 5 gm
  (Saturated Fat 0.8 gm,
  Trans Fat 0.0 gm,
  Polyunsat Fat 1.6 gm,
  Monounsat Fat 2.7 gm)
- Cholesterol 0 mg
- Sodium 45 mg
- Potassium 115 gm
- Total Carb 7 gm
- Dietary Fiber 2 gm
- Sugars 1 gm
- Protein 2 gm
- Phosphorus 30 gm

Dutch Green Beans

Edwina Stoltzfus
Narvon, PA

Makes 12 servings
Prep. Time: 20 minutes
Cooking Time: 4½ hours
Ideal slow-cooker size: 4- or 5-qt.

6 slices bacon

4 medium onions, sliced

2 Tbsp. canola oil

2 qts. fresh, frozen, or canned, green beans

4 cups diced, fresh tomatoes

½ tsp. salt

¼ tsp. pepper

1. Brown bacon until crisp in skillet. Drain. Crumble bacon into small pieces.

2. Sauté onions in canola oil.

3. Combine all ingredients in slow cooker.

4. Cover. Cook on Low 4½ hours.

Exchange List Values
- Vegetable 3.0
- Fat 0.5

Basic Nutritional Values
- Calories 99
  (Calories from Fat 39)
- Total Fat 4 gm
  (Saturated Fat 0.7 gm,
  Polyunsat Fat 1.1 gm,
  Monounsat Fat 2.1 gm)
- Cholesterol 3 mg
- Sodium 154 mg
- Total Carb 14 gm
- Dietary Fiber 4 gm
- Sugars 6 gm
- Protein 4 gm

Easy Flavor-Filled Green Beans

Paula Showalter
Weyers Cave, VA

Makes 10 servings
Prep. Time: 15 minutes
Cooking Time: 3–4 hours
Ideal slow-cooker size: 4- or 5-qt.

2 qts. canned green beans, drained

⅓ cup chopped onions

4-oz. can mushrooms, drained

1 Tbsp. brown sugar substitute to equal 1½ tsp. sugar

3 Tbsp. light, soft tub margarine

pepper, to taste

1. Combine beans, onions, and mushrooms in slow cooker.

2. Sprinkle with brown sugar.

3. Dot with margarine.

4. Sprinkle with pepper.

5. Cover. Cook on High 3–4 hours. Stir just before serving.

Exchange List Value
- Vegetable 2.0

Basic Nutritional Values
- Calories 47
  (Calories from Fat 14)
- Total Fat 2 gm
  (Saturated Fat 0.0 gm,
  Polyunsat Fat 0.4 gm,
  Monounsat Fat 0.8 gm)
- Cholesterol 0 mg
- Sodium 339 mg
- Total Carb 7 gm
- Dietary Fiber 3 gm
- Sugars 4 gm
- Protein 2 gm

Scalloped Corn

**Rhonda Freed
Croghan, NY**

Makes 6 servings, 3½-inch square per
serving
Prep. Time: 15 minutes
Baking Time: 30–50 minutes

2 eggs

1 cup fat-free milk

⅔ cup cracker crumbs (Ritz or Club crackers)

2 cups canned creamed corn

⅓ cup 75%-less-fat shredded cheddar
cheese

1 Tbsp. trans-fat-free tub margarine, melted

1 tsp. dried minced onion

1 Tbsp. sugar

¼ tsp. salt

⅛ tsp. pepper

1. In a medium bowl, beat eggs with a
whisk.

2. Add milk and cracker crumbs. Whisk
again.

3. Add the rest of the ingredients. Stir
together well.

4. Pour into greased 7×11-inch casserole
dish.

5. Bake at 350°F for 30–50 minutes,
checking at 30 minutes. If center is still jiggly,
bake for 5–10 more minutes. Check again.
Repeat checking and baking until center is
firm.

Exchange List Values
- Starch 1.0
- Carbohydrate 0.5
- Fat 1.0

Basic Nutritional Values
- Calories 160
  (Calories from Fat 55)
- Total Fat 6 gm
  (Saturated Fat 1.5 gm,
  Trans Fat 0.0 gm,
  Polyunsat Fat 1.2 gm,
  Monounsat Fat 2.7 gm)
- Cholesterol 65 mg
- Sodium 420 mg
- Potassium 190 gm
- Total Carb 20 gm
- Dietary Fiber 1 gm
- Sugars 10 gm
- Protein 7 gm
- Phosphorus 170 gm

Creamy Corn

**Lauren M. Eberhard
Seneca, IL**

Makes 8 servings
Prep. Time: 10 minutes
Cooking Time: 6 hours
Ideal slow-cooker size: 5-qt.

12 oz. fat-free cottage cheese

1 cup reduced-fat Colby cheese, shredded

1 egg

pepper, to taste

2 lbs. frozen corn

1. Cream cottage cheese, Colby cheese, and egg in food processor until well-mixed.

2. Stir in pepper and corn.

3. Pour mixture into slow cooker.

4. Cover. Cook on Low 6 hours.

Exchange List Values
- Starch 2.0
- Lean Meat 1.0

Basic Nutritional Values
- Calories 180
  (Calories from Fat 35)
- Total Fat 4 gm
  (Saturated Fat 2.0 gm,
  Polyunsat Fat 0.5 gm,
  Monounsat Fat 1.0 gm)
- Cholesterol 30 mg
- Sodium 265 mg
- Total Carb 27 gm
- Dietary Fiber 2 gm
- Sugars 4 gm
- Protein 12 gm

Sweet Onion Corn Bake

Rebecca B. Stoltzfus
Lititz, PA
Sherry Mayer
Menomonee Falls, WI

Makes 12 servings, 3-inch square per
  serving
Prep. Time: 30 minutes
Baking Time: 45–50 minutes

2 large sweet onions, thinly sliced

2 Tbsp. canola oil

1 cup fat-free sour cream

½ cup fat-free milk

½ tsp. dill weed

¼ tsp. salt

1 cup 75%-reduced-fat shredded cheddar
  cheese, *divided*

¼ cup egg substitute

14¾-oz. can cream-style corn

8½-oz. pkg. cornbread muffin mix

4 drops hot pepper sauce, or to taste

1. In a large skillet, sauté onions in oil
until tender.

2. In a small bowl, combine sour cream,
milk, dill, and salt until blended.

3. Stir in ½ cup cheese.

4. Stir cheese mixture into onion mixture;
remove from heat and set aside.

5. In a bowl, combine egg substitute, corn,
cornbread mix, and hot pepper sauce.

6. Pour into a greased 9×13-inch baking
dish.

7. Spoon onion mixture over top. Sprinkle
with remaining cheese.

8. Bake at 350°F for 45–50 minutes or
until top is set and lightly browned.

9. Let stand 10 minutes before cutting and
serving.

Exchange List Values
- Carbohydrate 2.0
- Fat 0.5

Basic Nutritional Values
- Calories 155
  (Calories from Fat 45)
- Total Fat 5 gm
  (Saturated Fat 1.5 gm,
  Trans Fat 0.0 gm,
  Polyunsat Fat 0.9 gm,
  Monounsat Fat 2.0 gm)
- Cholesterol 5 mg
- Sodium 380 mg
- Potassium 185 gm
- Total Carb 26 gm
- Dietary Fiber 1 gm
- Sugars 10 gm
- Protein 6 gm
- Phosphorus 205 gm

Super Creamed Corn

Ruth Ann Penner
Hillsboro, KS
Alix Nancy Botsford
Seminole, OK

Makes 12 servings
Prep. Time: 10 minutes
Cooking Time: 4 hours
Ideal slow-cooker size: 4-qt.

2 lbs. frozen corn

8-oz. pkg. fat-free cream cheese, cubed

2 Tbsp. margarine, melted

1 Tbsp. sugar substitute to equal ½ Tbsp.
sugar

2–3 Tbsp. water, *optional*

1. Combine ingredients in slow cooker.

2. Cover. Cook on Low 4 hours.

TIP

Serve with meatloaf, turkey, or
hamburgers. It's a great addition to a
holiday because it is easy and requires
no last-minute preparation. It also
frees the stove and oven for other food
preparation.

Exchange List Values

- Starch 1.0
- Fat 0.5

Basic Nutritional Values

- Calories 99
  (Calories from Fat 20)
- Total Fat 2 gm
  (Saturated Fat 0.4 gm,
  Polyunsat Fat 0.8 gm,
  Monounsat Fat 0.9 gm)
- Cholesterol 2 mg
- Sodium 129 mg
- Total Carb 17 gm
- Dietary Fiber 2 gm
- Sugars 3 gm
- Protein 5 gm

Baked Corn and Noodles

Ruth Hershey
Paradise, PA

Makes 6 servings
Prep. Time: 20 minutes
Cooking Time: 3–8 hours
Ideal slow-cooker size: 4-qt.

3 cups noodles, cooked al dente

2 cups fresh or frozen corn, thawed

¾ cup grated fat-free cheddar cheese

1 egg, beaten

2 Tbsp. light, soft tub margarine, melted

½ tsp. salt

1. Combine all ingredients in slow cooker.

2. Cover. Cook on Low 6–8 hours or on High 3–4 hours.

Exchange List Values
- Starch 2.0
- Fat 0.5

Basic Nutritional Values
- Calories 198
  (Calories from Fat 34)
- Total Fat 4 gm
  (Saturated Fat 0.6 gm,
  Polyunsat Fat 0.9 gm,
  Monounsat Fat 1.6 gm)
- Cholesterol 63 mg
- Sodium 343 mg
- Total Carb 32 gm
- Dietary Fiber 2 gm
- Sugars 3 gm
- Protein 11 gm

Mexican Corn

**Betty K. Drescher
Quakertown, PA**

Makes 8 servings
Prep. Time: 10 minutes
Cooking Time: 2¾–4¾ hours
Ideal slow-cooker size: 3- or 4-qt.

2 10-oz. pkgs. frozen corn, partially thawed

4-oz. jar chopped pimentos, drained

⅓ cup chopped green pepper

⅓ cup water

1 tsp. salt

¼ tsp. pepper

½ tsp. paprika

½ tsp. chili powder

1. Combine all ingredients in slow cooker.

2. Cover. Cook on High 45 minutes, then on Low 2–4 hours. Stir occasionally.

Variations:
For more fire, add ⅓ cup salsa to the ingredients, and increase the amounts of pepper, paprika, and chili powder to match your taste.

Exchange List Value
- Starch 1.0

Basic Nutritional Values
- Calories 63
  (Calories from Fat 3)
- Total Fat 0 gm
  (Saturated Fat 0.1 gm,
  Polyunsat Fat 0.2 gm,
  Monounsat Fat 0.1 gm)
- Cholesterol 0 mg
- Sodium 298 mg
- Total Carb 15 gm
- Dietary Fiber 2 gm
- Sugars 2 gm
- Protein 2 gm

Cornbread Casserole

Arlene Groff
Lewistown, PA

Makes 16 servings
Prep. Time: 15 minutes
Cooking Time: 3½–4 hours
Ideal slow-cooker size: 4-qt.

1 qt. frozen whole-kernel corn, thawed

1 qt. creamed corn

8.5-oz. pkg. corn muffin mix

1 egg

2 Tbsp. light, soft tub margarine

¼ tsp. garlic powder

2 Tbsp. sugar

¼ cup fat-free milk

½ tsp. salt

¼ tsp. pepper

1. Combine ingredients in greased slow cooker.

2. Cover. Cook on Low 3½–4 hours, stirring once halfway through.

Exchange List Value
- Starch 2.0

Basic Nutritional Values
- Calories 141
  (Calories from Fat 23)
- Total Fat 3 gm
  (Saturated Fat 0.7 gm,
  Polyunsat Fat 0.5 gm,
  Monounsat Fat 0.8 gm)
- Cholesterol 13 mg
- Sodium 412 mg
- Total Carb 31 gm
- Dietary Fiber 2 gm
- Sugars 10 gm
- Protein 3 gm

Zucchini Special

Louise Stackhouse
Benten, PA

Makes 8 servings
Prep. Time: 25 minutes
Cooking Time: 6–8 hours
Ideal slow-cooker size: 4-qt.

1 medium to large zucchini, peeled and sliced

1 medium onion, sliced

1 qt. stewed, no-added-salt tomatoes with juice, or 2 14-oz. cans stewed, no-added-salt tomatoes with juice

½ tsp. salt

1 tsp. dried basil

4 oz. (1 cup) reduced-fat mozzarella cheese, shredded

1. Layer zucchini, onion, and tomatoes in slow cooker.

2. Sprinkle with salt, basil, and cheese.

3. Cover. Cook on Low 6–8 hours.

Exchange List Values
- Vegetable 2.0
- Fat 0.5

Basic Nutritional Values
- Calories 79 (Calories from Fat 21)
- Total Fat 2 gm (Saturated Fat 1.3 gm, Polyunsat Fat 0.3 gm, Monounsat Fat 0.4 gm)
- Cholesterol 8 mg
- Sodium 273 mg
- Total Carb 11 gm
- Dietary Fiber 2 gm
- Sugars 5 gm
- Protein 6 gm

Cheesy Zucchini

**Louise Stackhouse
Benton, PA**

Makes 6 servings, about 3 oz. per serving
Prep. Time: 10 minutes
Cooking Time: 20 minutes

2 small to medium-sized zucchini, peeled, sliced

1 large onion, sliced

3 Tbsp. trans-fat-free tub margarine, sliced

salt and pepper, to taste

2 slices (¾-oz. each) reduced-fat American cheese

basil, fresh or dry

1. Spray casserole bowl with nonstick cooking spray.

2. Layer zucchini and onion in bowl, adding slices of margarine, salt, and pepper as you go.

3. Lay cheese on top. Sprinkle with basil.

4. Cover and microwave approximately 20 minutes until zucchini is tender when tested with a fork.

Variation:
Sauté onion and zucchini in margarine in a large skillet. Add cheese and basil on top. Cover and cook on low until tender.

Exchange List Values
- Vegetable 1.0
- Fat 1.0

Basic Nutritional Values
- Calories 75
  (Calories from Fat 45)
- Total Fat 5 gm
  (Saturated Fat 1.4 gm,
  Trans Fat 0.0 gm,
  Polyunsat Fat 1.8 gm,
  Monounsat Fat 1.6 gm)
- Cholesterol 5 mg
- Sodium 145 mg
- Potassium 185 gm
- Total Carb 6 gm
- Dietary Fiber 1 gm
- Sugars 3 gm
- Protein 2 gm
- Phosphorus 85 gm

Squash Apple Bake

Ruth Ann Swartzendruber
Hydro, OK

Makes 8 servings, about 3 oz. per serving
Prep. Time: 20 minutes
Baking Time: 45–60 minutes

4 cups cubed, peeled butternut squash

2 Tbsp. honey

⅓ cup orange, or apple, juice

2 apples, thinly sliced

¼ cup raisins

cinnamon

1. Slice butternut squash into ¾-inch rounds. Peel and remove any seeds. Cut into cubes.

2. Combine honey and juice.

3. In a greased 2-qt. casserole dish make 2 layers of squash, apples, and raisins. Sprinkle generously with cinnamon and pour juice mixture over layers.

4. Cover and bake at 350°F for 45–60 minutes or until tender.

Exchange List Values
- Starch 0.5
- Fruit 1.0

Basic Nutritional Values
- Calories 75
  (Calories from Fat 0)
- Total Fat 0 gm
  (Saturated Fat 0.0 gm,
  Trans Fat 0.0 gm,
  Polyunsat Fat 0.0 gm,
  Monounsat Fat 0.0 gm)
- Cholesterol 0 mg
- Sodium 0 mg
- Potassium 270 gm
- Total Carb 20 gm
- Dietary Fiber 3 gm
- Sugars 13 gm
- Protein 1 gm
- Phosphorus 25 gm

Baked Acorn Squash

Dale Peterson
Rapid City, SD

Makes 4 servings
Prep. Time: 25 minutes
Cooking Time: 5–6 hours
Ideal slow-cooker size: 3- or 4-qt.

2 small (1¼ lb. each) acorn squash

½ cup cracker crumbs

¼ cup coarsely chopped pecans

2 Tbsp. light, soft tub margarine, melted

2 Tbsp. brown sugar substitute to equal 1
  Tbsp. sugar

¼ tsp. salt

¼ tsp. ground nutmeg

2 Tbsp. orange juice

1. Cut squash in half. Remove seeds.

2. Combine remaining ingredients. Spoon
into squash halves. Place squash in slow
cooker.

3. Cover. Cook on Low 5–6 hours, or until
squash is tender.

Exchange List Values

- Starch 2.0
- Carbohydrate 0.5
- Fat 1.0

Basic Nutritional Values

- Calories 229
  (Calories from Fat 82)
- Total Fat 9 gm
  (Saturated Fat 0.8 gm,
  Polyunsat Fat 2.3 gm,
  Monounsat Fat 5.1 gm)
- Cholesterol 0 mg
- Sodium 314 mg
- Total Carb 38 gm
- Dietary Fiber 8 gm
- Sugars 15 gm
- Protein 3 gm

Stuffed Acorn Squash

Jean Butzer
Batavia, NY

Makes 6 servings
Prep. Time: 25 minutes
Cooking Time: 2½ hours
Ideal slow-cooker size: 4-qt.

3 small (1¼ lb. each) acorn squash

5 Tbsp. instant brown rice

3 Tbsp. dried cranberries

3 Tbsp. diced celery

3 Tbsp. onion, minced

pinch ground sage

1 tsp. butter, *divided*

3 Tbsp. orange juice

½ cup water

NOTES

To make squash easier to slice, microwave whole squash on High for 5 minutes to soften skin.

1. Slice off points on the bottoms of squash so they will stand in slow cooker. Slice off tops and discard. Scoop out seeds. Place squash in slow cooker.

2. Combine rice, cranberries, celery, onion, and sage. Stuff into squash.

3. Dot with butter.

4. Pour 1 Tbsp. orange juice into each squash.

5. Pour water into bottom of slow cooker.

6. Cover. Cook on Low 2½ hours.

Serving suggestion:
Serve with cooked turkey breast.

Exchange List Value
- Starch 2.0

Basic Nutritional Values
- Calories 131 (Calories from Fat 10)
- Total Fat 1 gm (Saturated Fat 0.4 gm, Polyunsat Fat 0.2 gm, Monounsat Fat 0.3 gm)
- Cholesterol 2 mg
- Sodium 18 mg
- Total Carb 31 gm
- Dietary Fiber 7 gm
- Sugars 11 gm
- Protein 2 gm

Squash Casserole

Sharon Anders
Alburtis, PA

Makes 9 servings
Prep. Time: 25 minutes
Cooking Time: 7–9 hours
Ideal slow-cooker size: 4-qt.

2 lbs. yellow summer squash or zucchini, thinly sliced (about 6 cups)

½ medium onion, chopped

1 cup peeled, shredded carrot

10¾-oz. can 98%-fat-free, lower-sodium, condensed cream of chicken soup

½ cup fat-free sour cream

2 Tbsp. flour

4-oz. (½ of 8 oz. pkg.) seasoned stuffing crumbs

2 Tbsp. canola oil

1. Combine squash, onion, carrot, and soup.

2. Mix together sour cream and flour. Stir into vegetables.

3. Toss stuffing mix with canola oil. Spread half in bottom of slow cooker. Add vegetable mixture. Top with remaining crumbs.

4. Cover. Cook on Low 7–9 hours.

Exchange List Values
- Starch 1.0
- Vegetable 1.0
- Fat 1.0

Basic Nutritional Values
- Calories 140 (Calories from Fat 38)
- Total Fat 4 gm (Saturated Fat 0.5 gm, Polyunsat Fat 1.4 gm, Monounsat Fat 2.1 gm)
- Cholesterol 4 mg
- Sodium 486 mg
- Total Carb 21 gm
- Dietary Fiber 3 gm
- Sugars 5 gm
- Protein 4 gm

Rosemary Roasted Potatoes

Pamela Pierce
Annville, PA

Makes 8 servings, 6 wedges per serving
Prep. Time: 10 minutes
Roasting Time: 45–60 minutes

8 medium red potatoes, scrubbed, dried, and
   cut into 6 wedges each

3 Tbsp. olive oil

1 tsp. dried rosemary

1 tsp. dried thyme

½ tsp. salt

⅛ tsp. pepper

1. Toss potato wedges in oil.

2. Place in shallow roasting pan in single layer. Sprinkle evenly with seasonings. Stir.

3. Roast in 375°F oven for 45–60 minutes, stirring and flipping every 10–15 minutes, until wedges are golden and fork-tender.

Good Go-Alongs:
Great with roast pork.

Exchange List Values
- Starch 2.0
- Fat 1.0

Basic Nutritional Values
- Calories 195
  (Calories from Fat 45)
- Total Fat 5 gm
  (Saturated Fat 0.8 gm,
  Trans Fat 0.0 gm,
  Polyunsat Fat 0.6 gm,
  Monounsat Fat 3.7 gm)
- Cholesterol 0 mg
- Sodium 155 mg
- Potassium 825 gm
- Total Carb 34 gm
- Dietary Fiber 4 gm
- Sugars 2 gm
- Protein 4 gm
- Phosphorus 110 gm

Bavarian Cabbage

Joyce Shackelford
Green Bay, WI

Makes 8 servings
Prep. Time: 30 minutes
Cooking Time: 3–8 hours
Ideal slow-cooker size: 4-qt.

1 small (1½ lb.) head red cabbage, sliced

1 medium onion, chopped

3 medium tart apples, unpeeled, cored and quartered

1 tsp. salt

1 cup hot water

1 Tbsp. sugar substitute to equal ½ Tbsp. sugar

⅓ cup vinegar

1½ Tbsp. bacon drippings

1. Place all ingredients in slow cooker in order listed.

2. Cover. Cook on Low 8 hours, or High 3 hours. Stir well before serving.

Variation:
Add 6 slices bacon, browned until crisp and crumbled.

—Jean Butzer, Batavia, NY

Exchange List Values
- Fruit 0.5
- Vegetable 1.0
- Fat 0.5

Basic Nutritional Values
- Calories 85
  (Calories from Fat 24)
- Total Fat 3 gm
  (Saturated Fat 1.1 gm,
  Polyunsat Fat 0.3 gm,
  Monounsat Fat 1.0 gm)
- Cholesterol 2 mg
- Sodium 313 mg
- Total Carb 16 gm
- Dietary Fiber 3 gm
- Sugars 12 gm
- Protein 1 gm

Cabbage Casserole

Edwina Stoltzfus
Narvon, PA

Makes 6 servings
Prep. Time: 40 minutes
Cooking Time: 4–5 hours
Ideal slow-cooker size: 4-qt.

1 large head cabbage, chopped

2 cups water

3 Tbsp. margarine

¼ cup flour

¼ tsp. salt

¼ tsp. pepper

1⅓ cups fat-free milk

1⅓ cups fat-free shredded cheddar cheese

Variation:
Replace cabbage with cauliflower.

1. Cook cabbage in saucepan in boiling water for 5 minutes. Drain. Place in slow cooker.

2. In saucepan, melt margarine. Stir in flour, salt, and pepper. Add milk, stirring constantly on low heat for 5 minutes. Remove from heat. Stir in cheese. Pour over cabbage.

3. Cover. Cook on Low 4–5 hours.

Exchange List Values
- Carbohydrate 0.5
- Vegetable 2.0
- Lean Meat 1.0
- Fat 0.5

Basic Nutritional Values
- Calories 179 (Calories from Fat 57)
- Total Fat 6 gm (Saturated Fat 1.1 gm, Polyunsat Fat 2.1 gm, Monounsat Fat 2.6 gm)
- Cholesterol 4 mg
- Sodium 400 mg
- Total Carb 19 gm
- Dietary Fiber 5 gm
- Sugars 10 gm
- Protein 13 gm

German Red Cabbage

Annie C. Boshart
Lebanon, PA

Makes 12 servings, about 5 oz. per serving
Prep. Time: 30–40 minutes
Cooking/Baking Time: 3–4 hours

3 Tbsp. water

3 apples, peeled and cored, sliced thin

1 medium onion, chopped or sliced

4 tsp. sugar

salt, to taste

1 large red cabbage, shredded

2 bay leaves

10 whole cloves

½ lb. bacon

2 Tbsp. white vinegar, or more to taste

1. Place water in bottom of Dutch oven or 4-qt. pot. Put in half the apples, half the onion, half the sugar, and some salt to taste.

2. Put in all the cabbage.

3. Top with the rest of the apples, onion, sugar, and any more salt desired. Add bay leaves and cloves.

4. Cover and cook on low heat.

5. Meanwhile, fry bacon until brown. Remove bacon and set aside on paper towels. Pat it dry. Chop.

6. Reserve 1½ Tbsp. bacon grease and discard the rest.

7. Add the chopped bacon and the reserved grease on top of the cabbage.

8. Add vinegar. Simmer 3–4 hours on low. Add more vinegar to your taste.

9. Remove bay leaves and cloves and discard.

Exchange List Values

- Fruit 0.5
- Vegetable 1.0
- Fat 1.0

Basic Nutritional Values

- Calories 100
  (Calories from Fat 35)
- Total Fat 4 gm
  (Saturated Fat 1.4 gm,
  Trans Fat 0.0 gm,
  Polyunsat Fat 0.5 gm,
  Monounsat Fat 1.7 gm)
- Cholesterol 5 mg
- Sodium 150 mg
- Potassium 305 gm
- Total Carb 14 gm
- Dietary Fiber 3 gm
- Sugars 9 gm
- Protein 4 gm
- Phosphorus 65 gm

Oven Brussels Sprouts

Gail Martin
Elkhart, IN

Makes 8 servings
Prep. Time: 15 minutes
Roasting Time: 15–20 minutes

1½ lbs. Brussels sprouts, halved

¼ cup plus 2 Tbsp. olive oil

juice of 1 lemon

½ tsp. salt

½ tsp. pepper

½ tsp. crushed red pepper flakes

1. In a large bowl, toss halved sprouts with 2 Tbsp. olive oil.

2. Place them on a single layer on a rimmed cookie sheet.

3. Roast sprouts in the oven at 450°F, stirring twice, until crisp and lightly browned, about 15–20 minutes.

4. Whisk together in a large bowl ¼ cup oil, lemon juice, salt, pepper, and red pepper flakes.

5. Toss sprouts with dressing and serve.

TIP

Don't overcook the sprouts.

Warm Memories:
This is a lovely dish for any meal but especially nice at Easter.

Good Go-Alongs:
Sliced ham and new potatoes.

Exchange List Values
- Vegetable 1.0
- Fat 2.0

Basic Nutritional Values
- Calories 120
  (Calories from Fat 100)
- Total Fat 11 gm
  (Saturated Fat 1.5 gm,
  Trans Fat 0.0 gm,
  Polyunsat Fat 1.3 gm,
  Monounsat Fat 7.4 gm)
- Cholesterol 0 mg
- Sodium 165 mg
- Potassium 280 gm
- Total Carb 7 gm
- Dietary Fiber 2 gm
- Sugars 2 gm
- Protein 2 gm
- Phosphorus 50 gm

Balsamic Glazed Brussels Sprouts

Hope Comerford
Clinton Township, MI

Makes 8 servings
Prep. Time: 15 minutes
Roasting Time: 20 minutes

1½ lbs. Brussels sprouts, halved
¼ cup olive oil
½ tsp. salt
½ tsp. garlic powder
½ tsp. onion powder
¼ tsp. pepper
1 Tbsp. balsamic vinegar

1. Line a baking sheet with parchment paper.

2. In a bowl, toss together the Brussels sprouts, olive oil, salt, pepper, garlic powder, onion powder, and pepper. Dump onto baking sheet and spread out evenly.

3. Place baking sheet in a 450°F oven for 15 minutes.

4. The last 5 minutes of roasting, drizzle the balsamic vinegar over the Brussels sprouts.

Exchange List Values
- Carbohydrate 1.5 (vegetable)
- Fat 1.5

Basic Nutritional Values
- Calories 99 (Calories from Fat 63)
- Total Fat 7 gm (Saturated Fat 1 gm, Trans Fat 0.0 gm, Polyunsat Fat 0.8 gm, Monounsat Fat 4.9 gm)
- Cholesterol 0 mg
- Sodium 141 mg
- Potassium 337 gm
- Total Carb 8 gm
- Dietary Fiber 3.3 gm
- Sugars 2 gm
- Protein 2.9 gm
- Phosphorus 60 gm

Janie's Vegetable Medley

Janie Steele
Moore, OK

Makes 8 servings
Prep. Time: 25–30 minutes
Cooking Time: 1½–2 hours
Ideal slow-cooker size: 4-qt.

large potato, peeled and cut into small cubes

2 onions, chopped

2 carrots, sliced thin

¾ cup uncooked long-grain rice

2 Tbsp. lemon juice

¼ cup olive oil

2 16-oz. cans diced tomatoes, *divided*

1 cup water, *divided*

large green pepper, chopped

2 zucchini, chopped

2 Tbsp. parsley, chopped

½ a 1-lb. pkg. frozen green peas

¾ tsp. salt

1 cup grated cheese

hot sauce, *optional*

1. Combine cubed potato, chopped onions, sliced carrots, uncooked rice, lemon juice, olive oil, 1 can of tomatoes, and ½ cup water in slow cooker.

2. Cover and cook on High 1 hour.

3. Stir in remaining ingredients except grated cheese and hot sauce. Cover and cook 30–60 minutes, or until vegetables are tender but not mushy.

4. Serve in bowls, topped with grated cheese. Pass hot sauce to be added individually.

Exchange List Values
- Starch 1.5
- Vegetable 2.0
- Fat 2.0

Basic Nutritional Values
- Calories 260
  (Calories from Fat 90)
- Total Fat 10 gm
  (Saturated Fat 2.5 gm,
  Polyunsat Fat 1.0 gm,
  Monounsat Fat 6.0 gm)
- Cholesterol 5 mg
- Sodium 580 mg
- Total Carb 36 gm
- Dietary Fiber 5 gm
- Sugars 9 gm
- Protein 9 gm

Aunt Jean's Potatoes

Jen Hoover
Akron, PA

Makes 8 servings, about 5½ oz. per serving
Prep. Time: 30 minutes
Baking Time: 30 minutes
Cooling Time: 1 hour

6 medium potatoes

½ Tbsp. canola oil

⅓ cup onion, chopped fine

1 cup shredded 75%-reduced-fat cheddar cheese

1 cup fat-free sour cream

½ tsp. salt

¼ tsp. pepper

1 Tbsp. trans-fat-free tub margarine

4 slices bacon, fried and crumbled

paprika

1. Microwave, cook, or bake potatoes in skins; cool at least an hour.

2. Peel and shred coarsely.

3. In saucepan over low heat, sauté onion in canola oil, about 8 minutes. Do not brown!

4. Add cheese and stir until almost melted.

5. Remove from heat. Blend in sour cream, salt, and pepper.

6. Fold in shredded potatoes.

7. Put in greased casserole.

8. Dot with margarine, and sprinkle with paprika and bacon.

9. Bake at 350°F for 30 minutes or until heated through.

Warm Memories:
Mom brings these potatoes to our Diener family gatherings. She is not allowed to *not* bring them!

Exchange List Values
- Starch 2.0
- Lean Meat 1.0

Basic Nutritional Values
- Calories 205 (Calories from Fat 45)
- Total Fat 5 gm (Saturated Fat 1.6 gm, Trans Fat 0.0 gm, Polyunsat Fat 0.9 gm, Monounsat Fat 1.7 gm)
- Cholesterol 10 mg
- Sodium 370 mg
- Potassium 565 gm
- Total Carb 32 gm
- Dietary Fiber 3 gm
- Sugars 3 gm
- Protein 10 gm
- Phosphorus 230 gm

TIP

1. Can be made the day before baking or frozen for later use.
2. Great dish for potluck picnics.
3. Use frozen shredded potatoes instead—this is more costly but quicker to prepare.

Ranch Potato Cubes

Charlotte Shaffer
East Earl, PA

Makes 8 servings, about 6 oz. per serving
Prep. Time: 20 minutes
Baking Time: 1 hour

6 medium potatoes, cut into ½-inch cubes

4 Tbsp. trans-fat-free tub margarine

1 cup fat-free sour cream

1-oz. packet ranch salad dressing mix

1 cup (4-oz.) 75%-less-fat shredded cheddar
  cheese

1. Place potatoes in a greased 11×7-inch baking dish. Dot with margarine.

2. Cover. Bake at 350°F for 1 hour.

3. Combine sour cream and salad dressing mix.

4. Spoon over potatoes. Sprinkle with cheese.

5. Bake uncovered 10 minutes until cheese is melted.

Exchange List Values
- Starch 2.0
- Fat-Free Milk 0.5
- Fat 0.5

Basic Nutritional Values
- Calories 215
  (Calories from Fat 55)
- Total Fat 6 gm
  (Saturated Fat 1.8 gm,
  Trans Fat 0.0 gm,
  Polyunsat Fat 1.8 gm,
  Monounsat Fat 1.6 gm)
- Cholesterol 10 mg
- Sodium 450 mg
- Potassium 675 gm
- Total Carb 33 gm
- Dietary Fiber 3 gm
- Sugars 2 gm
- Protein 9 gm
- Phosphorus 180 gm

Company Mashed Potatoes

Eileen Eash
Carlsbad, NM

Makes 12 servings
Prep. Time: 40 minutes
Cooking Time: 12–16 hours
Ideal slow-cooker size: 6-qt.

15 (5 lb. total) medium-sized potatoes

1 cup reduced-fat sour cream

1 small onion, diced fine

1 tsp. salt

¼ tsp. pepper

1 cup buttermilk

1 cup fresh, chopped spinach

1 cup grated Colby or cheddar cheese,
optional

1. Peel and quarter potatoes. Place in slow cooker. Barely cover with water.

2. Cover. Cook on Low 8–10 hours. Drain water.

3. Mash potatoes. Add remaining ingredients except cheese.

4. Cover. Heat on low 4–6 hours.

5. Sprinkle with cheese 5 minutes before serving.

NOTES

1. I save the water drained from cooking the potatoes and use it to make gravy or a soup base.
2. Small amounts of leftovers from this recipe add a special flavor to vegetable or noodle soup for another meal.

Exchange List Value
• Starch 2.0

Basic Nutritional Values
• Calories 160
  (Calories from Fat 18)
• Total Fat 2 gm
  (Saturated Fat 1.1 gm,
  Polyunsat Fat 0.1 gm,
  Monounsat Fat 0.5 gm)
• Cholesterol 7 mg
• Sodium 236 mg
• Total Carb 32 gm
• Dietary Fiber 3 gm
• Sugars 5 gm
• Protein 5 gm

TIP

Buttermilk gives mashed potatoes a unique flavor that most people enjoy. I often serve variations of this recipe for guests and they always ask what I put in the potatoes.

Potatoes Perfect

Naomi Ressler
Harrisonburg, VA

Makes 6 servings
Prep. Time: 35 minutes
Cooking Time: 3–10 hours
Ideal slow-cooker size: 4-qt.

¼ lb. bacon, diced and browned until crisp

2 medium-sized onions, thinly sliced

6–8 medium-sized potatoes, thinly sliced

4 oz. fat-free cheddar cheese, shredded

pepper, to taste

2 Tbsp. light, soft tub margarine

1. Layer half of bacon, onions, potatoes, and cheese in greased slow cooker. Season to taste.

2. Dot with margarine. Repeat layers.

3. Cover. Cook on Low 8–10 hours or on High 3–4 hours, or until potatoes are soft.

Exchange List Values
- Starch 2.0
- Vegetable 1.0
- Fat 1.0

Basic Nutritional Values
- Calories 224
  (Calories from Fat 38)
- Total Fat 4 gm
  (Saturated Fat 0.9 gm,
  Polyunsat Fat 0.7 gm,
  Monounsat Fat 2.1 gm)
- Cholesterol 6 mg
- Sodium 262 mg
- Total Carb 35 gm
- Dietary Fiber 4 gm
- Sugars 7 gm
- Protein 12 gm

Lotsa Scalloped Potatoes

**Fannie Miller
Hutchinson, KS**

Makes 25 servings
Prep. Time: 40 minutes
Cooking Time: 2–3 hours
Ideal slow-cooker size: 6-qt.

5 lbs. potatoes, cooked and sliced

2 lbs. extra-lean, lower-sodium cooked ham, cubed

¼ lb. light, soft tub margarine

½ cup flour

2 cups fat-free half-and-half

¼ lb. reduced-fat mild cheese, shredded

¼–½ tsp. pepper

1. Place layers of sliced potatoes and ham in slow cooker.

2. Melt margarine in saucepan on stove. Whisk in flour. Gradually add half-and-half to make a white sauce, stirring constantly until smooth and thickened.

3. Stir in cheese and pepper. Stir until cheese is melted. Pour over potatoes and ham.

4. Cover. Cook on Low 2–3 hours.

NOTES

A great way to free up oven space.

Exchange List Values
- Starch 1.0
- Lean meat 1.0

Basic Nutritional Values
- Calories 136
  (Calories from Fat 24)
- Total Fat 3 gm
  (Saturated Fat 1.0 gm,
  Polyunsat Fat 0.4 gm,
  Monounsat Fat 0.9 gm)
- Cholesterol 21 mg
- Sodium 379 mg
- Total Carb 19 gm
- Dietary Fiber 1 gm
- Sugars 4 gm
- Protein 10 gm

Shredded Baked Potatoes

**Alice Miller
Stuarts Draft, VA**

Makes 6 servings, about 7½ oz. per serving
Prep. Time: 35 minutes
Baking Time: 45 minutes

6 medium potatoes
1 cup fat-free sour cream
6–8 green onions, chopped
1 cup 75%-less-fat shredded cheddar cheese
½ tsp. salt
2 Tbsp. trans-fat-free tub margarine

1. Cook, cool, peel, and shred potatoes.

2. Combine potatoes, sour cream, onions, cheese, and salt.

3. Spoon into 2-qt. casserole dish.

4. Melt margarine and pour over top of casserole.

5. Bake at 400°F for 45 minutes, until light brown and bubbly.

Exchange List Values
- Starch 1.5
- Fat-Free Milk 0.5
- Fat 0.5

Basic Nutritional Values
- Calories 200
  (Calories from Fat 45)
- Total Fat 5 gm
  (Saturated Fat 1.8 gm,
  Trans Fat 0.0 gm,
  Polyunsat Fat 1.3 gm,
  Monounsat Fat 1.2 gm)
- Cholesterol 10 mg
- Sodium 430 mg
- Potassium 745 gm
- Total Carb 30 gm
- Dietary Fiber 3 gm
- Sugars 4 gm
- Protein 11 gm
- Phosphorus 220 gm

Creamy Hash Browns

Judy Buller
Bluffton, OH
Elaine Patton
West Middletown, PA
Melissa Raber
Millersburg, OH

Makes 14 servings
Prep. Time: 25 minutes
Cooking Time: 4–5 hours
Ideal slow-cooker size: 4- or 5-qt.

2-lb. pkg. frozen, cubed hash brown potatoes

2 cups cubed or shredded fat-free American cheese

12 oz. fat-free sour cream

10¾-oz. can cream of celery soup

10¾-oz. can 98%-fat-free, lower-sodium cream of chicken soup

¼ lb. sliced bacon, cooked and crumbled

1 medium onion, chopped

2 Tbsp. margarine, melted

¼ tsp. pepper

1. Place potatoes in slow cooker. Combine remaining ingredients and pour over potatoes. Mix well.

2. Cover. Cook on Low 4–5 hours, or until potatoes are tender.

Exchange List Values
- Starch 1.0
- Carbohydrate 0.5
- Fat 1.0

Basic Nutritional Values
- Calories 167 (Calories from Fat 44)
- Total Fat 5 gm (Saturated Fat 1.4 gm, Polyunsat Fat 1.5 gm, Monounsat Fat 1.6 gm)
- Cholesterol 9 mg
- Sodium 578 mg
- Total Carb 23 gm
- Dietary Fiber 2 gm
- Sugars 4 gm
- Protein 8 gm

Sour Cream Potatoes

**Renee Baum
Chambersburg, PA**

Makes 8 servings, about 7½ oz. per serving
Prep. Time: 30 minutes
Baking/Cooking Time: 1 hour

3½ lbs. potatoes, about 10 medium

4 oz. fat-free cream cheese

4 oz. Neufchâtel (⅓-less-fat) cream cheese

8 oz. fat-free sour cream

¼ cup fat-free milk

2 Tbsp. trans-fat-free tub margarine, *divided*

2 Tbsp. chopped fresh parsley or 1 Tbsp.
   dried parsley

1¼ tsp. garlic salt

¼ tsp. paprika

1. Peel and quarter potatoes. Place in a large saucepan and cover with water. Bring to a boil.

2. Reduce heat, cover partially, and cook 15–20 minutes until tender. Drain.

3. Mash the potatoes.

4. Add cream cheese, Neufchâtel cheese, sour cream, milk, 1 Tbsp. margarine, parsley, and garlic salt. Beat until smooth.

5. Spoon mixture into a greased 2-qt. baking dish.

6. Dot with remaining margarine. Sprinkle with paprika.

7. Bake, uncovered, at 350°F for 30–40 minutes or until heated through.

Exchange List Values
- Starch 2.0
- Fat-Free Milk 0.5
- Fat 0.5

Basic Nutritional Values
- Calories 225
  (Calories from Fat 55)
- Total Fat 6 gm
  (Saturated Fat 2.4 gm,
  Trans Fat 0.0 gm,
  Polyunsat Fat 1.1 gm,
  Monounsat Fat 1.5 gm)
- Cholesterol 15 mg
- Sodium 415 mg
- Potassium 610 gm
- Total Carb 36 gm
- Dietary Fiber 3 gm
- Sugars 4 gm
- Protein 7 gm
- Phosphorus 190 gm

Baked German Potato Salad

Bernice Hertzler
Phoenix, AZ

Makes 12 servings, about 6 oz. per serving
Prep. Time: 30 minutes
Baking Time: 30 minutes

8 strips bacon

1 cup chopped celery

1 cup chopped onion

3 Tbsp. flour

1⅓ cups water

1 cup cider vinegar

⅔ cup granulated Splenda

1 tsp. salt

¼ tsp. pepper

8 cups cooked potatoes, cubed

1 cup sliced radishes, *optional*

1. Fry, drain, and crumble bacon. Drain all bacon drippings from skillet, reserving 1½ Tbsp. Set bacon pieces aside.

2. Sauté celery and onion in bacon drippings for 1 minute. Blend in flour, stirring until bubbly. Add water and vinegar, stirring constantly until mixture is thick and bubbly. Stir in Splenda, salt, and pepper, cooking until Splenda dissolves.

3. Place cubed potatoes into greased 3-qt. casserole dish. Pour sauce over potatoes and mix lightly. Fold in bacon pieces.

4. Cover and bake at 350°F for 30 minutes.

5. Remove from oven and stir in radishes, if using. Serve immediately.

Exchange List Values
- Starch 1.5
- Fat 0.5

Basic Nutritional Values
- Calories 150
  (Calories from Fat 30)
- Total Fat 4 gm
  (Saturated Fat 1.2 gm,
  Trans Fat 0.0 gm,
  Polyunsat Fat 0.4 gm,
  Monounsat Fat 1.5 gm)
- Cholesterol 5 mg
- Sodium 305 mg
- Potassium 420 gm
- Total Carb 25 gm
- Dietary Fiber 2 gm
- Sugars 3 gm
- Protein 4 gm
- Phosphorus 70 gm

Pizza Potatoes

**Margaret Wenger Johnson
Keezletown, VA**

Makes 8 servings
Prep. Time: 20 minutes
Cooking Time: 6–10 hours
Ideal slow-cooker size: 4-qt.

6 (5¾ oz.) medium potatoes, sliced

1 large onion, thinly sliced

2 Tbsp. olive oil

6 oz. (1½ cups) grated fat-free mozzarella cheese

2 oz. sliced turkey pepperoni

8-oz. can pizza sauce

1. Sauté potato and onion slices in oil in skillet until onions appear transparent. Drain well.

2. In slow cooker, combine potatoes, onion, cheese, and pepperoni.

3. Pour pizza sauce over top.

4. Cover. Cook on Low 6–10 hours, or until potatoes are soft.

Exchange List Values
- Starch 2.0
- Lean Meat 1.0

Basic Nutritional Values
- Calories 205
  (Calories from Fat 43)
- Total Fat 5 gm
  (Saturated Fat 0.9 gm,
  Polyunsat Fat 0.8 gm,
  Monounsat Fat 2.9 gm)
- Cholesterol 12 mg
- Sodium 417 mg
- Total Carb 27 gm
- Dietary Fiber 3 gm
- Sugars 6 gm
- Protein 13 gm

Glazed Tzimmes

**Elaine Vigoda
Rochester, NY**

Makes 8 servings
Prep. Time: 40 minutes
Cooking Time: 10 hours
Ideal slow-cooker size: 6-qt.

1 sweet potato

6 carrots, sliced

1 potato, peeled and diced

1 onion, chopped

2 apples, peeled and sliced

1 medium (about 1½ lbs.) butternut squash, peeled and sliced

¼ cup dry white wine or apple juice

½ lb. dried apricots

1 Tbsp. ground cinnamon

1 Tbsp. apple pie spice

1 Tbsp. maple syrup or honey

1 tsp. salt

1 tsp. ground ginger

1. Combine all ingredients in large slow cooker, or mix all ingredients in large bowl and place in slow cooker.

2. Cover. Cook on Low 10 hours.

Exchange List Values
- Starch 1.0
- Fruit 1.5
- Vegetable 1.0

Basic Nutritional Values
- Calories 179 (Calories from Fat 5)
- Total Fat 1 gm (Saturated Fat 0.1 gm, Polyunsat Fat 0.2 gm, Monounsat Fat 0.1 gm)
- Cholesterol 0 mg
- Sodium 332 mg
- Total Carb 45 gm
- Dietary Fiber 6 gm
- Sugars 27 gm
- Protein 3 gm

Sweet Potato Casserole

Jean Butzer
Batavia, NY

Makes 10 servings
Prep. Time: 25 minutes
Cooking Time: 3–4 hours
Ideal slow-cooker size: 4- or 5-qt.

2 29-oz. cans no-sugar-added sweet
   potatoes, drained and mashed

2½ Tbsp. light, soft tub margarine

1 Tbsp. sugar

⅓ cup plus 2 Tbsp. brown sugar substitute,
   divided

1 Tbsp. orange juice

2 eggs, beaten

½ cup fat-free milk

⅓ cup chopped pecans

2 Tbsp. flour

2 tsp. light, soft tub margarine, melted

Exchange List Values
- Starch 2.0
- Carbohydrate 0.5
- Fat 0.5

Basic Nutritional Values
- Calories 218
  (Calories from Fat 51)
- Total Fat 6 gm
  (Saturated Fat 0.7 gm,
  Polyunsat Fat 1.4 gm,
  Monounsat Fat 2.9 gm)
- Cholesterol 43 mg
- Sodium 64 mg
- Total Carb 40 gm
- Dietary Fiber 5 gm
- Sugars 24 gm
- Protein 5 gm

1. Combine sweet potatoes, ⅓ cup
magarine, 2 Tbsp. sugar, and 2 Tbsp. brown
sugar substitute.

2. Beat in orange juice, eggs, and milk.
Transfer to greased slow cooker.

3. Combine pecans, ⅓ cup brown sugar
substitute, flour, and 2 tsp. margarine. Spread
over sweet potatoes.

4. Cover. Cook on High 3–4 hours.

Sweet Potatoes and Apples

Bernita Boyts
Shawnee Mission, KS

Makes 8 servings
Prep. Time: 25 minutes
Cooking Time: 6–8 hours
Ideal slow-cooker size: 4-qt.

3 large sweet potatoes, peeled and cubed

3 large tart and firm apples, peeled and sliced

½ tsp. salt

⅛–¼ tsp. pepper

1 tsp. dried sage

1 tsp. ground cinnamon

4 Tbsp. light, soft tub margarine, melted

2 Tbsp. maple syrup brown sugar substitute to equal 1 Tbsp. sugar

toasted sliced almonds or chopped pecans, *optional*

1. Place half the sweet potatoes in slow cooker. Layer in half the apple slices.

2. Mix together seasonings. Sprinkle half over apples.

3. Mix together margarine, maple syrup, and brown sugar. Spoon half over seasonings.

4. Repeat layers.

5. Cover. Cook on Low, stirring occasionally, 6–8 hours or until potatoes are soft.

6. To add a bit of crunch, sprinkle with toasted almonds or pecans when serving. Serve with pork or poultry.

Exchange List Values
- Starch 1.0
- Fruit 1.0
- Fat 0.5

Basic Nutritional Values
- Calories 152
  (Calories from Fat 24)
- Total Fat 3 gm
  (Saturated Fat 0.1 gm,
  Polyunsat Fat 0.7 gm,
  Monounsat Fat 1.3 gm)
- Cholesterol 0 mg
- Sodium 201 mg
- Total Carb 32 gm
- Dietary Fiber 3 gm
- Sugars 17 gm
- Protein 1 gm

Candied Sweet Potatoes

Julie Weaver
Reinholds, PA

Makes 8 servings
Prep. Time: 30 minutes
Cooking Time: 4 hours
Ideal slow-cooker size: 4-qt.

6 medium (6½ oz. each) sweet potatoes

½ tsp. salt

2 Tbsp. margarine, melted

20-oz. can crushed pineapples, undrained

2 Tbsp. brown sugar substitute to equal 1 Tbsp. sugar

1 tsp. nutmeg

1 tsp. cinnamon

1. Cook sweet potatoes until soft. Peel. Slice and place in slow cooker.

2. Combine remaining ingredients. Pour over sweet potatoes.

3. Cover. Cook on High 4 hours.

Exchange List Values
- Starch 1.5
- Fruit 1.0
- Fat 0.5

Basic Nutritional Values
- Calories 186
  (Calories from Fat 30)
- Total Fat 3 gm
  (Saturated Fat 0.7 gm,
  Polyunsat Fat 1.1 gm,
  Monounsat Fat 1.3 gm)
- Cholesterol 0 mg
- Sodium 193 mg
- Total Carb 39 gm
- Dietary Fiber 3 gm
- Sugars 19 gm
- Protein 2 gm

Orange-Glazed Sweet Potatoes

**Annabelle Kratz
Clarksville, MD**

Makes 12 servings, a 3-inch square per
  serving
Prep. Time: 20 minutes
Cooking/Baking Time: 1 hour

8 medium sweet potatoes, 6 oz. each

½ tsp. salt

¼ cup Splenda Brown Sugar Blend

2 Tbsp. cornstarch

½ tsp. shredded orange peel

2 cups orange juice

½ cup raisins

2 Tbsp. trans-fat-free tub margarine

¼ cup chopped walnuts

1. Cook potatoes in boiling, salted water until just tender. Drain.

2. Peel potatoes and cut lengthwise into ½-inch slices. Arrange in 9×13-inch baking dish. Sprinkle with ½ tsp. salt.

3. In a saucepan combine brown sugar substitute and cornstarch. Blend in orange peel and juice. Add raisins. Cook and stir over medium heat until thickened and bubbly. Cook 1 minute longer.

4. Add margarine and walnuts, stirring until margarine has melted. Pour sauce over sweet potatoes.

5. Bake at 325°F for 30 minutes or until sweet potatoes are well-glazed. Baste occasionally.

Variation:
Immediately before pouring sauce over sweet potatoes, fold in 2 cups apricot halves
—Dorothy Shank, Goshen, IN

Exchange List Values
- Starch 1.5
- Fruit 0.5
- Fat 0.5

Basic Nutritional Values
- Calories 160
  (Calories from Fat 25)
- Total Fat 3 gm
  (Saturated Fat 0.5 gm,
  Trans Fat 0.0 gm,
  Polyunsat Fat 1.8 gm,
  Monounsat Fat 0.7 gm)
- Cholesterol 0 mg
- Sodium 140 mg
- Potassium 375 gm
- Total Carb 32 gm
- Dietary Fiber 3 gm
- Sugars 15 gm
- Protein 2 gm
- Phosphorus 55 gm

Fruited Wild Rice with Pecans

Dottie Schmidt
Kansas City, MO

Makes 8 servings
Prep. Time: 15 minutes
Cooking Time: 2–2½ hours
Ideal slow-cooker size: 4-qt.

½ cup chopped onions

1 Tbsp. canola oil

6-oz. pkg. long-grain and wild rice

seasoning packet from wild rice pkg.

1½ cups hot water

⅔ cup apple juice

1 large tart apple, chopped

¼ cup raisins

¼ cup coarsely chopped pecans

1. Combine all ingredients except pecans in slow cooker sprayed with nonfat cooking spray.

2. Cover. Cook on High 2–2½ hours.

3. Stir in pecans. Serve.

Exchange List Values
- Starch 1.0
- Fruit 1.0
- Fat 0.5

Basic Nutritional Values
- Calories 154
  (Calories from Fat 43)
- Total Fat 5 gm
  (Saturated Fat 0.4 gm,
  Polyunsat Fat 1.3 gm,
  Monounsat Fat 2.7 gm)
- Cholesterol 0 mg
- Sodium 237 mg
- Total Carb 27 gm
- Dietary Fiber 2 gm
- Sugars 9 gm
- Protein 3 gm

Risi Bisi (Peas and Rice)

**Cyndie Marrara
Port Matilda, PA**

Makes 8 servings
Prep. Time: 15 minutes
Cooking Time: 2½–3½ hours
Ideal slow-cooker size: 4-qt.

1½ cups converted long-grain white rice, uncooked

¾ cup chopped onion

2 cloves garlic, minced

2 14½-oz. cans reduced-sodium chicken broth

⅓ cup water

¾ tsp. Italian herb seasoning

½ tsp. dried basil

½ cup frozen baby peas, thawed

¼ cup freshly grated Parmesan cheese

1. Combine rice, onion, and garlic in slow cooker.

2. In saucepan, mix together chicken broth and water. Bring to boil. Add Italian seasoning and basil. Stir into rice mixture.

3. Cover. Cook on Low 2–3 hours, or until liquid is absorbed.

4. Stir in peas. Cover. Cook 30 minutes. Stir in cheese.

Exchange List Value
• Starch 2.0

Basic Nutritional Values
• Calories 165
  (Calories from Fat 11)
• Total Fat 1 gm
  (Saturated Fat 0.5 gm,
  Polyunsat Fat 0.1 gm,
  Monounsat Fat 0.4 gm)
• Cholesterol 3 mg
• Sodium 409 mg
• Total Carb 32 gm
• Dietary Fiber 1 gm
• Sugars 2 gm
• Protein 6 gm

Slow-Cooker Stuffing

**Dede Peterson
Rapid City, SD**

Makes 12 servings
Prep. Time: 30 minutes
Cooking Time: 4 hours
Ideal slow-cooker size: 6-qt.

12 cups toasted bread crumbs, or dressing mix

4 oz. 50%-less-fat bulk sausage, browned and drained

2 Tbsp. canola oil

1 cup or more finely chopped onions

1 cup or more finely chopped celery

8-oz. can sliced mushrooms, with liquid

¼ cup chopped fresh parsley

2 tsp. poultry seasoning (omit if using dressing mix)

dash pepper

2 eggs, beaten

4 tsp. salt-free bouillon powder

4 cups water

1. Combine bread crumbs and sausage.

2. Put oil in skillet. Add onions and celery and sauté until tender. Stir in mushrooms and parsley. Add seasonings. Pour over bread crumbs and mix well.

3. Stir in eggs and bouillon mixed with water.

4. Pour into slow cooker and cook on High 1 hour, and on Low an additional 3 hours.

Variations:

1. For a less spicy stuffing, reduce the poultry seasoning to ½ tsp.
            —Dolores Metzler, Mechanicsburg, PA

2. Substitute 3½–4½ cups cooked and diced giblets in place of sausage. Add another can mushrooms and 2 tsp. sage in Step 2.
            —Mrs. Don Martins, Fairbank, IA

Exchange List Values
- Starch 2.0
- Fat 1.0

Basic Nutritional Values
- Calories 209
  (Calories from Fat 68)
- Total Fat 8 gm
  (Saturated Fat 1.5 gm,
  Polyunsat Fat 1.9 gm,
  Monounsat Fat 2.4 gm)
- Cholesterol 44 mg
- Sodium 423 mg
- Total Carb 28 gm
- Dietary Fiber 2 gm
- Sugars 4 gm
- Protein 8 gm

Slow-Cooker Cornbread Dressing

Marie Shank
Harrisonburg, VA

Makes 20 servings
Prep. Time: 45 minutes
Cooling Time: 2 hours
Cooking Time: 3–9 hours
Ideal slow-cooker size: 6-qt.

2 (8.5-oz.) boxes Jiffy Corn Muffin Mix

8 slices day-old bread

3 eggs

1 onion, chopped

½ cup chopped celery

2 10¾-oz. cans 98%-fat-free, lower-sodium cream of chicken soup

2 tsp. salt-free chicken bouillon powder

2 cups water

½ tsp. pepper

1½ Tbsp. sage or poultry seasoning

1. Prepare and bake cornbread according to package instructions. Cool.

2. Crumble cornbread and bread together.

3. In large bowl combine all ingredients and spoon into 6-qt. greased slow cooker, or 2 smaller cookers.

4. Cover. Cook on High 2–4 hours or on Low 3–8 hours.

Variations:

1. Prepare your favorite cornbread recipe in an 8-inch-square baking pan instead of using the boxed mix.

2. Serve with roast chicken or turkey drumsticks.

—Helen Kenagy, Carlsbad, NM

Exchange List Values
- Starch 1.5
- Fat 0.5

Basic Nutritional Values
- Calories 133
  (Calories from Fat 34)
- Total Fat 4 gm
  (Saturated Fat 1.5 gm,
  Polyunsat Fat 0.9 gm,
  Monounsat Fat 1.1 gm)
- Cholesterol 35 mg
- Sodium 387 mg
- Total Carb 26 gm
- Dietary Fiber 1 gm
- Sugars 6 gm
- Protein 4 gm

Baked Beans

Barbara Hershey
Lititz, PA

Makes 10 servings, about 6½ oz. per serving
Prep. Time: 30 minutes
Soaking Time: overnight
Cooking/Baking Time: 2–6 hours

1 lb. dry great northern beans

1 tsp. salt

½ tsp. baking soda

2 cups low-sodium V8 juice

1 small onion, minced

2 Tbsp. molasses

1 tsp. dry mustard

7 pieces bacon, fried and drained

½ cup ketchup

¼ cup Splenda Brown Sugar Blend

1. Cover beans with about 3 inches of water and allow to soak overnight.

2. In morning, add salt and baking soda.

3. Bring to boil. Cook about 20–25 minutes until beans are soft. Drain.

4. Pour beans into large baking dish.

5. Add juice, onion, molasses, mustard, bacon, ketchup, and Splenda. Mix.

6. Bake at 325°F for 2 hours or on Low in slow cooker for 5–6 hours.

Good Go-Alongs:
Hamburgers, hot dogs, coleslaw.

TIP

If you don't have time to soak dry beans, you could purchase 6 16-oz. cans of great northern beans and drain before adding other ingredients.

Exchange List Values
- Starch 1.5
- Carbohydrate 0.5
- Lean Meat 1.0

Basic Nutritional Values
- Calories 215 (Calories from Fat 20)
- Total Fat 2.5 gm (Saturated Fat 0.8 gm, Trans Fat 0.0 gm, Polyunsat Fat 0.4 gm, Monounsat Fat 0.9 gm)
- Cholesterol 5 mg
- Sodium 565 mg
- Potassium 685 gm
- Total Carb 37 gm
- Dietary Fiber 9 gm
- Sugars 11 gm
- Protein 12 gm
- Phosphorus 225 gm

Best-in-the-West Beans

Lorraine Martin
Dryden, MI

Makes 10 servings, about ⅔ cup per serving
Prep. Time: 20 minutes
Baking Time: 1–5 hours

½ lb. ground beef

5 slices bacon, chopped

½ cup chopped onion

¼ cup brown sugar

¼ cup white sugar

¼ cup no-salt ketchup

¼ cup low-sodium, low-carb barbecue sauce

2 Tbsp. prepared mustard

2 Tbsp. molasses

½ tsp. chili powder

½ tsp. pepper

16-oz. can kidney beans

16-oz. can butter beans

16-oz. can pork and beans

Exchange List Values
- Starch 1.5
- Carbohydrate 1.0
- Lean Meat 1.0

Basic Nutritional Values
- Calories 225
  (Calories from Fat 35)
- Total Fat 4 gm
  (Saturated Fat 1.3 gm,
  Trans Fat 0.1 gm,
  Polyunsat Fat 0.5 gm,
  Monounsat Fat 1.6 gm)
- Cholesterol 20 mg
- Sodium 470 mg
- Potassium 615 gm
- Total Carb 37 gm
- Dietary Fiber 6 gm
- Sugars 17 gm
- Protein 13 gm
- Phosphorus 190 gm

1. Brown ground beef and bacon. Drain. Add onion and cook until tender. Add all other ingredients except beans and mix well.

2. Drain kidney beans and butter beans. Add all beans to meat mixture. Pour into slow cooker or 3-qt. casserole dish.

3. To prepare in slow cooker, cook on High for 1 hour. Reduce heat to Low and cook for 4 hours. To prepare in oven, bake at 350°F for 1 hour.

Salads

BLT Salad

Alica Denlinger
Lancaster, PA

Makes 12 servings, about 3½ oz. per serving
Prep. Time: 30 minutes

Salad:
2 heads Romaine lettuce, torn
2 cups chopped tomatoes
4 bacon strips, cooked and crumbled
½ cup freshly grated Parmesan cheese
1 cup croutons

Dressing:
¼ cup olive oil
½ tsp. salt
½ tsp. pepper
¼ cup fresh lemon juice
2 cloves garlic, crushed

1. Toss together salad ingredients in a large bowl.

2. Shake together dressing ingredients.

3. Pour dressing over salad immediately before serving.

Exchange List Values
- Vegetable 1.0
- Fat 1.5

Basic Nutritional Values
- Calories 90
  (Calories from Fat 65)
- Total Fat 7 gm
  (Saturated Fat 1.5 gm,
  Trans Fat 0.0 gm,
  Polyunsat Fat 0.7 gm,
  Monounsat Fat 4.0 gm)
- Cholesterol 5 mg
- Sodium 220 mg
- Potassium 250 gm
- Total Carb 6 gm
- Dietary Fiber 2 gm
- Sugars 2 gm
- Protein 3 gm
- Phosphorus 60 gm

Lettuce Salad with Hot Bacon Dressing

Mary B. Sensenig
New Holland, PA

Makes 12 servings, about 3 oz. lettuce and 2 Tbsp. dressing per serving
Prep. Time: 5 minutes
Cooking Time: 15 minutes

5 pieces bacon

¼ cup sugar

1 Tbsp. cornstarch

½ tsp. salt

1 egg, beaten

1 cup fat-free milk

¼ cup vinegar

36 oz. ready-to-serve mixed lettuces, or 2 medium heads iceberg lettuce

Exchange List Values
- Carbohydrate
- 0.5 Fat 0.5

Basic Nutritional Values
- Calories 60 (Calories from Fat 15)
- Total Fat 2 gm (Saturated Fat 0.5 gm, Trans Fat 0.0 gm, Polyunsat Fat 0.3 gm, Monounsat Fat 0.7 gm)
- Cholesterol 20 mg
- Sodium 180 mg
- Potassium 180 gm
- Total Carb 9 gm
- Dietary Fiber 1 gm
- Sugars 7 gm
- Protein 3 gm
- Phosphorus 60 gm

1. Sautée bacon in skillet until crisp.

2. Remove bacon from heat and drain. Chop. Discard drippings.

3. Add sugar, cornstarch, and salt to skillet. Blend together well.

4. Add egg, milk, and vinegar, stirring until smooth.

5. Cook over low heat, stirring continually, until thickened and smooth.

6. When dressing is no longer hot, but still warm, toss with torn lettuce leaves and chopped bacon.

7. Serve immediately.

Mexican Salad

**Jan Pembleton
Arlington, TX**

Makes 10 servings, about 6 oz. per serving
Prep. Time: 20 minutes
Cooking Time: 15 minutes
Cooling Time: 30 minutes

1 head lettuce

¾ lb. 93%-lean ground beef

2 tomatoes, chopped

16-oz. can kidney beans, drained

¾ cup freshly grated cheddar cheese

¼ cup diced onion

¼ cup sliced black olives, sliced

1 avocado, diced

2 oz. tortilla chips, crushed

Sauce:

8 oz. fat-free Thousand Island dressing

1 Tbsp. dry low-sodium taco seasoning

1 Tbsp. hot sauce

1 Tbsp. sugar

1. Wash lettuce and tear into bite-size pieces.

2. Brown, drain, and cool ground meat.

3. Combine all salad ingredients except tortilla chips. Set aside.

4. Combine all sauce ingredients. Pour sauce over salad and toss thoroughly.

5. Immediately before serving, add tortilla chips.

Exchange List Values

- Starch 0.5
- Carbohydrate 0.5
- Vegetable 1.0
- Med-Fat Meat 1.0
- Fat 0.5

Basic Nutritional Values

- Calories 215
  (Calories from Fat 70)
- Total Fat 8 gm
  (Saturated Fat 2.5 gm,
  Trans Fat 0.1 gm,
  Polyunsat Fat 1.0 gm,
  Monounsat Fat 4.0 gm)
- Cholesterol 25 mg
- Sodium 380 mg
- Potassium 495 gm
- Total Carb 23 gm
- Dietary Fiber 5 gm
- Sugars 7 gm
- Protein 13 gm
- Phosphorus 180 gm

Italian Green Salad

Jane Geigley
Lancaster, PA

Makes 4 servings, about 7 oz. per serving
Prep. Time: 10 minutes

16-oz. pkg. green salad mix

1 oz. pastrami, chopped in ½-inch pieces

¼ cup shredded part-skim mozzarella cheese

4 plum tomatoes, chopped

1 tsp. Italian herb seasoning

3 Tbsp. fat-free Italian salad dressing

¼ cup sliced ripe olives

1 cup seasoned croutons

1. Combine salad mix, pastrami, mozzarella, tomatoes, and seasoning.

2. Drizzle with salad dressing; toss to coat.

3. Before serving, top with olives and croutons. Serve immediately.

Serving suggestion:
Garnish with fresh basil.

Warm Memories:
It's a great dish on a hot day. People just love this salad when I take it to gatherings.

Good Go-Alongs:
Great with a pizza party.

Exchange List Values
- Starch 0.5
- Vegetable 1.0
- Lean Meat 1.0
- Fat 0.5

Basic Nutritional Values
- Calories 125
  (Calories from Fat 45)
- Total Fat 5 gm
  (Saturated Fat 1.7 gm,
  Trans Fat 0.0 gm,
  Polyunsat Fat 0.6 gm,
  Monounsat Fat 2.2 gm)
- Cholesterol 10 mg
- Sodium 455 mg
- Potassium 530 gm
- Total Carb 14 gm
- Dietary Fiber 4 gm
- Sugars 4 gm
- Protein 7 gm
- Phosphorus 120 gm

Very Good Salad Dressing

Lydia K. Stoltzfus
Gordonville, PA

Makes 2⅔ cups, 24 servings, 2 Tbsp. per serving
Prep. Time: 10 minutes

2 cups mayonnaise

½ cup granulated Splenda

1 Tbsp. prepared mustard

1 Tbsp. vinegar

¼ tsp. salt

¼ tsp. celery seed

¼ tsp. dried parsley

dash pepper

¼ cup pickle juice

TIP

Use on tossed salad or coleslaw.

1. Mix together mayonnaise, Splenda, mustard, vinegar, salt, celery seed, parsley, and pepper to taste.

2. Add pickle juice last, to desired consistency.

Exchange List Value
• Fat 0.5

Basic Nutritional Values
• Calories 25
  (Calories from Fat 15)
• Total Fat 2 gm
  (Saturated Fat 0.2 gm,
  Trans Fat 0.0 gm,
  Polyunsat Fat 0.8 gm,
  Monounsat Fat 0.3 gm)
• Cholesterol 0 mg
• Sodium 235 mg
• Potassium 10 gm
• Total Carb 3 gm
• Dietary Fiber 0 gm
• Sugars 1 gm
• Protein 0 gm
• Phosphorus 5 gm

Crunchy Romaine Toss

Jolene Schrock
Millersburg, OH
Jamie Mowry
Arlington, TX
Lucille Hollinger
Richland, PA

Makes 8 servings, about 3 oz. per serving
Prep. Time: 20–30 minutes
Cooking Time: 10 minutes

Dressing:

1 Tbsp. sugar

2 Tbsp. canola oil

2 Tbsp. cider vinegar

1 tsp. reduced-sodium soy sauce

salt and pepper, to taste

3-oz. pkg. ramen noodles, broken up,
    seasoning packets discarded

½ Tbsp. trans-fat-free tub margarine

1½ cups chopped broccoli

1 small head romaine lettuce, torn up

4 green onions, chopped

½ cup chopped walnuts

1. In the blender, combine sugar, oil, vinegar, soy sauce, salt, and pepper. Blend until sugar is dissolved.

2. In a skillet, sauté ramen noodles in margarine until golden brown.

3. In a large bowl, combine broccoli, lettuce, onions, and noodles.

4. Just before serving, toss with nuts and dressing.

Variations:

1. Use 2 cups sliced fresh strawberries in place of broccoli. Increase walnuts to 1 cup.
—Janice Nolt, Ephrata, PA

2. Add 1 small can mandarin oranges, drained.
—Janet Derstine, Telford, PA

Exchange List Values

- Starch 0.5
- Vegetable 1.0
- Fat 2.0

Basic Nutritional Values

- Calories 150
  (Calories from Fat 100)
- Total Fat 11 gm
  (Saturated Fat 1.5 gm,
  Trans Fat 0.0 gm,
  Polyunsat Fat 5.6 gm,
  Monounsat Fat 3.8 gm)
- Cholesterol 0 mg
- Sodium 75 mg
- Potassium 185 gm
- Total Carb 12 gm
- Dietary Fiber 2 gm
- Sugars 3 gm
- Protein 3 gm
- Phosphorus 60 gm

TIP

Sometimes I like to set the dressing on the side and let everybody put their own dressing on. Plus, if you have any leftover salad it won't get soggy.

Lettuce and Egg Salad

Frances Kruba and Cathy Kruba
Dundalk, MD

Makes 6 servings, about 3½ oz. salad plus 2 Tbsp. dressing per serving
Prep. Time: 25 minutes

⅔ cup low-fat mayonnaise

1⅓ Tbsp. vinegar

2 tsp. sugar

1 head lettuce, washed and dried, torn

2 hard-boiled eggs, chopped

1–4 green onions, chopped

1. In a jar, mix mayonnaise, vinegar, and sugar and shake well.

2. Just before serving, mix lettuce, eggs, and onions. Add dressing, a little at a time, to your taste preference.

Exchange List Values
- Carbohydrate 0.5
- Fat 0.5

Basic Nutritional Values
- Calories 70 (Calories from Fat 30)
- Total Fat 4 gm (Saturated Fat 0.8 gm, Trans Fat 0.0 gm, Polyunsat Fat 1.4 gm, Monounsat Fat 1.0 gm)
- Cholesterol 60 mg
- Sodium 265 mg
- Potassium 165 gm
- Total Carb 8 gm
- Dietary Fiber 1 gm
- Sugars 4 gm
- Protein 3 gm
- Phosphorus 60 gm

Tortellini Caesar Salad

Rebecca Meyerkorth
Wamego, KS

Makes 10 servings, about 3 oz. per serving
Prep. Time: 30–35 minutes
Cooking Time: 15 minutes

9-oz. pkg. frozen cheese tortellini

½ cup low-fat mayonnaise

¼ cup fat-free milk

½ cup freshly shredded Parmesan cheese, *divided*

2 Tbsp. lemon juice

2 cloves garlic, minced

8 cups torn Romaine lettuce

1 cup seasoned croutons, *optional*

halved cherry tomatoes, *optional*

1. Cook tortellini according to package directions. Drain and rinse with cold water.

2. Meanwhile, in a small bowl, combine mayonnaise, milk, ⅓ cup Parmesan cheese, lemon juice, and garlic. Mix well.

3. Put cooled tortellini in large bowl.

4. Add Romaine and remaining 2⅔ Tbsp. Parmesan.

5. Just before serving, drizzle with dressing and toss to coat. Top with croutons and tomatoes, if desired.

Warm Memories:

Just plain delicious! This salad is especially good in hot summer weather. Our family loves it.

Exchange List Values
- Starch 0.5
- Carbohydrate 0.5
- Fat 0.5

Basic Nutritional Values
- Calories 95 (Calories from Fat 30)
- Total Fat 4 gm (Saturated Fat 1.4 gm, Trans Fat 0.0 gm, Polyunsat Fat 0.6 gm, Monounsat Fat 0.9 gm)
- Cholesterol 10 mg
- Sodium 225 mg
- Potassium 120 gm
- Total Carb 12 gm
- Dietary Fiber 1 gm
- Sugars 2 gm
- Protein 5 gm
- Phosphorus 85 gm

TIP

Tomatoes look great for color. Also, I don't always have seasoned croutons on hand. They are optional.

Festive Apple Salad

Susan Kasting
Jenks, OK

Makes 8 servings, about 5 oz. per serving
Prep. Time: 15 minutes

Dressing:

2 Tbsp. olive oil

2 Tbsp. Dijon mustard

1½–3 Tbsp. sugar

2 Tbsp. vinegar or lemon juice

salt and pepper

1 Granny Smith apple, chopped

4-6 Tbsp. chopped walnuts or cashews

1 large head Romaine lettuce, chopped

4 Tbsp. crumbled blue cheese, or shredded
baby Swiss, *optional*

1. In the bottom of a large salad bowl, make dressing by mixing together the oil, mustard, sugar, vinegar or lemon juice, salt, and pepper.

2. Add the apple and nuts and stir to coat. Put lettuce and cheese (if using) on top without stirring.

3. Mix it all together when ready to serve.

Exchange List Values

- Fruit 0.5
- Carbohydrate 0.5
- Fat 1.0

Basic Nutritional Values

- Calories 115
  (Calories from Fat 55)
- Total Fat 6 gm
  (Saturated Fat 0.7 gm,
  Trans Fat 0.0 gm,
  Polyunsat Fat 2.3 gm,
  Monounsat Fat 2.9 gm)
- Cholesterol 0 mg
- Sodium 95 mg
- Potassium 270 gm
- Total Carb 15 gm
- Dietary Fiber 3 gm
- Sugars 10 gm
- Protein 2 gm
- Phosphorus 45 gm

Orange-Spinach Salad

Esther Shisler
Lansdale, PA

Makes 8 servings, about 7 oz. per serving
Prep. Time: 25 minutes

Honey-Caraway Dressing:
¾ cup low-fat mayonnaise

2 Tbsp. honey

1 Tbsp. lemon juice

1 Tbsp. caraway seeds

Salad:
10-oz. bag spinach or Romaine lettuce

1 medium head iceberg lettuce, shredded

2 Tbsp. diced onion

2 Tbsp. diced canned pimento or red pepper

2 large oranges, peeled and chopped

1 small cucumber, sliced

1. In small bowl, whisk mayonnaise, honey, lemon juice, and caraway seeds until blended. Cover and refrigerate. Stir before using.

2. Into large salad bowl, tear spinach into bite-sized pieces.

3. Add lettuce, onion, pimento, oranges, and cucumber. Toss gently with dressing.

TIP

A 15-oz. can mandarin oranges, drained, can be used instead of the 2 oranges. I use Romaine and spinach instead of the iceberg lettuce sometimes.

Exchange List Values
- Fruit 0.5
- Carbohydrate 0.5
- Vegetable 1.0
- Fat 0.5

Basic Nutritional Values
- Calories 85
  (Calories from Fat 20)
- Total Fat 2 gm
  (Saturated Fat 0.3 gm,
  Trans Fat 0.0 gm,
  Polyunsat Fat 1.0 gm,
  Monounsat Fat 0.4 gm)
- Cholesterol 0 mg
- Sodium 240 mg
- Potassium 435 gm
- Total Carb 17 gm
- Dietary Fiber 3 gm
- Sugars 12 gm
- Protein 3 gm
- Phosphorus 55 gm

Spinach Salad

Ruth Zercher
Grantham, PA

Makes 15 servings
Prep. Time: 20 minutes

1 lb. fresh spinach with stems discarded

1 head Bibb lettuce

¼ cup salted cashew nuts, *divided*

½ cup olive oil

1 tsp. celery seed

2 Tbsp. sugar

1 tsp. salt

1 tsp. dry mustard

1 tsp. grated onion

3 Tbsp. vinegar

1. Wash spinach and lettuce and tear into bite-sized pieces. Combine spinach, lettuce, and nuts in serving bowl, reserving a few nuts for garnish.

2. Combine all other ingredients in blender and mix well.

3. Immediately before serving, pour dressing over greens and nuts. Sprinkle reserved nuts over top.

Exchange List Value
- Fat 2.0

Basic Nutritional Values
- Calories 95 (Calories from Fat 70)
- Total Fat 8 gm (Saturated Fat 1.2 gm, Trans Fat 0.0 gm, Polyunsat Fat 1.0 gm, Monounsat Fat 5.9 gm)
- Cholesterol 0 mg
- Sodium 195 mg
- Potassium 215 gm
- Total Carb 4 gm
- Dietary Fiber 1 gm
- Sugars 2 gm
- Protein 1 gm
- Phosphorus 30 gm

Our Favorite Dressing

Carol Eberly
Harrisonburg, VA

Makes 3½ cups, 28 servings, 2 Tbsp. per serving
Prep. Time: 10 minutes

1 cup granulated Splenda

1 cup ketchup

1½ tsp. paprika

1½ tsp. salt

1½ tsp. celery seed

1½ tsp. grated onion, *optional*

1½ cups vegetable oil

½ cup vinegar

Warm Memories:
This is our family's favorite salad dressing. I always have a jar in the refrigerator.

Good Go-Alongs:
This dressing is great on tossed salad or used as a dip for veggies.

1. Shake ingredients together well in a 1-qt. jar. Keep in refrigerator.

Exchange List Value
- Fat 2.5

Basic Nutritional Values
- Calories 115
  (Calories from Fat 110)
- Total Fat 12 gm
  (Saturated Fat 0.9 gm,
  Trans Fat 0.0 gm,
  Polyunsat Fat 3.3 gm,
  Monounsat Fat 7.4 gm)
- Cholesterol 0 mg
- Sodium 220 mg
- Potassium 40 gm
- Total Carb 3 gm
- Dietary Fiber 0 gm
- Sugars 3 gm
- Protein 0 gm
- Phosphorus 0 gm

Simple Salad Dressing

**Cynthia Morris
Grottoes, VA**

Makes 1½ cups, 12 servings, 2 Tbsp. per serving
Prep. Time: 5-10 minutes

¼ cup Splenda Brown Sugar Blend

½ cup oil

⅓ cup vinegar

⅓ cup ketchup

1 Tbsp. Worcestershire sauce

1. In a bottle or jar, combine ingredients. Cover and shake well to mix.

TIP

I use an empty ketchup bottle to keep the salad dressing in. Shake well before each use.

Exchange List Values
- Carbohydrate 0.5
- Fat 1.5

Basic Nutritional Values
- Calories 105
  (Calories from Fat 80)
- Total Fat 9 gm
  (Saturated Fat 0.7 gm,
  Trans Fat 0.0 gm,
  Polyunsat Fat 2.6 gm,
  Monounsat Fat 5.8 gm)
- Cholesterol 0 mg
- Sodium 90 mg
- Potassium 45 gm
- Total Carb 6 gm
- Dietary Fiber 0 gm
- Sugars 3 gm
- Protein 0 gm
- Phosphorus 0 gm

Russian Dressing

Frances Schrag
Newton, KS

Makes 9 servings, 1 Tbsp. per serving
Prep. Time: 10 minutes

½ cup reduced-fat mayonnaise

1 Tbsp. chili sauce, or ketchup

1 tsp. finely chopped onion

½ tsp. horseradish

¼ tsp. Worcestershire sauce

1 Tbsp. finely chopped parsley

1. Combine all ingredients and mix well.

2. Serve with choice of tossed salad.

Exchange List Value
- Fat 0.5

Basic Nutritional Values
- Calories 35
  (Calories from Fat 25)
- Total Fat 3 gm
  (Saturated Fat 0.4 gm,
  Trans Fat 0.0 gm,
  Polyunsat Fat 1.8 gm,
  Monounsat Fat 0.9 gm)
- Cholesterol 5 mg
- Sodium 140 mg
- Potassium 15 gm
- Total Carb 1 gm
- Dietary Fiber 0 gm
- Sugars 1 gm
- Protein 0 gm
- Phosphorus 5 gm

Tabouli

Ellen Helmuth
Debec, NB

Makes 8 servings, about 4 oz. per serving
Prep. Time: 20 minutes
Standing Time: 30–40 minutes
Chilling Time: 8 hours or overnight

1 cup dry bulgur wheat

1½ cups boiling water

1 tsp. salt

¼ cup lemon juice

¼ cup olive oil

1 cup chopped fresh parsley

1 cup chopped fresh mint

2–3 tomatoes, chopped

2 cloves garlic, crushed

½ cup chopped green onions, or chopped onions

pepper, to taste

1. Pour boiling water over bulgur wheat and let stand approximately ½ hour until wheat is fluffy. Drain or squeeze liquid from wheat.

2. Add all remaining ingredients and mix well.

3. Chill overnight before serving.

Exchange List Values
- Starch 0.5
- Vegetable 1.0
- Fat 1.0

Basic Nutritional Values
- Calories 120
  (Calories from Fat 65)
- Total Fat 7 gm
  (Saturated Fat 1.0 gm,
  Trans Fat 0.0 gm,
  Polyunsat Fat 0.8 gm,
  Monounsat Fat 5.0 gm)
- Cholesterol 0 mg
- Sodium 305 mg
- Potassium 215 gm
- Total Carb 13 gm
- Dietary Fiber 4 gm
- Sugars 1 gm
- Protein 2 gm
- Phosphorus 40 gm

Chinese Cabbage Salad

Kim McEuen
Lincoln University, PA

Makes 10 servings, about 4 oz. per serving
Prep. Time: 15–20 minutes
Cooking Time: 10 minutes

1 head bok choy, chopped

6 green onions, sliced

1 Tbsp. canola oil

1 pkg. ramen noodles, crunched up,
    seasoning packs discarded

2 oz. slivered almonds

2 oz. sunflower seeds

Dressing:

2 Tbsp. tarragon vinegar

½ Tbsp. light soy sauce

2 Tbsp. canola oil

2 Tbsp. granulated Splenda

1. Mix bok choy and onions in a large bowl. Set aside.

2. In a frying pan, heat oil. Sauté noodles, almonds, and sunflower seeds until lightly browned. Cool.

3. Mix dressing ingredients together.

4. Just before serving, mix together the bok choy mixture and noodle mixture.

5. Add the dressing, tossing to coat.

Exchange List Values
- Carbohydrate 1.0
- Fat 2.0

Basic Nutritional Values
- Calories 160
  (Calories from Fat 110)
- Total Fat 12 gm
  (Saturated Fat 1.5 gm,
  Trans Fat 0.0 gm,
  Polyunsat Fat 4.1 gm,
  Monounsat Fat 5.6 gm)
- Cholesterol 0 mg
- Sodium 110 mg
- Potassium 345 gm
- Total Carb 11 gm
- Dietary Fiber 3 gm
- Sugars 2 gm
- Protein 5 gm
- Phosphorus 140 gm

Creamy Coleslaw

Orpha M. Herr
Andover, NY

Makes 10 servings, about 4 oz. per serving
Prep. Time: 15 minutes

1 head cabbage, shredded

1 medium carrot, shredded

3 Tbsp. low-fat mayonnaise

½ cup fat-free milk

1 tsp. prepared mustard

¼ cup vinegar

½ cup granulated Splenda

⅛ tsp. salt

Good Go-Alongs:
Barbecue chicken and baked beans.

1. In a bowl, mix together cabbage and carrot. Set aside.

2. To make dressing, mix together mayonnaise, milk, mustard, vinegar, Splenda, and salt.

3. Pour dressing over cabbage and carrots. Stir.

Exchange List Value
• Vegetable 1.0

Basic Nutritional Values
• Calories 40
  (Calories from Fat 0)
• Total Fat 0 gm
  (Saturated Fat 0.1 gm,
  Trans Fat 0.0 gm,
  Polyunsat Fat 0.2 gm,
  Monounsat Fat 0.1 gm)
• Cholesterol 0 mg
• Sodium 100 mg
• Potassium 200 gm
• Total Carb 8 gm
• Dietary Fiber 2 gm
• Sugars 5 gm
• Protein 2 gm
• Phosphorus 40 gm

Apple Coleslaw

Joy Uhler
Richardson, TX

Makes 9 servings, about ½ cup per serving
Prep. Time: 20 minutes

2 cups coleslaw mix

1 unpeeled apple, cored and chopped

½ cup chopped celery

½ cup chopped green pepper

½ cup chopped broccoli, *optional*

¼ cup vegetable oil

2 Tbsp. lemon juice

1 Tbsp. honey

Good Go-Alongs:
This recipe is perfect beside salmon.
It is a family must-have for picnics!

1. In a bowl, combine coleslaw mix, apple, celery, green pepper, and broccoli (if using).

2. In a small bowl, whisk together oil, lemon juice, and honey. Pour over coleslaw and toss to coat evenly.

Exchange List Values
- Fruit 0.5
- Fat 1.0

Basic Nutritional Values
- Calories 80
  (Calories from Fat 55)
- Total Fat 6 gm
  (Saturated Fat 0.5 gm,
  Trans Fat 0.0 gm,
  Polyunsat Fat 1.7 gm,
  Monounsat Fat 3.8 gm)
- Cholesterol 0 mg
- Sodium 10 mg
- Potassium 85 gm
- Total Carb 6 gm
- Dietary Fiber 1 gm
- Sugars 5 gm
- Protein 0 gm
- Phosphorus 10 gm

TIP

1. This is a great recipe for potlucks, as it doesn't contain mayonnaise, so there's no need to worry about it sitting out.
2. Use red or yellow peppers for even more color.

Vegetables and Side Dishes   415

The Best Broccoli Salad

Sandra Haverstraw
Hummelstown, PA

Makes 12 servings, about 4 oz. per serving
Prep. Time: 20–25 minutes
Chilling Time: 8–12 hours

12 cups fresh broccoli florets, about 2
   bunches broccoli, large stems discarded

1 cup golden raisins

1 small onion, chopped

6 slices bacon, fried and chopped

½ cup chopped cashews

Dressing:

¼ cup sugar

4 Tbsp. Splenda

2 Tbsp. vinegar

1 cup reduced-fat Miracle Whip dressing

2 Tbsp. horseradish

¼ tsp. salt

½ tsp. prepared mustard

TIP

Precooked bacon works well.

Exchange List Values
- Fruit 0.5
- Carbohydrate 1.0
- Vegetable 1.0
- Fat 1.0

Basic Nutritional Values
- Calories 165
  (Calories from Fat 55)
- Total Fat 6 gm
  (Saturated Fat 1.4 gm,
  Trans Fat 0.0 gm,
  Polyunsat Fat 2.1 gm,
  Monounsat Fat 2.4 gm)
- Cholesterol 10 mg
- Sodium 375 mg
- Potassium 395 gm
- Total Carb 25 gm
- Dietary Fiber 3 gm
- Sugars 17 gm
- Protein 5 gm
- Phosphorus 110 gm

1. Mix broccoli florets, raisins, chopped onion, and bacon.

2. Prepare dressing by blending sugar, Splenda, vinegar, Miracle Whip, horseradish, salt, and mustard until smooth.

3. Pour dressing over broccoli mix and toss gently until evenly coated.

4. Cover and refrigerate 8–12 hours. Add cashews just before serving.

Broccoli, Cauliflower, and Carrot Salad

Clara L. Yoder
Wadsworth, OH

Makes 8 servings, about 6 oz. per serving
Prep. Time: 20 minutes
Cooking Time: 25 minutes
Chilling Time: 12 hours or overnight

2 10-oz. pkgs. broccoli florets

10-oz. pkg. cauliflower florets

3 large carrots, chopped

1 cup diced celery

1 cup diced onion

1 green bell pepper, sliced

½ tsp. dry mustard

¼ cup granulated Splenda

¾ Tbsp. cornstarch

½ cup vinegar

½ tsp. salt

1. Cook first three vegetables separately to a crisp stage. Drain each one and cool.

2. Combine all vegetables in large serving bowl.

3. In a saucepan combine mustard, Splenda, cornstarch, vinegar, and salt. Cook until clear. Pour over vegetables.

4. Cover and chill overnight or at least 12 hours before serving.

Exchange List Value
• Vegetable 3.0

Basic Nutritional Values
• Calories 75
  (Calories from Fat 5)
• Total Fat 0.5 gm
  (Saturated Fat 0.1 gm,
  Trans Fat 0.0 gm,
  Polyunsat Fat 0.2 gm,
  Monounsat Fat 0.0 gm)
• Cholesterol 0 mg
• Sodium 210 mg
• Potassium 535 gm
• Total Carb 16 gm
• Dietary Fiber 4 gm
• Sugars 9 gm
• Protein 4 gm
• Phosphorus 85 gm

Broccoli, Cauliflower, and Pea Salad

**Virginia Graber
Freeman, SD**

Makes 12 servings, about ¾ cup per serving
Prep. Time: 25 minutes
Chilling Time: 8–12 hours or overnight

2 cups chopped broccoli

2 cups chopped cauliflower

2 cups frozen peas, thawed

1 large onion, chopped

2 cups chopped celery

½ cup sour cream

½ cup low-fat mayonnaise

1½ Tbsp. sugar

2 Tbsp. vinegar

¼ tsp. salt

1. Combine all ingredients.

2. Refrigerate overnight and serve.

Variation:
Add 1 can sliced water chestnuts to ingredients.
—Jeanne Heyerly, Reedley, CA

Exchange List Values
- Carbohydrate 0.5
- Vegetable 1.0

Basic Nutritional Values
- Calories 60
  (Calories from Fat 10)
- Total Fat 1 gm
  (Saturated Fat 0.2 gm,
  Trans Fat 0.0 gm,
  Polyunsat Fat 0.5 gm,
  Monounsat Fat 0.2 gm)
- Cholesterol 0 mg
- Sodium 195 mg
- Potassium 220 gm
- Total Carb 12 gm
- Dietary Fiber 2 gm
- Sugars 5 gm
- Protein 3 gm
- Phosphorus 60 gm

Carrot Raisin Salad

Shelia Heil
Lancaster, PA

Makes 6 servings, about 4 oz. per serving
Prep. Time: 10 minutes
Chilling Time: 4–12 hours

5 large carrots, shredded

1 cup raisins

⅔ cup plain fat-free yogurt

4 Tbsp. reduced-fat mayonnaise

2 tsp. honey

1. Combine ingredients.

2. Chill for several hours or overnight. Serve cold.

Warm Memories:
My mother often made a recipe like this for guests in our home. Adds color to a meat-and-potato meal.

Exchange List Values
- Fruit 1.5
- Vegetable 1.0
- Fat 0.5

Basic Nutritional Values
- Calories 140
  (Calories from Fat 20)
- Total Fat 2.5 gm
  (Saturated Fat 0.4 gm,
  Trans Fat 0.0 gm,
  Polyunsat Fat 1.4 gm,
  Monounsat Fat 0.7 gm)
- Cholesterol 5 mg
- Sodium 145 mg
- Potassium 440 gm
- Total Carb 29 gm
- Dietary Fiber 3 gm
- Sugars 21 gm
- Protein 3 gm
- Phosphorus 90 gm

Fresh Corn and Tomato Salad

Dawn Landowski
Eau Claire, WI

Makes 12 servings, about ⅔ cup per serving
Prep. Time: 20 minutes
Standing Time: 15 minutes–2 hours

4¼ cups fresh, raw corn cut off the cob
  (about 6 medium ears corn, husked)

2 cups halved grape tomatoes

3 oz. fresh mozzarella, cut into small cubes

4-6 green onions, thinly sliced

3 Tbsp. white vinegar

2 tsp. salt

fresh ground pepper

¼ cup extra virgin olive oil

1½ cups fresh basil leaves, torn

Warm Memories:
People can't believe the corn is raw—there are always discussions!

TIP

For cutting corn off the cob, I put the end of the cob in a Bundt pan and cut down. Kernels fall into pan.

1. Stir together corn, tomatoes, mozzarella, and green onions in a large bowl.

2. Whisk vinegar, salt, and pepper together in a small bowl. Gradually whisk in oil to make a smooth dressing.

3. Pour vinaigrette over salad and toss to coat.

4. Cover and let set for 15 minutes to 2 hours. Right before serving, tear the basil over the salad and stir.

Exchange List Values
- Starch 1.0
- Fat 1.0

Basic Nutritional Values
- Calories 110
  (Calories from Fat 65)
- Total Fat 7 gm
  (Saturated Fat 1.5 gm,
  Trans Fat 0.0 gm,
  Polyunsat Fat 0.8 gm,
  Monounsat Fat 3.9 gm)
- Cholesterol 0 mg
- Sodium 435 mg
- Potassium 255 gm
- Total Carb 11 gm
- Dietary Fiber 2 gm
- Sugars 4 gm
- Protein 4 gm
- Phosphorus 85 gm

Sour Cream Cucumber Salad

Mary Jones
Marengo, OH

Makes 6 servings, about 5 oz. per serving
Prep. Time: 20–30 minutes

3 medium cucumbers, about 9 oz. each,
   unpeeled and sliced thinly

½ tsp. salt

½ cup finely chopped green onions

1 Tbsp. white vinegar

dash pepper, *optional*

¼ cup fat-free sour cream

1. Sprinkle cucumber with salt. Let stand 15 minutes. Drain liquid.

2. Add onions, vinegar, and pepper (if using).

3. Just before serving, stir in sour cream.

Exchange List Value
- Vegetable 1.0

Basic Nutritional Values
- Calories 30
  (Calories from Fat 0)
- Total Fat 0 gm
  (Saturated Fat 0.1 gm,
  Trans Fat 0.0 gm,
  Polyunsat Fat 0.0 gm,
  Monounsat Fat 0.0 gm)
- Cholesterol 0 mg
- Sodium 110 mg
- Potassium 220 gm
- Total Carb 7 gm
- Dietary Fiber 1 gm
- Sugars 3 gm
- Protein 1 gm
- Phosphorus 45 gm

Picnic Pea Salad

Mary Kathryn Yoder
Harrisonville, MO

Makes 6 servings, about 3½ oz. per serving
Prep. Time: 30 minutes
Chilling Time: 1 hour

10-oz. pkg. frozen peas, thawed

¼ cup chopped onion or green onions

½ cup chopped celery

½ cup fat-free sour cream

2 Tbsp. low-fat mayonnaise

¼ tsp. salt

1 tsp. dried dill weed

¼ tsp. pepper

⅓ cup Spanish peanuts

¼ cup fried and crumbled bacon

1 cup cherry tomatoes for garnish, *optional*

1. Mix peas, onion, celery, sour cream, mayonnaise, salt, dill weed, and pepper. Chill.

2. Just before serving, stir in peanuts. Garnish with bacon and tomatoes.

TIP

Fry bacon ahead of time and let cool.

Variation:
Omit celery, peanuts, and dill weed. Add a chopped hard-boiled egg and a dash of garlic powder.

—Dorothy VanDeest, Memphis, TN

Exchange List Values
- Starch 0.5
- Carbohydrate 0.5
- Med-Fat Meat 1.0

Basic Nutritional Values
- Calories 135
  (Calories from Fat 65)
- Total Fat 7 gm
  (Saturated Fat 1.4 gm,
  Trans Fat 0.0 gm,
  Polyunsat Fat 1.9 gm,
  Monounsat Fat 2.7 gm)
- Cholesterol 5 mg
- Sodium 365 mg
- Potassium 230 gm
- Total Carb 13 gm
- Dietary Fiber 3 gm
- Sugars 4 gm
- Protein 8 gm
- Phosphorus 120 gm

Mixed Vegetable Salad

Sharon Miller
Holmesville, OH

Makes 8 servings, about 4½ oz. per serving
Prep. Time: 15 minutes
Cooking Time: 10 minutes
Standing Time: 15 minutes
Chilling Time: 8–12 hours

16-oz. frozen mixed vegetables, thawed

15-oz. can kidney beans, rinsed and drained

½ cup chopped celery

½ cup chopped onion

½ cup chopped green or red pepper

¾ cup granulated Splenda

1 Tbsp. cornstarch

½ cup vinegar

TIP

The cornstarch-vinegar mix eliminates the oil usually used in a salad of this type. I use this same sauce in three-bean salad recipes or other similar recipes.

1. Cook mixed vegetables until crisp-tender. Drain.

2. Add kidney beans, celery, onion, and pepper.

3. In saucepan, combine Splenda and cornstarch. Add vinegar.

4. Cook over low heat until thick, stirring constantly. Or microwave uncovered until thickened, stirring once or twice.

5. Cool for 15 minutes. Pour over vegetables. Refrigerate overnight for best flavor.

Exchange List Value
- Starch 1.0

Basic Nutritional Values
- Calories 105
  (Calories from Fat 0)
- Total Fat 0 gm
  (Saturated Fat 0.1 gm,
  Trans Fat 0.0 gm,
  Polyunsat Fat 0.2 gm,
  Monounsat Fat 0.0 gm)
- Cholesterol 0 mg
- Sodium 80 mg
- Potassium 295 gm
- Total Carb 20 gm
- Dietary Fiber 5 gm
- Sugars 5 gm
- Protein 5 gm
- Phosphorus 85 gm

Going Away Salad

Judith Govotsos
Frederick, MD

Makes 15 servings, about 7 oz. per serving
Prep. Time: 30–45 minutes
Chilling Time: 8–12 hours

15-oz. can kidney beans, drained

15-oz. can wax beans, drained

15-oz. can string beans, drained

15-oz. can garbanzo beans, drained

1 English cucumber, thinly sliced, 1 lb. total

2 carrots, thinly sliced

2–3 ribs celery, thinly sliced

1 medium to large onion, thinly sliced

1 medium cabbage shredded or 2 1 lb.
   packages coleslaw mix

Marinade:

1¾ tsp. salt

2 tsp. black pepper

⅔ cup white vinegar

½ cup canola oil

½ cup granulated Splenda

1. Combine beans and vegetables in a large lidded container.

2. In saucepan, combine salt, black pepper, vinegar, oil, and Splenda. Bring to boil. Allow to cool.

3. Pour cooled marinade over vegetables.

4. Let the vegetables marinate in the refrigerator at least overnight before serving.

Warm Memories:
My mom used to make this and it would last 1–2 weeks at home or we would take it to family reunions.

Good Go-Alongs:
Fried chicken or ham.

TIP

I use a large orange Tupperware bowl with lid to take to church lunches (covered dish) or to family reunions.

Exchange List Values
- Starch 0.5
- Vegetable 2.0
- Fat 1.5

Basic Nutritional Values
- Calories 155
  (Calories from Fat 70)
- Total Fat 8 gm
  (Saturated Fat 0.6 gm,
  Trans Fat 0.0 gm,
  Polyunsat Fat 2.3 gm,
  Monounsat Fat 4.7 gm)
- Cholesterol 0 mg
- Sodium 440 mg
- Potassium 370 gm
- Total Carb 18 gm
- Dietary Fiber 5 gm
- Sugars 5 gm
- Protein 5 gm
- Phosphorus 90 gm

Green Bean and Walnut Salad

**Mary Wheatley
Mashpee, MA.**

Makes 4 servings, about 3¼ oz. per serving
Prep. Time: 20 minutes
Cooking Time: 5-7 minutes

¾ lb. fresh green beans, trimmed

¼ cup walnut pieces

3 Tbsp. finely chopped fresh parsley

3 Tbsp. finely chopped onion

1 Tbsp. walnut or olive oil

1½ tsp. red wine vinegar

1 tsp. Dijon mustard

salt, to taste

freshly ground pepper, to taste

TIP

1. You'll want to double or triple the recipe, since people come back for more.
2. Pecans or almonds can be substituted for the walnuts.

1. Steam beans in basket over boiling water for 4 minutes. Transfer to a medium serving bowl.

2. Toast walnuts in a small dry skillet, stirring frequently until fragrant, 3–5 minutes. Chop the toasted walnuts finely.

3. Stir parsley and onion into walnuts.

4. Whisk together oil, vinegar, and mustard. Add to green beans. Season with salt and pepper and top with walnut mixture.

5. Serve warm or at room temperature.

Good Go-Alongs:

This is a good alternative to the soggy green bean casseroles so often used for holidays.

Exchange List Values
- Vegetable 2.0
- Fat 1.5

Basic Nutritional Values
- Calories 110
  (Calories from Fat 80)
- Total Fat 9 gm
  (Saturated Fat 0.8 gm,
  Trans Fat 0.0 gm,
  Polyunsat Fat 5.8 gm,
  Monounsat Fat 1.5 gm)
- Cholesterol 0 mg
- Sodium 35 mg
- Potassium 170 gm
- Total Carb 8 gm
- Dietary Fiber 3 gm
- Sugars 2 gm
- Protein 3 gm
- Phosphorus 50 gm

Summer Salad

June S. Groff
Denver, PA

Makes 8 servings, about 6 oz. per serving
Prep. Time: 20 minutes
Cooking Time for Couscous: 10 minutes

Salad:
1½ cups cooked garbanzo beans
½ cup chopped onion
½ cup chopped celery
½ cup chopped cucumber
½ cup chopped red grapes
2 medium tomatoes, chopped
2¼-oz. can sliced black olives, drained
¾ cup couscous, cooked and cooled

Dressing:
½ cup olive oil
½ cup lemon juice or vinegar
⅛ tsp. minced garlic
1 Tbsp. Dijon mustard
¼ tsp. dried oregano
¼ tsp. dried basil
1 Tbsp. sugar
⅛ tsp. coriander
⅛ tsp. onion powder
1 tsp. dried parsley
2 Tbsp. freshly grated Parmesan cheese

1. Toss salad ingredients together.

2. Mix the dressing ingredients together. Pour dressing over salad mixture and toss.

3. Top with Parmesan cheese.

Exchange List Values
- Starch 1.5
- Carbohydrate 0.5
- Fat 3.0

Basic Nutritional Values
- Calories 270
  (Calories from Fat 145)
- Total Fat 16 gm
  (Saturated Fat 2.3 gm,
  Trans Fat 0.0 gm,
  Polyunsat Fat 2.0 gm,
  Monounsat Fat 10.9 gm)
- Cholesterol 0 mg
- Sodium 130 mg
- Potassium 285 gm
- Total Carb 28 gm
- Dietary Fiber 4 gm
- Sugars 7 gm
- Protein 6 gm
- Phosphorus 85 gm

Corn and Black Bean Salad

Jamie Mowry
Arlington, TX

Makes 5 cups, 1 cup per serving
Prep. Time: 15 minutes
Chilling Time: 30 minutes

4 medium ears sweet corn, kernels cut off (2 cups)

1 large red bell pepper, diced

½ cup thinly sliced green onions

½ cup chopped fresh cilantro

15½-oz. can black beans, rinsed and drained

¼ cup red wine vinegar

2 tsp. canola oil

1 tsp. sugar

½ tsp. garlic powder

½ tsp. ground cumin

½ tsp. freshly ground black pepper

salt, to taste

1. Combine corn, bell pepper, onions, cilantro, and beans in a medium bowl.

2. Whisk together vinegar, oil, sugar, garlic powder, cumin, black pepper, and salt.

3. Stir dressing gently into corn mixture.

4. Cover and chill for 30 minutes.

Exchange List Values
- Starch 1.5
- Lean Meat 1.0

Basic Nutritional Values
- Calories 160 (Calories from Fat 25)
- Total Fat 3 gm (Saturated Fat 0.3 gm, Trans Fat 0.0 gm, Polyunsat Fat 1.1 gm, Monounsat Fat 1.4 gm)
- Cholesterol 0 mg
- Sodium 70 mg
- Potassium 435 gm
- Total Carb 29 gm
- Dietary Fiber 7 gm
- Sugars 6 gm
- Protein 7 gm
- Phosphorus 135 gm

Southwestern Bean Salad

**Ellie Oberholtzer
Ronks, PA**

Makes 7 cups, 1 cup per serving
Prep. Time: 20 minutes
Chilling Time: 2 hours

15-oz. can kidney beans, rinsed and drained

15-oz. can black beans, rinsed and drained

15-oz. can garbanzo beans, rinsed and drained

2 celery ribs, sliced

1 medium red onion, diced

1 medium tomato, diced

1 cup frozen corn, thawed

Dressing:

¾ cup thick and chunky salsa

¼ cup vegetable oil or olive oil

¼ cup lime juice

1–2 tsp. chili powder

½ tsp. ground cumin

1. In a bowl, combine beans, celery, onion, tomato, and corn.

2. Mix together salsa, oil, lime juice, chili powder, and cumin.

3. Pour over bean mixture and toss. Cover and chill 2 hours.

Exchange List Values
- Starch 2.0
- Lean Meat 1.0
- Fat 1.5

Basic Nutritional Values
- Calories 265
  (Calories from Fat 80)
- Total Fat 9 gm
  (Saturated Fat 0.8 gm,
  Trans Fat 0.0 gm,
  Polyunsat Fat 3.0 gm,
  Monounsat Fat 5.3 gm)
- Cholesterol 0 mg
- Sodium 350 mg
- Potassium 645 gm
- Total Carb 37 gm
- Dietary Fiber 10 gm
- Sugars 6 gm
- Protein 11 gm
- Phosphorus 205 gm

Greek Pasta Salad

Edie Moran
West Babylon, NY
Judi Manos
West Islip, NY

Makes 8 servings, about 4½ oz. per serving
Prep. Time: 15 minutes
Cooking Time for Pasta: 15 minutes
Chilling Time: 2–3 hours

2 cups cooked macaroni or bow-tie pasta (1 cup dry), rinsed and cooled

4 medium plum tomatoes, chopped

15-oz. can garbanzo beans, rinsed and drained

1 medium onion, chopped

6-oz. can pitted black olives, drained

1 oz. crumbled reduced-fat feta cheese

1 clove garlic, minced

¼ cup olive oil

2 Tbsp. lemon juice

½ tsp. salt

½ tsp. pepper

TIP

1. I like to serve it in a clear glass salad bowl.
2. Add some baby spinach leaves. Combine vegetables with hot pasta right after draining it. Kraft Greek Vinaigrette is a good dressing, too.
—Judi Manos, West Islip, NY

1. In a large bowl, combine macaroni, tomatoes, garbanzo beans, onion, olives, and feta cheese.

2. In a small bowl, whisk together garlic, oil, lemon juice, salt, and pepper. Pour over salad and toss to coat.

3. Cover and chill 2–3 hours in refrigerator. Stir before serving.

Exchange List Values
- Starch 1.0
- Vegetable 1.0
- Fat 2.0

Basic Nutritional Values
- Calories 200 (Calories from Fat 90)
- Total Fat 10 gm (Saturated Fat 1.5 gm, Trans Fat 0.0 gm, Polyunsat Fat 1.3 gm, Monounsat Fat 6.1 gm)
- Cholesterol 0 mg
- Sodium 340 mg
- Potassium 220 gm
- Total Carb 23 gm
- Dietary Fiber 4 gm
- Sugars 4 gm
- Protein 6 gm
- Phosphorus 100 gm

Serving suggestion:
Garnish with chopped parsley.

Warm Memories:
When visiting my husband's family on the island of Samos, Greece, this was made with all fresh ingredients grown in their garden.
—Judi Manos, West Islip, NY

Five-Bean Salad

Jeanne Heyerly
Shipshewana, IN

Makes 10 servings, about 6 oz. per serving
Prep. Time: 20 minutes
Chilling Time: 12 hours

15-oz. can green beans

15-oz. can wax beans

15-oz. can lima beans

15-oz. can kidney beans

15-oz. can garbanzo beans

¼ cup canola or light olive oil

¼ cup apple cider vinegar

6 Tbsp. granulated Splenda

½ tsp. salt

½ tsp. pepper

½ tsp. dry mustard

¾ tsp. celery seed

1 medium onion, chopped

1 green or red pepper, chopped

1 large clove garlic, minced

1. Drain all beans and combine in a large bowl.

2. Heat until hot (but do not boil) the oil, vinegar, Splenda, salt, pepper, mustard, and celery seed.

3. Mix with bean mixture and let stand overnight.

4. Add onion, green pepper, and garlic about 1 hour before serving.

Good Go-Alongs:
This always tastes so good along with casseroles that people bring to a church supper.

TIP

1. Omit dry mustard, celery seed, and garlic. Serve with a slotted spoon. If there is another type of bean you like that's not listed, add it; or you could double up on the kinds you do like.
—Jean Halloran, Green Bay, WI

2. Add ½ cup chopped celery and 2-oz. jar pimento.
—Joyce Kaut, Rochester, NY

Exchange List Values
- Starch 1.5
- Lean Meat 1.0
- Fat 0.5

Basic Nutritional Values
- Calories 180 (Calories from Fat 55)
- Total Fat 6 gm (Saturated Fat 0.5 gm, Trans Fat 0.0 gm, Polyunsat Fat 2.0 gm, Monounsat Fat 3.6 gm)
- Cholesterol 0 mg
- Sodium 420 mg
- Potassium 430 gm
- Total Carb 24 gm
- Dietary Fiber 7 gm
- Sugars 4 gm
- Protein 8 gm
- Phosphorus 130 gm

Macaroni Salad

Frances Kruba and Cathy Kruba
Dundalk, MD
Marcia S. Myer
Manheim, PA

Makes 12 servings, about 7 oz. per serving
Prep. Time: 30 minutes
Cooking Time for Pasta: 15 minutes

1 lb. macaroni, cooked and cooled

1 cup diced celery

1 cup diced onion

1 cup diced carrots

8 hard-boiled eggs, diced

3 Tbsp. sugar

3 Tbsp. vinegar or lemon juice

½ cup low-fat mayonnaise

1¼ cups egg substitute

1 Tbsp. prepared mustard

1 Tbsp. trans-fat-free tub margarine

1. Mix together macaroni, celery, onion, carrots, hard-boiled eggs, sugar, and vinegar or lemon juice. Add mayonnaise.

2. In a saucepan, mix egg substitute, mustard, and margarine. Cook on medium heat until thickened and steaming, stirring constantly. Do not boil.

3. Remove from heat and cool 5 minutes. Add to macaroni mixture.

Serving suggestion:
Top with fresh cracked black pepper.

Exchange List Values

- Starch 2.0
- Carbohydrate 0.5
- Med-Fat Meat 1.0

Basic Nutritional Values

- Calories 250
  (Calories from Fat 45)
- Total Fat 5 gm
  (Saturated Fat 1.5 gm,
  Trans Fat 0.0 gm,
  Polyunsat Fat 1.6 gm,
  Monounsat Fat 1.8 gm)
- Cholesterol 125 mg
- Sodium 315 mg
- Potassium 205 gm
- Total Carb 37 gm
- Dietary Fiber 2 gm
- Sugars 6 gm
- Protein 13 gm
- Phosphorus 140 gm

Chicken Pasta Salad

Esther Gingerich
Kalona, IA

Makes 10 servings, about 7 oz. per serving
Prep. Time: 15 minutes
Cooking Time for Pasta: 15 minutes
Chilling Time: 1 hour or more

2¼ cups diced cooked chicken

2 cups cooked (1 cup dry) small pasta or macaroni

2 cups diced celery

2 cups seedless grape halves

4 hard-boiled eggs, diced

15-oz. can pineapple tidbits, drained

Dressing:

¾ cup low-fat mayonnaise

½ cup fat-free sour cream

½ cup fat-free frozen whipped topping, thawed

1 Tbsp. lemon juice

1 Tbsp. sugar

½ tsp. salt

½ cup cashew pieces

1. In a large bowl, combine chicken, macaroni, celery, grapes, eggs, and pineapple.

2. Whisk dressing ingredients until smooth. Pour dressing over salad; toss to coat.

3. Chill at least one hour. Just before serving, fold in cashews.

Warm Memories:
I often take this to summer potlucks for a "cooler" dish. This could be a one-dish meal.

TIP

It's simple to put this together if chicken is cooked and diced, macaroni is cooked, and eggs are boiled ahead of time.

Exchange List Values
- Starch 0.5
- Fruit 0.5
- Carbohydrate 1.0
- Lean Meat 2.0
- Fat 0.5

Basic Nutritional Values
- Calories 250 (Calories from Fat 80)
- Total Fat 9 gm (Saturated Fat 2.2 gm, Trans Fat 0.0 gm, Polyunsat Fat 2.3 gm, Monounsat Fat 3.8 gm)
- Cholesterol 105 mg
- Sodium 360 mg
- Potassium 325 gm
- Total Carb 28 gm
- Dietary Fiber 2 gm
- Sugars 12 gm
- Protein 15 gm
- Phosphorus 185 gm

Creamy Pasta Salad

Irma Wengerd
Dundee, OH

Makes 15 servings, about 7 oz. per serving
Prep. Time: 30 minutes
Cooking Time for Pasta: 15 minutes

1½ lbs. uncooked spiral pasta

½ cup chopped celery

2 tomatoes, chopped

1 small onion, chopped

1 green pepper, chopped

3-oz. can black olives, drained, sliced

10-oz. lower-sodium, lean ham, diced

8 oz. 75%-less-fat cheddar cheese, diced

Dressing:

¾ cup reduced-fat Miracle Whip

1 Tbsp. spicy brown mustard

3 Tbsp. canola oil

1 Tbsp. vinegar

5 Tbsp. sugar

¼ tsp. onion salt

½ tsp. celery seed

1. Cook pasta in boiling, unsalted water. Drain and rinse with cold water.

2. In large bowl, toss together pasta, celery, tomatoes, onion, green pepper, olives, ham, and cheese.

3. In a separate bowl, blend the dressing ingredients together.

4. Pour dressing over pasta and toss.

Good Go-Alongs:
This salad is delicious with grilled chicken.

Exchange List Values
- Starch 1.0
- Carbohydrate 2.0
- Med-Fat Meat 1.0

Basic Nutritional Values
- Calories 295
  (Calories from Fat 70)
- Total Fat 8 gm
  (Saturated Fat 1.7 gm,
  Trans Fat 0.0 gm,
  Polyunsat Fat 2.1 gm,
  Monounsat Fat 3.0 gm)
- Cholesterol 20 mg
- Sodium 475 mg
- Potassium 190 gm
- Total Carb 42 gm
- Dietary Fiber 2 gm
- Sugars 8 gm
- Protein 15 gm
- Phosphorus 185 gm

Almond-Apricot Pasta Salad

Tracey Hanson Schramel
Windom, MN

Makes 8 servings, about 9 oz. per serving
Prep. Time: 15 minutes
Cooking Time for Pasta: 15 minutes

Salad:
½ lb. bow-tie pasta, cooked, rinsed, and drained
3 cups chopped broccoli
2½ cups chopped cooked chicken
1 cup chopped celery
1 cup dried apricots, cut into ¼-inch strips
¾ cup toasted whole almonds
½ cup finely chopped green onions

TIP

1. You can leave the almonds out and sprinkle them on top if you like that look better.
2. Pass the dressing in a small pitcher so each person can put on the amount they like. The leftovers don't get soggy then either!

Dressing:
¾ cup low-fat mayonnaise
¾ cup fat-free sour cream
2 tsp. grated lemon peel
1 Tbsp. lemon juice
1 Tbsp. Dijon mustard
¾ tsp. salt
¼ tsp. pepper

1. In a large bowl, combine salad ingredients.

2. In another bowl, combine dressing ingredients.

3. Pour dressing over pasta mixture and toss.

Exchange List Values
- Starch 1.5
- Fruit 1.0
- Carbohydrate 0.5
- Lean Meat 2.0
- Fat 1.5

Basic Nutritional Values
- Calories 370 (Calories from Fat 110)
- Total Fat 12 gm (Saturated Fat 1.8 gm, Trans Fat 0.0 gm, Polyunsat Fat 3.6 gm, Monounsat Fat 5.8 gm)
- Cholesterol 40 mg
- Sodium 545 mg
- Potassium 635 gm
- Total Carb 46 gm
- Dietary Fiber 5 gm
- Sugars 15 gm
- Protein 22 gm
- Phosphorus 260 gm

Spaghetti Salad

Lois Stoltzfus
Honey Brook, PA

Makes 8 servings, about 5 oz. per serving
Prep. Time: 15 minutes
Cooking Time: 15 minutes
Cooling Time: 30 minutes

16 oz. angel-hair pasta or spaghetti

¼ cup canola oil

¼ cup lemon juice

1 tsp. Accent

1 tsp. seasoned salt

¼ cup low-fat mayonnaise

1 green bell pepper, chopped

1 cup grape tomatoes

1 red onion, chopped

1 cup shredded 75%-less-fat cheddar cheese

½ cup sliced black olives

pepperoni, *optional*

1. Cook pasta according to directions.

2. Mix oil, lemon juice, Accent, seasoned salt, and mayonnaise together. Add to drained pasta while it is still warm.

3. When pasta mixture has cooled at least 30 minutes, stir in pepper, tomatoes, onion, cheese, olives, and optional pepperoni. Chill.

Exchange List Values
- Starch 3.0
- Lean Meat 1.0
- Fat 1.5

Basic Nutritional Values
- Calories 335
  (Calories from Fat 100)
- Total Fat 11 gm
  (Saturated Fat 1.6 gm,
  Trans Fat 0.0 gm,
  Polyunsat Fat 2.7 gm,
  Monounsat Fat 5.6 gm)
- Cholesterol 5 mg
- Sodium 420 mg
- Potassium 225 gm
- Total Carb 48 gm
- Dietary Fiber 3 gm
- Sugars 4 gm
- Protein 12 gm
- Phosphorus 170 gm

Tomato Basil Couscous

Amber Martin
Mount Joy, PA

Makes 6 servings, 3½ oz. per serving
Prep. Time: 25 minutes
Cooking Time for Couscous: 10 minutes
Chilling Time: 2 hours or more

2 cups cooked couscous, cooled

1 cup chopped tomato

2 Tbsp. chopped basil

1 oz. reduced-fat feta cheese, crumbled fine

3 Tbsp. olive oil

2 Tbsp. lemon juice

1 tsp. Dijon mustard

1 clove garlic, crushed

fresh black pepper, to taste

1. Mix together couscous, tomato, basil, and feta cheese.

2. In separate bowl, mix together olive oil, lemon juice, mustard, garlic, and black pepper. Pour over couscous mixture and toss.

3. Chill at least 2 hours before serving.

TIP

To cook couscous, boil 1½ cups water and ½ tsp. salt. Remove from heat. Add 1 cup couscous, stir, and cover. Let stand 5 minutes. Fluff couscous lightly with fork. Cool before using in salad.

Exchange List Values
- Starch 1.0
- Fat 1.5

Basic Nutritional Values
- Calories 135
  (Calories from Fat 70)
- Total Fat 8 gm
  (Saturated Fat 1.4 gm,
  Trans Fat 0.0 gm,
  Polyunsat Fat 0.8 gm,
  Monounsat Fat 5.1 gm)
- Cholesterol 0 mg
- Sodium 90 mg
- Potassium 120 gm
- Total Carb 14 gm
- Dietary Fiber 1 gm
- Sugars 1 gm
- Protein 3 gm
- Phosphorus 35 gm

Apple Chicken Salad

Marlene Fonken
Upland, CA

Makes 6 servings, about 6 oz. per serving
Prep. Time: 30–40 minutes
Chilling Time: 2–12 hours

Dressing:

½ cup light mayonnaise

2 Tbsp. cider vinegar

2 Tbsp. lemon juice

2–3 Tbsp. Dijon mustard

2 cups chopped, cooked chicken breast

2 ribs celery, chopped

¼ cup diced onion

1 green apple, chopped

1 red apple, chopped

⅓ cup dried cranberries

salt and pepper, to taste

1. Whisk together mayonnaise, vinegar, lemon juice, and mustard. Set aside.

2. Mix together chicken, celery, onion, apples, cranberries, salt, and pepper.

3. Pour on dressing and toss to mix. Refrigerate until serving. Flavor develops with longer chilling.

Serving suggestion:
Top with fresh cracked pepper and parsley.

Warm Memories:
At a church dinner, a man found out who had made my dish, found me, and asked for the recipe.

TIP

1. Break up and soften a handful of rice sticks; drain and add to the finished salad. This salad is gluten-free!
2. If you're starting with raw chicken, chop it into bite-sized pieces. In a saucepan, cover the chicken pieces with water or chicken broth. Cover and cook on medium heat until the chicken pieces are white through, 10–20 minutes. Drain. This can be done ahead of time.
3. You can substitute 12½-oz. can chicken, drained and broken up, for this salad.

Exchange List Values
- Fruit 1.0
- Lean Meat 2.0
- Fat 1.0

Basic Nutritional Values
- Calories 190
  (Calories from Fat 65)
- Total Fat 7 gm
  (Saturated Fat 1.2 gm,
  Trans Fat 0.0 gm,
  Polyunsat Fat 3.2 gm,
  Monounsat Fat 2.0 gm)
- Cholesterol 45 mg
- Sodium 340 mg
- Potassium 270 gm
- Total Carb 17 gm
- Dietary Fiber 2 gm
- Sugars 13 gm
- Protein 15 gm
- Phosphorus 130 gm

Chicken Salad with Blue Cheese

Susan Smith
Monument, CO

Makes 6 servings, about 5 oz. per serving
Prep. Time: 15 minutes

2½ cups cooked chicken breast, diced or julienned

6 cups shredded lettuce

¾ cup low-fat mayonnaise

2 Tbsp. tarragon vinegar

2½ Tbsp. chili sauce

2 Tbsp. chopped green pepper

1 oz. reduced-fat blue cheese, crumbled

whole lettuce leaves

TIP

It is best made and eaten on the same day.

1. Mix chicken with lettuce.

2. Mix mayonnaise, vinegar, chili sauce, and green pepper. Add crumbled cheese.

3. Gently combine chicken and mayonnaise mixtures.

4. Place salad in a bowl lined with lettuce or in individual lettuce cups.

Exchange List Values
- Carbohydrate 0.5
- Lean Meat 3.0

Basic Nutritional Values
- Calories 155 (Calories from Fat 45)
- Total Fat 5 gm (Saturated Fat 1.5 gm, Trans Fat 0.0 gm, Polyunsat Fat 1.7 gm, Monounsat Fat 1.4 gm)
- Cholesterol 50 mg
- Sodium 470 mg
- Potassium 275 gm
- Total Carb 7 gm
- Dietary Fiber 1 gm
- Sugars 2 gm
- Protein 20 gm
- Phosphorus 175 gm

Unique Tuna Salad

**Brenda J. Hochstedler
East Earl, PA**

Makes 8 servings, about 9 oz. per serving
Prep. Time: 10 minutes
Cooking Time (for potatoes and eggs):
    20–30 minutes
Cooling Time: 30 minutes

10 medium potatoes

Dressing:
¼ cup reduced-fat mayonnaise
1¼ tsp. salt
¼ tsp. pepper
¼ tsp. paprika
2 Tbs. sweet pickle relish

Salad:
4 eggs, hard-boiled, chopped
6-oz. pouch water-packed tuna, drained and
    flaked
½ cup chopped celery
½ head lettuce, torn
2 tomatoes, cut into wedges
Parmesan cheese, grated

1. Chop potatoes (peeled if you wish). Boil over medium heat until fork-tender but not mushy. Drain and cool.

2. Mix dressing ingredients. Stir gently into potatoes.

3. Add eggs, tuna, celery, and lettuce. Toss lightly.

4. Garnish with tomato wedges and Parmesan cheese.

TIP

This is like a potato salad loaded, or a simplified salade niçoise. If you already have potato salad in the refrigerator, use it instead of the potatoes and dressing. Just add the other ingredients and garnishes. This transforms a leftover completely!

Exchange List Values
- Starch 2.0
- Lean Meat 1.0

Basic Nutritional Values
- Calories 210
  (Calories from Fat 40)
- Total Fat 4.5 gm
  (Saturated Fat 1.1 gm,
  Trans Fat 0.0 gm,
  Polyunsat Fat 1.7 gm,
  Monounsat Fat 1.5 gm)
- Cholesterol 105 mg
- Sodium 585 mg
- Potassium 695 gm
- Total Carb 31 gm
- Dietary Fiber 4 gm
- Sugars 4 gm
- Protein 11 gm
- Phosphorus 160 gm

Italian-Way Tuna Salad

Hope Comerford
Clinton Township, MI

Makes 2 servings
Prep. Time: 5 minutes

5 oz. can of light tuna in water, drained

1 Tbsp. fresh minced onion

¼ tsp. garlic powder

¼ tsp. salt

⅛ tsp. pepper

1 Tbsp. olive oil

2 tsp. lemon juice

1. Mix together all ingredients.

Serving suggestion:
Serve with crackers or on bread.

Warm Memories:
This was how my Meme (grandma) used to always make tuna for us when she didn't have any mayo. She said her mother (from Italy) always made tuna with olive oil and lemon and never with mayo.

Exchange List Values
- Carbohydrate 0
- Lean Meat 1.0
- Fat 1.0

Basic Nutritional Values
- Calories 210
  (Calories from Fat 113)
- Total Fat 12.5 gm
  (Saturated Fat 2 gm,
  Trans Fat 0.0 gm,
  Polyunsat Fat 2.8 gm,
  Monounsat Fat 7 gm)
- Cholesterol 13 mg
- Sodium 531 mg
- Potassium 202 gm
- Total Carb 3 gm
- Dietary Fiber 1 gm
- Sugars 0 gm
- Protein 21 gm
- Phosphorus 227 gm

Grandpa Steve's Potato Salad

Nanci Keatley
Salem, OR

Makes 8 servings, about 7 oz. per serving
Prep. Time: 20 minutes
Cooking Time for Potatoes: 20 minutes

6 russet potatoes, peeled, cooked, and cubed

1 cup finely chopped onion

1 cup thinly sliced celery

1 cup sliced black olives (reserve 1 Tbsp. for top of salad)

1 large carrot, grated

6 hard-boiled eggs (4 chopped, 2 sliced for top of salad)

1 cup low-fat mayonnaise

salt and pepper, to taste

Tabasco sauce, *optional*

Good Go-Alongs:
I helped Grandpa cater a few weddings with this recipe along with ham, beans, rolls, and green salad.

Exchange List Values
- Starch 1.0
- Carbohydrate 0.5
- Vegetable 1.0
- Fat 1.5

Basic Nutritional Values
- Calories 205 (Calories from Fat 70)
- Total Fat 8 gm (Saturated Fat 1.8 gm, Trans Fat 0.0 gm, Polyunsat Fat 2.2 gm, Monounsat Fat 3.4 gm)
- Cholesterol 140 mg
- Sodium 455 mg
- Potassium 460 gm
- Total Carb 27 gm
- Dietary Fiber 3 gm
- Sugars 4 gm
- Protein 7 gm
- Phosphorus 135 gm

1. Gently mix potatoes, onion, celery, olives, carrot, and chopped eggs together.

2. Add the mayonnaise and blend.

3. Season with salt and pepper to taste. Add Tabasco sauce to taste, if desired. Garnish with egg slices and reserved olives.

German Potato Salad

Rhonda Burgoon
Collingswood, NJ

Makes 4 servings, about 6 oz. per serving
Prep. Time: 15 minutes
Cooking Time: 20 minutes

3 cups diced, peeled potatoes

4 slices bacon

1 small onion, diced

1 rib celery, chopped

¼ cup white vinegar

2 Tbsp. water

2 Tbsp. sugar

½ tsp. salt

⅛ tsp. ground black pepper

1. Place potatoes in pot and just cover with water. Bring to boil and cook about 11 minutes or until tender. Drain and set aside to cool.

2. Fry bacon in a large skillet until browned and crisp. Remove from pan and set aside. Save 1 tsp. of bacon grease and discard the rest.

3. Add onion and celery to bacon grease and sauté for 5 minutes.

4. Mix together vinegar, water, sugar, salt, and pepper.

5. Over low heat, add vinegar mixture to the onion and celery in the skillet. Bring to a boil; pour over potatoes and stir gently to combine.

Warm Memories:
This has been a family Easter tradition for over fifty years. My grandmother taught me how to make this when I was a teen.

TIP

My family prefers this cold; however you can serve right away warm.

Exchange List Values
- Carbohydrate 0.5
- Vegetable 1.0
- Fat 0.5

Basic Nutritional Values
- Calories 185
  (Calories from Fat 35)
- Total Fat 4 gm
  (Saturated Fat 1.3 gm,
  Trans Fat 0.0 gm,
  Polyunsat Fat 0.5 gm,
  Monounsat Fat 1.7 gm)
- Cholesterol 10 mg
- Sodium 455 mg
- Potassium 490 gm
- Total Carb 32 gm
- Dietary Fiber 3 gm
- Sugars 9 gm
- Protein 5 gm
- Phosphorus 90 gm

Pink Potato Salad

Dawn Landowski
Eau Claire, WI

Makes 10 servings, about 8 oz. per serving
Prep. Time: 30 minutes
Cooking Time: 20 minutes
Cooling Time: 1 hour

3 lbs. baby red potatoes

1 medium onion, diced

Dressing:

¼ cup chili sauce

1 cup light, reduced-fat mayonnaise

½ cup light, reduced-fat French dressing

3 tsp. onion powder

½ tsp. pepper

¼ tsp. garlic powder

Salad:

6 hard-boiled eggs, sliced, *divided*

½ green pepper, diced

6 sliced radishes

1 cucumber, peeled and diced

½ cup frozen peas, thawed

3 Tbsp. parsley

paprika for garnish

1. Boil potatoes until tender but firm. Allow to cool. Peel and dice potatoes.

2. Mix dressing ingredients together and add to potatoes.

3. Fold in 5 sliced eggs, green pepper, radishes, cucumber, peas, and parsley.

4. Refrigerate. Garnish with reserved sliced egg and paprika.

Warm Memories:
My granny always made this for me.

Exchange List Values
- Starch 1.5
- Carbohydrate 0.5
- Fat 2.0

Basic Nutritional Values
- Calories 240
  (Calories from Fat 90)
- Total Fat 10 gm
  (Saturated Fat 1.9 gm,
  Trans Fat 0.0 gm,
  Polyunsat Fat 4.4 gm,
  Monounsat Fat 3.3 gm)
- Cholesterol 120 mg
- Sodium 470 mg
- Potassium 730 gm
- Total Carb 30 gm
- Dietary Fiber 4 gm
- Sugars 7 gm
- Protein 7 gm
- Phosphorus 165 gm

Cherry Wild Rice Salad

Edie Moran
West Babylon, NY

Makes 8 servings, about 1 cup per serving
Prep. Time: 20 minutes
Cooking Time (for rice): 35 minutes
Chilling Time: 30 minutes

¾ cup cashews, halved

2 cups snow peas, chopped in half

2 cups cooked wild rice, cooled

1 cup cooked long grain rice, cooled

8-oz. can sliced water chestnuts, drained

1 cup dried cherries

½ cup celery, sliced thin

¼ cup chopped green onions

Dressing:

3 Tbsp. sugar

3 Tbsp. cider vinegar

4½ tsp. light soy sauce

1 clove garlic, peeled

¾ tsp. minced fresh ginger root

1. Toast the cashews in a medium oven or toaster oven for 5 minutes or until fragrant. Cool.

2. In a large bowl, combine peas, cooled rice, water chestnuts, cherries, celery, onions, and cashews.

3. Combine dressing ingredients in the blender and process until well blended.

4. Pour dressing over rice mixture and toss to coat. Cover and refrigerate until serving.

Warm Memories:
We always serve it at our annual cousins' reunion. I double the recipe for that.

TIP

It can be made the day before and add dressing an hour before serving.

Exchange List Values
- Starch 1.0
- Fruit 1.0
- Carbohydrate 0.5
- Vegetable 1.0
- Fat 1.0

Basic Nutritional Values
- Calories 250
  (Calories from Fat 55)
- Total Fat 6 gm
  (Saturated Fat 1.2 gm,
  Trans Fat 0.0 gm,
  Polyunsat Fat 1.1 gm,
  Monounsat Fat 3.6 gm)
- Cholesterol 0 mg
- Sodium 205 mg
- Potassium 290 gm
- Total Carb 44 gm
- Dietary Fiber 4 gm
- Sugars 20 gm
- Protein 5 gm
- Phosphorus 235 gm

Cranberry Relish

Winifred Erb Paul
Scottdale, PA

Makes 7 cups, 28 servings, ¼ cup per serving
Prep. Time: 20 minutes
Chilling Time: a week or more

4 cups cranberries

2 apples, cored but not peeled, quartered

2 oranges, including rind, quartered

1 lemon, including rind, quartered

2 cups granulated Splenda

1. Grind the whole fruit together using meat grinder. Alternatively, use a food processor and pulse just until most fruits are diced, but not mushy.

2. Be sure to keep the juice after fruits are ground. Add Splenda and let it set a week in the refrigerator before serving.

Warm Memories:
The Tillman Erb family emigrated to Hesston, Kansas, in 1885. They brought this recipe with them from Lancaster County, Pennsylvania. It was always served at the Erb Christmas get-together. My husband makes it every year and it goes well with turkey, chicken, or ham on Christmas Day.

TIP

To get a good grind from a food processor, put in only a few pieces of fruit—do not fill up the processor bowl. Push the pulse button once and allow everything to come to a stop before pushing the button again. Look at the size of the fruit carefully after each pulse.

Exchange List Value
• Fruit 0.5

Basic Nutritional Values
• Calories 30 (Calories from Fat 0)
• Total Fat 0 gm (Saturated Fat 0.0 gm, Trans Fat 0.0 gm, Polyunsat Fat 0.0 gm, Monounsat Fat 0.0 gm)
• Cholesterol 0 mg
• Sodium 0 mg
• Potassium 55 gm
• Total Carb 7 gm
• Dietary Fiber 2 gm
• Sugars 4 gm
• Protein 0 gm
• Phosphorus 5 gm

Red Bliss Potato Salad

Tim Smith
Wynnewood, PA

Makes 12 servings, about 5½ oz. per serving
Prep. Time: 15 minutes
Cooking Time: 20–25 minutes
Chilling Time: 2 hours

12 medium Red Bliss potatoes, about 5 oz. each

3 ribs celery, diced

2 hard-boiled eggs, diced

¼ cup light, reduced-fat mayonnaise

2 Tbsp. white vinegar

1 Tbsp. dry mustard

1 tsp. celery seed

1 tsp. white pepper

1 tsp. black pepper

salt, to taste

1. Cook whole potatoes until medium soft, but still firm. Drain. Allow to cool, then dice.

2. Put diced potatoes in large bowl. Add rest of ingredients and stir gently.

3. Chill in refrigerator for 2 hours before serving.

Warm Memories:
Everybody in my family loves this potato salad. My nieces and nephews always ask if I'm bringing it.

TIP

Do not overcook the potatoes! You want them soft but not soft like you're making mashed potatoes!

Exchange List Values
- Starch 2.0
- Fat 0.5

Basic Nutritional Values
- Calories 170 (Calories from Fat 20)
- Total Fat 2 gm (Saturated Fat 0.4 gm, Trans Fat 0.0 gm, Polyunsat Fat 0.9 gm, Monounsat Fat 0.6 gm)
- Cholesterol 30 mg
- Sodium 75 mg
- Potassium 650 gm
- Total Carb 33 gm
- Dietary Fiber 3 gm
- Sugars 2 gm
- Protein 4 gm
- Phosphorus 165 gm

Thanksgiving Fruit Salad

Mary Vaughn Warye
West Liberty, OH

Makes 10 servings, about 1 cup per serving
Prep. Time: 20 minutes
Chilling Time: 2 hours

1 cup canned pineapple tidbits packed in juice, drained, with ⅓ cup juice reserved

2 3-oz. pkgs. sugar-free cherry gelatin

2 cups hot water

1 cup cold water

2 Tbsp. lemon juice

¾ cup granulated Splenda

1½ cups coarsely ground fresh cranberries

½ cup finely ground orange with peel

1 cup orange sections, halved

¾ cup diced celery

⅓ cup chopped walnuts

Variation:
Add 1 cup red grapes to the partially set gelatin.

—Betty Rutt, Elizabethtown, PA

1. Drain pineapple, reserving ⅓ cup juice.

2. Dissolve gelatin in hot water. Stir in cold water, reserved pineapple juice, and lemon juice. Chill until partially set.

3. Meanwhile, stir Splenda into ground cranberries and orange.

4. Stir ground fruit mixture, pineapple, orange sections, celery, and walnuts into partially set gelatin.

5. Pour into mold and chill until set, at least 2 hours.

Exchange List Values
- Fruit 1.0
- Fat 0.5

Basic Nutritional Values
- Calories 80
  (Calories from Fat 20)
- Total Fat 2.5 gm
  (Saturated Fat 0.3 gm,
  Trans Fat 0.0 gm,
  Polyunsat Fat 1.9 gm,
  Monounsat Fat 0.4 gm)
- Cholesterol 0 mg
- Sodium 60 mg
- Potassium 150 gm
- Total Carb 13 gm
- Dietary Fiber 2 gm
- Sugars 9 gm
- Protein 2 gm
- Phosphorus 55 gm

Cranberry Salad

Eileen M. Landis
Lebanon, PA

Makes 10 servings, about 7 oz. per serving
Prep. Time: 15 minutes
Chilling Time: 2–4 hours

2 0.3-oz. pkgs. sugar-free cherry or raspberry gelatin

1½ cups boiling water

20-oz. can crushed pineapple, packed in juice, undrained

14-oz. can whole cranberry sauce

1½ cups halved red seedless grapes

½ cup chopped pecans or walnuts, *optional*

1. Dissolve gelatin in boiling water.

2. Add pineapple, cranberry sauce, and grapes. Add nuts, if desired.

3. Chill until set.

Exchange List Values
- Fruit 1.0
- Carbohydrate 0.5

Basic Nutritional Values
- Calories 115 (Calories from Fat 0)
- Total Fat 0 gm (Saturated Fat 0.0 gm, Trans Fat 0.0 gm, Polyunsat Fat 0.1 gm, Monounsat Fat 0.0 gm)
- Cholesterol 0 mg
- Sodium 50 mg
- Potassium 115 gm
- Total Carb 26 gm
- Dietary Fiber 1 gm
- Sugars 21 gm
- Protein 2 gm
- Phosphorus 40 gm

Desserts

Desserts

Zesty Pears

Barbara Walker
Sturgis, SD

Makes 8 servings
Prep. Time: 35 minutes
Cooking Time: 4–6 hours
Ideal slow-cooker size: 3- or 4-qt.

6 fresh pears

½ cup raisins

¼ cup brown sugar

1 tsp. grated lemon peel

¼ cup brandy

½ cup Sauternes wine

½ cup crumbled macaroons

fat-free sour cream, *optional*

1. Peel and core pears. Cut into thin slices.

2. Combine raisins, sugar, and lemon peel. Layer alternately with pear slices in slow cooker.

3. Pour brandy and wine over top.

4. Cover. Cook on Low 4–6 hours.

5. Spoon into serving dishes. Cool. Sprinkle with macaroons. Serve plain or topped with sour cream.

Exchange List Value

- Carbohydrate 2.0

Basic Nutritional Values

- Calories 140
  (Calories from Fat 13)
- Total Fat 1 gm
  (Saturated Fat 0.9 gm,
  Polyunsat Fat 0.1 gm,
  Monounsat Fat 0.1 gm)
- Cholesterol 0 mg
- Sodium 11 mg
- Total Carb 33 gm
- Dietary Fiber 3 gm
- Sugars 28 gm
- Protein 1 gm

Caramel Apples

Elaine Patton
West Middletown, PA
Rhonda Lee Schmidt
Scranton, PA
Renee Shirk
Mount Joy, PA

Makes 8 servings
Prep. Time: 30 minutes
Cooking Time: 4–6 hours
Ideal slow-cooker size: 4-qt.

4 very large tart apples, cored

½ cup apple juice

8 Tbsp. brown sugar substitute

12 hot cinnamon candies

4 Tbsp. light, soft tub margarine

8 caramel candies

¼ tsp. ground cinnamon

whipped cream, *optional*

1. Remove ½-inch-wide strip of peel off the top of each apple and place apples in slow cooker.

2. Pour apple juice over apples.

3. Fill the center of each apple with 2 Tbsp. brown sugar substitute, 3 hot cinnamon candies, 1 Tbsp. margarine, and 2 caramel candies. Sprinkle with cinnamon.

4. Cover and cook on Low 4–6 hours, or until tender.

5. Serve hot with juice from bottom of slow cooker and optional whipped cream.

Exchange List Value
- Carbohydrate 2.0

Basic Nutritional Values
- Calories 130 (Calories from Fat 26)
- Total Fat 3 gm (Saturated Fat 0.6 gm, Polyunsat Fat 0.6 gm, Monounsat Fat 1.3 gm)
- Cholesterol 0 mg
- Sodium 63 mg
- Total Carb 28 gm
- Dietary Fiber 3 gm
- Sugars 23 gm
- Protein 1 gm

Easy Baked Apples

Willard E. and Alice Roth
Elkhart, IN

Makes 12 servings, 1 apple per serving
Prep. Time: 20 minutes
Cooking Time: 6–8 hours
Ideal slow-cooker size: 7-qt.

12 medium baking apples, 4 lbs. total

½ cup raisins

½ cup chopped nuts

½ cup Splenda Brown Sugar Blend

½ tsp. nutmeg

1 tsp. cinnamon

3 slices fresh lemon

1¼ cups boiling water

1. Wash and core whole apples. Starting at the stem, peel about ⅓ of the way down.

2. Fill each apple with raisins and nuts. Stack into slow cooker.

3. Combine Splenda, nutmeg, and cinnamon in small saucepan. Add lemon slices and pour boiling water over everything. Boil ingredients together for about 5 minutes. Pour over apples in slow cooker.

4. Cover and cook on Low 6–8 hours. Serve hot or cold.

Exchange List Values
- Fruit 1.5
- Carbohydrate 0.5
- Fat 0.5

Basic Nutritional Values
- Calories 155
  (Calories from Fat 30)
- Total Fat 4 gm
  (Saturated Fat 0.4 gm,
  Trans Fat 0.0 gm,
  Polyunsat Fat 2.4 gm,
  Monounsat Fat 0.5 gm)
- Cholesterol 0 mg
- Sodium 0 mg
- Potassium 230 gm
- Total Carb 33 gm
- Dietary Fiber 4 gm
- Sugars 22 gm
- Protein 1 gm
- Phosphorus 40 gm

Desserts

Apple Crisp

Michelle Strite
Goshen, IN

Makes 12 servings
Prep. Time: 15 minutes
Cooking Time: 2–3 hours
Ideal slow-cooker size: 4-qt.

⅔ cup sugar

1¼ cups water

3 Tbsp. cornstarch

4 cups sliced, peeled apples

½ tsp. ground cinnamon

¼ tsp. ground allspice

¾ cup quick oatmeal

¼ cup brown sugar substitute to equal 2
   Tbsp. sugar

½ cup flour

¼ cup light, soft tub margarine, at room
   temperature

1. Combine ⅔ cup sugar, water, cornstarch, apples, cinnamon, and allspice. Place in cooker.

2. Combine remaining ingredients until crumbly. Sprinkle over apple filling.

3. Cover. Cook on Low 2–3 hours.

Exchange List Value
• Carbohydrate 2.0

Basic Nutritional Values
• Calories 134
  (Calories from Fat 18)
• Total Fat 2 gm
  (Saturated Fat 0.2 gm,
  Polyunsat Fat 0.5 gm,
  Monounsat Fat 0.9 gm)
• Cholesterol 0 mg
• Sodium 34 mg
• Total Carb 29 gm
• Dietary Fiber 2 gm
• Sugars 15 gm
• Protein 1 gm

Slow-Cooker Pumpkin Pie

Colleen Heatwole
Burton, MI
Joette Droz
Kalona, IA

Makes 8 servings
Prep. Time: 10 minutes
Cooking Time: 3–4 hours
Cooling Time: 2–4 hours
Ideal slow-cooker size: 3-qt.

15-oz. can solid-pack pumpkin

12-oz. can fat-free evaporated milk

¾ cup sugar

½ cup low-fat buttermilk baking mix

2 eggs, beaten

2 Tbsp. tub-type margarine, melted

1½ tsp. cinnamon

¾ tsp. ground ginger

¼ tsp. ground nutmeg

whipped topping

Variation:
You can substitute 2½ Tbsp. pumpkin-pie spice in place of cinnamon, ginger, and nutmeg.

1. Spray slow cooker with cooking spray.

2. Mix all ingredients together in slow cooker, except whipped topping.

3. Cover. Cook on Low 3–4 hours, or until a toothpick inserted in center comes out clean.

4. Allow to cool to warm, or chill, before serving with whipped topping.

Exchange List Values
- Carbohydrate 2.0
- Fat 1.0

Basic Nutritional Values
- Calories 200
  (Calories from Fat 45)
- Total Fat 5 gm
  (Saturated Fat 1.5 gm,
  Polyunsat Fat 1.0 gm,
  Monounsat Fat 1.5 gm)
- Cholesterol 50 mg
- Sodium 175 mg
- Total Carb 34 gm
- Dietary Fiber 2 gm
- Sugars 26 gm
- Protein 6 gm

Black-and-Blue Cobbler

Renee Shirk
Mount Joy, PA

Makes 12 servings
Prep. Time: 30 minutes
Cooking Time: 2–2½ hours
Standing Time: 30 minutes
Ideal slow-cooker size: 5-qt.

1 cup flour

6 Tbsp. sugar substitute to equal 3 Tbsp. sugar

1 tsp. baking powder

¼ tsp. salt

¼ tsp. ground cinnamon

¼ tsp. ground nutmeg

2 eggs, beaten

2 Tbsp. milk

2 Tbsp. vegetable oil

2 cups fresh, or frozen, blueberries

2 cups fresh, or frozen, blackberries

¾ cup water

1 tsp. grated orange peel

6 Tbsp. sugar substitute to equal 3 Tbsp. sugar

whipped topping or ice cream, *optional*

1. Combine flour, sugar substitute, baking powder, salt, cinnamon, and nutmeg.

2. Combine eggs, milk, and oil. Stir into dry ingredients until moistened.

3. Spread the batter evenly over bottom of greased 5-qt. slow cooker.

4. In saucepan, combine berries, water, orange peel, and sugar substitute. Bring to boil. Remove from heat and pour over batter. Cover.

5. Cook on High 2–2½ hours, or until toothpick inserted into batter comes out clean. Turn off cooker.

6. Uncover and let stand 30 minutes before serving. Spoon from cooker and serve with whipped topping or ice cream, if desired.

Exchange List Values
- Carbohydrate 2.0
- Fat 0.5

Basic Nutritional Values
- Calories 170 (Calories from Fat 31)
- Total Fat 3 gm (Saturated Fat 0.5 gm, Polyunsat Fat 0.9 gm, Monounsat Fat 1.7 gm)
- Cholesterol 36 mg
- Sodium 92 mg
- Total Carb 34 gm
- Dietary Fiber 2 gm
- Sugars 23 gm
- Protein 3 gm

Quick Yummy Peaches

Willard E. Roth
Elkhart, IN

Makes 8 servings
Prep. Time: 20 minutes
Cooking Time: 5 hours
Ideal slow-cooker size: 4-qt.

⅓ cup buttermilk baking mix

⅔ cup dry quick oats

¼ cup brown sugar substitute to equal 2 Tbsp. sugar

1 tsp. cinnamon

4 cups sliced peaches, canned or fresh

½ cup peach juice or water

1. Mix together baking mix, oats, brown sugar substitute, and cinnamon in greased slow cooker.

2. Stir in peaches and peach juice.

3. Cook on Low for at least 5 hours. If you like a drier cobbler, remove lid for last 15–30 minutes of cooking.

Exchange List Value
- Carbohydrate 2.0

Basic Nutritional Values
- Calories 131
  (Calories from Fat 11)
- Total Fat 1 gm
  (Saturated Fat 0.1 gm,
  Polyunsat Fat 0.5 gm,
  Monounsat Fat 0.4 gm)
- Cholesterol 0 mg
- Sodium 76 mg
- Total Carb 29 gm
- Dietary Fiber 3 gm
- Sugars 20 gm
- Protein 2 gm

Desserts

Peach Crumble

Nathan LeBeau
Rapid City, SD

Makes 8 servings, 2×4-inch rectangle per
  serving
Prep. Time: 10 minutes
Baking Time: 20–30 minutes

4 cups peeled, sliced fresh peaches

6 Tbsp. Splenda Brown Sugar Blend

⅓ cup (5⅓ Tbsp.) trans-fat-free tub margarine

¾ tsp. nutmeg

¾ tsp. cinnamon

1 cup crushed graham crackers

Variation:
Use apples instead of peaches.

1. Mix peaches and Splenda together.

2. Place in a greased 8-inch pan.

3. Combine margarine, nutmeg, cinnamon, and graham crackers.

4. Sprinkle mixture over top of peaches.

5. Bake at 375°F for 20–30 minutes until bubbling.

Exchange List Values
- Carbohydrate 2.0
- Fat 1.0

Basic Nutritional Values
- Calories 165
  (Calories from Fat 65)
- Total Fat 7 gm
  (Saturated Fat 1.4 gm,
  Trans Fat 0.0 gm,
  Polyunsat Fat 2.8 gm,
  Monounsat Fat 2.3 gm)
- Cholesterol 0 mg
- Sodium 125 mg
- Potassium 195 gm
- Total Carb 26 gm
- Dietary Fiber 2 gm
- Sugars 15 gm
- Protein 2 gm
- Phosphorus 30 gm

Jumbleberry Crumble

Joanna Harrison
Lafayette, CO

Makes 10 servings, 2×3½-inch rectangle per serving
Prep. Time: 20 minutes
Baking Time: 50 minutes

3 cups strawberries

1½ cups blueberries

1½ cups raspberries

3 Tbsp. quick-cooking tapioca

⅓ cup Splenda Sugar Blend

½ cup flour

½ cup quick oats

¼ cup Splenda Brown Sugar Blend

1 tsp. cinnamon

5 Tbsp. trans-fat-free tub margarine

1. In large bowl, combine berries, tapioca, and Splenda Sugar Blend.

2. Pour into a greased 11×7-inch baking dish. Let stand 15 minutes.

3. Combine flour, oats, brown sugar blend, and cinnamon in small bowl.

4. Stir in melted margarine.

5. Sprinkle over berry mixture.

6. Bake at 350°F for 45–50 minutes or until filling is bubbly and topping is golden brown. Serve warm.

TIP

I've used fresh or frozen berries depending on the season. Yummy with vanilla ice cream.

Exchange List Values
- Carbohydrate 2.0
- Fat 1.0

Basic Nutritional Values
- Calories 165
  (Calories from Fat 45)
- Total Fat 5 gm
  (Saturated Fat 1.0 gm,
  Trans Fat 0.0 gm,
  Polyunsat Fat 2.0 gm,
  Monounsat Fat 1.5 gm)
- Cholesterol 0 mg
- Sodium 45 mg
- Potassium 145 gm
- Total Carb 30 gm
- Dietary Fiber 3 gm
- Sugars 14 gm
- Protein 2 gm
- Phosphorus 45 gm

Zucchini Strudel

Judith Houser
Hershey, PA

Makes 20 servings, 2½-inch square per serving
Prep. Time: 30 minutes
Cooking/Baking Time: 50 minutes

4 cups flour

¾ cup Splenda Sugar Blend

½ tsp. salt

1 cup trans-fat-free tub margarine

Filling:

4 cups peeled and cubed zucchini

½ to ⅔ cup lemon juice

¾ cup granulated Splenda

¼ tsp. nutmeg

½ tsp. cinnamon

1. Cut together flour, Splenda, salt, and margarine until crumbly.

2. Press half of the mixture into a 9×13-inch baking pan to make a crust.

3. Bake at 375°F for 10 minutes.

4. For filling: Combine zucchini and lemon juice in saucepan. Bring to a boil, covered.

5. Add Splenda and nutmeg. Simmer 5 minutes.

6. Add ½ cup reserved crumbs and stir over low heat until thickened.

7. Spread zucchini mixture over baked dough.

8. Cover with remaining crumbs. Sprinkle with cinnamon.

9. Bake at 375°F for 30 minutes.

Good Go-Alongs:

This is delicious served warm with vanilla ice cream.

TIP

Use smaller amount of lemon juice if you want a less tart dessert. A great way to use extra zucchini—people will think it's an apple strudel.

Exchange List Values

- Carbohydrate 2.0
- Fat 1.0

Basic Nutritional Values

- Calories 190 (Calories from Fat 65)
- Total Fat 7 gm (Saturated Fat 1.5 gm, Trans Fat 0.0 gm, Polyunsat Fat 2.9 gm, Monounsat Fat 2.2 gm)
- Cholesterol 0 mg
- Sodium 135 mg
- Potassium 100 gm
- Total Carb 28 gm
- Dietary Fiber 1 gm
- Sugars 9 gm
- Protein 3 gm
- Phosphorus 40 gm

German Blueberry Kuchen

Mrs. A. Krueger
Richmond, BC

Makes 20 servings, 3-inch square per serving
Prep. Time: 30 minutes
Baking Time: 40–45 minutes

3 cups flour

¾ cup Splenda Sugar Blend

4 tsp. baking powder

½ tsp. salt

½ cup trans-fat-free tub margarine

1⅓ cups milk

2 eggs

2 tsp. vanilla extract

1 tsp. nutmeg

grated rind of 1 lemon

4 cups fresh, or frozen blueberries

Crumb Topping:

½ cup granulated Splenda

½ cup flour

¼ cup trans-fat-free tub margarine

1. To prepare batter, combine flour, Splenda, baking powder, salt, margarine, and milk in large bowl.

2. Beat 2 minutes with electric mixer or 300 strokes by hand. Add eggs, vanilla, nutmeg, and lemon rind. Mix thoroughly.

3. Pour batter into greased and floured 12×16-inch baking pan. (Do not use a smaller pan.) Sprinkle with blueberries.

4. To prepare crumb topping, rub together Splenda, flour, and margarine until mixture is crumbly. Sprinkle over layer of blueberries.

5. Bake at 350°F for 40–45 minutes. Cut into squares.

Exchange List Values
- Carbohydrate 2.0
- Fat 1.0

Basic Nutritional Values
- Calories 190 (Calories from Fat 55)
- Total Fat 6 gm (Saturated Fat 1.3 gm, Trans Fat 0.0 gm, Polyunsat Fat 2.3 gm, Monounsat Fat 1.9 gm)
- Cholesterol 20 mg
- Sodium 200 mg
- Potassium 80 gm
- Total Carb 30 gm
- Dietary Fiber 1 gm
- Sugars 12 gm
- Protein 4 gm
- Phosphorus 145 gm

Desserts

Blackberry Rolypoly

Elaine Gibbel
Lititz, PA

Makes 12 servings, 1 slice per serving
Prep. Time: 30 minutes
Baking Time: 30 minutes

2 cups flour

2 tsp. baking powder

1 tsp. salt, *divided*

1 Tbsp. sugar

dash nutmeg

4 Tbsp. trans-fat-free tub margarine

¾ cup milk

3–4 sprays of cooking spray

6 cups blackberries

1 cup granulated Splenda

whipped topping, *optional*

1. Combine flour, baking powder, ½ tsp. salt, sugar, and nutmeg. Work 4 Tbsp. margarine into dry ingredients with fingers.

Gradually stir in milk until dough holds together but is soft. Turn out onto floured board and roll into a ½-inch thick rectangle.

2. Spray with cooking spray.

3. Combine berries, Splenda, and ½ tsp. salt. Sprinkle ½ fruit mixture over dough. Roll up like a jelly roll.

4. Place in greased 8×12-inch pan, seam-side down. Spoon remaining fruit mixture around roll.

5. Bake at 425°F for 30 minutes. Cut into 12 slices. Serve with whipped topping if your diet allows.

Exchange List Values
- Carbohydrate 2.0
- Fat 0.5

Basic Nutritional Values
- Calories 150
  (Calories from Fat 30)
- Total Fat 4 gm
  (Saturated Fat 0.7 gm,
  Trans Fat 0.0 gm,
  Polyunsat Fat 1.5 gm,
  Monounsat Fat 1.0 gm)
- Cholesterol 0 mg
- Sodium 290 mg
- Potassium 165 gm
- Total Carb 27 gm
- Dietary Fiber 4 gm
- Sugars 8 gm
- Protein 4 gm
- Phosphorus 130 gm

No-Added-Sugar Apple Pie

Faye Pankratz
Inola, OK

Makes 1 9-inch pie, 8 slices, 1 slice per
serving
Prep. Time: 30 minutes
Chilling Time: 1 hours
Baking Time: 45 minutes

Pastry:

½ cup low-fat ricotta cheese

5 pkgs. artificial sweetener

3 Tbsp. fat-free milk

1 egg white

2 Tbsp. cooking oil

1½ tsp. vanilla extract

dash salt

2 cups flour

2 tsp. baking powder

2 Tbsp. water

Filling:

6–8 apples

¼ cup flour

½ tsp. cinnamon

10–12 pkgs. artificial sweetener

1. Mix pastry ingredients in the order given. Divide pastry into two equal pieces. Chill dough.

2. Roll each piece of dough into a 10-inch circle. Place 1 piece of pastry in pie pan.

3. Peel and slice apples. Toss with flour, cinnamon, and sweetener. Spoon into pie shell.

4. Use remaining pastry for a top crust. Slit in several places.

5. Bake at 375°F for 20 minutes. Reduce temperature to 325°F and bake 25 minutes longer. (The edges of this pastry tend to get hard.)

Exchange List Values
- Starch 2.0
- Fruit 0.5
- Fat 1.0

Basic Nutritional Values
- Calories 230 (Calories from Fat 40)
- Total Fat 4.5 gm (Saturated Fat 0.8 gm, Trans Fat 0.0 gm, Polyunsat Fat 1.3 gm, Monounsat Fat 2.4 gm)
- Cholesterol 5 mg
- Sodium 140 mg
- Potassium 160 gm
- Total Carb 42 gm
- Dietary Fiber 2 gm
- Sugars 12 gm
- Protein 6 gm
- Phosphorus 195 gm

New England Blueberry Pie

Krista Hershberger
Elverson, PA

Makes 8 servings, 1 slice per serving
Prep. Time: 15 minutes
Cooking Time: 12 minutes
Chilling Time: 1 hour

4 cups fresh blueberries, *divided*

pre-baked 9-inch pie shell

½ cup Splenda Sugar Blend

3 Tbsp. cornstarch

¼ tsp. salt

¼ cup water

1 Tbsp. trans-fat-free tub margarine

whipped cream, *optional*

1. Place 2 cups of blueberries in a baked pie shell.

2. In medium saucepan, cook Splenda, cornstarch, salt, water, remaining 2 cups blueberries, and margarine. Stir continuously until thick.

3. Cool blueberry mixture for ½ hour. Pour cooled mixture over berries in pie crust. Chill.

4. Top with whipped cream before serving if you wish.

Warm Memories:
We have our own blueberry bushes so this is the first recipe to come out when we pick our first batch!

Exchange List Values
- Carbohydrate 2.0
- Fat 0.5

Basic Nutritional Values
- Calories 150
  (Calories from Fat 25)
- Total Fat 3 gm
  (Saturated Fat 0.6 gm,
  Trans Fat 0.2 gm,
  Polyunsat Fat 1.0 gm,
  Monounsat Fat 1.2 gm)
- Cholesterol 0 mg
- Sodium 105 mg
- Potassium 65 gm
- Total Carb 30 gm
- Dietary Fiber 2 gm
- Sugars 19 gm
- Protein 1 gm
- Phosphorus 15 gm

Lemon Pie for Beginners

Jean Butzer
Batavia, NY

Makes 8 servings
Prep. Time: 10 minutes
Cooking Time: 10–12 minutes
Cooling Time: 15 minutes

½ cup Splenda

4 Tbsp. cornstarch

¼ tsp. salt

1¾ cups water, *divided*

3 egg yolks, slightly beaten

2 Tbsp. trans-fat-free tub margarine

⅓ cup lemon juice

9-inch baked pastry shell

meringue or whipped cream, *optional*

1. Combine Splenda, cornstarch, salt, and ¼ cup water in 1½-qt. microwave safe bowl.

2. Microwave remaining ¼ cup water on High until boiling. Stir into Splenda mixture.

3. Microwave 4–6 minutes until very thick, stirring every 2 minutes.

4. Mix a little hot mixture into egg yolks. Blend yolks into sugar mixture.

5. Microwave 1 minute more.

6. Stir in margarine and lemon juice.

7. Cool for 15 minutes and pour into pie shell.

TIP

1. To make a meringue, beat 3 egg whites adding ¼ tsp. cream of tartar and 3 Tbsp. sugar slowly. Continue beating until stiff peaks form. Cover the lemon filling with meringue to edge of crust. Bake in 350°F oven for 10–12 minutes or until meringue is golden.
2. Using the microwave is so much easier than cooking the filling on the top of the stove. You don't have to worry about it burning or sticking to the bottom of the pan.

Exchange List Values
- Carbohydrate 1.5
- Fat 1.0

Basic Nutritional Values
- Calories 140 (Calories from Fat 55)
- Total Fat 6 gm (Saturated Fat 1.4 gm, Trans Fat 0.2 gm, Polyunsat Fat 1.6 gm, Monounsat Fat 2.3 gm)
- Cholesterol 70 mg
- Sodium 125 mg
- Potassium 25 gm
- Total Carb 21 gm
- Dietary Fiber 0 gm
- Sugars 12 gm
- Protein 2 gm
- Phosphorus 30 gm

Fresh Peach Delight

Jan Mast
Lancaster, PA

Makes 20 servings, 2¼-inch square per serving
Prep. Time: 20 minutes
Cooking/Baking Time: 35 minutes
Cooling Time: 1½ hours

½ cup trans-fat-free tub margarine

2 Tbsp. Splenda Brown Sugar Blend

1 cup chopped pecans

1 cup plus 2 Tbsp. flour

8 oz. fat-free cream cheese, softened

1 cup confectioners' sugar

1 tsp. vanilla extract

2 cups frozen whipped topping, thawed

2 Tbsp. cornstarch

⅓ cup granulated Splenda

1½ cups water

0.3-oz. box sugar-free peach gelatin

4 cups sliced fresh peaches

1. To make a crust, combine margarine, Splenda Brown Sugar Blend, pecans, and flour. Press into a 9×13-inch baking pan.

2. Bake at 350°F for 25 minutes. Cool at least 30 minutes.

3. Beat cream cheese until soft and smooth. Beat in vanilla and confectioners' sugar.

4. Fold in whipped topping.

5. Spread filling on cooled crust.

6. To make topping, combine cornstarch and granulated Splenda in a saucepan. Add water.

7. Cook until boiling. Boil and stir for 2 minutes.

8. Add gelatin and stir well. Allow to cool at least 30 minutes.

9. Combine gelatin mixture with sliced peaches and stir gently.

10. Refrigerate until cool but not gelled, between 15–30 minutes.

11. Pour cooled topping over filling.

12. Chill and cut into squares to serve.

Warm Memories:
Everyone loves this yummy dessert. It works well with fresh strawberries, fresh blueberries, etc. Just change the gelatin flavor and fruit for your own variation!

Exchange List Values
- Carbohydrate 1.5
- Fat 1.5

Basic Nutritional Values
- Calories 165
  (Calories from Fat 70)
- Total Fat 8 gm
  (Saturated Fat 1.1 gm,
  Trans Fat 0.0 gm,
  Polyunsat Fat 2.6 gm,
  Monounsat Fat 3.5 gm)
- Cholesterol 0 mg
- Sodium 125 mg
- Potassium 140 gm
- Total Carb 21 gm
- Dietary Fiber 1 gm
- Sugars 11 gm
- Protein 3 gm
- Phosphorus 105 gm

Desserts

Creamy Peanut Butter Dessert

Kristine Martin
Newmanstown, PA

Makes 16 servings, 2¼×3¼-inch rectangle
  per serving
Prep. Time: 15 minutes
Chilling Time: 30 minutes + 3 hours

Crust:

1¾ cups graham cracker crumbs

¼ cup trans-fat-free tub margarine

2 Tbsp. peanut butter

8 oz. fat-free cream cheese, softened

½ cup peanut butter

½ cup granulated Splenda

2 tsp. vanilla extract

16 oz. fat-free frozen whipped topping,
  thawed

3 Tbsp. chocolate syrup

1. Combine graham cracker crumbs, margarine, and peanut butter. Mix well. Set aside ½ cup for topping.

2. Press remaining crumb mixture into greased 9×13-inch baking dish.

3. Cover and refrigerate 30 minutes.

4. Meanwhile, make the filling. In a mixing bowl, beat cream cheese and peanut butter until smooth.

5. Beat in Splenda and vanilla. Fold in whipped topping.

6. Spoon filling over chilled crust.

7. Drizzle with chocolate syrup. Sprinkle with reserved ½ cup crumbs.

8. Cover. Freeze for at least 3 hours before serving.

9. Remove from freezer 15 minutes before serving.

Warm Memories:

I take this often to hot and cold dish dinners. Everyone always thinks it has ice cream in it, but it doesn't, so it's a lot easier to keep from melting than something with ice cream. I always get requests for the recipe.

TIP

This dessert can be frozen up to three months, so it's convenient to make ahead for many occasions.

Exchange List Values
- Carbohydrate 1.5
- Fat 1.5

Basic Nutritional Values
- Calories 180
  (Calories from Fat 70)
- Total Fat 8 gm
  (Saturated Fat 1.6 gm,
  Trans Fat 0.0 gm,
  Polyunsat Fat 2.6 gm,
  Monounsat Fat 3.4 gm)
- Cholesterol 5 mg
- Sodium 225 mg
- Potassium 145 gm
- Total Carb 21 gm
- Dietary Fiber 1 gm
- Sugars 9 gm
- Protein 5 gm
- Phosphorus 140 gm

Lemon Pudding Cake

Jean Butzer
Batavia, NY

Makes 6 servings
Prep. Time: 30 minutes
Cooking Time: 2–3 hours
Ideal slow-cooker size: 3- or 4-qt.

3 eggs, separated

1 tsp. grated lemon peel

¼ cup lemon juice

1 Tbsp. melted light, soft tub margarine

1½ cups fat-free half-and-half

½ cup sugar substitute to equal 2 Tbsp. sugar

¼ cup flour

⅛ tsp. salt

1. Beat egg whites until stiff peaks form. Set aside.

2. Beat egg yolks. Blend in lemon peel, lemon juice, margarine, and half-and-half.

3. In separate bowl, combine sugar substitute, flour, and salt. Add to egg-lemon mixture, beating until smooth.

4. Fold into beaten egg whites.

5. Spoon into slow cooker.

6. Cover and cook on High 2–3 hours.

7. Serve with spoon from cooker.

Exchange List Values
- Carbohydrate 2.0
- Fat 0.5

Basic Nutritional Values
- Calories 169
  (Calories from Fat 37)
- Total Fat 4 gm
  (Saturated Fat 1.5 gm,
  Polyunsat Fat 0.5 gm,
  Monounsat Fat 1.4 gm)
- Cholesterol 111 mg
- Sodium 185 mg
- Total Carb 27 gm
- Dietary Fiber 0 gm
- Sugars 20 gm
- Protein 5 gm

Raw Apple Cake

Kathryn Yoder
Minot, ND

Makes 15–20 servings
Prep. Time: 20 minutes
Baking Time: 40–50 minutes

Cake:

4 cups diced apples

1 cup Splenda Brown Sugar Blend

½ cup canola oil

1 cup nuts, *optional*

2 eggs, beaten

2 tsp. vanilla extract

2 cups whole wheat flour

2 tsp. baking soda

2 tsp. cinnamon

1 tsp. salt

Hard Sauce:

¼ cup margarine

6 Tbsp. Splenda Brown Sugar Blend

1⅓ Tbsp. flour

dash salt

1½ cups water

1 tsp. maple flavoring

1. To prepare cake, combine apples and brown sugar and mix thoroughly. Add oil, nuts, eggs, and vanilla.

2. Mix all dry ingredients and add to batter. Place in greased and floured 9×13-inch pan.

3. Bake at 350°F for 40–50 minutes or until done.

4. To prepare hard sauce, melt margarine in saucepan. Add all other ingredients and cook until mixture thickens.

5. Pour over warm cake. Serve.

Exchange List Values
- Carbohydrate 2.0
- Fat 1.0

Basic Nutritional Values
- Calories 180
  (Calories from Fat 70)
- Total Fat 8 gm
  (Saturated Fat 1.0 gm,
  Trans Fat 0.0 gm,
  Polyunsat Fat 2.4 gm,
  Monounsat Fat 4.2 gm)
- Cholesterol 20 mg
- Sodium 275 mg
- Potassium 105 gm
- Total Carb 26 gm
- Dietary Fiber 2 gm
- Sugars 9 gm
- Protein 2 gm
- Phosphorus 55 gm

Desserts

Dark Apple Cake

Amy Bauer
New Ulm, MN

Makes 24 servings, 2-inch square per
serving
Prep. Time: 30 minutes
Baking Time: 50 minutes

1 cup Splenda Sugar Blend

½ cup trans-fat-free tub margarine

4 eggs

1 cup cold coffee

⅓ cup canola oil

3 cups all-purpose flour

1½ tsp. baking soda

1½ tsp. ground cinnamon

½ tsp. ground nutmeg

½ tsp. ground cloves

½ tsp. salt

1 tsp. vanilla extract

1 cup chopped nuts

½ cup raisins

2 cups chopped apples

Exchange List Values

- Carbohydrate 1.5
- Fat 2.0

Basic Nutritional Values

- Calories 200
  (Calories from Fat 90)
- Total Fat 10 gm
  (Saturated Fat 1.4 gm,
  Trans Fat 0.0 gm,
  Polyunsat Fat 4.6 gm,
  Monounsat Fat 3.6 gm)
- Cholesterol 30 mg
- Sodium 170 mg
- Potassium 90 gm
- Total Carb 25 gm
- Dietary Fiber 1 gm
- Sugars 11 gm
- Protein 4 gm
- Phosphorus 55 gm

1. Cream Spenda, margarine, and eggs. Blend in coffee.

2. Add rest of ingredients. Mix well.

3. Pour into greased 9×13-inch pan. Bake at 350°F for 50 minutes.

Royal Raspberry Cake

Miriam Christophel
Battle Creek, MI

Makes 20 servings
Prep. Time: 25 minutes
Baking Time: 30–35 minutes

Cake:

2 cups flour

½ tsp. salt

1 Tbsp. baking powder

⅓ cup trans-fat-free tub margarine, softened

½ cup Splenda Sugar Blend

1 egg, room temperature

1 cup fat-free milk, room temperature

1 tsp. vanilla extract

3½ cups red raspberries

Glaze:

1½ cups granulated Splenda

¼ cup cornstarch

½ tsp. vanilla extract

1⅔ Tbsp. water

1. Sift together flour, salt, and baking powder. Set aside.

2. Cream margarine with mixer. Add Splenda gradually, beating well after each addition. Stir in egg.

3. Combine milk and vanilla.

4. Add dry ingredients to margarine mixture, alternating with milk and vanilla and beating well after each addition.

5. Spread cake batter into greased 9×13-inch pan. Spread berries evenly over the top.

6. Bake at 350°F for 30–35 minutes or until center of cake springs back when lightly touched. Cool 5 minutes.

7. To make glaze, blend Splenda and cornstarch to a very fine powder. Pour into a small bowl. Add vanilla and water and stir well. Spread over cake.

Exchange List Values

- Carbohydrate 1.5
- Fat 0.5

Basic Nutritional Values

- Calories 120
  (Calories from Fat 20)
- Total Fat 2.5 gm
  (Saturated Fat 0.6 gm,
  Trans Fat 0.0 gm,
  Polyunsat Fat 1.1 gm,
  Monounsat Fat 0.8 gm)
- Cholesterol 10 mg
- Sodium 145 mg
- Potassium 70 gm
- Total Carb 21 gm
- Dietary Fiber 2 gm
- Sugars 8 gm
- Protein 2 gm
- Phosphorus 105 gm

Carrot Cake

Colleen Heatwole
Burton, MI

Makes 10 servings
Prep. Time: 35 minutes
Cooking Time: 3–4 hours
Cooling Time: 10 minutes
Ideal slow-cooker size: 4- or 5-qt.

⅓ cup canola oil

2 eggs

1 Tbsp. hot water

½ cup grated raw carrots

¾ cup flour

¾ cup sugar

½ tsp. baking powder

⅛ tsp. salt

¼ tsp. ground allspice

½ tsp. ground cinnamon

⅛ tsp. ground cloves

½ cup chopped nuts

½ cup raisins or chopped dates

2 Tbsp. flour

1. In large bowl, beat oil, eggs, and water for 1 minute.

2. Add carrots. Mix well.

3. Stir together flour, sugar, baking powder, salt, allspice, cinnamon, and cloves. Add to creamed mixture.

4. Toss nuts and raisins in bowl with 2 Tbsp. flour. Add to creamed mixture. Mix well.

5. Pour into greased and floured 3-lb. coffee can, 9×5-inch bread pan, or slow cooker baking insert. Place can, pan, or baking insert in slow cooker.

6. Cover insert with its lid, or cover can/pan with 8 paper towels, folded down over edge of slow cooker to absorb moisture. Cover paper towels with cooker lid. Cook on High 3–4 hours.

7. Remove can, pan, or insert from cooker and allow to cool on rack for 10 minutes. Run knife around edge of cake. Invert onto serving plate.

Exchange List Values
- Carbohydrate 2.0
- Fat 3.0

Basic Nutritional Values
- Calories 274 (Calories from Fat 147)
- Total Fat 16 gm (Saturated Fat 1.5 gm, Polyunsat Fat 6.4 gm, Monounsat Fat 7.6 gm)
- Cholesterol 43 mg
- Sodium 66 mg
- Total Carb 30 gm
- Dietary Fiber 1 gm
- Sugars 20 gm
- Protein 4 gm

Dump Cake

Janice Muller
Derwood, MD

Makes 15 servings
Prep. Time: 20 minutes
Cooking Time: 2–3 hours
Ideal slow-cooker size: 4- or 5-qt.

20-oz. can crushed pineapple

21-oz. can light blueberry or cherry pie filling

18½-oz. pkg. yellow cake mix

cinnamon

⅓ cup light, soft tub margarine

⅓ cup chopped walnuts

1. Grease bottom and sides of slow cooker.

2. Spread layers of pineapple, blueberry or cherry pie filling, and dry cake mix. Be careful not to mix the layers.

3. Sprinkle with cinnamon.

4. Top with thin layers of margarine chunks and nuts.

5. Cover. Cook on High 2–3 hours.

Variation:

Use a package of spice cake mix and apple pie filling.

Exchange List Values
- Carbohydrate 2.5
- Fat 1.0

Basic Nutritional Values
- Calories 219 (Calories from Fat 57)
- Total Fat 6 gm (Saturated Fat 1.5 gm, Polyunsat Fat 2.4 gm, Monounsat Fat 2.2 gm)
- Cholesterol 0 mg
- Sodium 250 mg
- Total Carb 41 gm
- Dietary Fiber 1 gm
- Sugars 28 gm
- Protein 2 gm

Desserts

Chocolate Chip Applesauce Cake

Lois Cressman
Plattsville, ON
Ruby Lehman
Towson, MD

Makes 20 servings
Prep. Time: 25 minutes
Baking Time: 40 minutes

¾ cup Splenda Sugar Blend

½ cup cooking oil

2 eggs

2 cups unsweetened applesauce

2 cups flour

1½ tsp. baking soda

½ tsp. cinnamon

2 Tbsp. unsweetened cocoa

Topping:
½ cup chopped nuts

½ cup chocolate chips

1. To prepare cake batter, combine Splenda, oil, eggs, and applesauce. Beat lightly.

2. Add all dry ingredients and stir to mix.

3. Pour into greased 9×13-inch pan. Mix topping ingredients and sprinkle over batter.

4. Bake at 350°F for 40 minutes. When cool, cut in 4 rows lengthwise and 5 rows crosswise to yield 20 pieces.

Exchange List Values
- Carbohydrate 1.5
- Fat 2.0

Basic Nutritional Values
- Calories 185
  (Calories from Fat 80)
- Total Fat 9 gm
  (Saturated Fat 1.6 gm,
  Trans Fat 0.0 gm,
  Polyunsat Fat 3.1 gm,
  Monounsat Fat 4.4 gm)
- Cholesterol 20 mg
- Sodium 105 mg
- Potassium 75 gm
- Total Carb 23 gm
- Dietary Fiber 1 gm
- Sugars 12 gm
- Protein 3 gm
- Phosphorus 45 gm

Chocolate Peanut Butter Cake

Ruth Ann Gingerich
New Holland, PA

Makes 11 servings
Prep. Time: 20 minutes
Cooking Time: 2–3 hours
Cooling Time: 2 hours
Ideal slow-cooker size: 4-qt.

2 cups (half a package) milk chocolate cake mix

½ cup water

¼ cup peanut butter

1 egg

2 egg whites

6 Tbsp. chopped walnuts

1. Combine all ingredients. Beat 2 minutes in electric mixer.

2. Pour into greased and floured 3-lb. coffee can or 9×5-inch bread pan. Place can/pan in slow cooker.

3. Cover top of can/pan with 8 paper towels.

4. Cover cooker. Cook on High 2–3 hours.

5. Allow to cool for 10 minutes. Run knife around edge and invert cake onto serving plate. Cool completely before slicing and serving.

Exchange List Values
- Carbohydrate 1.5
- Fat 1.5

Basic Nutritional Values
- Calories 165 (Calories from Fat 75)
- Total Fat 8 gm (Saturated Fat 1.5 gm, Polyunsat Fat 3.6 gm, Monounsat Fat 2.8 gm)
- Cholesterol 19 mg
- Sodium 255 mg
- Total Carb 20 gm
- Dietary Fiber 1 gm
- Sugars 11 gm
- Protein 4 gm

Hot Fudge Cake

**Maricarol Magil
Freehold, NJ**

Makes 10 servings
Prep. Time: 25 minutes
Cooking Time: 2–3 hours
Ideal slow-cooker size: 4-qt.

¾ cup packed brown sugar, *divided*

brown sugar substitute to equal ½ cup sugar, *divided*

1 cup flour

¼ cup plus 3 Tbsp. unsweetened cocoa powder, *divided*

2 tsp. baking powder

½ tsp. salt

½ cup fat-free half-and-half

2 Tbsp. melted butter

½ tsp. vanilla extract

1¾ cups boiling water

vanilla ice cream, *optional*

1. Mix together ½ cup brown sugar, ¼ cup brown sugar substitute, flour, 3 Tbsp. cocoa, baking powder, and salt.

2. Stir in half-and-half, butter, and vanilla. Spread over the bottom of slow cooker.

3. Mix together ¼ cup brown sugar, ¼ cup brown sugar substitute, and ¼ cup cocoa. Sprinkle over mixture in slow cooker.

4. Pour in boiling water. Do not stir.

5. Cover and cook on High 2–3 hours, or until a toothpick inserted comes out clean.

6. Serve warm with vanilla ice cream, if desired.

Exchange List Value
- Carbohydrate 2.0

Basic Nutritional Values
- Calories 143
  (Calories from Fat 11)
- Total Fat 1 gm
  (Saturated Fat 0.4 gm,
  Polyunsat Fat 0.2 gm,
  Monounsat Fat 0.4 gm)
- Cholesterol 1 mg
- Sodium 226 mg
- Total Carb 32 gm
- Dietary Fiber 2 gm
- Sugars 21 gm
- Protein 2 gm

Gingerbread with Lemon Sauce

Fran Sauder
Mount Joy, PA

Makes 12 servings, 2¼×3-inch rectangle per serving
Prep. Time: 20 minutes
Baking Time: 45 minutes
Cooking Time: 20 minutes

2 cups flour
½ cup Splenda Sugar Blend
1 tsp. ginger
1 tsp. cinnamon
⅓ cup shortening
1 egg, beaten
2 Tbsp. molasses
½ tsp. salt
1 tsp. baking soda
1 cup 1% milkfat buttermilk
whipped cream, *optional*

Lemon Sauce:
2 cups water
4 Tbsp. cornstarch
1½ cups granulated Splenda
¼ tsp. salt
3 egg yolks
juice of 2 lemons
zest of 1 lemon
4 tsp. butter

1. Sift together flour, Splenda, ginger, and cinnamon.

2. Cut shortening into flour mixture to make fine crumbs. Take out ½ cup crumbs and set aside.

3. To remaining, add egg, molasses, salt, baking soda, and buttermilk. Beat well.

4. Pour into 9×9-inch greased and floured cake pan. Sprinkle with reserved crumbs.

5. Bake at 350°F for 45 minutes.

6. To make the lemon sauce, bring water to boil in covered saucepan.

7. Combine cornstarch, Splenda, and salt. Mix well. Add to boiling water, stirring constantly. Cook about 5 minutes on low heat. Mixture should be thickened.

8. Stir a small amount of hot sugar mixture into beaten egg yolks, whisking continuously. Return the whole mixture to pan and cook 1 more minute, stirring constantly.

9. Remove from heat; add lemon juice, zest, and butter.

10. Serve the gingerbread with the lemon sauce and optional whipped cream.

Exchange List Values
- Carbohydrate 2.0
- Fat 2.0

Basic Nutritional Values
- Calories 235 (Calories from Fat 80)
- Total Fat 9 gm (Saturated Fat 1.9 gm, Trans Fat 0.1 gm, Polyunsat Fat 2.1 gm, Monounsat Fat 4.8 gm)
- Cholesterol 65 mg
- Sodium 295 mg
- Potassium 125 gm
- Total Carb 34 gm
- Dietary Fiber 1 gm
- Sugars 14 gm
- Protein 4 gm
- Phosphorus 70 gm

Apple Cupcakes

Phyllis Good
Lancaster, PA

Makes 24 servings, 1 cupcake per serving
Prep. Time: 20 minutes
Baking Time: 20–25 minutes

1 cup whole wheat flour

1¼ cups white flour

½ cup Splenda Sugar Blend

1½ tsp. baking soda

⅜ tsp. baking powder

1 tsp. ground cinnamon

½ tsp. ground cloves

⅔ cup canola oil

2 eggs

⅔ cup fat-free milk

1½ tsp. vanilla extract

3 cups chopped apples

½ cup raisins, *optional*

Topping:

1 Tbsp. trans-fat-free tub margarine, melted

2⅔ Tbsp. Splenda Brown Sugar Blend

½ cup chopped nuts

2 tsp. cinnamon

2 tsp. flour

¼ cup quick oats

1. Combine flours, Splenda, baking soda, baking powder, and spices in a bowl.

2. Add canola oil, eggs, milk, and vanilla and beat well. Fold in apples and, if using, raisins.

3. Fill greased and floured muffin cups at least ½ full.

4. Mix all topping ingredients and put 1 tsp. topping on each cupcake.

5. Bake at 350°F for 20–25 minutes.

Exchange List Values
- Carbohydrate 1.0
- Fat 2.0

Basic Nutritional Values
- Calories 160 (Calories from Fat 80)
- Total Fat 9 gm (Saturated Fat 0.9 gm, Trans Fat 0.0 gm, Polyunsat Fat 3.2 gm, Monounsat Fat 4.4 gm)
- Cholesterol 15 mg
- Sodium 100 mg
- Potassium 80 gm
- Total Carb 18 gm
- Dietary Fiber 2 gm
- Sugars 7 gm
- Protein 3 gm
- Phosphorus 60 gm

Pumpkin Cupcakes

Shelley Burns
Elverson, PA

Makes 24 cupcakes, 1 cupcake per serving
Prep. Time: 20 minutes
Baking Time: 20–25 minutes

1 cup Splenda Sugar Blend

2 cups cooked pumpkin

1 cup canola oil

¼ cup fat-free milk

4 eggs

2 cups flour

1 tsp. salt

2 tsp. baking powder

2 tsp. baking soda

2 tsp. cinnamon

dash nutmeg

½ cup coconut, *optional*

cinnamon and sugar, *optional*

1. Mix together Splenda, pumpkin, oil, milk and eggs.

2. Add flour, salt, baking powder, baking soda, cinnamon, and nutmeg. Fold in coconut if you wish.

3. Line 24 muffin cups with cupcake papers.

4. Divide batter among them.

5. Sprinkle cinnamon and sugar on tops of cupcakes if you wish.

6. Bake at 350°F for 20–25 minutes or until inserted toothpick comes out clean.

TIP

You can use canned or frozen pumpkin. I use frozen pumpkin. I get it out of the freezer a few hours before I am going to use it. I let it thaw and drain any excess water off before using it in the recipe.

Exchange List Values
- Carbohydrate 1.0
- Fat 2.0

Basic Nutritional Values
- Calories 170
  (Calories from Fat 90)
- Total Fat 10 gm
  (Saturated Fat 1.0 gm,
  Trans Fat 0.0 gm,
  Polyunsat Fat 2.8 gm,
  Monounsat Fat 6.1 gm)
- Cholesterol 30 mg
- Sodium 245 mg
- Potassium 70 gm
- Total Carb 18 gm
- Dietary Fiber 1 gm
- Sugars 9 gm
- Protein 2 gm
- Phosphorus 75 gm

Cheesecake

Dot Hess
Willow Street, PA

Makes 15 servings
Prep. Time: 30 minutes
Baking Time: 1 hour 10 minutes
Chilling Time: 3 hours

Crust:

1½ cups crushed graham crackers

2 Tbsp. Splenda Sugar Blend

¼ cup trans-fat-free tub margarine

Filling:

3 8-oz. pkgs. fat-free cream cheese, softened

5 eggs

½ cup Splenda Sugar Blend

1½ tsp. vanilla extract

Topping:

1½ pints fat-free sour cream

⅓ cup granulated Splenda

1½ tsp. vanilla extract

1. Combine graham crackers, Splenda, and margarine. Press into bottom of 9-inch springform pan.

2. Beat cream cheese well with mixer. Add eggs, one at a time, mixing well after each one.

3. Add Splenda and vanilla.

4. Pour gently over prepared crust.

5. Bake at 300°F for 1 hour. Cool 5 minutes. Do not turn off oven.

6. As the cake cools, mix sour cream, Splenda, and vanilla.

7. Spread topping on cake and bake 5 minutes more.

8. Chill for at least 3 hours before serving.

Good Go-Alongs:
Good with canned pie filling on top.

Variation:
Omit crust. Bake at 350°F for 35 minutes and proceed with topping.

—Renée Hankins, Narvon, PA

Exchange List Values
- Fat-Free Milk 0.5
- Carbohydrate 1.5
- Fat 1.0

Basic Nutritional Values
- Calories 200 (Calories from Fat 45)
- Total Fat 5 gm (Saturated Fat 1.3 gm, Trans Fat 0.0 gm, Polyunsat Fat 1.6 gm, Monounsat Fat 1.7 gm)
- Cholesterol 75 mg
- Sodium 440 mg
- Potassium 230 gm
- Total Carb 26 gm
- Dietary Fiber 0 gm
- Sugars 15 gm
- Protein 10 gm
- Phosphorus 330 gm

Chocolate Brownies

Sandy Zeiset Richardson
Leavenworth, WA

Makes 16 servings, 2-inch square per serving
Prep. Time: 20 minutes
Baking Time: 30 minutes

2 eggs

6 Tbsp. Splenda Sugar Blend

½ tsp. vanilla extract

½ cup light (50% less calories and sugar) chocolate syrup

⅓ cup canola oil

¾ cup flour

½ tsp. salt

½ cup chopped nuts

1. Beat eggs until foamy. Add Splenda and vanilla. Beat.

2. Add chocolate syrup and oil. Beat.

3. Add flour and salt. Mix thoroughly. Fold in nuts.

4. Spread into 8-inch square nonstick pan.

5. Bake at 350°F for 30 minutes.

Exchange List Values
- Carbohydrate 1.0
- Fat 1.5

Basic Nutritional Values
- Calories 125 (Calories from Fat 70)
- Total Fat 8 gm (Saturated Fat 0.8 gm, Trans Fat 0.0 gm, Polyunsat Fat 3.2 gm, Monounsat Fat 3.4 gm)
- Cholesterol 25 mg
- Sodium 95 mg
- Potassium 50 gm
- Total Carb 13 gm
- Dietary Fiber 1 gm
- Sugars 7 gm
- Protein 2 gm
- Phosphorus 35 gm

White Chip Pumpkin Cookies

Joanna Harrison
Lafayette, CO

Makes 60 cookies, 1 cookie per serving
Prep. Time: 15 minutes
Baking Time: 11–14 minutes

2 sticks (8 Tbsp.) butter

¼ cup Splenda Brown Sugar Blend

¼ cup Splenda Sugar Blend

1 egg

2 tsp. vanilla extract

1 cup cooked, puréed pumpkin

2 cups flour

1 tsp. ground cardamom

2 tsp. ground cinnamon

1 tsp. baking soda

1¼ cups white chocolate chips

⅔ cup chopped nuts, *optional*

1. Using a mixer, cream together butter, Splenda, egg, and vanilla. Beat in pumpkin.

2. Separately, stir together flour, cardamom, cinnamon, and baking soda.

3. Stir flour mixture into butter mixture. Stir in chocolate chips and optional nuts.

4. Drop spoonfuls onto greased cookie sheet.

5. Bake at 350°F for 11–14 minutes.

Exchange List Values
- Carbohydrate 0.5
- Fat 1.0

Basic Nutritional Values
- Calories 70
  (Calories from Fat 30)
- Total Fat 4 gm
  (Saturated Fat 1.5 gm,
  Trans Fat 0.0 gm,
  Polyunsat Fat 1.0 gm,
  Monounsat Fat 1.2 gm)
- Cholesterol 5 mg
- Sodium 50 mg
- Potassium 30 gm
- Total Carb 8 gm
- Dietary Fiber 0 gm
- Sugars 4 gm
- Protein 1 gm
- Phosphorus 15 gm

Forgotten Cookies

Penny Blosser
New Carlisle, OH

Makes 30 cookies, 1 cookie per serving
Prep. Time: 20 minutes
Baking Time: until oven cools or overnight

2 egg whites

⅔ cup sugar

pinch salt

1 tsp. vanilla extract

½ cup chopped nuts

½ cup chocolate chips

1. Preheat oven to 350°F.

2. Beat egg whites until foamy. Gradually add sugar, beating until stiff. Fold in remaining ingredients.

3. Drop cookies onto foil-lined cookie sheet. Place in 350°F oven.

4. Turn oven off immediately. Leave cookies in oven until cooled completely or overnight.

Exchange List Values
- Carbohydrate 0.5
- Fat 0.5

Basic Nutritional Values
- Calories 45 (Calories from Fat 20)
- Total Fat 2 gm (Saturated Fat 0.6 gm, Trans Fat 0.0 gm, Polyunsat Fat 1.0 gm, Monounsat Fat 0.5 gm)
- Cholesterol 0 mg
- Sodium 0 mg
- Potassium 25 gm
- Total Carb 7 gm
- Dietary Fiber 0 gm
- Sugars 6 gm
- Protein 1 gm
- Phosphorus 10 gm

No-Bake Chocolate Cookies

Penny Blosser
Beavercreek, OH

Makes 3 dozen, 36 servings, 1 cookie per
  serving
Prep. Time: 20 minutes
Cooking Time: 15 minutes
Cooling Time: 30 minutes

½ cup trans-fat-free tub margarine

½ cup fat-free milk

1 cup Splenda Sugar Blend

1 cup chocolate chips

½ cup peanut butter

1 tsp. vanilla extract

3 cups quick oats

1. Put margarine, milk, Splenda, and chocolate chips in a saucepan.

2. Bring to boil; boil 1 minute. Remove from heat.

3. Stir in peanut butter and vanilla until melted.

4. Add oats. Mix.

5. Drop by heaping tablespoon onto wax paper lined baking sheet.

6. Let cool until set.

Exchange List Values
- Carbohydrate 1.0
- Fat 1.0

Basic Nutritional Values
- Calories 110
  (Calories from Fat 55)
- Total Fat 6 gm
  (Saturated Fat 1.7 gm,
  Trans Fat 0.0 gm,
  Polyunsat Fat 1.5 gm,
  Monounsat Fat 2.1 gm)
- Cholesterol 0 mg
- Sodium 40 mg
- Potassium 70 gm
- Total Carb 14 gm
- Dietary Fiber 1 gm
- Sugars 9 gm
- Protein 2 gm
- Phosphorus 50 gm

Desserts

Apricot Bars

Shirley Thieszen
Lakin, KS
Virginia Bender
Dover, DE

Makes 20 servings, 2½×2¼-inch bar per
  serving
Prep. Time: 20 minutes
Baking Time: 40–45 minutes

½ cup egg substitute, *divided*

½ cup + 2 Tbsp. trans-fat-free tub margarine,
  divided

1 tsp. baking powder

1 cup flour

6 Tbsp. Splenda Sugar Blend

1¼ cups quick oats

1 cup sugar-free apricot jam, or preserves

½ cup granulated Splenda

⅔ cup unsweetened coconut flakes

Variation:
Add ⅓ cup pecan or walnut pieces and ½ tsp.
vanilla extract to ingredients in Step 3.
  —Loren J. Zehr, Fort Myers, FL

1. Combine ¼ cup egg substitute, ½ cup
margarine, baking powder, flour, Splenda
Sugar Blend, and quick oats. Press into
greased 9×13-inch baking pan.

2. Spread batter with apricot jam.

3. Mix together granulated Splenda, ¼
cup egg substitute, 2 Tbsp. margarine, and
coconut. Spread this mixture over apricot
jam.

4. Bake at 350°F for 40–45 minutes. Cut
when cool.

Exchange List Values
- Carbohydrate 1.0
- Fat 1.0

Basic Nutritional Values
- Calories 125
  (Calories from Fat 55)
- Total Fat 6 gm
  (Saturated Fat 2.0 gm,
  Trans Fat 0.0 gm,
  Polyunsat Fat 1.9 gm,
  Monounsat Fat 1.5 gm)
- Cholesterol 0 mg
- Sodium 80 mg
- Potassium 55 gm
- Total Carb 18 gm
- Dietary Fiber 1 gm
- Sugars 6 gm
- Protein 2 gm
- Phosphorus 55 gm

Date Nut Bars

Anna A. Yoder
Millersburg, OH

Makes 24 servings, 2-inch square per
  serving
Prep. Time: 20 minutes
Baking Time: 15–20 minutes

2 eggs

6 Tbsp. Splenda Sugar Blend

½ cup trans-fat-free tub margarine, melted

¾ cup whole wheat flour

¼ tsp. baking powder

1 cup chopped nuts

1 cup chopped dates

1. Beat eggs and add Splenda, mixing well.
Add melted margarine.

2. Sift together flour and baking powder
and add to batter. Beat gently. Fold in nuts
and dates. Pour into greased 9×13-inch pan.

3. Bake at 350°F for about 15–20 minutes.
Cool, cut, and serve.

Exchange List Values

- Carbohydrate 1.0
- Fat 1.0

Basic Nutritional Values

- Calories 105
  (Calories from Fat 65)
- Total Fat 7 gm
  (Saturated Fat 1.1 gm,
  Trans Fat 0.0 gm,
  Polyunsat Fat 3.6 gm,
  Monounsat Fat 1.5 gm)
- Cholesterol 15 mg
- Sodium 40 mg
- Potassium 85 gm
- Total Carb 11 gm
- Dietary Fiber 1 gm
- Sugars 7 gm
- Protein 2 gm
- Phosphorus 50 gm

Bread Pudding

Winifred Ewy
Newton, KS
Helen King
Fairbank, IA
Elaine Patton
West Middletown, PA

Makes 9 servings
Prep. Time: 35 minutes
Cooking Time: 4–5 hours
Ideal slow-cooker size: 4-qt.

Desserts

8 slices bread (raisin bread is especially good), cubed

3 eggs

2 egg whites

2 cups fat-free half-and-half

2 Tbsp. sugar substitute to equal 1 Tbsp. sugar

½ cup raisins (use only ¼ cup if using raisin bread)

½ tsp. cinnamon

Sauce:

2 Tbsp. light, soft tub margarine

2 Tbsp. flour

1 cup water

6 Tbsp. sugar substitute to equal 3 Tbsp. sugar

1 tsp. vanilla extract

1. Place bread cubes in greased slow cooker.

2. Beat together eggs, egg whites, and half-and-half. Stir in sugar substitute, raisins, and cinnamon. Pour over bread and stir.

3. Cover and cook on High 1 hour. Reduce heat to Low and cook 3–4 hours, or until thermometer reaches 160°F.

4. Make sauce just before pudding is done baking. Begin by melting margarine in saucepan. Stir in flour until smooth. Gradually add water, sugar substitute, and vanilla. Bring to boil. Cook, stirring constantly for 2 minutes, or until thickened.

5. Serve sauce over warm bread pudding.

Variations:

1. Use dried cherries instead of raisins. Use cherry flavoring in sauce instead of vanilla extract.
—Char Hagnes, Montague, MI

2. Use ¼ tsp. ground cinnamon and ¼ tsp. ground nutmeg, instead of ½ tsp. ground cinnamon in pudding.

3. Use 8 cups day-old unfrosted cinnamon rolls instead of the bread.
—Beatrice Orgist, Richardson, TX

4. Use ½ tsp. vanilla and ¼ tsp. ground nutmeg instead of ½ tsp. cinnamon.
—Nanci Keatley, Salem, OR

Exchange List Values
- Carbohydrate 2.0
- Fat 1.0

Basic Nutritional Values
- Calories 200 (Calories from Fat 40)
- Total Fat 4 gm (Saturated Fat 1.4 gm, Polyunsat Fat 0.6 gm, Monounsat Fat 1.7 gm)
- Cholesterol 75 mg
- Sodium 221 mg
- Total Carb 34 gm
- Dietary Fiber 1 gm
- Sugars 21 gm
- Protein 6 gm

Simple Bread Pudding

Melanie L. Thrower
McPherson, KS

Makes 8 servings
Prep. Time: 25 minutes
Cooking Time: 3 hours
Ideal slow-cooker size: 4-qt.

6–8 slices bread, cubed

2 cups fat-free milk

2 eggs

¼ cup sugar

1 tsp. ground cinnamon

1 tsp. vanilla extract

Sauce:
6-oz. can concentrated grape juice

1 Tbsp. cornstarch

TIP

This is a fine dessert with a cold salad main dish.

1. Place bread in slow cooker.

2. Whisk together milk, eggs, sugar, cinnamon, and vanilla. Pour over bread.

3. Cover. Cook on High 2–2½ hours, or until mixture is set.

4. Combine concentrated juice and cornstarch in saucepan. Heat until boiling, stirring constantly, until sauce is thickened. Serve drizzled over bread pudding.

Exchange List Value
- Carbohydrate 2.5

Basic Nutritional Values
- Calories 179 (Calories from Fat 19)
- Total Fat 2 gm (Saturated Fat 0.7 gm, Polyunsat Fat 0.6 gm, Monounsat Fat 0.6 gm)
- Cholesterol 55 mg
- Sodium 153 mg
- Total Carb 35 gm
- Dietary Fiber 1 gm
- Sugars 24 gm
- Protein 5 gm

Mama's Rice Pudding

Donna Barnitz
Jenks, OK
Shari Jensen
Fountain, CO

Makes 8 servings
Prep. Time: 10 minutes
Cooking Time: 6–7 hours
Chilling Time: minimum 4 hours
Ideal slow-cooker size: 4-qt.

½ cup white rice, uncooked

¼ cup sugar substitute to equal 2 Tbsp. sugar

1 tsp. vanilla extract

1 tsp. lemon extract

1 cup plus 2 Tbsp. fat-free milk

1 tsp. butter

2 eggs, beaten

1 tsp. cinnamon

½ cup raisins

1 cup fat-free whipped topping

nutmeg for garnish

Exchange List Value
• Carbohydrate 2.0

Basic Nutritional Values
• Calories 148
  (Calories from Fat 17)
• Total Fat 2 gm
  (Saturated Fat 0.8 gm,
  Polyunsat Fat 0.2 gm,
  Monounsat Fat 0.7 gm)
• Cholesterol 55 mg
• Sodium 43 mg
• Total Carb 28 gm
• Dietary Fiber 1 gm
• Sugars 15 gm
• Protein 4 gm

1. Combine all ingredients except whipped topping and nutmeg in slow cooker. Stir well.

2. Cover crock. Cook on Low 6–7 hours, until rice is tender and milk absorbed. Be sure to stir once every 2 hours during cooking.

3. Pour into serving bowl. Cover and chill at least 4 hours.

4. Before serving, fold in whipped topping and sprinkle with nutmeg.

Chocolate Rice Pudding

Michele Ruvola
Selden, NY

Makes 12 servings
Prep. Time: 20 minutes
Cooking Time: 2½-3½ hours
Ideal slow-cooker size: 3- or 4-qt.

4 cups cooked white rice

½ cup sugar substitute to equal 2 Tbsp. sugar

¼ cup baking cocoa powder

2 Tbsp. light, soft tub margarine, melted

1 tsp. vanilla extract

2 12-oz. cans fat-free evaporated milk

whipped cream, *optional*

sliced toasted almonds, *optional*

maraschino cherries, *optional*

1. Combine first 6 ingredients in greased slow cooker.

2. Cover. Cook on Low 2½–3½ hours, or until liquid is absorbed.

3. Serve warm or chilled. Top individual servings with a dollop of whipped cream, sliced toasted almonds, and a maraschino cherry, if desired.

Exchange List Value
- Carbohydrate 2.5

Basic Nutritional Values
- Calories 180 (Calories from Fat 15)
- Total Fat 2 gm (Saturated Fat 0.3 gm, Polyunsat Fat 0.3 gm, Monounsat Fat 0.8 gm)
- Cholesterol 0 mg
- Sodium 104 mg
- Total Carb 35 gm
- Dietary Fiber 1 gm
- Sugars 18 gm
- Protein 7 gm

Desserts

Slow-Cooker Tapioca

Nancy W. Huber
Green Park, PA

Makes 12 servings
Prep. Time: 10 minutes
Cooking Time: 3½ hours
Chilling Time: minimum 4 hours
Ideal slow-cooker size: 4-qt.

2 qts. fat-free milk

1 cup small pearl tapioca

½ cups sugar substitute to equal ¼ cup sugar

4 eggs, beaten

1 tsp. vanilla extract

fruit of choice, *optional*

1. Combine milk, tapioca, and sugar substitute in slow cooker. Cook on High 3 hours.

2. Mix together eggs, vanilla, and a little hot milk from slow cooker. Add to slow cooker. Mix. Cook on High 20 more minutes.

3. Chill thoroughly, at least 4 hours. Serve with fruit, if desired.

Exchange List Value
- Carbohydrate 2.0

Basic Nutritional Values
- Calories 160 (Calories from Fat 16)
- Total Fat 2 gm (Saturated Fat 0.9 gm, Polyunsat Fat 0.2 gm, Monounsat Fat 0.7 gm)
- Cholesterol 74 mg
- Sodium 93 mg
- Total Carb 28 gm
- Dietary Fiber 0 gm
- Sugars 17 gm
- Protein 8 gm

Fruit Tapioca

Anna Weber
Atmore, AL

Makes 20 servings
Prep. Time: 15 minutes
Cooling Time: 1 hour
Cooking Time: 5 minutes

7 cups water

1 cup instant tapioca

1 cup granulated Splenda

12-oz. can frozen orange concentrate

2 bananas, sliced

2 oranges, peeled, segments diced

1. Bring water to a boil and add tapioca and Splenda. Boil for 1 minute or until tapioca appears clear.

2. Remove from heat and add frozen concentrate. Mix well and cool, at least 1 hour.

3. Immediately before serving, fold in fruit slices.

Exchange List Values
- Starch 0.5
- Fruit 1.0

Basic Nutritional Values
- Calories 85
  (Calories from Fat 0)
- Total Fat 0 gm
  (Saturated Fat 0.0 gm,
  Trans Fat 0.0 gm,
  Polyunsat Fat 0.0 gm,
  Monounsat Fat 0.0 gm)
- Cholesterol 0 mg
- Sodium 0 mg
- Potassium 230 gm
- Total Carb 21 gm
- Dietary Fiber 1 gm
- Sugars 13 gm
- Protein 1 gm
- Phosphorus 20 gm

Chocolate Almond Mousse

Hope Comerford
Clinton Township, MI

Makes 6 servings
Prep. Time: 5 minutes
Cooling Time: 1 hour

Desserts

3.9 oz. pkg. sugar-free chocolate instant pudding

2 cups cold heavy whipping cream

¼ tsp. almond extract

1. Combine all ingredients in a bowl.

2. Using a hand mixer, beat on Low until all ingredients are well-combined, then continue on High for 2–3 minutes, or until the pudding is thick and fluffy.

Exchange List Values
- Carbohydrate 1.0
- Lean Meat 0
- Fat 6

Basic Nutritional Values
- Calories 330
  (Calories from Fat 261)
- Total Fat 29 gm
  (Saturated Fat 18 gm,
  Trans Fat 1 gm,
  Polyunsat Fat 1.2 gm,
  Monounsat Fat 7 gm)
- Cholesterol 90 mg
- Sodium 537 mg
- Potassium 76 gm
- Total Carb 16 gm
- Dietary Fiber 2 gm
- Sugars 2 gm
- Protein 4 gm
- Phosphorus 46 gm

Strawberry Rhubarb Sauce

Tina Snyder
Manheim, PA

Makes 8 servings
Prep. Time: 15 minutes
Cooking Time: 6–7 hours
Chilling Time: 4 hours or more
Ideal slow-cooker size: 4-qt.

Desserts

6 cups chopped rhubarb

1 cup sugar

1 cinnamon stick

½ cup white grape juice

2 cups sliced strawberries

Serving suggestion:
Serve over cake or ice cream.

1. Place rhubarb in slow cooker. Pour sugar over rhubarb. Add cinnamon stick and grape juice. Stir well.

2. Cover and cook on Low 5–6 hours, or until rhubarb is tender.

3. Stir in strawberries. Cook 1 hour longer.

4. Remove cinnamon stick. Chill at least 4 hours.

Exchange List Value
• Carbohydrate 2.0

Basic Nutritional Values
• Calories 132
  (Calories from Fat 3)
• Total Fat 0 gm
  (Saturated Fat 0.0 gm,
  Polyunsat Fat 0.1 gm,
  Monounsat Fat 0.0 gm)
• Cholesterol 0 mg
• Sodium 5 mg
• Total Carb 33 gm
• Dietary Fiber 3 gm
• Sugars 29 gm
• Protein 1 gm

Frozen Fruit

Anna A. Yoder
Millersburg, OH

Makes 20 servings, 2¼-inch square per serving
Prep. Time: 15 minutes
Freezing Time: 3 hours or more
Standing Time: 2 hours

3 cups water

1½ cups granulated Splenda

8 medium bananas, sliced

20-oz. can crushed pineapple packed in juice

6-oz. can frozen orange juice, undiluted

1. Combine water and Splenda and let stand to dissolve.

2. Combine bananas and pineapple. Set aside.

3. Add orange juice to sugar water. Pour mixture over bananas and pineapple, stirring gently until mixed. Pour into 9×13-inch baking dish with a lid. Cover dish and freeze for at least 3 hours.

4. Remove from freezer 2 hours before serving.

Variation:
Add some sliced fresh peaches and a small bottle of maraschino cherries. Pour ginger ale over slush immediately before serving.
—Veva Zimmerman Mumaw, Hatfield, PA

Exchange List Value
- Fruit 1.5

Basic Nutritional Values
- Calories 85 (Calories from Fat 0)
- Total Fat 0 gm (Saturated Fat 0.1 gm, Trans Fat 0.0 gm, Polyunsat Fat 0.1 gm, Monounsat Fat 0.0 gm)
- Cholesterol 0 mg
- Sodium 0 mg
- Potassium 285 gm
- Total Carb 21 gm
- Dietary Fiber 2 gm
- Sugars 15 gm
- Protein 1 gm
- Phosphorus 20 gm

Homemade Applesauce

Renita Denlinger
Denver, PA

Makes 8 servings
Prep. Time: 10–20 minutes
Cooking Time: 3½ hours
Ideal slow-cooker size: 5- or 6-qt.

10 large apples, halved, cored, and peeled

½ tsp. cinnamon

dash nutmeg

dash ground cloves

1 Tbsp. water

NOTES

This makes the whole house smell wonderful.

1. Spray slow cooker with nonstick spray.

2. Put apples in slow cooker.

3. Sprinkle cinnamon, nutmeg, cloves, and water over apples. Stir.

4. Cover. Cook on Low 3½ hours, or until apples are soft. If you're home and available, stir the apples after they've cooked for 2 hours. It's okay to mash them up a bit as you stir.

5. Serve warm or chilled.

Exchange List Value
- Fruit 2.0

Basic Nutritional Values
- Calories 115 (Calories from Fat 0)
- Total Fat 0 gm (Saturated Fat 0 gm, Polyunsat Fat 0 gm Monounsat Fat 0 gm
- Cholesterol 0 mg),
- Sodium 0 mg
- Total Carb 31 gm
- Dietary Fiber 3 gm
- Sugars 24 gm
- Protein 1 gm

Spiced Apple Butter

Hope Comerford
Clinton Township, MI

Makes 12 (¼-cup) servings
Prep. Time: 10 minutes
Cooking Time: 12–13 hours
Ideal slow-cooker size: 6-qt.

7 large Gala apples

2 tsp. cinnamon

¼ tsp. nutmeg

¼ tsp. ground ginger

¼ tsp. ground cloves

¼ tsp. allspice

¼ cup water

1. Core the apples and roughly chop them. You can choose to leave the skin on or off.

2. Place the apples and all remaining ingredients into the crock. Stir.

3. Cover and cook on Low for 10 hours.

4. Using an immersion blender, blend the apples until they're smooth.

5. Cover and cook on High for an additional 2–3 hours, stirring every 30 minutes until thickened. You may need to prop the lid open with a wooden spoon the last hour or so to help the apple butter thicken.

Exchange List Values
- Fruit 0.5

Basic Nutritional Values
- Calories 31
  (Calories from Fat 0)
- Total Fat 0 gm
  (Saturated Fat 0 gm,
  Trans Fat 0.0 gm,
  Polyunsat Fat 0 gm,
  Monounsat Fat 0 gm)
- Cholesterol 0 mg
- Sodium 1 mg
- Potassium 60 gm
- Total Carb 8 gm
- Dietary Fiber 1 gm
- Sugars 6 gm
- Protein 0 gm
- Phosphorus 6 gm

Lime Poppy Seed Fruit Salad

Diann Dunham
State College, PA

Makes 4½ cups, 9 servings total, ½ cup per serving
Prep. Time: 20 minutes

2 cups pineapple chunks, fresh or canned, juice reserved

1 orange, peeled and chopped

1 kiwi fruit, peeled and sliced

1 cup red or green grapes

1 cup quartered strawberries

Dressing:

¼ cup reserved pineapple juice

¼ tsp. grated lime peel

2 Tbsp. fresh lime juice

1 Tbsp. honey

1 tsp. poppy seeds

whole strawberries, *optional*

Warm Memories:

People can't tell why it tastes better than other fruit salads. The lime juice and peel with the honey gives it a refreshing taste. I have used it for many years. I first made it for a special Mother & Daughter brunch.

Good Go-Alongs:

It's lovely for a simple dessert with shortbread cookies or coconut macaroons.

1. Mix pineapple chunks, orange, kiwi, grapes, and strawberries in a bowl.

2. In a separate bowl, mix dressing ingredients. Add dressing to salad.

3. If desired, garnish with a few whole strawberries before serving.

TIP

1. It looks very pretty in a clear bowl.
2. The salad is best made and eaten the same day. Strawberries get mushy if stored too long.

Exchange List Value
- Fruit 1.0

Basic Nutritional Values
- Calories 70 (Calories from Fat 0)
- Total Fat 0 gm (Saturated Fat 0.0 gm, Trans Fat 0.0 gm, Polyunsat Fat 0.2 gm, Monounsat Fat 0.0 gm)
- Cholesterol 0 mg
- Sodium 0 mg
- Potassium 180 gm
- Total Carb 17 gm
- Dietary Fiber 2 gm
- Sugars 14 gm
- Protein 1 gm
- Phosphorus 20 gm

Desserts

Healthy Fruit Salad

Ida C. Knopp
Salem, OH

Makes 8 servings, about ½ cup per serving
Prep. Time: 15 minutes

3 tart red apples, chopped

3 oranges, peeled, chopped

½ cup chopped celery

⅓ cup raisins

⅓ cup chopped nuts

2 Tbsp. honey

2 Tbsp. lemon juice

1. In a serving bowl toss apples, oranges, celery, raisins, and nuts.

2. In a small bowl combine honey and lemon juice. Drizzle over fruit salad and serve.

Exchange List Values
- Fruit 1.5
- Fat 0.5

Basic Nutritional Values
- Calories 120 (Calories from Fat 30)
- Total Fat 4 gm (Saturated Fat 0.3 gm, Trans Fat 0.0 gm, Polyunsat Fat 2.4 gm, Monounsat Fat 0.5 gm)
- Cholesterol 0 mg
- Sodium 5 mg
- Potassium 250 gm
- Total Carb 24 gm
- Dietary Fiber 3 gm
- Sugars 19 gm
- Protein 2 gm
- Phosphorus 40 gm

Grandma Moley's Fruit Salad

Elva Evers
North English, IA

Makes 8 servings, about 6½ oz. per serving
Prep. Time: 15 minutes
Cooking Time: 8–10 minutes
Standing Time: 20 minutes

20-oz. can juice-packed pineapple chunks

1 orange

1 lemon

6–8 pkgs. sugar substitute

2 Tbsp. instant tapioca

6 small apples, cored and diced

2 bananas

1. Drain pineapple chunks, reserving juice.

2. Squeeze juice from orange and lemon. Combine all juices, sugar substitute, and tapioca. Let stand for about 5 minutes.

3. Heat mixture in microwave for 8–10 minutes, stirring every 2 minutes, until it thickens and tapioca is transparent. Cool.

4. Combine apples and pineapple chunks. Fold in cooled dressing.

5. Immediately before serving, slice in bananas.

Exchange List Value
- Fruit 2.0

Basic Nutritional Values
- Calories 130
  (Calories from Fat 0)
- Total Fat 0 gm
  (Saturated Fat 0.1 gm,
  Trans Fat 0.0 gm,
  Polyunsat Fat 0.1 gm,
  Monounsat Fat 0.0 gm)
- Cholesterol 0 mg
- Sodium 0 mg
- Potassium 310 gm
- Total Carb 33 gm
- Dietary Fiber 3 gm
- Sugars 24 gm
- Protein 1 gm
- Phosphorus 20 gm

Fruit Slush

Julette Rush
Harrisonburg, VA

Makes 16 servings, about 6 oz. per serving
Prep. Time: 20 minutes
Freezing Time: 5–12 hours

½ cup granulated Splenda

2 cups boiling water

6-oz. can frozen orange juice

12-oz. can apricot nectar

6 bananas, firmly ripe

1 Tbsp. lemon juice

20-oz. can crushed pineapple, undrained

16-oz. frozen no-sugar-added strawberries

TIP

For a potluck event, make this a day or more in advance. Get it out of the freezer 2–3 hours ahead of time to get to the right slushy consistency. Time to thaw may vary greatly depending on your home's temperature. The slush keeps indefinitely in the freezer.

1. In large bowl, dissolve Splenda in 2 cups boiling water.

2. Add frozen orange juice and 2 cans of water. Add apricot nectar.

3. Mash the bananas with the lemon juice to prevent browning. Add them to the bowl.

4. Add pineapple and strawberries. Stir all gently together.

5. Put bowl in freezer. Stir once an hour for 5 hours until slushy.

Exchange List Value
- Fruit 2.0

Basic Nutritional Values
- Calories 105 (Calories from Fat 0)
- Total Fat 0 gm (Saturated Fat 0.1 gm, Trans Fat 0.0 gm, Polyunsat Fat 0.1 gm, Monounsat Fat 0.0 gm)
- Cholesterol 0 mg
- Sodium 0 mg
- Potassium 365 gm
- Total Carb 27 gm
- Dietary Fiber 3 gm
- Sugars 18 gm
- Protein 1 gm
- Phosphorus 25 gm

Snacks
and Beverages

Snacks and Beverages

Chili Nuts

Barbara Aston
Ashdown, AR

Makes 80 (1 Tbsp.) servings
Prep. Time: 10 minutes
Cooking Time: 2½–3 hours
Ideal slow-cooker size: 3-qt.

half stick (4 Tbsp.) melted butter

2 12-oz. cans cocktail peanuts

1⅝-oz. pkg. chili seasoning mix

1. Pour butter over nuts in slow cooker. Sprinkle in dry chili mix. Toss together.

2. Cover. Heat on Low 2–2½ hours. Turn to High. Remove lid and cook 10–15 minutes.

3. Serve warm or cool.

Exchange List Value
- Fat 1.0

Basic Nutritional Values
- Calories 56
  (Calories from Fat 43)
- Total Fat 5 gm
  (Saturated Fat 1.0 gm,
  Polyunsat Fat 1.4 gm,
  Monounsat Fat 2.3 gm)
- Cholesterol 2 mg
- Sodium 104 mg
- Total Carb 2 gm
- Dietary Fiber 1 gm
- Sugars 0 gm
- Protein 2 gm

Snacks and Beverages

Orange Pecans

Janice Muller
Derwood, MD

Makes 44 servings, 2 Tbsp. per serving, 5½
cups total
Prep. Time: 3 minutes
Cooking Time: 10 minutes
Cooling Time: 30 minutes

¼ cup orange juice

1 Tbsp. grated orange rind

½ tsp. cinnamon

¼ tsp. allspice

¼ tsp. ginger

pinch salt

1 cup sugar

1 lb. pecan halves, whole

1. Combine orange juice, orange rind, cinnamon, allspice, ginger, salt, and sugar in a large flat pot so that it will be easy to coat pecans with the hot mixture.

2. Cook on medium heat until mix comes to a full boil.

3. Stir in pecans. Keep stirring until the pecans are well coated and the syrup is absorbed.

4. Remove from heat; stir until pecans separate. Spread onto wax paper to cool.

Warm Memories:
I can't keep enough of these in the house during the holidays, and they're fun to take to gatherings. People can take as few or as many as they want. The orange flavor and pecan crunch make them addictive. I've also packaged these in pretty bags as gifts for neighbors during the holidays.

Good Go-Alongs:
The sugared pecans are good by themselves, or you can sprinkle them over a dish of vanilla ice cream, or in a green salad.

Exchange List Values
- Carbohydrate 0.5
- Fat 1.5

Basic Nutritional Values
- Calories 90
  (Calories from Fat 70)
- Total Fat 8 gm
  (Saturated Fat 0.6 gm,
  Trans Fat 0.0 gm,
  Polyunsat Fat 2.1 gm,
  Monounsat Fat 4.5 gm)
- Cholesterol 0 mg
- Sodium 0 mg
- Potassium 45 gm
- Total Carb 6 gm
- Dietary Fiber 1 gm
- Sugars 5 gm
- Protein 1 gm
- Phosphorus 30 gm

TIP

I always double this recipe because I buy the pecans in a 2 lb. bag at a club/warehouse, and once you assemble your ingredients, why not? They go fast when you serve them.

Curried Almonds

Barbara Aston
Ashdown, AR

Makes 64 (1 Tbsp.) servings
Prep. Time: 5 minutes
Cooking Time: 3–4½ hours
Ideal slow-cooker size: 3-qt.

2 Tbsp. butter, melted
1 Tbsp. curry powder
½ tsp. seasoned salt
1 lb. blanched almonds

1. Combine butter with curry powder and seasoned salt.

2. Pour over almonds in slow cooker. Mix to coat well.

3. Cover. Cook on Low 2–3 hours. Turn to High. Uncover cooker and cook 1–1½ hours.

4. Serve warm or room temperature.

Exchane List Value
- Fat 1.0

Basic Nutritional Values
- Calories 45
  (Calories from Fat 36)
- Total Fat 4 gm
  (Saturated Fat 0.5 gm,
  Polyunsat Fat 0.9 gm,
  Monounsat Fat 2.4 gm)
- Cholesterol 1 mg
- Sodium 18 mg
- Total Carb 1 gm
- Dietary Fiber 1 gm
- Sugars 0 gm
- Protein 2 gm

Apple Peanut Butter Rings

Hope Comerford
Clinton Township, MI

Makes 4 servings
Prep. Time: 5 minutes

2 large apples of your choice, cored, cut into rings

⅔ cup natural peanut butter

⅛ cup shredded coconut

¼ cup dark chocolate chips

1. Spread the peanut butter evenly over the top of each apple slice.

2. Sprinkle the shredded coconut evenly over each apple slice.

3. Divide the chocolate chips evenly over the apple slices.

Exchange List Values
- Bread/Starch 1.0
- Fruit 1.0
- Fat 4.5

Basic Nutritional Values
- Calories 353 (Calories from Fat 207)
- Total Fat 23 gm (Saturated Fat 6.5 gm, Trans Fat 0.0 gm, Polyunsat Fat 0.2 gm, Monounsat Fat 1.4 gm)
- Cholesterol 1 mg
- Sodium 96 mg
- Potassium 182 gm
- Total Carb 30 gm
- Dietary Fiber 6 gm
- Sugars 19 gm
- Protein 9 gm
- Phosphorus 43 gm

All-American Snack

Doris M. Coyle-Zipp
South Ozone Park, NY
Melissa Raber
Millersburg, OH
Ada Miller
Sugarcreek, OH
Nanci Keatley
Salem, OR

Makes 48 (¼ cup) servings
Prep. Time: 15 minutes
Cooking Time: 3 hours
Ideal slow-cooker size: 4-qt.

3 cups thin pretzel sticks

4 cups Wheat Chex

4 cups Cheerios

12-oz. can salted peanuts

¼ cup melted butter, or margarine

1 tsp. garlic powder

1 tsp. celery salt

½ tsp. seasoned salt

2 Tbsp. grated Parmesan cheese

1. Combine pretzels, cereals, and peanuts in large bowl.

2. Melt butter. Stir in garlic powder, celery salt, seasoned salt, and Parmesan cheese. Pour over pretzels and cereal. Toss until well mixed.

3. Pour into large slow cooker. Cover. Cook on Low 2½ hours, stirring every 30 minutes.

4. Remove lid and cook another 30 minutes on Low.

5. Serve warm or at room temperature. Store in tightly covered container.

Variations:

1. Use 3 cups Wheat Chex (instead of 4 cups) and 3 cups Cheerios (instead of 4 cups). Add 3 cups Corn Chex.
— Marcia S. Myer, Manheim, PA

Exchange List Values
- Starch 0.5
- Fat 1.0

Basic Nutritional Values
- Calories 77 (Calories from Fat 44)
- Total Fat 5 gm (Saturated Fat 1.2 gm, Polyunsat Fat 1.2 gm, Monounsat Fat 2.1 gm)
- Cholesterol 3 mg
- Sodium 174 mg
- Total Carb 7 gm
- Dietary Fiber 1 gm
- Sugars 1 gm
- Protein 3 gm

Snacks and Beverages

Red and Green Snack Mix

Hope Comerford
Clinton Township, MI

Makes 20 servings
Prep. Time: 5 minutes
Cooking Time: 20 minutes

4 cups rice square cereal

½ cup shelled pistachios

2 Tbsp. melted butter

¼ tsp. salt

¼ tsp. cinnamon

⅛ tsp. nutmeg

⅛ tsp. allspice

1 cup dried cranberries

1. Preheat oven to 300°F.

2. Line a baking sheet with parchment paper.

3. Combine the rice cereal and pistachios on the baking sheet.

4. In a small bowl, mix together the melted butter and spices. Pour over the rice cereal and pistachios and toss to coat evenly.

5. Bake for 20 minutes, stirring halfway through.

6. Remove from oven. Carefully remove the parchment paper and all its contents and place on a cooling rack for about 20 minutes.

7. Stir in the cranberries. Let it cool completely. Store in an airtight container for 1–2 weeks.

Exchange List Values
- Bread/Starch 0.5
- Fat 0.5

Basic Nutritional Values
- Calories 62
  (Calories from Fat 23)
- Total Fat 2.5 gm
  (Saturated Fat 0.8 gm,
  Trans Fat 0.0 gm,
  Polyunsat Fat 0.4 gm,
  Monounsat Fat 1 gm)
- Cholesterol 2.9 mg
- Sodium 70 mg
- Potassium 12 gm
- Total Carb 10 gm
- Dietary Fiber 0.6 gm
- Sugars 4.7 gm
- Protein 1 gm
- Phosphorus 7 gm

Popcorn

Rosetta Martin
Columbiana, OH

Makes 17 servings, about 2 cups per serving
Prep. Time: 15 minutes

Snacks and Beverages

2 tsp. salt

2 tsp. garlic powder

2 Tbsp. cheese powder

½ cup trans-fat-free tub margarine, melted

8 qts. air-popped popcorn with no salt or butter

1 cup small cheese crackers

1. Mix together salt, garlic powder, and cheese powder.

2. Pour melted margarine over popcorn, mixing so it's spread evenly. Pour seasonings over popcorn and mix well.

3. Add cheese crackers and serve.

Exchange List Values
- Starch 1.0
- Fat 1.0

Basic Nutritional Values
- Calories 115
  (Calories from Fat 55)
- Total Fat 6 gm
  (Saturated Fat 1.4 gm,
  Trans Fat 0.0 gm,
  Polyunsat Fat 2.0 gm,
  Monounsat Fat 1.9 gm)
- Cholesterol 0 mg
- Sodium 385 mg
- Potassium 60 gm
- Total Carb 14 gm
- Dietary Fiber 2 gm
- Sugars 0 gm
- Protein 3 gm
- Phosphorus 70 gm

Soft Pretzels

Lydia K. Stoltzfus
Gordonville, PA

Makes 24 pretzels, 1 pretzel per serving
Prep. Time: 15 minutes
Rising Time: 30 minutes
Cooking/Baking Time: 15 minutes

4 tsp. active dry yeast

3 cups lukewarm water

⅓ cup brown sugar

pinch salt

7½ cups flour

3 Tbsp. baking soda

2 cups water

pretzel salt

1. Dissolve yeast in water.

2. Add brown sugar and pinch salt.

3. Stir in flour slowly. Knead well.

4. Cover and let rise 30 minutes.

5. Divide dough into small pieces and form into pretzel shapes.

6. Meanwhile mix baking soda and 2 cups water in a saucepan and heat until hot.

7. Dip each twisted pretzel in hot solution and rub back side on paper towels, so it will not stick to pan.

8. Lay dipped pretzels on greased baking sheets.

9. Sprinkle salt on pretzels.

10. Bake at 500°F for 7–10 minutes.

Exchange List Value
- Starch 2.0

Basic Nutritional Values
- Calories 150 (Calories from Fat 0)
- Total Fat 0 gm (Saturated Fat 0.1 gm, Trans Fat 0.0 gm, Polyunsat Fat 0.2 gm, Monounsat Fat 0.0 gm)
- Cholesterol 0 mg
- Sodium 175 mg
- Potassium 55 gm
- Total Carb 32 gm
- Dietary Fiber 1 gm
- Sugars 3 gm
- Protein 4 gm
- Phosphorus 50 gm

Crisp Snack Bars

Norma Saltzman
Shickley, NE

Makes 16 servings, 1 bar per serving
Prep. Time: 30 minutes
Cooking Time: 10 minutes

¼ cup honey

½ cup chunky peanut butter

½ cup nonfat dry milk

4 cups crisp rice cereal

1. In a large saucepan, combine honey, peanut butter, and milk powder.

2. Cook and stir over low heat until peanut butter is melted and mixture is warm. Remove from heat. If the mixture is too thick to stir easily, thin with a little milk.

3. Stir in cereal.

4. Press into an 8-inch square dish coated with nonstick cooking spray. Let stand until set.

5. Cut into 16 square bars.

Variations:
Melt chocolate chips along with the peanut butter mixture. Reduce the cereal to 2 cups.
—Karen Burkholder, Narvon, PA

Exchange List Values
- Carbohydrate 1.0
- Fat 1.0

Basic Nutritional Values
- Calories 100
  (Calories from Fat 40)
- Total Fat 4.5 gm
  (Saturated Fat 0.8 gm,
  Trans Fat 0.0 gm,
  Polyunsat Fat 1.2 gm,
  Monounsat Fat 2.0 gm)
- Cholesterol 0 mg
- Sodium 120 mg
- Potassium 100 gm
- Total Carb 13 gm
- Dietary Fiber 1 gm
- Sugars 7 gm
- Protein 3 gm
- Phosphorus 60 gm

Power Smoothie

Hope Comerford
Clinton Township, MI

Makes 4 servings
Prep. Time: 10 minutes

1 cup spinach

1 cup kale

⅓ cup blueberries

⅓ cup raspberries

⅓ cup chopped strawberries

½ cup frozen grapes

½ frozen banana

1 Tbsp. honey

1 cup water

1. Place all ingredients in a blender.

2. Cover and blend for about 3 minutes, or until smooth.

Exchange List Values
- Fruit 1.0
- Vegetable 0.5

Basic Nutritional Values
- Calories 90 (Calories from Fat 11.7)
- Total Fat 1.3 gm (Saturated Fat 0 gm, Trans Fat 0.0 gm, Polyunsat Fat 0.7 gm, Monounsat Fat 0 gm)
- Cholesterol 0 mg
- Sodium 72 mg
- Potassium 705 gm
- Total Carb 17 gm
- Dietary Fiber 3 gm
- Sugars 12 gm
- Protein 4 gm
- Phosphorus 73 gm

Raspberry Punch

Gloria Martin
Ephrata, PA

Makes 4 qts., 32 servings, ½ cup per serving
Prep. Time: 20 minutes

3 3-oz. pkgs. sugar-free raspberry gelatin

4 cups boiling water

¾ cup granulated Splenda

4 cups cold water

2¼ cups orange juice concentrate

1¼ cups lemonade concentrate

1 qt. diet ginger ale

10-oz. pkg. frozen raspberries

1. Dissolve gelatin in boiling water.

2. Add Splenda and cold water and stir to dissolve.

3. In a punch bowl, mix orange juice concentrate, lemonade concentrate, ginger ale, and raspberries.

4. Pour gelatin mixture into punch bowl. Stir. Serve with ice.

Variation:
Float scoops of raspberry sherbet on top of the punch.

Exchange List Value
- Carbohydrate 1.0

Basic Nutritional Values
- Calories 70
  (Calories from Fat 0)
- Total Fat 0 gm
  (Saturated Fat 0.0 gm,
  Trans Fat 0.0 gm,
  Polyunsat Fat 0.0 gm,
  Monounsat Fat 0.0 gm)
- Cholesterol 0 mg
- Sodium 30 mg
- Potassium 155 gm
- Total Carb 17 gm
- Dietary Fiber 1 gm
- Sugars 16 gm
- Protein 1 gm
- Phosphorus 25 gm

Very Simple Punch

Mrs. Lewis L. Beachy
Sarasota, FL

Makes 60 servings, a scant ½ cup per serving
Prep. Time: 10 minutes

46-oz. can pineapple juice

46-oz. can grapefruit juice

46-oz. can orange juice

2 qts. diet ginger ale

1 qt. orange sherbet

1. Mix all liquids together.

2. Immediately before serving, cut sherbet into chunks and add to punch.

Exchange List Value
- Carbohydrate 0.5

Basic Nutritional Values
- Calories 45
  (Calories from Fat 0)
- Total Fat 0 gm
  (Saturated Fat 0.1 gm,
  Trans Fat 0.0 gm,
  Polyunsat Fat 0.0 gm,
  Monounsat Fat 0.1 gm)
- Cholesterol 0 mg
- Sodium 10 mg
- Potassium 110 gm
- Total Carb 10 gm
- Dietary Fiber 0 gm
- Sugars 8 gm
- Protein 0 gm
- Phosphorus 10 gm

Snacks and Beverages

My Mother's Holiday Punch

Geraldine A. Ebersole
Hershey, PA

Makes 32 servings, ½ cup per serving
Prep. Time: 15 minutes
Cooking Time: 10 minutes

2 cups granulated Splenda

3 cups water

4 cups diet cranberry juice drink

6-oz. can frozen lemon juice

6-oz. can frozen orange juice

3 cups pineapple juice

ice

1 qt. diet ginger ale

sprigs of mint, *optional*

1. Make a sugar syrup with Splenda and water: Place Splenda and water in a saucepan and bring to a boil. Boil 1 minute and take off heat. Cool.

2. Add all fruit juices to cooled syrup. When ready to serve, pour mixture over ice in punch bowl and add ginger ale.

3. If desired, garnish with sprigs of mint.

Exchange List Value
- Fruit 0.5

Basic Nutritional Values
- Calories 30 (Calories from Fat 0)
- Total Fat 0 gm (Saturated Fat 0.0 gm, Trans Fat 0.0 gm, Polyunsat Fat 0.0 gm, Monounsat Fat 0.0 gm)
- Cholesterol 0 mg
- Sodium 10 mg
- Potassium 80 gm
- Total Carb 8 gm
- Dietary Fiber 0 gm
- Sugars 7 gm
- Protein 0 gm
- Phosphorus 5 gm

Orange Lemon Drink

Rhonda Freed
Croghan, NY

Makes 1 gallon, 16 servings of 1 cup each
Prep. Time: 10 minutes

Snacks and Beverages

12-oz. can frozen orange juice concentrate

1 cup granulated Splenda

½ cup lemon juice

1 gallon water, *divided*

1. Mix juice concentrate, Splenda, lemon juice, and ½ gallon water.

2. Add enough water to make a full gallon. Serve cold.

Exchange List Value
- Fruit 1.0

Basic Nutritional Values
- Calories 50
  (Calories from Fat 0)
- Total Fat 0 gm
  (Saturated Fat 0.0 gm,
  Trans Fat 0.0 gm,
  Polyunsat Fat 0.0 gm,
  Monounsat Fat 0.0 gm)
- Cholesterol 0 mg
- Sodium 10 mg
- Potassium 185 gm
- Total Carb 12 gm
- Dietary Fiber 0 gm
- Sugars 12 gm
- Protein 1 gm
- Phosphorus 15 gm

Lemonade

Ruth R. Nissley
Mount Joy, PA

Makes 60 servings, about ¾ cup per serving
Prep. Time: 10 minutes

3 cups ReaLemon

6 oz. frozen orange juice

4 cups granulated Splenda

water to fill 3 gallons

1. Mix ReaLemon, orange juice, and Splenda.

2. Add water and ice to make an ice-cold drink.

Exchange List Value
- Free food

Basic Nutritional Values
- Calories 15
  (Calories from Fat 0)
- Total Fat 0 gm
  (Saturated Fat 0.0 gm,
  Trans Fat 0.0 gm,
  Polyunsat Fat 0.0 gm,
  Monounsat Fat 0.0 gm)
- Cholesterol 0 mg
- Sodium 10 mg
- Potassium 35 gm
- Total Carb 4 gm
- Dietary Fiber 0 gm
- Sugars 3 gm
- Protein 0 gm
- Phosphorus 0 gm

Hot Mulled Cider

Phyllis Attig, Reynolds, IL
Jean Butzer, Batavia, NY
Doris G. Herr, Manheim, PA
Mary E. Martin, Goshen, IN
Leona Miller, Millersburg, OH
Marjora Miller, Archbold, OH
Janet L. Roggie, Lowville, NY
Shirley Sears, Tiskilwa, IL
Charlotte Shaffer, East Earl, PA
Berenice M. Wagner, Dodge City, KS
Connie B. Weaver, Bethlehem, PA
Maryann Westerberg, Rosamond, CA
Carole Whaling, New Tripoli, PA

Makes 16 (½-cup) servings
Prep. Time: 15 minutes
Cooking Time: 2–8 hours
Ideal slow-cooker size: 4-qt.

¼ cup brown sugar

2 qts. apple cider

1 tsp. whole allspice

1½ tsp. whole cloves

2 cinnamon sticks

2 oranges, sliced, with peels on

1. Combine brown sugar and cider in slow cooker.

2. Put spices in tea strainer or tie in cheesecloth. Add to slow cooker. Stir in orange slices.

3. Cover and simmer on Low 2–8 hours.

Variation:
Add a dash of ground nutmeg and salt.
—Marsha Sabus, Fallbrook, CA

Exchange List Value
- Fruit 1.0

Basic Nutritional Values
- Calories 76 (Calories from Fat 1)
- Total Fat 0 gm (Saturated Fat 0.0 gm, Polyunsat Fat 0.0 gm, Monounsat Fat 0.0 gm)
- Cholesterol 0 mg
- Sodium 5 mg
- Total Carb 19 gm
- Dietary Fiber 0 gm
- Sugars 18 gm
- Protein 0 gm

Snacks and Beverages

Maple Mulled Cider

Leesa Lesenski
Wheately, MA

Makes 10 servings
Prep. Time: 10 minutes
Cooking Time: 2 hours
Ideal slow-cooker size: 4-qt.

½ gallon apple cider

3–4 cinnamon sticks

2 tsp. whole cloves

2 tsp. whole allspice

1–2 Tbsp. orange juice concentrate, *optional*

1 Tbsp. maple syrup

1. Combine ingredients in slow cooker.

2. Cover. Heat on Low for 2 hours. Serve warm.

Exchange List Value
- Fruit 1.5

Basic Nutritional Values
- Calories 98
  (Calories from Fat 1)
- Total Fat 0 gm
  (Saturated Fat 0.0 gm,
  Polyunsat Fat 0.1 gm,
  Monounsat Fat 0.0 gm)
- Cholesterol 0 mg
- Sodium 7 mg
- Total Carb 25 gm
- Dietary Fiber 0 gm
- Sugars 23 gm
- Protein 0 gm

NOTES

Serve at Halloween, Christmas caroling, or sledding parties.

Deep Red Apple Cider

Judi Manos
West Islip, NY

Makes 16 (½ cup) servings
Prep. Time: 10 minutes
Cooking Time: 3–4 hours
Ideal slow-cooker size: 4-qt.

5 cups apple cider
3 cups dry red wine
¼ cup brown sugar
½ tsp. whole cloves
¼ tsp. whole allspice
1 stick cinnamon

1. Combine all ingredients in slow cooker.

2. Cover. Cook on Low 3–4 hours.

3. Remove cloves, allspice, and cinnamon before serving.

Variation:
You can use 8 cups apple cider and no red wine.

Exchange List Value
- Fruit 1.0

Basic Nutritional Values
- Calories 58
  (Calories from Fat 1)
- Total Fat 0 gm
  (Saturated Fat 0.0 gm,
  Polyunsat Fat 0.0 gm,
  Monounsat Fat 0.0 gm)
- Cholesterol 0 mg
- Sodium 7 mg
- Total Carb 14 gm
- Dietary Fiber 0 gm
- Sugars 14 gm
- Protein 0 gm

Snacks and Beverages

Hot Wassail Drink

Dale Peterson
Rapid City, SD

Makes 54 (½-cup) servings
Prep. Time: 15 minutes
Cooking Time: 1–2 hours
Ideal slow-cooker size: 6-qt.

12-oz. can frozen orange juice

12-oz. can frozen lemonade

2 qts. apple juice

1 cup sugar substitute to equal ½ cup sugar

3 Tbsp. whole cloves

2 Tbsp. ground ginger

4 tsp. ground cinnamon

10 cups hot water

6 cups strong tea

1. Mix juices, sugar substitute, and spices in slow cooker.

2. Add hot water and tea.

3. Heat on High 1–2 hours or until hot, then on Low while serving.

Exchange List Value
• Fruit 1.0

Basic Nutritional Values
• Calories 61
  (Calories from Fat 1)
• Total Fat 0 gm
  (Saturated Fat 0.0 gm,
  Polyunsat Fat 0.0 gm,
  Monounsat Fat 0.0 gm)
• Cholesterol 0 mg
• Sodium 3 mg
• Total Carb 16 gm
• Dietary Fiber 0 gm
• Sugars 15 gm
• Protein 0 gm

Cocoa for a Crowd

Joy Reiff
Mount Joy, PA

Makes 65 (1-cup) servings
Prep. Time: 5 minutes
Cooking Time: 20–30 minutes

5 cups unsweetened cocoa powder

4 cups granulated Splenda

2 tsp. salt

5 qts. (20 cups) water, *divided*

10 qts. (2½ gallons) fat-free milk

1 qt. fat-free half-and-half

2 Tbsp. vanilla extract

whipped cream and additional cocoa for
   garnish, *optional*

1. In each of two large stockpots, combine
2½ cups cocoa, 2 cups Splenda, and 1
teaspoon salt.

2. Gradually stir 5 cups water into each
pot.

3. Bring to a boil, covered. Turn heat to
low.

4. Whisk in milk, half-and-half, and
remaining 10 cups water, half in each pot;
heat through, but do not boil.

5. Turn off heat. Stir 1 Tbsp. vanilla
extract into each pot. Taste, and add sugar to
your taste.

6. Garnish with whipped topping and
additional cocoa.

Warm Memories:
I like to serve this at my open house in the
winter.

Exchange List Value
- Fat-Free Milk 1.0

Basic Nutritional Values
- Calories 80
  (Calories from Fat 10)
- Total Fat 1 gm
  (Saturated Fat 0.7 gm,
  Trans Fat 0.0 gm,
  Polyunsat Fat 0.0 gm,
  Monounsat Fat 0.4 gm)
- Cholesterol 5 mg
- Sodium 150 mg
- Potassium 365 gm
- Total Carb 14 gm
- Dietary Fiber 2 gm
- Sugars 10 gm
- Protein 7 gm
- Phosphorus 225 gm

Snacks and Beverages

Crockery Cocoa

Betty Hostetler
Allensville, PA

Makes 12 servings
Prep. Time: 10 minutes
Cooking Time: 1–4 hours
Ideal slow-cooker size: 4- or 5-qt.

½ cup sugar

½ cup unsweetened cocoa powder

2 cups boiling water

3½ cups nonfat dry milk powder

6 cups water

1 tsp. vanilla extract

1 tsp. ground cinnamon

1. Combine sugar and cocoa powder in slow cooker. Add 2 cups boiling water. Stir well to dissolve.

2. Add dry milk powder, 6 cups water, and vanilla. Stir well to dissolve.

3. Cover. Cook on Low 4 hours or High 1–1½ hours.

4. Before serving, beat with rotary beater to make frothy. Ladle into mugs. Sprinkle with cinnamon.

Variations:

1. Add ⅛ tsp. ground nutmeg along with ground cinnamon in Step 4.
2. Mocha-style: Stir ¾ tsp. coffee crystals into each serving in Step 4.
3. Coffee-Cocoa: Pour half-cups of freshly brewed, high-quality coffee; top with half-cups of Crockery Cocoa.

Exchange List Values
- Fat-Free Milk 1.0
- Carbohydrate 0.5

Basic Nutritional Values
- Calories 111 (Calories from Fat 6)
- Total Fat 1 gm (Saturated Fat 0.3 gm, Polyunsat Fat 0.0 gm, Monounsat Fat 0.2 gm)
- Cholesterol 4 mg
- Sodium 110 mg
- Total Carb 21 gm
- Dietary Fiber 1 gm
- Sugars 19 gm
- Protein 8 gm

Snacks and Beverages

Johnny Appleseed Tea

Sheila Plock
Boalsburg, PA

Makes 9 cups
Prep. Time: 15 minutes
Cooking Time: 2–3 hours
Ideal slow-cooker size: 4-qt.

2 qts. water, *divided*

6 tea bags of your favorite flavor

6 oz. frozen apple juice, thawed

3 Tbsp. packed brown sugar substitute to equal 2 Tbsp. sugar

1. Bring 1 qt. water to boil. Add tea bags. Remove from heat. Cover and let steep 5 minutes. Pour into slow cooker.

2. Add remaining ingredients and mix well.

3. Cover. Heat on Low until hot, 2–3 hours. Continue on Low while serving from slow cooker.

Exchange List Value
- Fruit 1.0

Basic Nutritional Values
- Calories 60 (Calories from Fat 1)
- Total Fat 0 gm (Saturated Fat 0.0 gm, Polyunsat Fat 0.0 gm, Monounsat Fat 0.0 gm)
- Cholesterol 0 mg
- Sodium 12 mg
- Total Carb 15 gm
- Dietary Fiber 0 gm
- Sugars 14 gm
- Protein 0 gm

NOTES

I serve this wonderful hot beverage with cookies at our Open House Tea and Cookies afternoon, which I host at Christmastime for friends and neighbors.

Snacks and Beverages

Almond Tea

Frances Schrag
Newton, KS

Makes 12 (1-cup) servings
Prep. Time: 10 minutes
Cooking Time: 1 hour
Ideal slow-cooker size: 4-qt.

10 cups boiling water

1 Tbsp. instant tea

⅔ cup lemon juice

½ cup sugar

½ cup granulated Splenda

1 tsp. vanilla extract

1 tsp. almond extract

1. Mix together all ingredients in slow cooker.

2. Turn to High and heat thoroughly, about 1 hour. Turn to Low while serving.

Exchange List Value
- Carbohydrate 0.5

Basic Nutritional Values
- Calories 40
  (Calories from Fat 0)
- Total Fat 0 gm
  (Saturated Fat 0.0 gm,
  Polyunsat Fat 0.0 gm,
  Monounsat Fat 0.0 gm)
- Cholesterol 0 mg
- Sodium 3 mg
- Total Carb 10 gm
- Dietary Fiber 0 gm
- Sugars 9 gm
- Protein 0 gm

Metric Equivalent Measurements

If you're accustomed to using metric measurements, I don't want you to be inconvenienced by the imperial measurements I use in this book.

Use this handy chart, too, to figure out the size of the slow cooker you'll need for each recipe.

Weight (Dry Ingredients)

1 oz		30 g
4 oz	¼ lb	120 g
8 oz	½ lb	240 g
12 oz	¾ lb	360 g
16 oz	1 lb	480 g
32 oz	2 lbs	960 g

Volume (Liquid Ingredients)

½ tsp.		2 ml
1 tsp.		5 ml
1 Tbsp.	½ fl oz	15 ml
2 Tbsp.	1 fl oz	30 ml
¼ cup	2 fl oz	60 ml
⅓ cup	3 fl oz	80 ml
½ cup	4 fl oz	120 ml
⅔ cup	5 fl oz	160 ml
¾ cup	6 fl oz	180 ml
1 cup	8 fl oz	240 ml
1 pt	16 fl oz	480 ml
1 qt	32 fl oz	960 ml

Slow Cooker Sizes

1-quart	0.96 l
2-quart	1.92 l
3-quart	2.88 l
4-quart	3.84 l
5-quart	4.80 l
6-quart	5.76 l
7-quart	6.72 l
8-quart	7.68 l

Length

¼ in	6 mm
½ in	13 mm
¾ in	19 mm
1 in	25 mm
6 in	15 cm
12 in	30 cm

Extra Information

Abbreviations used in *Welcome Home Diabetic Cookbook*

lb. = pound
oz. = ounce
pkg. = package
pt. = pint
qt. = quart
Tbsp. = tablespoon
tsp. = teaspoon
9 x 13 baking pan = 9 inches wide by 13 inches long
8 x 8 baking pan = 8 inches wide by 8 inches long
5 x 9 loaf pan = 5 inches wide by 9 inches long
Assumptions
flour = unbleached or white, and all-purpose
oatmeal or oats = dry, quick or rolled (old-fashioned), unless specified
pepper = black, finely ground
rice = regular, long-grain (not Minute or instant)
salt = table salt
shortening = solid, not liquid
spices = all ground, unless specified otherwise
sugar = granulated sugar (not brown and not confectioners')
Equivalents
dash = little less than ⅛ tsp.
3 teaspoons = 1 Tablespoon
2 Tablespoons = 1 oz.
4 Tablespoons = ¼ cup
5 Tablespoons plus 1 tsp. = ⅓ cup
8 Tablespoons = ½ cup
12 Tablespoons = ¾ cup
16 Tablespoons = 1 cup
1 cup = 8 oz. liquid
2 cups = 1 pint
4 cups = 1 quart
4 quarts = 1 gallon

1 stick butter = ¼ lb.

1 stick butter = ½ cup

1 stick butter = 8 Tbsp.

Beans, 1 lb. dried = 2–2½ cups (depending upon the size of the beans)

Bell peppers, 1 large = 1 cup chopped

Cheese, hard (for example, cheddar, Swiss, Monterey Jack, mozzarella), 1 lb. grated = 4 cups

Cheese, cottage, 1 lb. = 2 cups

Chocolate chips, 6-oz. pkg. = 1 scant cup

Coconut, 3-oz. pkg., grated = 1 cup, lightly filled

Crackers, graham, 12 single crackers = 1 cup crumbs

Crackers (butter, saltines, snack), 20 single crackers = 1 cup crumbs

Herbs, 1 Tbsp. fresh = 1 tsp. dried

Lemon, 1 medium-sized = 2–3 Tbsp. juice

Lemon, 1 medium-sized = 2–3 tsp. grated rind

Mustard, 1 Tbsp. prepared = 1 tsp. dry or ground mustard

Oatmeal, 1 lb. dry = about 5 cups dry

Onion, 1 medium-sized = ½ cup chopped

Pasta: Macaroni, penne, and other small or tubular shapes, 1 lb. dry = 4 cups uncooked Noodles, 1 lb. dry = 6 cups uncooked spaghetti, linguine, fettucine, 1 lb. dry = 4 cups uncooked

Potatoes, white, 1 lb. = 3 medium-sized potatoes = 2 cups mashed

Potatoes, sweet, 1 lb. = 3 medium-sized potatoes = 2 cups mashed

Rice, 1 lb. dry = 2 cups uncooked

Sugar, confectioners', 1 lb. = 3½ cups sifted

Whipping cream, 1 cup un-whipped = 2 cups whipped

Whipped topping, 8-oz. container = 3 cups

Yeast, dry, 1 envelope (¼ oz.) = 1 Tbsp.

About the Author

Hope Comerford is a mom, wife, elementary music teacher, blogger, recipe developer, public speaker, FitAddict Training fit leader, Young Living Essential Oils essential oil enthusiast/educator, and published author. In 2013, she was diagnosed with a severe gluten intolerance and since then has spent many hours creating easy, practical and delicious gluten-free recipes that can be enjoyed by both those who are affected by gluten and those who are not.

Growing up, Hope spent many hours in the kitchen with her Meme (grandmother), and her love for cooking grew from there. While working on her master's degree when her daughter was young, Hope turned to her slow cookers for some salvation and sanity. It was from there she began truly experimenting with recipes and quickly learned she had the ability to get a little more creative in the kitchen and develop her own recipes.

In 2010, Hope started her blog, *A Busy Mom's Slow Cooker Adventures*, to simply share the recipes she was making with her family and friends. She never imagined people all over the world would begin visiting her page and sharing her recipes with others as well. In 2013, Hope self-published her first cookbook, *Slow Cooker Recipes 10 Ingredients or Less and Gluten-Free*, and then later wrote *The Gluten-Free Slow Cooker*.

Hope became the new brand ambassador and author of Fix-It and Forget-It in mid-2016. She is excited to bring her creativeness to the Fix-It and Forget-It brand. Through Fix-It and Forget-It, she has written *Fix-It and Forget-It Lazy & Slow*, *Fix-It and Forget-It Healthy Slow Cooker Cookbook*, *Fix-It and Forget-It Favorite Slow Cooker Recipes for Mom*, *Fix-It and Forget-It Favorite Slow Cooker Recipes for Dad*, *Fix-It and Enjoy-It Welcome Home Cookbook*, *Fix-It and Forget-It Holiday Favorites*, *Fix-It and Forget-It Cooking for Two*, *Fix-It and Forget-It Crowd Pleasers for the American Summer*, and *Fix-It and Forget-It Dunp Dinners and Dump Desserts*.

Hope lives in the city of Clinton Township, Michigan, near Metro Detroit. She has lived Michigan her whole life. She has been happily married to her husband and best friend, Justin, since 2008. Together they have two children, Ella and Gavin, who are her motivation, inspiration, and heart. In her spare time, Hope enjoys traveling, singing, cooking, reading books, spending time with friends and family, and relaxing.

Index

Index

Index

Index

Index